GREAT MEN AND WOMEN
OF POLAND

THE MACMILLAN COMPANY
NEW YORK · BOSTON · CHICAGO · DALLAS
ATLANTA · SAN FRANCISCO

MACMILLAN AND CO., Limited
LONDON · BOMBAY · CALCUTTA · MADRAS
MELBOURNE

THE MACMILLAN COMPANY
OF CANADA, Limited
TORONTO

GREAT MEN AND WOMEN OF POLAND

Edited by

STEPHEN P. MIZWA

New York

THE MACMILLAN COMPANY

1942

PRINTED IN THE UNITED STATES OF AMERICA
BY J. J. LITTLE & IVES COMPANY, NEW YORK

11732

TO THE MEMORY OF

Dr. John H. Finley
Henry Sieminski
Samuel M. Vauclain

MODEST BUT EFFECTIVE CO-WORKERS IN THE PROMOTION OF
CULTURAL RELATIONSHIPS BETWEEN THE UNITED STATES
OF AMERICA AND THE NEW POLAND—
THIS VOLUME IS GRATEFULLY DEDICATED

KEY TO PRONUNCIATION

Unlike the English, the Polish vowels have only one sound each.

Polish vowels:

a ..... like "a" in the English word "Mars."
ą ..... nasal like "on" in French "mon."
e ..... like "e" in "met."
ę ..... nasal like "in" in French "fin."
i ..... like "ee" in "see."
o ..... like "o" in "horse."
ó ..... like "oo" in "book."
u ..... like "u" in "true."

Consonants:

c ..... like "ts."
ć ..... like "ch" in "church."
ch ..... like "h."
cz ..... nearest to "ch."
j ..... like the English "y."
ń ..... like "n" in "new "
ś ..... like "sh" in "sheep."
sz ..... nearest to "sh."
ł ..... like "l" in "look."
w ..... at the beginning of a word, like "v," but at the end of a word and before or after a voiceless consonant like "f."
y ..... like "i" in "it."
ź, ż and rz ..... nearest to "z" in "azure."

Polish accent falls as a rule on the last syllable but one.

Bolesław Chrobry.....Bo-les'-laf Hro'bry.

Casimir the Great.....(Kazimierz Wielki).....Ka-zee'-myez Vyel'-kee.

Queen Jadwiga.....Yad-vee'ga.

Nicolas Copernicus.....(Mikołaj Kopernik).....Mee-ko'-lay Koper'-neek.

A. Frycz Modrzewski.....Fritch Mo-dzef'-skee.

Jan Kochanowski.....Yan Ko-ha-nof'-skee.

Piotr Skarga..... Pyotr Skar'-ga.

Jan Zamoyski..... Yan Za-moy'-skee.

Jan Sobieski..... Yan Sob-yes'-kee.

Stanisław Konarski..... Sta-nees'-laf Ko-nar'-skee.

Tadeusz Kościuszko..... Ta-de'-oosh Kosh-choosh'-ko.

Kazimierz Pułaski..... Ka-zee'-myez Poo-las'-kee.

Stanisław Staszic..... Sta-nees'-laf Sta'-sheets.

Prince Adam Czartoryski..... Char-to-ri'-skee.

Joachim Lelewel..... Yo-a'-heem Le-le'-vel.

Adam Mickiewicz..... Meets-kye'-vich.

Juliusz Słowacki..... Yul'-yoosh Slo-vats'-kee.

Fryderyk Chopin..... Friderik Sho'-pen.

Jan Matejko..... Yan Ma-tey'-ko.

Helena Modjeska..... (Modrzejewska)..... Mo-dje-yef'-ska.

Zygmunt Wróblewski..... Zig'-munt Vroob-lef'-skee.

Karol Olszewski..... Ol-shef'-skee.

Henryk Sienkiewicz..... Shen-kye'-vich.

Józef Chełmoński...... Yoo'-zef Hel-mon'-skee

Joseph Conrad..... (Józef Korzeniowski)..... Yoo'-zef Ko-ze-nyof'-skee.

Ignace (Ignacy) Jan Paderewski..... Ig-na'-tsy Yan Pa-de-ref'-skee.

Marie Skłodowska Curie..... Sklo-dof'-ska Curie.

Józef Piłsudski..... Yoo'-zef Peel-soods'-kee.

Władysław Reymont..... Vla-di'-slaf Ray'-mont.

Stanisław Wyspiański..... Sta-nees'-laf Vis-pyan'-skee.

INTRODUCTION

Toward the close of the first century of our Christian era, a Greek historian and biographer named Plutarch wrote forty-six parallel biographies of famous Greeks and Romans for the edification of generations that were and that were to follow. Plutarch made his own selection of the great men of the ancient Greco-Roman world, and his primary aim was to tell the story of each with a didactic purpose in view: to instill in the new generations an admiration for the virtues of his heroes.

Eighteen centuries later (to be exact, in the year 1900) Chancellor Henry Mitchell MacCracken of New York University conceived and brought to fruition the idea of the Hall of Fame for Great Americans as a national memorial, "a noble shrine of the nation's greatness," also with a view to "educational use." Twenty-nine great Americans were elected for the first roster. This Hall of Fame is the "American Plutarch."

President Henry Noble MacCracken (of Vassar College), son of the illustrious Chancellor of New York University, by a juncture of circumstances is the spiritual father of this "Polish Plutarch." In one of numerous conversations and conferences with the present writer President MacCracken mentioned a general need of a single volume, "manageable in size and intelligible to the average intelligent reader," of biographical stories of great men and women of Poland.

Actually, the present volume does not pretend to be either a Polish Plutarch or the Polish Hall of Fame, yet it is hoped that it may prove to be a little of both. The number of biographies, thirty, was arbitrarily arrived at long before the final selection was made. Why thirty, and not forty, fifty or sixty? In fact, as the problem of selection of names unfolded, it was felt that, the more exclusive fifteen or the more inclusive sixty names would

ix

have been easier to select than thirty. However, this arbitrary number of names was determined for purely practical reasons: thirty short biographies would make a manageable volume.

How were those thirty great Poles to be selected? Was an attempt to be made to determine and select the thirty greatest Poles in history or simply thirty "typical" great Poles, in the various fields of constructive human endeavor—rulers and statesmen, scientists, artists, men of letters, social reformers, etc.? There was no national or international jury or "Board of Electors" as in the case of the American Hall of Fame. The final responsibility rests on the present writer and his jury composed of the following: an outstanding Polish scholar of the University of Kraków; Dr. Oscar Halecki, Professor of History at the University of Warsaw and Visiting Professor of History at Vassar College; Dr. William J. Rose, formerly of Dartmouth College and now head of the Slavonic Department at the University of London; and Dr. Frank Nowak, Professor of Modern European History at Boston University. The final selection was made by this jury,[1] from among hundreds of names submitted by Polish scholars, heads of higher institutions of learning in Poland, and others.

No claim is made that the thirty names selected are the greatest names in the one thousand years of Polish history. Fifteen of them would be selected by any jury as such; substitutes might be found for the other fifteen. Some of the possible substitutes will be mentioned hereunder. But this claim can be made: that "not one name has found a place here which does not rightly deserve it by virtue of great talents and great public services"—or great services in some field of spiritual or intellectual endeavor. Some great intellects were left out, because their contributions lay in some highly specialized sphere understood only by specialists.[2] Other great intellects, also working in specialized spheres, were included because it was felt that their contributions were of more general benefit, were more generally understood or were believed to be of greater substantive value.

The final selection of thirty names was made by the jury

[1] Professor Nowak strenuously objected to the omission of King Stefan Batory.

[2] Marian Smoluchowski, one of the outstanding theoretical physicists in Europe of his generation, belongs in this category.

from a composite list of one hundred and thirty-three names submitted by the following:

The Polish Academy of Sciences in Kraków, Rector of the University of Poznań, Rector of the Free University of Warsaw, History Seminary at the University of Poznań, Dean of the School of Agriculture and Forestry at the University of Poznań, Rector of the Graduate School of Business Administration at Warsaw, Rector of the Polytechnic Institute at Lwów, Director of the Kraków Graduate School of Commerce, Rector of the Academy of Veterinary Medicine at Lwów, Rector of the Catholic University at Lublin, Director of the Graduate School of Political Science at Warsaw, Director of the Silesian Conservatory of Music at Katowice, Rector of the University of Lwów, Dean of the Department of Theology at the University of Kraków, also Deans at the same University of the Departments of Law, Medicine and Philosophy; and by Dr. Stanisław Kot,[3] Professor of the History of Polish Culture at the University of Kraków jointly with another prominent Polish scholar at the same university.

The first sixty names (including living Poles) from a list of one hundred and thirty-three submitted by the aforementioned eighteen individuals and institutions, with the number of votes each received, were as follows (italicized names are those that were finally selected):

NAME	NUMBER OF VOTES	REMARKS
1. *Fryderyk Chopin*	18	Composer (1810-49)
2. *Mikołaj Kopernik* (Nicolas Copernicus)	18	Astronomer, Mathematician (1473-1543)
3. *Tadeusz Kościuszko*	18	Patriot, Soldier (1746-1817)
4. *Adam Mickiewicz*	18	National Poet of Poland (1798-1855)
5. *Maria Skłodowska Curie*	18	Scientist (1867-1934)
6. *Henryk Sienkiewicz*	18	Novelist, Nobel Prize Winner (1846-1916)
7. *Jan Matejko*	16	Painter (1839-93)
8. *Jan Sobieski*	15	King, Statesman, Soldier (1624-96)

[3] From September 1939, Minister in the Polish Government in Exile, in Paris, Angers and London.

NAME	NUMBER OF VOTES	REMARKS
9. *Ignace Jan Paderewski*	13	Composer, Musician, Patriot, Statesman, Humanitarian (1860-1941)
10. *Władysław Reymont*	13	Novelist, Nobel Prize Winner (1868-1925)
11. *Juljusz Słowacki*	13	Poet (1809-49)
12. *Bolesław Chrobry*	12	King, Statesman, Soldier (966-1025)
13. *Queen Jadwiga*	12	"Poland's Great Queen" (1373-99)
14. *Jan Kochanowski*	12	Poet (1530-84)
15. *Joachim Lelewel*	12	Historian, Teacher of Patriotism (1786-1861)
16. *Józef Piłsudski*	12	Patriot, Statesman, Soldier (1867-1935)
17. *Casimir the Great*	11	King, Statesman (1310-70)
18. *Karol Olszewski*	11	Scientist (1846-1915)
19. *Casimir Pułaski*	11	Patriot, Soldier (1747-79)
20. Wit Stwosz	11	Artist (Wood Carver and Painter) (1438-1533)
21. Stefan Batory	10	King, Statesman, Soldier (1533-86)
22. *Helena Modjeska*	10	Dramatic Artist (1842-1908)
23. *Prince Adam Czartoryski*	9	Statesman (1770-1861)
24. Jan Henryk Dąbrowski	9	Soldier (1755-1818)
25. Prince Józef Poniatowski	9	Soldier, Hero (1762-1813)
26. *Piotr Skarga*	9	Preacher of Prophetic Vision (1536-1612)
27. *Stanisław Staszic*	9	Political Thinker and Reformer (1755-1826)
28. *Jan Zamoyski*	9	Statesman, Soldier (1542-1605)
29. Artur Grottger	8	Painter (1837-67)
30. Zygmunt Krasiński	8	Poet, Philosopher (1812-59)
31. *Stanisław Wyspiański*	8	Poet, Dramatist, Painter (1869-1907)
32. *Zygmunt Wróblewski*	8	Scientist (1845-88)
33. Stanisław Moniuszko	7	Composer of National Operas (1819-72)
34. Marian Smoluchowski	7	Physicist (1872-1917)
35. Stefan Żeromski	7	Novelist (1864-1925)
36. Henryk Siemiradzki	6	Painter (1843-1902)
37. Jędrzej Śniadecki	6	Physiologist, Physician (1768-1838)

NAME	NUMBER OF VOTES	REMARKS
38. Stanisław Żółkiewski	6	Soldier, Statesman (1547-1620)
39. Zygmunt II August	5	King, Statesman (1520-72)
40. Benedykt Dybowski	5	Naturalist, Explorer, Zoologist (1835-1930)
41. Oswald Balzer	4	Political Scientist (1858-1933)
42. Jan Baudouin de Courtanay	4	Philologist (1845-1929)
43. General Józef Bem	4	Soldier (1794-1850)
44. Jan Długosz	4	Historian (1415-80)
45. Cardinal Stanisław Hoziusz	4	Churchman (1504-79)
46. Władysław Jagiełło	4	King, Statesman (1348-1434)
47. Józef Kraszewski	4	Novelist, Historian (1812-87)
48. Stanisław Leszczyński	4	King, Statesman (1677-1766)
49. Marceli Nencki	4	Physiologist, Chemist (1847-1901)
50. *Józef Chełmoński*	3	Painter (1850-1914)
51. Ignacy Domeyko	3	Explorer, Chemist, Geologist, Mineralogist (1801-89)
52. Józef Hoene-Wroński	3	Philosopher, Mathematician (1776-1853)
53. *Stanisław Konarski*	3	Educational Reformer (1700-1773)
54. Ignacy Łukasiewicz	3	Chemist, Inventor (1822-82)
55. *A. Frycz Modrzewski*	3	Political Thinker and Social Reformer (1503-72)
56. Ignacy Mościcki	3	Scientist, Inventor, President of Poland 1926-39 (1867-)
57. Karol Szymanowski	3	Composer (1883-1937)
58. Tadeusz Czacki	2	Patriot, Historian, Educator (1765-1813)
59. Hugo Kołłątaj	2	Educator, Statesman, Patriot (1750-1812)
60. *Konrad Korzeniowski* (Joseph Conrad)	2	Novelist in the English language (1851-1924)

Two things are obvious from the table given above:

First: That twenty-four (or eighty per cent) out of the thirty names finally selected by the jury were recommended by nine or more of the eighteen Polish savants, heads of higher institutions of learning in Poland and the Polish Academy.

Second: That no name was selected by the jury unless it was

recommended by at least two independent votes from among the eighteen above mentioned.

It may not be obvious to the general reader, but it was obvious to the jury, that on every one of the eighteen lists of thirty or more great Poles, submitted from Poland, there were a few names that loomed large in the light of regional pride, or of professional brotherhood. Thus the Krakovians submitted more names that emanated from Kraków; and learned Poles in some branch of science submitted relatively more names (not always known to the general public) identified with that branch of science than with any other single field.

In addition to the thirty great Poles finally selected or, as many a reader may possibly suggest, names worthy as substitutes for some of those on the list, the following ten deserve special mention:

Stefan Batory	Zygmunt Krasiński
Wit Stwosz	Stanisław Moniuszko
Jan Henryk Dąbrowski	Stefan Żeromski
Prince Józef Poniatowski	Władysław Jagiełło
Artur Grottger	Hugo Kołłątaj

In the process of selection and elimination these ten names were left out simply because in each group there were other kings and rulers, soldiers and statesmen, artists and writers, painters and composers who, it was felt, were not less important.

Stefan Batory is great, but so is Casimir (the only Polish king the Poles call Great), Bolesław the Brave, Queen Jadwiga, and Sobieski. These could not be moved from the niches they so eminently deserve. And there was no more room for kings, unless others were deprived of their seats. Władysław Jagiełło, the founder of the Jagiellonian Dynasty, was a great ruler, soldier and statesman, but it was felt that Queen Jadwiga was the prime cause of what they both did jointly and individually. Wit Stwosz was a great artistic genius; but his contribution was mainly confined to the masterpiece at St. Mary's and he could not, it was felt, displace either Jan Matejko or Józef Chełmoński. Jan Henryk Dąbrowski and Prince Józef Poniatowski were set opposite Tadeusz Kościuszko and Casimir Pułaski respectively, and the

Polish and American heroes won out. As to why Artur Grottger was left out, there may be no apparent justification. The Polish Academy submitted all three names—Jan Matejko, Artur Grottger and Józef Chełmoński. There was room for only two painters. Matejko could not possibly be left out. Hence, Chełmoński or Grottger. The latter had more votes, because, presumably, of the patriotic appeal of his canvases. Upon further consultation with critics of Polish art it was felt that Chełmoński perhaps showed greater innate genius. Zygmunt Krasiński is generally regarded as highly as Juliusz Słowacki. But there was room for only one poet besides Mickiewicz, whose position is secure beyond any question. The Polish Academy's vote for Słowacki solved the problem of choice. Stanisław Moniuszko, best known as a composer of national operas, was left out through the following reasoning: Rightly or wrongly, Poland is known abroad as a nation of musicians. If Polish music is to be represented, it should be represented at its best; hence Fryderyk Chopin and Ignace Jan Paderewski. If Moniuszko were to be their companion, then Karol Szymanowski and a few others could not be justifiably left out. Stefan Żeromski or Władysław Reymont—one or the other—that was the question in the final analysis, concerning writers. Although Reymont was a Nobel Prize winner, many Poles regard Żeromski as the greater of the two. However, the majority vote decided in favor of Reymont. Last but not least—of the left out but not forgotten ten—was Hugo Kołłątaj. Konarski, Staszic, and Kołłątaj seem to belong in the same category of Polish national esteem. Only two of these three could be considered, finally. The first two, having a slightly larger number of votes, were put on the list.

It is not always easy to allocate certain personalities into definite categories. Zamoyski was not only a great statesman and soldier but at the same time perhaps the outstanding educator in sixteenth-century Poland. And where can we place the great Paderewski: among musicians, statesmen, diplomats, orators, patriots or humanitarians?

For the sake of convenience and general orientation, even though arbitrary method be used to achieve a sense of proportion, the thirty biographies may be reduced to the following six groups:

I. RULERS, STATESMEN, SOLDIERS AND HEROES

1. Bolesław the Brave (966-1025)
2. Casimir the Great (1310-70)
3. Jadwiga (1373-99)
4. Jan Zamoyski (1542-1605)
5. Jan Sobieski (1624-96)
6. Tadeusz Kościuszko (1746-1817)
7. Casimir Pułaski (1747-79)
8. Prince Adam Czartoryski (1770-1861)
9. Józef Piłsudski (1867-1935)

II. POETS, WRITERS, HISTORIANS AND DRAMATIC ARTISTS

1. Jan Kochanowski (1530-84)
2. Joachim Lelewel (1786-1861)
3. Adam Mickiewicz (1798-1855)
4. Juliusz Słowacki (1809-49)
5. Helena Modjeska (1840-1908)
6. Henryk Sienkiewicz (1846-1916)
7. Joseph Conrad (1851-1924)
8. Władysław Reymont (1868-1925)
9. Stanisław Wyspiański (1869-1907)

III. SOCIAL, POLITICAL, EDUCATIONAL AND RELIGIOUS THINKERS, LEADERS AND REFORMERS

1. A. Frycz Modrzewski (1503-72)
2. Piotr Skarga (1536-1612)
3. Stanisław Konarski (1700-1773)
4. Stanisław Staszic (1755-1826)

IV. SCIENTISTS

1. Nicolas Copernicus (1473-1543)
2. Zygmunt Wróblewski (1845-88)
3. Karol Olszewski (1846-1915)
4. Maria Skłodowska Curie (1867-1934)

V. PAINTERS

1. Jan Matejko (1838-93)
2. Józef Chełmoński (1850-1914)

VI. MUSICIANS AND COMPOSERS

1. Fryderyk Chopin (1810-49)
2. Ignace Jan Paderewski (1860-1941)

The problem of selecting thirty great Poles, truly representative of the versatile genius of the sons and daughters of Sarmatia, was not an easy one. That of selecting the author or authors to tell the story of each in an authoritative manner, was not any easier. Obviously it is impossible for any one author to write, with equal competence, about Casimir the Great and Skłodowska Curie, Copernicus and Chopin, Sienkiewicz and Matejko. The only alternative was a composite authorship, a biographical symposium. It is the Editor's conviction that he has been successful in enrolling in this co-operative effort a highly competent group of scholars and authors from Poland, England and the United States. Most of them are outstanding authorities on their respective subjects.

This work was started and most of it was completed before the War of September 1939 broke out. In fact all the contributions herein contained by authors now in Europe, were received by the Editor before the outbreak of the War. A few chapters were intercepted by war conditions and substitute authors were found.

A joint product of Polish, British and American scholars and collaborators, the book as a whole does not possess the uniform literary quality and penetrating acumen that is apparent in a number of individual chapters. Several chapters were originally written in Polish and translated into the English. A number of authors and translators were at one time or another exchange professors or exchange students under the auspices of the Kosciuszko Foundation.[4]

Comparatively little is known of Poland in America; still less of a good many of her great sons and daughters. Because of the partitions of Poland during the eighteenth century, many a Pole had been "appropriated" by the ruling nations. The more adventurous, like Konrad Korzeniowski, or the more restless, like Maria Skłodowska, who found no opportunity for growth or expression at home, sought freer atmosphere in other countries and added to the luster of their adopted fatherlands. Thus the former emerged as a man of letters in England under the adopted and more easily

---

[4] The Kosciuszko Foundation, with headquarters in New York, was organized in 1925-26 as a "Living Memorial" to Tadeusz Kościuszko on the occasion of the 150th anniversary of his enrollment in the American Revolutionary Army. Its essential purposes are to promote the exchange of students and professors between Poland and the United States, to encourage cultural relationships between the two countries and to serve as a clearing house of information pertaining to such relationships.

pronounced name of Joseph Conrad; and the latter, as the greatest woman scientist of all time, under the married name of Madame Curie in France. Both became household names everywhere, but how many people know that one adventurous genius hailed from the ancient capital of Poland, Kraków, and the other from the later capital, Warsaw?

The "Polish Plutarch," if one should be inclined to call it that, is more, we hope, than a mere series of success stories or accumulations of individual achievements. It is in a way the history of Polish culture presented in biographical form. The brightness of these thirty shining stars is almost invariably heightened against the background of shadows that enveloped their countrymen practically in every age and generation. The words of the great Paderewski, so frequently and eloquently spoken during the first World War, easily come to mind: "Far from pretending that the Polish nation was made up of angels, I willingly admit that my compatriots, though exceptionally richly endowed, full of imagination, laborious, brave, chivalrous, kind-hearted, broad-minded, were and naturally still are extremely temperamental, excessively emotional, and consequently subject to passion, to errors." It is then not only against the complimentary background painted by Paderewski in the first portion, but primarily on the canvas of his "compatriots" that "were and naturally still are extremely temperamental, subject to passion, to errors"—that these portraits are drawn.

There are two "schools" of Polish historiography that interpret Poland's national experience—especially the gloomy pages of her annals—from two different and somewhat opposite points of view. The Warsaw school minimizes the weaknesses of the Poles and emphasizes the faults of Poland's aggressive neighbors. The Kraków school, on the other hand, takes for granted that these neighbors cannot possibly be endowed with disinterested intentions and tries to find sources of Poland's weakness and downfall in the Poles themselves. Both schools are undoubtedly right. It is only a question of emphasis. It is not impossible that the adherents of both these schools try to stand so straight that they lean backward by overemphasis. Most of the authors represented in this volume tend to lean toward the Kraków school; and that for three reasons. In the first place, the University of Kraków has had an uninterrupted existence (the only Polish university in this happy position) since the day it was founded by Casimir the Great in 1364, to 1939; and its influence on Polish historiography has been the greatest, both quantitatively and qualitatively. Secondly, most of the authors have been either professors or students at that ancient seat of learning. Others had more direct contacts with that university than with any other Polish higher institution of learning. Thirdly, the achievements of their respective biographical subjects are enhanced in the light (or rather the shadow) of realistic background as interpreted by the Kraków School.

About a good many of these thirty Great Men and Women of Poland there is a great deal of information available to the American and English reader, in encyclopedias, in books and in periodical literature. Some of it is excellent and highly reliable, some of it is very complimentary but exceedingly untrustworthy, and the rest is out of tune with ascertained facts. At best, with several notable exceptions, the available information is fragmentary and scattered.

This is the first attempt [5] to gather in one volume and in the English language, short biographies of men and women of Poland who achieved fame, greatness and immortality in their own coun-

---

[5] In 1938 the Unique Press, Inc., of Detroit, Michigan, brought out a small volume (186 pp.) entitled *Notable Personages of Polish Ancestry*, compiled by W. Moore McLean. This biographical dictionary, limited as it is and not devoid of errors, is a useful compendium. It identifies 1474 Poles, telling who they were or are (kings, statesmen, scientists, historians, poets, etc.), and giving the dates of their birth and death. Its obvious shortcoming lies in its containing an unduly large number of names whose degree of notability met with generous interpretation on the part of the compiler and omitting a good many names that are really "notable."

In Polish, there is an abbreviated *Who's Who in Poland*, limited mostly to the fields of science, literature and art, entitled: *Współczesna Kultura Polska (Contemporary Polish Culture)*, prepared by Dr. A. Peretiatkowicz and Dr. M. Sobeski, Professors at the University of Poznań (Poznań, 1932, 319 pp.).

For scholars and research workers the best and only work of this type in the field of Polish biography is the monumental biographical dictionary published by the Polish Academy under the title of *Polski Słownik Biograficzny*. By September 1, 1939, only four complete volumes had appeared, and four-fifths of volume V, up to Jan Drohojowski. It was to contain ultimately 20,000 biographies, in twenty large volumes 40 (= quarto), 480 pages each. No living Poles are included. Bibliographical references accompany every important biography.

try, and some of whom earned the recognition and gratitude of the entire civilized world.

With all its shortcomings and sins of commission and omission, we hope this volume will fulfill a need and will serve a useful purpose.

As to the difficult question of nomenclature and the use of Polish diacritical marks, the Editor's practice has been to give the Polish version of Christian names and names of places with the usual diacritical signs—except in cases best known in the Anglicised form or when the several authors expressed preference for the English version. By way of personal predilection we have used *Kraków* throughout instead of Cracow. Names quoted or in a narrative in the first person have been left as given by the author, even though occasionally misspelled and thus giving the appearance of inconsistency.

The Editor desires to express his gratitude to the various contributors and collaborators for their "labor of love"; to Professor Oscar Halecki—"who remembers more historical dates than any other Polish historian"—for reading the manuscript and making helpful suggestions; and above all, to the Publisher's Editorial Staff for their vigilance, their patience, and their cheerful co-operation, all of which made the Editor's task decidedly a pleasure.

STEPHEN P. MIZWA
Editor

CONTENTS

PAGE

PAGE

by Stanisław Łempicki

Born in 1886. Ph.D., University of Lwów. Professor of History of Education at the University of Lwów and a recognized authority of the "Golden Age" in Poland in the sixteenth century. Member of the Polish Academy. Author, among others, of: JAN ZAMOYSKI's *Contributions in the Field of Education 1573-1605, Renaissance and Humanism in Poland.*

by Frank Nowak

A.B., University of Rochester, 1917; Ph.D., Harvard, 1924; Instructor, Assistant Professor and Professor of European History, Boston University, since 1922; Kosciuszko Foundation research fellow in Polish History, University of Kraków, 1933-34; Author *Medieval Slavdom and the Rise of Russia,* 1930.

by William J. Rose

A.B., University of Winnipeg; Rhodes Scholar and A.B. at Oxford; Ph.D., University of Kraków, 1926; Professor of Sociology, Dartmouth College, 1927-35; Kosciuszko Foundation Fellow in Poland, 1933-34; Reader and Professor of Polish language and literature, School of Slavonic studies, University of London, since 1935; Author, among others, of: *Stanisław Konarski—Preceptor of Poland, The Drama of Upper Silesia.*

by Stephen P. Mizwa

by Helena Waniczek

Ph.D., University of Kraków. Prepared under the direction of a Polish historian who is an outstanding authority on Pułaski.

A.B., Wesleyan University (Conn.), 1920; Ph.D., Columbia,
1925; Studied Slavonic Philology at Charles University,
Praha, and Polish language and literature at Kraków and
Warsaw; Teacher of Polish, Lecturer in Slavonic and East
European Languages at Columbia since 1928; Author, among
others, of monographs: *A Great Bard's 400th Anniversary*
(Jan Kochanowski); *The Basic Vocabulary in Polish; Po-
lonisms in Conrad's "Chance"; Language as a Factor in Polish Nationalism; Pushkin and Mickiewicz.* Frequent con-
tributor to book reviews on current Polish and Slavonic
literatures.

and MARION MOORE COLEMAN

A.B., New York State College, 1920; Co-author with Dr.
A. P. Coleman, of: *The Polish Insurrection of 1863 in the
Light of New York Editorial Opinion,* 1935; verse transla-
tion of Malczewski's *Marya,* 1937; translation of Słowacki's
Mary Stuart, 1940; translation of Fredro's *Maiden's Vows*
(Śluby Panieńskie), 1940; *Mickiewicz in English,* 1940.

Music studies in Lwów and Vienna; Privat-Dozent and Professor of History and Theory of Music, University of Kraków, since 1911; Member of the Polish Academy. Author,
among others, of: *Mozart,* 1906; *The Development of Musical Culture in Poland,* 1914; *Stanisław Moniuszko,* 1921;
Richard Wagner, 1922; *Fredric Chopin et son Œuvre,* 1930.

  Historian of Polish Art.

A.B., A.M., Dartmouth College; First worked as reporter,
etc., on various papers: *Springfield Union, Boston Herald,
Boston Transcript,* from 1906 to 1921. Instructor in English,

PAGE

1921-29, and Professor of Journalism since 1929, Dartmouth College; Kosciuszko Foundation Fellow, University of Kraków, 1925-26; Author of numerous stories and articles on Polish topics and, among others, of the following books: *The Trumpeter of Kraków; The Blacksmith of Wilno; The Golden Star of Halicz.* Awarded the John Newbury Medal "for the most distinguished contribution to the American literature for children," 1928.

Ph.D., University of Kraków; Privat-Dozent in Organic and Analytical Chemistry, University of Kraków, 1904-06; Professor of Inorganic Chemistry, University of Fribourg, 1906-19; Professor of Inorganic Chemistry, University of Kraków since 1919; Author of several monographic works in chemistry, especially on properties of gases and on low temperatures.

An English author, who for over thirty years devoted herself to the study and the interpretation of Polish history, literature and culture. Author of: *Adam Mickiewicz, the National Poet of Poland,* 1911; *Poland, A Study in National Idealism,* 1915; *Poland,* "Peeps at Many Lands" series, 1917; *Zygmunt Krasiński, the Anonymous Poet of Poland,* 1919; *Kościuszko, A Biography,* 1920; *Henryk Sienkiewicz, the Patriot Novelist of Poland,* 1926.
She was killed in the Spring of 1941 when a German bomb completely demolished her London house and destroyed her rich Polonica library, which was intended for the British Museum.

Ph.D., University of Kraków; Painter and teacher in Polish secondary schools from 1919 to 1928; Custodian of the Wawel Ethnographic Museum in Kraków since 1928; Author of books and monographic works dealing with ethnography and Polish folk art.

GREAT MEN AND WOMEN
OF POLAND

BOLESŁAW CHROBRY
An oil painting by Lucja Dzieszkowska
(on basis of half-tone from Jan Matejko)

I

BOLESŁAW CHROBRY

*The Founder of the Unified Kingdom of Poland and Precursor
of the Idea of East Central European Federation*

966-1025

by

OSCAR HALECKI

THE brave prince (Chrobry means brave in old Polish) who
was to die as Poland's first king, was born in or near the very year
of 966 when the Poles, becoming Christians, entered the European
community of nations. Even then, almost a thousand years ago,
Poland was not at all a new state. According to a contemporary
description by a foreign traveler, Bolesław's father, Mieszko I, was
already a powerful monarch, ruling over one of the largest Slavonic
countries, with a remarkable military and economic organization.
We also know the names of Mieszko's three predecessors, mentioned in the oldest Polish chronicle, and of the legendary founder
of the dynasty, Piast, who must have lived in the middle of the
ninth century. In contradistinction to the Norman dynasty which
simultaneously founded the Russian state, the Piasts were of purely
Polish stock, and the state which they governed through five
centuries was not a product of foreign conquest, but simply resulted from the unification of all the various Polish tribes, which
since Mieszko's time had extended as far north as the Baltic shore.
Bolesław's mother, Dubravka, was a Czech princess, and it was
through her and her country that Poland received the Christian
faith, not from Byzantium as the Russians did some twenty years
later, but from Rome, so that thenceforth Poland was closely connected with the Latin West.

The only information regarding the childhood of Mieszko's and Dubravka's son tells us that he had been sent temporarily as a hostage to Germany. He therefore had an early opportunity of becoming acquainted with the mighty neighbor country which he was to fight during most of his reign. Already under Mieszko dangerous clashes, the first one being mentioned in the historical sources as having taken place in 963, alternated with attempts at appeasement. The numerous Slavonic tribes, next of kin to the Poles and living between the Elbe and the Oder, had not yet been conquered. But the eastern marches of Germany, recently established on their territory, already entered into their first frontier disputes with the Poles. Moreover, the German kings, who since 962 were at the same time Roman Emperors, claimed a feudal overlordship over Poland, which Mieszko felt obliged to recognize to a certain extent. The chief task which he left to his successor was, therefore, to obtain Poland's full independence and the security of her western boundaries.

When Mieszko died in 992, Bolesław was not more than twenty-six, but already had his own family. He started his reign by expelling his German stepmother and her sons, to whom Mieszko had bequeathed a large part of his heritage. This first step was in the obvious interest of the country, which later on was to suffer so much from dynastic divisions and which, at the beginning of its political development, was particularly in need of unity under a single ruler. For a long time it has been admitted in Polish and foreign historiography that, in order to achieve territorial unity, Bolesław had also to recover from the Czechs the southern part of Poland, the so-called Little Poland which includes Kraków; it appears, however, from modern research, that this had already been done by his father, so that after getting rid of his younger half-brothers Bolesław could devote the first years of his rule to more peaceful activities, still avoiding a break with the Germans and even co-operating with them against some of the pagan Slavs.

The most urgent thing was, of course, to promote Christian civilization in a country quite recently converted. Bolesław did his best to attract to Poland distinguished clergymen and members of monastic orders not only from Germany and Bohemia, but even from the Romance countries, especially from Italy, thus strengthening cultural ties with Rome. This religious and cultural program was not without political significance. Before his death, Mieszko himself had placed his country under the protection of the Holy See, anticipating the support of the highest spiritual authority in the unavoidable conflict with the Empire. And Bolesław remained faithful to a principle which was to be one of the leading policies of medieval Poland. But not only in this respect did he follow the lines drafted by his father; Bolesław proved farsighted in dealing with ecclesiastical matters in all their medieval implications. He perfectly realized that Poland, owing to her geographical position at the eastern limits of the Latin world, had an important part to play both in the defense and in the expansion of Catholicism and Western culture. Therefore, without limiting himself to the development of the young church organization in Poland proper, he at once attempted to make it the basis for a systematic missionary activity beyond the frontiers of the country, among its northeastern neighbors. He never ceased to be interested in encouraging Western influences in Russia, which culturally depended on the Byzantine East and soon was to be severed from Rome by the accomplishment of the Eastern Schism. And as to the conversion of the pagan Baltic tribes of Lithuania and old Prussia, he approached that problem as early as 997, when he assisted the former bishop of Prague, the famous Adalbert, in his venture as a missionary to the Prussians. Soon after leaving Danzig, a place which at that date appears for the first time under its old Slavonic name of "Gyddanyzc" and under Polish control, Adalbert was killed by the heathens, but the martyrdom of the patron saint of both Bohemia and Poland was to have an unexpected result for Bolesław's foreign policy.

Adalbert's death leads us to the most striking event in Chrobry's life and to an exceptional moment not only in his but also in Poland's relations with Germany, when it seemed that thanks to an agreement between two outstanding personalities some cooperation might be established in the common interest of Christianity. The young Emperor Otto III, different from his predecessors and successors, inspired by his almost mystical conception of imperial universalism and by his special devotion to St. Adalbert whom he had met in Rome in connection with an ecclesiastical reform movement, decided to make a pilgrimage to the tomb of the martyr whose body had been ransomed by Bolesław and buried in Gniezno, Poland's first capital. Just before Easter time in 1000, the closing year of the first Christian millennium, the Emperor of the Romans, accompanied by some of his highest dignitaries and by representatives of Pope Sylvester II, his former preceptor and collaborator, was received by Bolesław at the frontier of Poland and led to Gniezno amidst ceremonies which the German witnesses called "indescribable and incredible." After having walked barefoot to the sepulcher of their common friend and piously venerated his reliquiae, Otto III discussed with Bolesław all the important problems of their mutual relations. This pilgrimage resulted not only in an official visit of courtesy, but in something like a first international conference on Polish soil.

One of the issues decided in common was connected with the religious purpose of the journey. With the Pope's assent, Poland, where hitherto there had been only one bishopric (founded at Poznań soon after Mieszko's conversion), now became an independent ecclesiastical province with an archbishop in Gniezno. The first archbishop nominated under the new arrangement was a brother of St. Adalbert, and he had three new bishops under his authority: at Kraków, whither the political capital was to be transferred in the same century, at Wrocław (Breslau) in the province of Silesia, and at Kołobrzeg (Kolberg) in Polish Pomerania, on the Baltic Sea.

It is hardly necessary to emphasize that such a decision was extremely favorable not only to the progress of religious life, but also to the political position of the country and of its able ruler. But even in this respect Bolesław obtained much more. The contemporaneous German chronicler, after having described the meeting with some obvious reluctancy, expresses the regret that Otto III elevated a former tributary prince to the rank of a "dominus," i.e., an independent lord. The Polish chronicle, written a hundred years later, certainly goes too far in saying that at the Gniezno congress the Emperor made Bolesław a king; but it seems probable that, by calling him "brother and co-operator" and "friend and ally of the Roman people," he recognized Bolesław as the representative of the Empire and protector of the Church in the whole region east of Germany. And in accordance with such a conception of an European order, Otto III seems to have authorized Bolesław to approach the Holy See for the purpose of obtaining the royal crown. After having received from his host precious gifts, including 300 knights, he was escorted as far as Magdeburg.

However, before their promising scheme materialized, the Emperor's premature death, in 1002, changed the situation entirely. His successor, Henry II, reassumed the already traditional policy of Germany with the object of subduing all her Slavonic neighbors, and Bolesław had to fight for sixteen years against the imperial pretensions. His own ambition was not only to safeguard the independence of Poland, but to unite under her direction all the Western Slavs in a state strong enough to check the German advance. The treaties concluded with Henry II during this period of Chrobry's rule proved to be only truces which, twice interrupting for some time the actual struggle, did not decide the real issue. The first question was whether the minor and still pagan Slavonic peoples between Germany and Poland would be conquered by the former or join the latter; the second, whether German or Polish influence would predominate among the Czechs. And Bolesław was fully aware how decisive these problems were for the future of Central Europe, and therefore he displayed all his strategic abilities, his diplomatic skill, and above all his bold spirit of initiative in order to secure a favorable solution of both of them.

Still in 1002, profiting by troubles in Bavaria which first absorbed the new Emperor, and also by the death of the Margrave of Meissen, Bolesław occupied not only this German outpost at the gates of Silesia, but also the whole of Lusatia as far as the Elbe river. The southern group of the Slavs living along that river was liberated from German rule. The following year, after the failure of his negotiations with Henry II, the Polish prince gained a still more important success. In Bohemia, where his father-in-law had died in 999 and civil war broke out between his sons, Chrobry seized the opportunity of supporting the anti-German party and of taking hold of the whole country, which he hoped to federate with Poland. This undertaking proved, however, to be beyond

Poland's possibilities. In 1004 Henry II entered Bohemia, bringing it again under German control and leaving only Moravia with Poland, and then he turned against Bolesław himself. As usual, only part of the Slavonic tribes in the Elbe basin took the Polish side, and they were defeated by the Germans who invaded Poland in the direction of Poznań. After the country had been devastated, peace was concluded in 1005. Bolesław had to give up his recent acquisitions, but tension continued between him and Henry II, and after only two years war began again.

The Emperor, convinced of its necessity, did not hesitate to utilize against the Poles the support of pagan tribes that lived in the center of the territory between the Elbe and the Oder. This decision was indignantly criticized by St. Bruno of Querfurt who, although a German himself, had a grateful appreciation of Bolesław's support of his missionary endeavors east of Poland. This time the war lasted four years. At the outset Chrobry once more entered Lusatia, where the Margrave of Bautzen had to surrender on honorable conditions, while the Poles conquered the whole region east of the Elbe in the direction of Magdeburg. It was not until 1010 that the Emperor could prepare for another campaign, and when he had eventually established a strong military basis near the Polish frontier, Bolesław raided the fortress in August 1012, before the German army was ready. After this splendid Polish victory, Henry II was glad to enter into negotiations which resulted in a new treaty, concluded at Merseburg in 1013. Chrobry kept the whole of Lusatia, but recognized the German overlordship over that province. That agreement seemed to lay the ground for a more lasting understanding, for Bolesław's son and successor, Mieszko II, who participated in the negotiation, married a niece of Emperor Otto III, while Henry II consented to furnish German auxiliary troops for Poland's eastern campaigns.

Nevertheless, the truce, as in previous cases, did not last more than two years. It is difficult to ascertain who was responsible for the failure of renewed negotiations which were to settle new misunderstandings. However, when in 1015 the Emperor claimed the restitution of Lusatia, Bolesław, with his usual pride, as the German chronicle says, answered that he would not cede his own; and not only had he halted the German invasion on the Oder, but pushed forward beyond the Thuringian frontier. After two years of fighting, in which even the Bohemians had to participate side by side with the Saxon and Bavarian troops of Henry II, the latter attempted in 1017 to invade Silesia and besieged two of its main fortresses. But he failed entirely, and Bolesław's forces, after having repulsed the large imperial army, crossed the Elbe, reaching the extreme southwestern limits of Slavonic settlements, whilst the northwestern tribes in what is now Mecklenburg rose against the Germans. The final peace treaty signed on January 30, 1018, at Bautzen, the capital of Lusatia where Bolesław received the imperial ambassadors, confirmed him definitely in the possession of the long-disputed province, and this time without any limitation by German sovereignty. His sixteen years' war had ended with an undoubted victory.

Yet the victory was not quite complete. Bohemia was to remain connected with the German Empire and only the Czechs of Moravia were united with Poland. North of the Sudeten Mountains, in the plain between the Elbe and the Oder, only the southern sector was reconquered from Germany. The situation of the other Slavonic tribes from Lusatia to the Baltic continued to be most precarious, especially as they were stubbornly attached to their paganism, which offered a convenient pretext for German conquest. But even so the results of Bolesław's heroic struggle were stupendous. A bare enumeration of his raids, battles and negotiations can scarcely give an adequate idea of the difficulties he had to face in opposing the greatest power of medieval Europe. The fact is that the German advance toward the East, almost uninterrupted from Charlemagne to our times, was not only stopped during Chrobry's reign, but suffered an exceptional and very serious setback, while the co-operation of at least a part of the Western Slavs made an equally exceptional progress. Moreover, the two choice territories which Bolesław succeeded in retaining were not at all an accidental consequence of the vicissitudes of war. Both Lusatia and Moravia were to be very useful marches of the realm of Chrobry who, imitating the German system of progressive defense, wanted to have such outposts on the main roads of access to Silesia, the most exposed of the Polish provinces—protecting at the same time Great Poland (Poznań) against the eastern marches of Germany and Little Poland (Kraków) against German-dominated Bohemia. From the viewpoint of political geography, the new western frontier which Bolesław gave to Poland, in addition to the natural boundary of the lower Oder, certainly was the best possible one.

Simultaneously he applied similar methods in his eastern policy. For it should be emphasized here that the greatness of his achievements with respect to Germany cannot be duly appreciated without taking into account the fact that Poland, even under such a powerful ruler as Chrobry, was under a permanent threat from both the West and the East, with open frontiers and aggressive neighbors on both sides. Mieszko I had experienced this danger when, while concerned with western affairs, he lost the region of Przemyśl with what much later was to be called Eastern Galicia, by an invasion of Vladimir of Kiev. This prince, who had made old Russia a great power, had been a constant danger for Bolesław at the critical moment of his second war with Henry II when for the first time the possibility of a German-Russian understanding directed against Poland arose. For that very reason even the limited support in the East which the Emperor felt obliged to promise to Chrobry in their peace negotiations was another real success of Polish diplomacy.

However, Vladimir the Great died in 1015 and his succession was disputed among his sons, the oldest of whom had married a daughter of Chrobry. Expelled from Kiev, he was restituted by Polish aid and Bolesław victoriously entered that capital of Russia, just as he had entered Prague fifteen years before. An annexation of the country, much larger than Poland, was of course out of the question and Bolesław's son-in-law remained in power only for one year. What Chrobry wanted was only to recover the eastern territory lost by his father, and to establish some kind of cooperation between the two greatest Slavonic countries, facilitated by the family ties between their rulers. He hoped of course that he would himself direct their common policy, and in that spirit he sent from occupied Kiev proud messages to the two Emperors: to Henry II of Germany, who now realized the growth of Poland's power in its full extent, and to Basil II of Constantinople, who considered Russia as his own sphere of influence and for the first time came in touch with a state hitherto scarcely known in the Byzantine world. To him, too, Bolesław offered his friendship, but at the same time declared himself ready to meet any possible opposition.

The real meaning of this procedure was that Chrobry was establishing in East Central Europe a new political system entirely independent of the two rival Empires and of their pretensions to universality. Was he dreaming of a third, Slavonic Empire, under his control? Certainly not. Realistic as he was, he must have been fully aware that it would have been utterly impossible to carry out such a scheme, hardly acceptable to the non-Polish populations, and inconsistent with the whole political conception of the Middle Ages, which recognized only the Roman Empire, either Western or Eastern. And although the differences between the various Slavonic peoples were at this time not yet as profound as later on, and the old Kievan Russia was much nearer to Poland than the Muscovite Russia of the future, it would be quite anachronistic to see in Bolesław something like a first representative of the pan-Slavic idea. He was rather a precursor of all those who later made attempts at some federal organization of that part of Europe without necessarily limiting it to peoples of Slavonic origin.

Directed by his broad political outlook, by geographical conditions and also by relationship with other dynasties, Bolesław was carefully following the developments not only west and east, but also south and north of his own country. His great contemporaries, St. Stephen of Hungary and Knut of Denmark, were his nephews, and he could not be disinterested in what was going on in their countries. Looking into Hungarian affairs, he probably extended Poland's frontiers over Slovakia and obtained also some Hungarian reinforcements in his Russian campaigns. And continuing his father's close relationships with all the Scandinavian nations, he must have been interested, in connection with Knut the Great's policy, even in far remote England. It might be said, therefore, that Poland's relations with the Anglo-Saxon world started under the first Polish king.

The desire of really becoming a king, as one of the great European rulers, outside the Empire, not only in practice, but legally, through a solemn coronation authorized by the Pope, was another of his life's great ambitions for himself and for Poland. This plan, advanced for the first time at the Gniezno congress, had to be postponed because of the hostility of the new Emperor; and not until after the death of Henry II, in 1024, could it be resumed successfully. There is no precise account of the renewed negotiations which must have been conducted with the Holy See, but its approval certainly was granted when, in 1025, Bolesław was crowned in Gniezno. Poland was now a kingdom, equal to the others which somewhat earlier had come into existence beyond the frontiers of the German Empire; the royal title was a symbol and a guarantee of her independence, a final consecration of her position in the Christian family of nations, crowning at the same time Bolesław's lifelong achievements.

These achievements, so conspicuous in the political sphere, were hardly less brilliant in other fields. Unfortunately, the last years of his reign, when he had more opportunity to deal with cultural, constitutional and economic problems, are much less known than the troublesome period of his tremendous military efforts and energetic foreign policy. Seriously concerned with the promoting of Christian religion and civilization since the earliest days of his rule, anxious to strengthen the frontiers he had reached in order to protect the security of the country, he also wanted to improve its government and administration by appointing a council which, according to tradition, numbered twelve members. The same tradition sees in Bolesław an energetic monarch, ready to punish severely any disobedience, but at the same time a protector of the peasants and an extremely popular ruler. When he died soon after his coronation, on June 17, 1025, he was deeply mourned by his people, who never ceased to consider his reign as a "golden age."

The tradition just referred to was recorded with a great deal of anecdotic detail, almost a hundred years after Chrobry's death, in the first chronicle of Poland written by an anonymous foreigner, probably of French origin. And it was not only a foreigner, but a harsh enemy, the German bishop of Merseburg and collaborator of Henry II, who left us the most abundant contemporary information on Bolesław until 1018, the year when his chronicle ends. But in spite of his one-sided and biased approach, he drafted a picture of the dangerous Polish leader which is an involuntary proof of his real greatness. Of course, more than anything else, Bolesław was for his opponent a personification of Polish resistance against German domination and influence, and that was indeed one of the main tasks of his life. But certainly not the only one. On the groundwork laid by his father he had to develop every side of Polish life, and it appears that he did it with the same creative genius which led him through his fierce struggle with the Emperor. To what extent were all these achievements the result of his personal merits, in what measure due to contributions of his collaborators? If, in the case of Bolesław, we know so very little of such collaborators (except a few representatives of the high clergy and just one Polish lord mentioned in the course of diplomatic relations with Germany), this lack of information largely results from the scarcity of source material. But as far as we are able to judge, Bolesław really was himself the leading personality of his epoch, and the splendor of his reign seems to be indeed the outcome of his own efforts.

The best proof of this may be seen in the rapid decline of Poland's power soon after his death. Although Mieszko II inherited a flowering and undivided kingdom, and was crowned immediately, he could not maintain his father's brilliant position for more than a few years. His reign ended in a series of catastrophes, after which his son, Casimir, without even assuming the royal title, had to restore the situation the best he could; and only his grandson, another Bolesław, called the Bold, who was crowned as king of Poland and, in general, followed Chrobry's footsteps, exercised during several years a similar influence in East Central Europe. But he proved much less successful. After a serious conflict with his own nation he died in exile, and in spite of the achievements of some of his successors it was not until 1295 that the royal dignity was re-established in Poland, to be finally confirmed in the fourteenth century by the last two Piasts—Władysław Łokietek (1306-33) and Casimir the Great (1333-70).

With these later developments in mind, the historian may wonder whether Bolesław Chrobry, obviously in advance of his time, had not been too ambitious in his attempts and whether his restless activity had any durable value for his country. Such assumptions would be entirely wrong. Through all the troubles and divisions from which the following generations had to suffer, the memory of his unforgotten glory and of the great, united Poland of his days remained an inspiration and a stimulation for the members of his dynasty, who frequently were given his illustrious name, and for the whole nation, which owed to him the consciousness of the dangers which were to be faced, of the possibilities of progress and expansion, and, above all, of its unity.

Considered from this viewpoint, the importance of Bolesław's coronation, to which all his earlier efforts had led, could scarcely be overrated. Even when no Polish prince felt strong enough to claim the royal crown for himself, the country still continued to be the "Regnum Poloniae" with its traditional rank in the hierarchy of the European powers; and the unity of its independent ecclesiastical organization, as it had cleared the way to Chrobry's royalty, later on mitigated the political disintegration, guaranteeing the continuity of an indivisible Poland not only in the eyes of the Holy See, but also in those of the whole Catholic world. Thanks to the timely initiative of Bolesław, his country had become one of the largest kingdoms on the continent, before the Norman conquest of England and before the first crusaders had founded the kingdom of Jerusalem.

In the field of foreign policy, Poland had fully learned from her first king the reality of persistent German danger and at the same time the possibility of resisting it. And she had also been taught to be aware of the necessity of strengthening her defensive position by close co-operation with related neighbor nations. The leading idea of the Jagellonian Poland: the idea of a federal system including the Baltic peoples, converted to Catholicism, as well as Kievan Russia—Ruthenia as it used to be called to distinguish it from Muscovy, or the Ukraine as it is called today—including also, if possible, at least in some looser form, Bohemia and Hungary, this idea, thanks again to Chrobry, made its first appearance in the early years of historic Poland. Impracticable under his rule, yet it was a great program for some distant future.

But there remains a last and probably conclusive argument for Bolesław's greatness. Poland had joined the Latin world at an early date, but nevertheless later than the nations of Western

Europe. Therefore, what she most urgently needed was an acceleration of her cultural evolution in order to reach an equal standing as soon as possible. Of course it was out of the question to get all this done entirely within the thirty-three years of Bolesław's rule, but he accelerated this evolution in a greater measure than anybody else before Casimir the Great and he did it in the first and decisive stage, utilizing foreign influences, but without submitting to any of them and without giving up the national individuality. And that was definitely a contribution not only to Poland's welfare, but also to the general progress of civilization in Christian Europe, in a community whose greatness always was in its diversity and which was enlarged and enriched by gaining in Bolesław Chrobry's kingdom a useful and enthusiastic member.

II

CASIMIR the GREAT

("*Kazimierz Wielki*")

1310-70

"Who found the Polish cities built of wood,
and left them built of stone and brick."

by

A. BRUCE BOSWELL

CASIMIR,[1] "the only king the Poles call Great," was born in
1310 in Kraków, the chief city of Lesser Poland, and was crowned
king at Kraków in 1333. We know very little about his early life.
He must have studied politics under the Archbishop of Gniezno
and the magnates of Lesser Poland in whose charge his father
left him.

This, however, we know full well, that he grew up during
one of the darkest periods in Polish history. A Polish state
scarcely existed, and throughout his life he had to endure from
his enemies the half-derisive title of "King of Kraków." Although
the Empire had declined and was no longer a formidable neighbor, the growing dissolution of Germany had given a great opportunity to the Czechs. Their new king of the Luxemburg dynasty
had revived his claims with such success that his dynasty became
the greatest menace to Polish independence, especially under his
son Charles IV, who became Emperor and made Bohemia the
greatest political and cultural force in central Europe. Along the
Baltic from the Narva almost to the Oder stretched the territories

[1] The son of Władysław the Short ("Lokietek"), one of the princes of
Kuyavia.

14

CASIMIR THE GREAT

(From painting by Jan Matejko)

acquired by the Teutonic Order, then at the height of its military power, exploiting Poland commercially by its occupation of the seaboard and acting as her enemy in politics, particularly in its alliance with the House of Luxemburg. In the East, Russia was in a state of complete decline, but interference there involved the aggressor in war with the Tartar khan, at that time the formidable Uzbeg, and in rivalry with the vigorous Lithuanian ruler Gedymin. In the south, Hungary was being raised by the Angevins from the political prostration that followed the extinction of her native dynasty. Charles Robert,[2] Casimir's brother-in-law and only ally, was a great cultural force in East Central Europe, and through his Court Italian civilization was permeating the backward clergy and magnates of Hungary and Poland. Charles IV of Bohemia had been educated at the French court and made Prague, where he entertained such men as Petrarch and Rienzi, the greatest city of Central Europe. Now Poland had always suffered from the fact that civilization had come to her from the West and implied German domination. As a result of the depopulation of the Tartar invasions her countryside was covered with villages of German settlers, many of her towns were populated by Germans, and even among her clergy and monks Germans were numerous. Casimir, though he never showed any antipathy to Germans personally, welcomed the chance of deriving cultural inspiration from other sources.

The two main objects which Casimir set before himself were the internal consolidation of Poland and her material and moral advancement. But first it was essential to secure her position externally. His preoccupation with this problem soon revealed him as a consummate diplomatist, and his achievements in this sphere form one of his chief titles to fame. He had to deal with the trained diplomats of the Empire, the Papacy and the Teutonic Order and with equally skilled statesmen taught in France and Italy. He had one great advantage in the decline of the German aggression in the West, especially after the extinction of the Ascanian dynasty in Brandenburg, which alone made possible the rise of national states in Central Europe. In the diplomatic game

[2] Charles Robert, the Angevin king of Hungary, married Casimir's sister Elizabeth in 1320.—*Ed.*

with his two great neighbors, his intuition enabled him to exploit two great weaknesses. The Czechs, culturally and economically so strong, were almost surrounded by German states, and could only find a field for expansion in Silesia, which they gradually acquired under John. They were naturally sensitive to any threat to the newly won province. Casimir exploited this feeling, and also the ambition of the Hungarian kings to succeed him in Poland. In fact Casimir had a great advantage over both his neighbors in that he had no sons and was free from the dynastic tangle that impeded the political developments of the age. Casimir's nephew, Louis,[3] was the most ambitious ruler of the day. He dominated the Adriatic, the northern Balkans and the lower Danube and wished to extend his power to the Baltic. Casimir drew from the Hungarian Court many new ideas and used its ruler's ambitions to his own profit. The Teutonic Order, however, was implacable and could only be satisfied by the cession of the seaboard. In a series of pacts, then, ending at Kalisz in 1343, Casimir, by renouncing all claim to Pomerania and Silesia, refounded a Polish state consisting of Lesser Poland, Greater Poland and Kuyavia. His policy has been criticized in subsequent times. But it is hard to see how the attenuated and exhausted lands of Poland could raise an army against the powerful combination of the Bohemian ruler and the Order. Moreover, the large German minorities in the lost provinces would have made their assimilation by the Polish element doubtful. Casimir himself never intended the concessions made in these sacrificial treaties to be permanent. He not only schemed and fought for the recovery of Silesia for the rest of his reign, but he exacted from Louis the promise to recover both Silesia and Pomerania.

To compensate Poland for these losses in the West, Casimir decided to annex Southwest Russia. He had a dynastic claim to these provinces, and the death of Gedymin as well as of Uzbeg, the last great khan of the Golden Horde, favored his plan. Moreover, while he had to fight one Lithuanian prince, another prince was defeating the Tartars further East. Secure in the West and supported by his ally from Hungary, Casimir inaugurated that great

[3] Louis the Great, King of Hungary, father of Jadwiga who later became "Poland's Great Queen."—*Ed.*

expansion of Poles, chiefly from Lesser Poland, into the Russian lands, partly as crusaders, partly as traders and settlers, which restored civilization to a land ruined by internal weakness and Tartar ravages. This Eastern policy also enabled him to add Mazovia to his group of Polish provinces, and to begin the attempts to convert Lithuania which had such successful results later on. This Eastern policy makes the year 1343 decisive in European history. Although Pomerania was recovered in the next generation, Silesia became largely German, so that Poland made a definite retreat from the Oder and acquired Eastern lands which made her a much greater, but less Western power, in contact with a new world of Tartars, Rumanians and Turks. This revolution was mainly due to the creative statesmanship of Casimir. Having satisfied the nobility of Lesser Poland, who began to spread not only over Galicia, but into Volhynia and Podolia, Casimir did not neglect the Northwest. He annexed two border towns from Brandenburg and a small territory which cut off that state from the territory of the Order. He gave his daughter in marriage to a prince of West Pomerania, and the son of this marriage, Casimir, was adopted by his grandfather and was regarded as the future successor of Louis to the crown of Poland. In fact Casimir the Great was actively evolving a new scheme for reaching the sea on the Oder instead of the Vistula, and his negotiations with Denmark, Mecklenburg and especially the princes of Pomerania, which was still largely a Slavonic land, show the fertility of his conceptions. The diplomatic activity of Casimir is remarkable. Whereas the great schemes of Charles IV and Louis perished with them, or their children, Casimir, building on firmer foundations, national rather than dynastic, left a more permanent edifice. The son of the little, hard-fighting prince of Brześć in Kuyavia handed over to his pupils a Poland which they could maintain and extend under his sister [4] and her Hungarian son,[5] under his grandniece [6] and her Lithuanian husband.[7]

As soon as he felt secure from his external foes, Casimir turned his attention to one of the main objects of his reign—in-

[4] Elizabeth.
[5] Louis the Great of Hungary.
[6] Jadwiga.
[7] Jagiełło.

ternal consolidation. Like his father, he based his authority on Lesser Poland. It must be realized that during the period of disunion the great principalities had become separate states with no bond of union except the ecclesiastical organization. These provinces, representing original tribal distinctions, had developed political separation and were divided by bitter antagonisms. Particularly keen was the rivalry between Greater and Lesser Poland, the one interested in the Germanic world on the Oder and the Baltic, and the other occupied with the rivalries of Bohemia, Hungary and Russia in the Carpathian area. Casimir had a double task—to strengthen his position as king in each of the provinces and to bring the provinces into closer constitutional union. In the first object he was completely successful; in the second less so. It is greatly to his credit that he refrained from exerting pressure that might have antagonized the provinces and have thrown them into the hands of Bohemia. Any real union was premature under the circumstances of the time. In Lesser Poland he was from the first an unquestioned ruler. Throughout his reign there was no opposition to him. The development of the monarchy was welcomed and supported by the magnates and gentry, especially when it gave them a field of adventure and settlement in Russia and close and friendly contact with their neighbors and cultural models at the Hungarian court. With its rapid economic development and the settlement of a rich court in its capital city, Lesser Poland became one of the wealthiest districts of central Europe, and Kraków, with its handicrafts and wealthy citizens, with its situation on three great trade routes, with its great buildings and its ostentatious court, became one of the great capitals of Europe. The princes continued to rule in Kuyavia, but their relationship to Casimir, their fear of aggression from the Order in the North, led them to view with growing favor the powerful monarchy rising in the South. The main opposition came from Greater Poland, which viewed with envy the rise of its rival. The early kings of Poland had reigned at Poznań. Gniezno was the seat of the Polish archbishop and the scene of the coronation of the kings. Civilization had penetrated to Poland from the West and there was a tendency among some of the clans of Greater Poland to imitate the institutions and manners of Brandenburg. Whereas the

Hungarian Entente and the occupation of Russia had enhanced the power of Lesser Poland, they were still exposed to the menace of aggression from the Czechs and the Order. Casimir had a strong link with Greater Poland through the descent of his mother from the princes of Kalisz and in the support of the higher clergy. But he had opposed several of the clans, especially when he put down private war. His tact and patience did much, but he had to crush a confederation and to execute its leader, Maćko Borkowic. It was partly to win the favor of the nobles of Greater Poland that he pursued his schemes in Pomerania, since it was largely the loss of the seaboard and the resulting commercial domination of the Order which weakened the province. The attraction of the Court and of service in a wider field gradually drew the gentry from their provincialism. The fourth great province, Mazovia, long a remote and backward district, ruled by princes who had even served the Teutonic Order, was brought into more active touch with Casimir through his Eastern advance. Its rulers were persuaded to swear feudal allegiance to Casimir as King of Poland, and gained by contact with their former rivals of Lesser Poland, especially in the rebuilding of their capital, Płock. In Russia there was no opposition to Casimir after the occupation of the province, which received Polish institutions and recognition of its customs and religion. In the lost provinces of Silesia and Pomerania, Casimir continued to support the Polish elements, and they remained part of the ecclesiastical organization of Poland. But in Silesia the process of Germanization, especially among the princes and nobles, proceeded rapidly.

Between these provinces the king was almost the only link, but he developed the office of Starosta to represent him in Greater Poland, Kuyavia and Russia. This official was responsible for justice, finance and military organization, and soon superseded the old Voyevoda and Kasztelan, who became territorial officials with nominal duties. The officials of Lesser Poland, especially the Chancellor and Treasurer, being constantly at Casimir's side, tended to become central ministers for the whole kingdom. The presence of the Court and the holding of Royal Councils also increased the influence of the center at the expense of the provinces. The Wiece or councils were still purely local assemblies and had not yet developed into representative institutions. If it was impracticable to give any real cohesion to his realm, Casimir did induce the magnates and gentry of the provinces to look beyond their limited horizon and watch and even participate in the affairs of a Poland no longer ruled by a "King of Kraków."

If Casimir's attempts to consolidate his provinces seem to have been frustrated by the separatism peculiar to the age, if the results of his diplomacy have been criticized, his efforts to secure material prosperity for his people and to direct their social and cultural advancement were entirely successful, and there is no great exaggeration in the legend that grew up of "the peasant king," the friend of the Jews, the ruler who "found a country of wood and left a country of brick." Casimir is rightly distinguished among all the kings of Poland by the title of "The Great." Like other great rulers he saw to it that justice was obeyed, he put down brigandage, respected and widened the legal rights of citizen and peasant as well as of nobleman. His great task of codifying the customary law of the different provinces gave him the opportunity of improving judicial procedure and bringing different codes into some sort of harmony. He encouraged the process of transforming the peasant groups into communities under German law. He respected the German law of the towns and founded towns, especially in Russia, with similar rights. But he showed a sound instinct in forbidding appeal to Magdeburg, and by setting up a court of appeals in Kraków began a process which was to transform the German citizens of Poland into Poles. He reformed the coinage, developed the salt mines, the source of the economic prosperity of Lesser Poland, and by judicious measures enabled Poland to obtain a leading position on the great Eastern trade route through Kraków and Lwów to the Genoese posts on the Black Sea. He built new churches, founded new towns and gave ancient cities strong walls and castles. In particular Kraków and Lwów benefited by his patronage. The castle on the Wawel was built by him and the Cathedral finished, while the lofty parish Church of St. Mary was built by a citizen of Kraków. New cathedrals at Gniezno and elsewhere testify to the royal support of architecture.

Casimir was not a learned man like his rival Charles IV, but he soon realized the importance of education. His chief churchmen were educated at Bologna or Padua, and a fresh impulse to imitate Italian civilization came through the Hungarian Court. Another current of civilization came from France through Prague and the Papal Court at Avignon, but when Casimir obtained permission to found an educational center in Poland it was Bologna, not Paris, that he took as his model. The University of Kraków was founded in 1364, sixteen years after the University of Prague and a few years before the Universities of Vienna, Pecs and Cologne.

About the personal life of Casimir we know very little. Of full habit, long-bearded and with a dignified carriage, he held a noble conception of his office that made his court admired and respected abroad. On the other hand, he liked good living, was genial and merry and a great lover of women. If he won the respect of the clergy and magnates by his qualities as a ruler, his benevolence, accessibility and love of good cheer gained him the affection of the gentry, burgesses and peasants. Rumor has it that he ran away at the battle of Plowce, like Charles IV at Crécy. But he was a competent soldier and generally a successful one. Like Richard II of England, Charles and Casimir had seen so much of the futility of war without statesmanship under their fathers that they preferred to gain their ends by diplomacy. Casimir revived kingship in Poland, made it a workable institution and surrounded it with prestige and glamour. He may be compared to contemporary rulers like Edward III or Charles V of France, but he left a legend that likens him to Charlemagne, Barbarossa, Vladimir and Robert Bruce. In an age when Empire and Papacy were losing their hold over states, it required a great personality to emerge from the feudal underworld into the open isolation of national monarchy. Casimir created a national state like France, England or Spain. To him it is due that the disunited provinces of Poland were not merged into the feudal anarchy of the Empire or absorbed by stronger neighbors like the Czechs or Magyars, leaving fragments to be overrun by Lithuanians and Tartar Khans. His achievements were due to his deep faith in the Polish people and confidence in his ability to teach and guide them. He was not a heroic figure, a dashing general or a doctrinaire reformer. He was a stern realist, and succeeded by infinite patience, tact and tenacity in conducting his people out of the more immediate dangers that threatened them, adapting and equipping them for the tasks of the future. The last of the native dynasty, he created a national tradition which survived centuries of foreign rulers, and with the exception of the development of representative government he sketched out almost all the lines of development which his country was destined to follow in the future. The fertility of his diplomacy is shown in the many schemes he left for experiment by his successors—the recovery of Silesia by diplomatic methods, the recovery of the seaboard either at Stettin or at Danzig, Russian colonization with its trade routes and a possible extension over the Podolian plateau and into Moldavia, the entry into a vast sphere of influence in Northwest Russia and the Baltic by the peaceful conversion of the Lithuanians. All these schemes were attempted and most of them realized by his successors. One is amazed at the wide sweep of them as compared with the petty intrigues of the former Piast princes. It is always dangerous to exaggerate the importance of a great man. We know that Casimir owed a great deal to the clergy and the magnates of Lesser Poland. He gained much from his elder sister at the Hungarian Court. But from the very first he towers over his compatriots, even though he left no great chronicler to praise him. He is the restorer of the Polish state, the creator of stable government, of material prosperity and cultural progress in what had been a very backward part of Europe.

It would be unjust to Casimir to regard him as a narrow nationalist. He is as much a European figure as a Polish ruler. He visited the Grandmaster of the Teutonic Order, attracted German knights to his Court and always supported the German burgesses in his towns. It is not for nothing that his patronage was sought by the fabulous Till Eulenspiegel. He was a good servant of the Church, and though he refused to embark on a crusade against the Turks—as indeed did all rulers who had no political interest in the Balkans—he spread the gospel among the Lithuanians in the last great center of paganism in Europe, and followed a policy which effected their conversion by peaceful methods where the violence of the Teutonic Knights had failed. In an age when heretics were burned and peasants oppressed, he set a striking example of toleration. We only hear of one anti-Semitic riot in

Poland (in the year of the Black Death), and the charter he conferred on the Jews at a time when they were being persecuted and expelled from most Western countries, attracted the great bulk of that race to Poland, which was for several centuries their homeland. He favored the Armenian community at Lwów and gave them religious liberty under their own bishop. He conferred on the Russian boyars equal rights with the Polish nobility, maintained the Orthodox church and gave it a new hierarchy. This great King of Poland was also a great and good European.

III

JADWIGA
"Poland's Great Queen"

1373-99

by
CHARLOTTE KELLOGG

JADWIGA was born at Buda, Hungary, in 1373. She was the grandniece of Casimir the Great, the last of the Piast kings of Poland, and the youngest daughter of Louis the Great, King of Hungary, who was also absentee ruler of Poland from 1370 to 1382.

In Jadwiga, strong heredities met, for King Louis' father was that Charles Robert of the family of Saint Louis of France who carried the Angevin line from Naples to Hungary, and Louis' mother, Elizabeth, was of Poland's Piast line—the sister of Casimir the Great.

I heard Jadwiga's story first from women at work in war-desolated Warsaw, then in that southern Kraków region whose loveliness not even war can destroy, and later, farther away in the Ukraine marches. I followed her down the corridor of the mind and heart of her people. And so struck was I by the position she holds in Polish thought and aspiration that I determined to know more about this young woman, who, during five hundred years, has been regarded by succeeding millions of Poles as their greatest queen.

I set out to discover the true Jadwiga. I found that the first event in which she played a major role was a "false marriage" ceremony, which, in the summer of 1378, celebrated the betrothal

QUEEN JADWIGA

(From painting by Jan Matejko)

of Hungary's younger princess to Prince William, son of the Hapsburg Duke Leopold of Austria.

When, in 1382, her beloved father died—after a rule of forty years in Hungary where he won glory and honor, and an absentee rule of twelve years in Poland where he won little of either—his wife and her two young daughters faced a future dark with uncertainty.

In Poland, during the latter years of Louis' rule, his extraordinary mother, Elizabeth, had acted as regent. After her death, one and a half years before his own, a triumvirate replaced her. During these regencies, disruption and misery grew, until they threatened the very foundations of the Polish state. Now, the uncertainty following Louis' death precipitated chaos. He had, to be sure, won from the Poles their promise to choose his daughter Mary and her future husband to succeed him. But after Mary's hurried coronation at Buda, Poland saw itself again dangerously facing absentee rule. And, too, the people had little relish for Mary's betrothed, Sigismund of Luxemburg, who had offended them in various ways. A strong group demanded that the Mazovian duke, Ziemowit, be crowned king; other forces pushed toward other objectives; many were ready to annul their promises to King Louis.

Then in November 1382, at Radom, in Greater Poland, the controlling nobles definitely decided against Mary and her German Sigismund. They were done with absenteeism. After terrible experiences with the Teutonic Knights, entrenched on their northern frontier, they wanted no German at their head. Asserting their privilege to select the successor within the reigning family, they would, while remaining true to Louis, reject Mary, and turn to his second daughter, Jadwiga, who must, on coming to them agree to remain forever in Poland. Unfortunately, Jadwiga also was betrothed to a German prince. But neither she nor William had yet reached their majorities. They would take care of William! They demanded that Jadwiga come at once to Kraków.

Now began a mother's desperate battle for time. For Elizabeth was determined to keep her beloved Jadwiga with her for several years' further education and physical development. She played an amazing game of subterfuge and evasion to hold her child, without forfeiting the Polish crown.

And as desperately, the Poles fought to end what amounted to civil war in their country. Near the close of February 1383, they called a great meeting at Sieradź. To it Elizabeth sent representatives, who demanded that after Jadwiga's coronation, she be allowed to return to Hungary, there to remain three years longer with her mother.

It was a stormy session, in which Hungary all but lost the crown to Ziemowit; but in the end the delegates again swung to Jadwiga. They declared her queen, and requested that she come to them at Pentecost to be crowned. Once again Elizabeth accomplished a delay. Then Polish nobles met on March 2, 1384, at Radom, and sent a final ultimatum. This time, Elizabeth, convinced that further equivocation meant certain defeat, capitulated. At any rate she had gained two years.

Space does not permit to depict here an adequate picture of the progress of Jadwiga and her Hungarian-Polish escort from Buda to Kraków, although it forms a part of the most brilliant pageantry of the time. For centuries girls had ridden across the eastern European plain unnoticed. Now, in this autumn of 1384, fate selected one to be the servant of high destinies.

She was met outside Kraków's great gate—the Kazimierz Gate —by a delegation of clergy and nobles. Advancing joyously came the high clergy with their banners, *chanoines* of convents, guilds with their insignia, the municipal council in silken robes and silver belts and round velvet bonnets. Strong men bore the city flag on which was embroidered, in gold, three square towers, the outer ones crowned by Poland's patron saints, Stanislaus and Wenceslaus, and the middle one by the Polish eagle. The city presented a gift, symbol of submission and homage; then to the music of trumpets and flutes and the cries of the hilarious crowd, Jadwiga entered the capital.

There she found that all that had passed so far had been only prelude. Great bells sounded, bonfires flared in the market place, lanterns illumined the streets. Girls in white, rose-garlanded and carrying lighted candles, came to meet their girl queen. She encountered a very delirium of welcome. No more absenteeism! She belonged to them—they would love her!

The rejoicing followed her to the royal Wawel Hill. There,

according to custom, she went first to the Cathedral, to kneel before the high altar, where the holy relics were brought out and kissed by her. Then she was offered gifts. At last, beneath her gorgeous robes, she crossed the wide court that separated the Cathedral from the royal castle, and retired into her stone chamber, which every tourist to Kraków today views with reverence.

Let us visualize Jadwiga, stranger in a strange land, as she lay down to sleep this first night in the gray stone room. She could not, looking forward, see that her reign would gloriously continue that of Casimir. She could not, mercifully, see the way she must walk in order to write her bright page in Poland's history.

In Hungary her world had seemed vast enough; but the boundaries of the new now widened. West, north, were the powerful Germans. She and William knew well the record of the Teutonic Knights as hunters of pagans. But henceforth she must hold her mind to a different view of them. Their name meant terror to Poland. Now pagan Lithuania was her next-door neighbor. To the east lay Muscovy. Beyond it ranged the Golden Horde. She was still too young to comprehend the problems these proximities presented.

Nor was she yet, actually to rule; though her preparation to do so had begun in very babyhood. Poland, a progressive among medieval European countries, was moving in the direction of an elective monarchy and parliamentary government. It had an advisory council of the crown and a national diet in which, theoretically, all the people, but actually for the time being, only the nobility or numerous gentry and clergy were represented. All of this, however, did not mean that the great provinces were yet committed to a strongly centralized government now that Casimir the Great was gone; each was still jealous of its sovereignty.

During the disastrous interregnum which Jadwiga's coming had ended, rivalries of provincial heads had reduced the land to almost hopeless disunion. The church synods alone, which represented the whole of Poland, had seemed to keep alive the idea of national solidarity. For the moment, the nobles of the province of Lesser Poland, who were her ardent supporters, were the dominant power in the land. She was to be under their tutelage, and directly in the care of Castellan Dobiesław, military commander of Kraków and mayor of the royal castle. Everything had been properly arranged—her dames of honor and maidens-in-waiting were ready to serve her.

During this very week of her arrival—on October 15, 1384, Jadwiga was crowned. After a preliminary ceremony in the castle, the archbishop, castellan, governor, and other high dignitaries escorted her across the courtyard to the Cathedral. As she walked, preceded by palatines who carried the royal scepter and coronation sword and followed by abbesses and prioresses and a crowd of courtiers holding lighted candles, a wave of intense emotion swept over the watching multitude. Here was glowing youth whose feet were forced from the carefree path of childhood into the road that wise maturity rarely traveled successfully.

Inside the candle-starred Cathedral gloom, the scene was one of medieval splendor. Before the gospel, Jadwiga approached the altar to hear the age-old question, winged with inextinguishable faith and hope—would she promise to respect the rights, the liberties, and privileges of the people? Her "Yes" was clear, firm. She meant to keep that promise as she understood it. She was crowned king, not queen; but because her mother had neglected to return the king's crown which her father had taken to Hungary, the heavy gold one with its pendant ribbons had been hurriedly made in Kraków for this day. After she mounted the throne erected in the nave, two dignitaries held the crown over her head during the remainder of the ceremony. Later, an image of her as she appeared at her coronation was stamped on one of the seals which she attached to her documents.

The ceremony was not yet complete, for in all that had passed so far, Kraków burghers had had no part. The following day, again royally robed and attended, Jadwiga went from Wawel Hill down to the town, and in another richly colorful ceremony was a second time crowned, before the city hall.

Three days later she was already signing documents—first signatures, seemingly of no especial importance, but today how venerated! Historians like to point out that the initial act of her reign confirmed the right of a man of the middle class, one Sidel, to certain lands. The people looked on this as a sign that their beautiful young queen was indeed kin of their great Casimir, the only king the Poles call Great.

The crown was on her head, the scepter in her hand. No hope, now, to run away, back to mother, sister, William! Messages were infrequent, letters took long to come, to go.

Daily she was going to school, to church and state. The council of the crown saw to the latter lessons; priests directed those of the Church. All found at once that they had in her an unusual mind to deal with—keen, intuitive, and at the same time logical. They were surprised by her knowledge of history. They were especially impressed to find this girl already an accomplished theologian, delighting in the sermons of the fathers and the lives of the saints. The deeds of Saint Bridget and Saint Catherine thrilled her; she was later to have certain of their utterances translated into Polish, so that her people could follow them directly, for she regarded Poland now as her true home.

The good tidings of her concern for her least subject, of her tender-heartedness, ran across the country. Scarcely a day passed but some sufferer appealed to her charity, and never in vain. She began early to endow altars and hospitals, and to give personal service to the sick.

But while love of her, belief in her, grew, yet foremost in her people's mind was the obsessing question—who will reign with her? If Poland was to stand against enemies, there must be a king, a strong king. In Jadwiga's mind there was no question. She was sacredly betrothed to her loved comrade William.

But William did not come. Her own problem, which was Poland's, too, reached a crisis. There was open talk of the dread Jagiełło, ruler of pagan Lithuania; of Jagiełło, scourge of Poland, the "hairy barbarian" as pictured by minstrels. Polish nobles were carrying on incredible negotiations with Jagiełło. Not only would he, if he became king of Poland, unite the vast Lithuanian territories with hers, restore her lost lands, release Polish prisoners of both sexes, and with her defend the united countries against the Order of Teutonic Knights, but Jagiełło would, if he came, embrace Christianity and bring his whole people into the Catholic fold! No such offer was to be found in the annals of Europe. For Lithuania, too, it meant tremendous things; a bulwark against

Germanism, the Christian religion, admission into the family of western Europe.

During succeeding weeks, magnates, priests, worked to force her to accept their plan. Then just as they seemed to be winning, Prince William, in gleaming mail and long-plumed helmet, a picture of the very flower of young knighthood, accompanied by a magnificent retinue and gift-laden wagons, arrived at Kraków Gate. Jadwiga's blood bounded. In Kraków there was consternation. The nobles could scarcely lock the city gate before Austria's heir, but they did bar him from Wawel Hill. However, the good Franciscans came to the aid of their young queen and her betrothed; they offered their convent, near the base of the royal hill, as a meeting-place. Then for months, while the leaders who supported Jagiełło and those who supported William fought their desperate battles outside, inside the convent refectory the young comrades and their friends met to feast and hope. The betrothed believed they were winning. But on August 14, 1385, a Polish mission stood before Jagiełło, near his capital, Wilno, to inform him that all Poland had agreed to accept him as king!

And now came that culminating scene about which chroniclers differ. Some assert that William, despite surveillance, managed to gain Wawel Hill—that he was actually fifteen days within the palace before a humiliating escape. Others tell us that he tried to force an entry to the royal castle, but the council placed guards at every door. All agree that a tide too strong for a control was carrying her to a great decision. With the news that Jagiełło had started with a strong following for Kraków, she decided to try to escape from Wawel Hill.

But how was she to escape? She must rely on a narrow stairway leading to a door usually unguarded. But this time, to her dismay, she found it barred, and guards posted. "Open," she commanded. "We are forbidden." "By whom?" "The Seigneurs." "But I am your queen." Throwing back her long mantle, she demanded an ax, and while they stood stupefied, the young queen beat on the door's hinges. Then suddenly her hand was stayed. Dimitri of Goray, aged treasurer of her father and her uncle, fell on his knees and implored her to respect the memory of her great ancestors. With power he pictured the greater Polish empire and its happy millions who would call her blessed. He showed the favor of heaven descending upon the queen who would bring a whole people into the Christian fold. Was not this conversion more important in heaven than any betrothal pact, however attested? In the end she agreed and he led her back to her chamber. She would send a message at once to William, begging him to leave the city. She would never see him again.

The next morning she went desolately to the Cathedral, where she remained all day on her knees below the pitying Christ on a great wooden crucifix, where today is set the inscription, "Here knelt Jadwiga." There she sealed her renunciation.

Through more than five centuries of troubled, of tragic history, this scene on the Wawel has remained fixed in Polish memory. Indeed, for Poland, the figure of Jadwiga possesses much of the vivid significance that Jeanne d'Arc has for France. Called to splendid and terrible sacrifice, these two maids, one a princess, the other a peasant, have become the symbols of the noblest in national hopes and national faith.

On Monday, February 12, 1386, as the thirty-eight-year-old Jagiełło entered Kraków, an excited populace hailed him as their deliverer from the nightmare of ever threatening invasion. It would be difficult to describe the pageantry of the succeeding days, during which, by ceremonies whose import shook the Christian world, he advanced to kingship. He was baptized, along with relatives and a large number of boyars. By this baptism the Order of Teutonic Knights became an anachronism. A territory stretching from the Baltic toward the Black Sea and eastward almost to Moscow would now turn its face to the West, toward Rome and occidental culture. Some were already calling Jagiełło a second Constantine.

On Sunday, February 18, the Church having declared itself free of all responsibility to William (Jagiełło was to pay Austria the 200,000 florins promised William's father by King Louis, as Jadwiga's *dot*), the now Christian ruler of the last pagan country in Europe and Poland's beautiful young queen were married.

March 4 was the coronation day. The Piast dynasty was ended; that of the great Jagiellonians began, and with it that heroic age of Poland, which was to last two hundred years, culminating in the Golden Age of the sixteenth century. All this was made possible by Jadwiga's sacrifice, and without the shedding of a single drop of blood.

Soon Jadwiga and Jagiełło made their first tour of the realm. Excited throngs all along the way pressed to see this procession. Here was the most beautiful, the most holy, the saddest queen in the world—the little queen who had given them her heart. Beside her rode the "wolf," the "infidel"; tamed, become Christian, because of her. The people recognize and love poetry; here was living poetry.

From the initial review, events of the double reign moved impressively forward. By January ice bridges had formed over the trackless northern marshes, and Jagiełło could prepare to fulfill his promise to make Lithuania Christian. What a spectacle at Wilno, on the plain and the low hills beside the Wilya river during this winter of 1387! On Sunday, February the seventeenth, while the crowd, scarcely breathing, watched, Christian priests quenched the fire on the pagan altar, and planted a cross where the statue of the pagan god had stood, Jagiełło himself aided the priests to interpret the new religion to his people. The pagan temple near his chateau was destroyed, and beside the ruins he laid the cornerstone of the Catholic Cathedral. From Wilno out over the land the good work spread. Three days after the laying of the cornerstone, he signed an edict which became the charter of Lithuanian liberty, based on Polish institutions. It secured to his people property rights and equality before the law, assured them a share in the results of their labor and in the joys of the family. All this was brought about without the unsheathing of a single sword, simply as a consequence of Jadwiga's sacrifice. This was her victory and her reward.

While Jagiełło astonished the world with this swift and sweeping emancipation of his people, Jadwiga thrilled it by riding at the head of her troops in an intrepid movement to recover from Hungary—from her sister, Mary—fertile Red Ruthenia, crossed by the great trade routes seeking out Lwów. The enthusiasm of her troops as the young queen rode with them swept all before it. In a short time the leaders of the Hungarian troops garrisoned on the land were forced to flee. Volhynia, Podolia, and subse-

quently other provinces were retrieved. This territory offered
Poland agrarian expansion; it promised commerce with the Orient.
The Black Sea would now be an assured economic objective;
Polish enterprise could link it with the Baltic. Jadwiga gave much
thought now to the development of this eastern territory, which
had been so ravaged by the Tatars; she sent there priests and
teachers.

While she was giving her energies to her royal duties, the
queen was increasingly having to endure personal grief. Each letter
from Buda brought darker news; not only the throne, but her
mother's and her sister's very lives were in danger. She heard
rumors of William's bitterness and unhappiness. There were persistent reports that her experience with her older, less cultivated
husband, was none too easy. But more than from all these things,
she suffered because the child she yearned for, prayed for, did
not come.

It took time to heal disruption. Poland was still divided. In
December 1387, Queen Jadwiga issued a decree which was of
great importance in the struggle toward unity. In it she asked
Kraków to swear to be as loyal and obedient to Jagiełło as to herself; and should she die, to take him as king. Similar decrees were
issued in other cities. The ambitious nobles were not quieted; on
all sides plots were hatching. And chiefly there was Jagiełło's
valorous but disturbing cousin, Prince Witowt, to watch. During
this period he turned a favorable ear toward the Teutonic Knights.
His plans did not stop with his visioned control of Lithuania, but
included fantastic plans of conquest in Russia, in Tatar-held lands.
There seemed to be little hope that he and Jagiełło would arrive
at a successful working agreement.

To Jagiełło, fate had assigned a double role. Not only was he
to develop a Slavic state strong enough to withstand the German
pressure eastward, but the former pagan now saw himself standing
as a defender of Europe against two powerful pagan forces, the
Golden Horde of Kipchak on whom Witowt's chivalric zeal was
centered, and the Osman Turks. He must work, therefore, with
Witowt, and yet restrain him. In this drama of opposition and
reconciliation enacted by Jagiełło and Witowt, Jadwiga held an
extraordinary relationship with both. Her reputation for wisdom

and fairness had grown steadily, until people from far away came
to seek her advice. And now, more and more frequently, Jagiełło
and Witowt turned to her in their conflicts. Intensely moving is
the picture of this young woman, dedicated to high and holy
tasks, as we see her standing between these two men, both willing
to accept her judgment, where they rejected each other's.

But more difficult than these problems was that of shaping
Poland's policy toward the Teutonic Knights, and the way in
which Queen Jadwiga tried to solve this problem—this, alone,
would have lifted her to the level of greatness. The Order must
be driven beyond all Polish-Lithuanian frontiers; Polish-Lithuanian
objectives must be secured against encroachment. But this, she determined, must be accomplished, not by fighting, but by negotiation. Her faith was so strong that, despite the sword-brandishing
spirit of her age, she believed she could succeed. And so, using
all her influence to win Jagiełło's support, she embarked on a
course of persistent, unwearying effort for a peaceful solution of
an international difficulty which bears comparison with any similar
undertaking of our own time. Indeed, her diplomatic struggle to
bring the Order to reason and justice stands as one of the extraordinary episodes of European history. That she did not in the end
succeed as she had hoped to, does not dim the values in this picture
of her as the early advocate of negotiation, the early pleader for
peace.

Jagiełło's turbulent family made Lithuanian affairs increasingly difficult for him. Early in the last decade of the fourteenth
century, he and his brothers and cousin asked Queen Jadwiga
to act as arbitress in all future disagreements which might arise
between them. A new period of settlement by arbitration, with
Jadwiga as arbitress, began. Five documents registered the concilia-
tory steps by which the final broad agreement was reached. The
little girl, who with her boy-friend had listened shiveringly, beside
the Danube, to tales of the heathen of the dark north, now as
queen accepted this extraordinary investiture.

Jadwiga had filled with good works the year 1390, declared
a holy year by Pope Boniface IX. She increased her study of the
church fathers and the saints; she added more days of self-denial;
though already she and Jagiełło limited themselves, two days a

week, to bread and water. At certain seasons she dressed almost
as a nun, wearing a dark veil and a rough garment next to her skin.

It was at this time that she and Jagiełło summoned Benedictines from Prague to found an abbey near Kleparz, where in their
Church of the Holy Cross the daily service would be recited in
the Slavic language. And for other foundations she now insisted
that at certain seasons both mass and song should be rendered in
Polish. She was an enthusiast in church music and did much to
improve it. During five hundred years Poland has been reverently
grateful to Jadwiga for her effort to bring religion and learning
within the reach of all; and for being, as she was, one of the first
to appreciate the beauty and importance of the Polish language.

To the two dominant forces of this century, those of the
Empire and the Church, has been added a third, that of the University. The Holy See knew and approved of Queen Jadwiga's
plan to give Kraków the thoroughly grounded university which
Casimir had attempted to establish in 1364. Unwearyingly she
labored for this; that she succeeded as she did in helping to recreate
Kraków University is one other reason for her position in Polish
history.

April 1397 brought further testimony of the people's confidence in their queen. She was sent as Ambassadress of the whole
nation to treat directly with the Grand Master of the Teutonic
Knights for the restoration of occupied Polish lands.

Then, as the last year of the century approached (for Jadwiga,
whose mother had been murdered, whose only sister had been
killed by a fall from a horse, who had borne grief upon grief),
suddenly the whole world was changed. She was with child! The
great of Europe crowded to Kraków to be present at the birth.
On June 22, 1399, when news spread that a baby girl was born,
shouts echoed from city wall to wall. The following day, in the
Cathedral, the child was baptized, and christened Elizabeth Boni-
facia, for Jadwiga's mother, and for the Pope. Succeeding fes-
tivities were not to continue long. Cutting like a sword across
them came the word that Jadwiga's baby, their heir to the throne,
was dead.

Jadwiga made her supreme effort, tried to plan for Poland's
future. She asked Jagiełło, if she should die, to marry Anna, daugh-

ter of the Count of Cilly and grand-daughter of King Casimir the Great. This marriage would further secure his position. He promised, and later fulfilled that promise, though he wore Jadwiga's ring until his death. Then she made her will. "My will is simple," she said. "One half of the proceeds of the sale of all I have, jewels, clothes, ornaments, possessions of every kind, I leave to the University of Kraków; the other half to be divided among the poor. Little must be spent on funeral ceremonies. I wish no elaborate service or eulogy, no monument of any kind. Let my body be placed beside that of my baby on the gospel side of the altar, with a plain inscription on the facing marble to mark the place." So, for the last time, she revealed the greatness of her spirit.

On the day of her death, July 17, 1399, the following words were inscribed in the Wawel's Latin calendar: "Today, at noon, died Jadwiga, Queen of Poland—unwearied creator of divine culture, protectress of the Church, administrator of justice, servant of all virtues, humble and beneficent mother of orphans, who in her time had had no equal of royal blood in the eyes of men in the whole world."

NICOLAS COPERNICUS

(From steel engraving by E. de Boulanois)

IV

NICOLAS COPERNICUS
"The Father of Modern Astronomy"

1473-1543

Wstrzymał słońce, wzruszył ziemię,
Polskie wydało go plemię

("The Sun he bade to stop, and at his bidding
the earth began to spin—
Poland has nurtured him.")

by

A POLISH SCIENTIST

NICOLAS COPERNICUS came of Polish Silesian stock. The documents of the fourteenth and fifteenth centuries mention several members of the Copernicus family living in Silesia. One of its branches moved (about 1350) to Kraków, the capital of Poland at that time. In 1396, the namesake of our astronomer, most likely his great-grandfather Nicholas, became a citizen of Kraków. The astronomer's grandfather was probably Jan Kopernik, a wealthy Kraków merchant. His name is mentioned several times in the historical documents of 1433-41. We know more about his son, who bore the traditional family name of Nicholas. To distinguish him from his famous son we will call him Nicholas Copernicus the Elder. As a rich merchant on the Vistula, he was widely known along the river from Kraków to Toruń (Thorn) and Danzig. Documents quote his name first in 1448, and then more often from 1454, the year when the union of Prussian territories and towns together with Danzig and Toruń revolted against the Teutonic Order and asked the Polish king Casimir II for protection. The revolt resulted in the Thirteen Years' War, after which the

Treaty of Toruń was concluded in 1466, giving all the land between Danzig and Toruń and also the Varmian territory back to
Poland. Nicholas Copernicus the Elder is known to have participated actively in the political events of those days. He moved from
Kraków to Toruń, became a citizen of that city and married
Barbara Watzelrode about the year 1460. Barbara's family had
also been originally Silesian, but had been settled in Toruń for a
century. Barbara's father, Lucas Watzelrode the Elder, belonged
to the richest patricians of the city. An old and inveterate enemy
of the Teutonic Order, he took an active part in the war and in
political events from 1454 until his death in 1462. Besides Barbara,
he had another daughter and a son, Lucas. The latter, having entered the Church and finished his studies at Bologna University
(1473), quickly began to advance in the hierarchy, holding in a
short time three canonries in Northwestern Poland (Włocławek,
Varmia and Gniezno). In 1489, being elected Bishop of Varmia,
he reached the height of his Church career.

Nicholas Copernicus the Elder passed away about 1483, leaving four children, the youngest of whom was his namesake,[1] the
famous astronomer, with whose life and work we are concerned
here. He was born in Toruń on February 19, 1473, and spent his
childhood there. After his father's death he was put under the
guardianship of his uncle Lucas Watzelrode and was educated most
probably in Włocławek Cathedral School. In the autumn of 1491
Nicolas was sent to continue his studies in Kraków. The University of Kraków was then famous for its high standard of science,
especially mathematics and astronomy, and attracted a great number of scholars from all over the world. Among its most famous
professors of astronomy were Jan z Głogowa (John of Głogów)
and Wojciech z Brudzewa (Albertus of Brudzewo). An old academic tradition maintains that the latter was Copernicus' principal
teacher. Throughout his whole life Nicolas Copernicus acknowledged his indebtedness to his Kraków Alma Mater, where most
probably he spent four years of his life, up to the spring or summer of 1495.

---

[1] Throughout this chapter we shall use the generally known and accepted
latinized form of *Nicolas*, without the "h," when we refer to the famous
astronomer.

After a short stay in Licbark (Heilsberg, the chief seat of the Varmian bishopric), Copernicus went to Italy about the middle of the year 1496. According to his uncle's wish he matriculated as a student of canon law at Bologna University, without, however, giving up his scientific preferences. There he became acquainted with a professor of astronomy named Domenico Maria Novara (1454-1504), whom he remembered ever after with love and gratitude. Even toward the end of his life, Copernicus often recollected the days when as a young scholar he "was less of a student than a collaborator and witness of Novara's astronomical observations." The earliest of Copernicus' extant observations are actually of Bolognian origin. This fact is not a mere coincidence, but the logical consequence of the evolution of his ideas. While still a student at the University of Kraków, he discovered several logical contradictions in the existing astronomical system taught in schools and used to calculate the tables of celestial motions. Bologna offered him a splendid opportunity to examine the existing system, no longer only by means of theoretical reasoning but by direct observation, though in only one but a very important detail. It concerned the theory of the motion of the moon. The occultation of Aldebaran (the brightest star in Taurus) by the moon in its first quarter offered an excellent occasion for this examination. Copernicus calculated that the phenomenon would take place in the evening of March 9, 1497. His observation, made with the greatest precision, turned out a success. It proved that the distance between the earth and the moon is the same no matter whether the moon is full or in one of its quarters. This was in contradiction to the Ptolemaic theory generally accepted in the lifetime of Copernicus.

This memorable observation of March 1497, closed the first period of evolution in the mind of our great scholar and opened the second. The period of criticism was over, and then began the period of research leading to the creation of a new astronomical system built upon the ruins of the Ptolemaic one. It is quite likely that for a while Copernicus himself did not realize what the principles of his new system would be. He very eagerly started to read various ancient authors, Greek and Latin, searching for some other conceptions of the universe besides those of Ptolemy. Studying thus the history of astronomy, he discovered, about 1498, that in Cicero, Plutarch and other writers, there was some obscure mention concerning certain Greek philosophers, especially those of the Pythagorean school, who thought the earth might be moving. This gave Copernicus the idea that the immobility of the earth was not such an indisputable axiom as was generally accepted.

In the meantime, thanks to the endeavors of his uncle, Bishop Lucas, Copernicus was elected a canon of Varmia (about 1497). This made him financially independent and gave more opportunity for scientific work. He did not leave Bologna, however, until the spring of the Jubilee Year of 1500, when he moved to Rome to work in the Pope's chancery, lecturing at the same time on mathematics and astronomy. Late in the spring of 1501 he went North to his canonry attached to the Varmian cathedral church in Frombork (Frauenburg), which had been granted him four years before, but in July of the same year the Varmian Chapter gave him special permission to return to Italy to study there the art of medicine. For this purpose Copernicus chose Padua University, where he remained from the autumn of 1501 till the autumn of 1503, except for a few weeks which he spent in Ferrara to obtain the doctor's degree in canon law (May 31, 1503). There are reasons to suppose that during those years spent in Padua he definitely came to the conclusion that the new system must be based on the principle of the mobility of the earth.

Having returned to Varmia at the end of 1503, Copernicus spent a short time in Frombork, and finally settled in Licbark Castle as physician and personal secretary to his uncle, Bishop Lucas. He took an active part in the political events of the duchy-bishopric of Varmia and accompanied the bishop on his frequent journeys. In his leisure time Copernicus continued his astronomical studies. It was in those days (and certainly before 1515) that he composed the first general outline of his new system and presented it in his opuscule: "Copernicus' Short Treatise concerning the principles established by him for the explanation of celestial motions" (*Nicolai Copernici de hypothesibus motuum caelestium a se constitutis commentariolus*). He did not, however, publish it but showed it only to his friends, for he considered the *Commentariolus* only a sketch, to be altered and completed. In fact, the celestial mechanism explained in the *Commentariolus* differs considerably from that presented in the chief work of his life (1543), although both of them are of course heliocentric.

There came a serious change in the astronomer's life in 1512. His uncle and protector, Bishop Lucas Watzelrode, passed away on March 30. Copernicus had to move to Frombark, where around the cathedral church there were scattered the houses of the Varmian canons. In one of these houses he settled down and arranged his scientific laboratory which was connected with the astronomical observatory. However, political events soon hindered his work. Albert of Hohenzollern, the young Grand Master of the Teutonic Order, could not forget the loss of the Order's territories and began scheming to regain them. He fomented disorders in the Polish provinces, especially in that of Varmia, which was encircled by the Teutonic possessions and was governed at that time by the weak and indolent prince-bishop Fabian Luzjański, the opposite of his energetic predecessor Lucas Watzelrode. All over the territory of the duchy there spread gangs of robbers and bandits organized by the Teutonic Order and openly backed by its Grand Master for the destruction of the country with fire and sword. This was only a prelude to the new Polish-Teutonic war that was to break out in 1520. In 1516 conditions in Varmia became so critical that its Chapter decided to complain to King Sigismund I. Copernicus, being Watzelrode's nephew, naturally belonged to the most inveterate enemies of the Teutonic Order. Commissioned by the Varmian Cathedral Chapter, he wrote the complaint to the king (July 22, 1516). It was the first but not the last protest of the astronomer against the violence of the Teutonic Knights. A few weeks later, chosen by his colleagues to be administrator of all the Church property, Copernicus settled at Olsztynek, the only fortress of Varmia, situated close to the Teutonic territory. On this dangerous and exposed outpost he spent three years of his life and returned there again as its Commander-in-Chief during the war. There has been preserved a letter of his, written at that time (in October 1518) to his Varmian colleagues, warning them to be cautious in their answer to the Grand Master's address, to avoid his "perverse interpretation." In the same letter Copernicus rejoices at the diplomatic defeat of the

Teutonic Order. It was also he who wrote a solemn censure presented by the Varmian Chapter to the "dietine" (provincial assembly) of Grudziądz (July 25, 1521) accusing the Grand Master Albert and his Order of invading and devastating Varmia in spite of the armistice treaty.

For a more complete picture of Copernicus' activities outside his main scientific work, his important part in the currency reform conferences of Varmia and its neighboring provinces (1519-1522) and his administration of the whole duchy after the death of Bishop Fabian (1523) must be mentioned. In this connection he wrote a special treatise concerning currency. It was twice revised by the author (the last edition dates from 1525 or 1526). In the second, and much more clearly in the third edition, Copernicus formulated an economic law, stating that the worst form of currency in circulation regulates the value of the whole and drives all good currency out of circulation. It is the so-called "Law of bad money" (also erroneously termed Gresham's law).[2] Copernicus was preceded in this discovery only by an anonymous French author of the fifteenth century, whose pamphlet, however, was unknown to him. He discovered that currency law quite independently and formulated it much more precisely than his French predecessor. Therefore, although not the very first to be a discoverer of one of the most important monetary laws, Copernicus cannot be denied his merit in the field of economics. This is why the well-known Scottish economist, Henry Dunning Macleod, calls him "one of the founders of a most important branch of economics."

It is amazing that in spite of such a busy life Copernicus was able to go on with his scientific work. Many of his observations were made during those stormy years. He began to write the first books of his great work *De Revolutionibus* about 1515. The principal aim of this work was to develop the idea of the heliocentric system already outlined in the *Commentariolus*. To prove the truth of his statements, Copernicus had to show their conformity with astronomical observations. It was not enough to proclaim the sun to be a "center of the universe" and the earth one of its planets; it was indispensable to develop his idea, work it out in all its details, get a definitive point of view on various contradic-

[2] Thomas Gresham was born in 1519.

11732

tory theories of those times, repudiate existing doubts, calculate the quantitative "elements" of celestial orbits and motions and verify them by subsequent observation. It was a stupendous and very difficult task, especially since Copernicus, far from all scientific centers, was left to himself and had no help whatsoever. As his work progressed, he found the mechanism of celestial motions more complicated than that outlined in the *Commentariolus*. His observations of 1515 resulted, for instance, in the unexpected discovery that the orbit of the earth had variable excentricity and that the apogee of the sun moved toward the fixed stars. Because of this the writing of *De Revolutionibus* was much delayed and became the subject of many changes and alterations.

And even when all his books were completed, Copernicus did not consider them to be ready for print, but perused them over and over again, verifying all the details and calculations with new observations. He felt a kind of moral obligation to perfect his astronomical system all his life long before he could think of its publication. Bold and independent as a thinker, he was not of a militant nature. Although deeply convinced of the truth of his heliocentric system, he did not dare to publish it, being (as he himself acknowledges) "afraid of contempt brought about by the novelty and inconceivableness" of his new theory. The mobility of our globe was in opposition to the testimony of the senses. He preferred therefore to keep the precious results of his work for himself and for his few chosen friends.

But intelligence began slowly to penetrate Europe. Yonder in distant Varmia, there lived a scientist working out a new astronomical theory. News of this reached Rome in 1533 and was the subject of a conversation between Pope Clement VII and a German orientalist, John Albert Widmanstadt. In the autumn of 1535, a friend of Copernicus, Bernard Wapowski, a canon of Kraków, obtained his permission to print the astronomical calendar for 1536, based on the heliocentric tables. It was to show to the educated public how much more exact were these Copernican tables than the old geocentric ones. Unfortunately, Wapowski's death prevented that plan from being put into practice. A year later, in October 1536, Cardinal Nicholas Schomberg sent a letter to Copernicus from Rome encouraging him to publish his work, or at least to send him a copy of the manuscript. The most ardent among those who advocated the publication of *De Revolutionibus* was Copernicus' good friend, Tiedeman Giese, at one time canon of the Varmian Chapter, then a bishop of Chełmno.

All those endeavors might have been fruitless had it not been for the intervention of a young Wittenberg astronomer, George Joachim von Lauchen, universally known as Georgius Joachimus Rheticus (b. 1514). The latter, having heard of Copernicus and his original, new system of the world, decided to go to Frombark and learn from the master himself the secret of his theory. Rheticus, full of youthful enthusiasm, came to Varmia in May 1539, and at once won the confidence and sympathy of the aged astronomer. Thanks to his own and Giese's persuasions, the doubts and scruples that kept Copernicus from publishing the work of his life were finally overcome. Once more he revised the priceless manuscript and commissioned Rheticus to publish only its summary in order to prepare minds for the new, revolutionary idea. This summary, "The first Announcement of Nicolas Copernicus' Revolutions" (*De libris Revolutionum D. Doctoris Nicolai Copernici Narratio Prima*), appeared in Danzig in 1540 and was reprinted a year later in Basle. In the same year (1541) Rheticus left Varmia with the manuscript of the whole work for the printer John Petrejus in Nuremberg. Andrew Osiander, a Lutheran theologian, was entrusted with its proofreading. Unfortunately he did not deserve the confidence which Rheticus and Copernicus had placed in him. Influenced by Melanchthon, he had tried even earlier to persuade Copernicus to write a foreword to his work, presenting the new astronomical theory as a mere hypothesis, useful for calculations but not necessarily true. Copernicus rejected this proposition with great indignation and by way of reasserting the truth of his system he wrote (in June 1542) a splendid dedicatory letter to Pope Paul III to be printed as a preface to *De Revolutionibus*. Osiander, however, would not agree to it. Finally he made the compromise that, besides the preface of Copernicus, he should print anonymously another one of his own contradicting the former.

Copernicus' letter to Pope Paul III was his swan song. A few months later he fell mortally ill, became paralyzed, deprived of memory and consciousness, and died on May 24, 1543. It was a curious coincidence, that on the very same day there came to Frombark the first printed copy of *De Revolutionibus*, so that the last dimmed glance of the creator might fall on his great book, which was to immortalize his name.

Thanks to Copernicus, "the father of modern astronomy," humanity got the key to the riddle which had been puzzling and troubling it for many thousand years. Since the very dawn of history, when *homo sapiens* began to turn his eyes toward the sky above him, he perceived there several bright and dim lights moving ceaselessly to and fro. On closer observation, he learned that the great majority of these celestial bodies (the "fixed stars") were always moving in one group and in one direction (from east to west) as if they were permanently fastened to a huge ball whirling rapidly around the earth. Other celestial bodies, i.e., the sun, moon and the "wandering stars" (planets), although also taking part in that whirling motion, had peculiar motions of their own: continually changing their position relatively to the "fixed stars" and their constellations. Further observations of these movements proved them to be extremely complicated, their routes were found to go in oblique directions across the sky, making occasional loops; the movement of planets on those routes was at times quicker, at other times slower, sometimes from west to east (toward "the fixed stars") and sometimes from east to west. There arose the question in human minds of how to explain and solve this amazing intricacy of celestial motions? It continually puzzled hundreds of scientists, from Babylonia and Greece to the Islam world and medieval Europe. There appeared in succession various "astronomical systems," more and more complicated, but none of them could explain all these observed phenomena. At last there came a man who proclaimed to the astonished world that the solution of the problem was comparatively simple, had only certain seemingly unbelievable principles been accepted. This man was Nicolas Copernicus.

To realize fully the significance of Copernicus' work we must go back to certain facts of astronomical history preceding it. We do not, however, need to go further back than to the days of Plato (fourth century B.C.), because Plato was the forefather of all those astronomical theories (more exactly the theories concerning the structure of the universe), which were still believed in the lifetime of Copernicus. This does not mean that they were preserved without any change for the two thousand years separating these great thinkers. On the contrary, they became subject to constant evolution and ever-growing complication. But there were certain cosmological axioms, which remained almost unchanged. The most important among them stated the earth to be a fixed center of the universe. In other words the world, according to this theory, was "geocentric." Another theory originated from the conviction that the celestial bodies were of a much more perfect nature than the earth and all that directly surrounded it (water, air, etc.). This suggested to Plato his conception of celestial bodies as endowed with circular and uniform motion, "the most excellent" of movements. Only such a movement, Plato admitted, could be the movement of celestial bodies. This thesis (which in short we call the axiom of Plato) may be formulated as follows: "All the observed motions of heavenly bodies, although seemingly more or less complicated, may be reduced to a certain combination of uniform motions around the circle."

Assumptions like these became the backbone of all the later astronomical theories of Greece, inherited by the Mohammedans and the Christian world of medieval Europe. The most perfect of those and the only one worked out in detail and adaptable to astronomical calculations was the so-called "system of excentrics and epicycles," generally known as the Ptolemaic system, because the Alexandrian astronomer Claude Ptolemy, author of *The Almagest*, had been one of its most famous adherents, although not its creator.[3]

The circular movements considered by Ptolemy were not altogether, but only seemingly, uniform. Between the "axiom of

[3] The mechanism of planetary motions, explained in *The Almagest*, consists of two kinds of circles. There are excentrics, i.e., circular orbits, the centers of which are slightly displaced from the center of the earth (which is fixed in the center of the universe), and there are epicycles, the small circles, the centers of which move around on the circumference of those excentric orbits. Thus, for instance, the planet Mars revolves around the circumference of the epicycle describing it in a certain time (the so-called "synodical period of Mars"), while the center of the epicycle moves around on the circumference of the excentric, describing it in a certain time (the so-called "period of the zodiacal revolution

Plato," accepted unquestionably by the "prince of ancient astronomers" and its practical application, there was a doubtful contradiction. Ptolemy's successors, who could not overlook it, tried to hide it with various deceitful and sophisticated arguments.

The celestial mechanism explained in *The Almagest* reflected the knowledge of astronomy in the second century A.D. In spite of the original sin of logical inconsistency, it explained fairly well the astronomical phenomena known in those days. Only the later observations, especially those of Arabian scientists, found the conformity between *The Almagest* and the sky to be merely approximate. They began to correct and amend the work of the Alexandrian astronomer. "Corrections" were limited to small numeral changes made in the concrete values accepted by Ptolemy (such as the length of the tropical year, of the obliquity of the ecliptic). "Amendments," on the other hand, introduced new additional circles and circlets to the old "system of excentrics and epicycles." The celestial mechanism thus grew more and more complicated. At the same time there appeared deep divergences between various astronomers; some of them accepted certain "corrections" or "amendments," some rejected them or introduced others. Theoretical astronomy fell into the dark period of chaos, as observations continually proved the striking incongruity between the calculations and the sky.

Nicolas Copernicus put an end to this confusion. In this brief story of his life we have already shown how, slowly and gradually,

of Mars"). The movement of Mars around the earth is therefore composite, the result of two motions around the circle (or rather three if we add the diurnal motion of the celestial sphere).

The question arises now: what kind of motion do those two circular movements present? Ptolemy disagrees here with himself. Fundamentally, he believes in the above-mentioned "axiom of Plato," admitting only circular and uniform movements in the sky. In the third book of *The Almagest* we find their complete definition: the uniform motion around the circle is such a motion in which the radius-vector (i.e., the straight line uniting the center of the circle to the point moving on its circumference) describes equal angles in equal periods of time. However, when the author passes to the more detailed description of planetary motions, the matter looks slightly different; the center of the epicycle moves on the circumference of the excentric so that equal angles in equal periods of time are described by the radius-vector coming not from the center of the excentric, but from a certain other point of space, called later "the center of the equant circle," which means the center of "the circle equalizing movements." The same point also regulates the velocity of the planet on the circumference of the epicycle.—*Author.*

his thoughts progressed until he completed his work, the foundation of modern astronomy.

Had Copernicus been satisfied with the creation of this schematic heliocentric system (as presented in the *Commentariolus*), he would have brought about the same revolution in astronomy and in our entire conception of the universe. As we know, he did not stop there, but undertook another, much more difficult task. He knew perfectly well that the revolutionary idea of a movable earth would be immediately repudiated by all who were unable to understand its simplicity and its direct logic and who preferred to adhere to the old, traditional geocentric system, based on the supposedly "obvious" testimony of the senses. To fight successfully those prejudices and convince at least "those mathematicians (astronomers) who were scholarly and ingenious," it was necessary to prove in detail that the heliocentric system actually solved that problem of celestial motions which had continually disturbed the human mind since its very beginning. Because of that, Copernicus spent the latter part of his life (1515-43) observing the sky and completing his work, the new *Almagest*, a much simpler work, free from logical incongruities, utilizing at the same time the positive results of the astronomical researches made since Ptolemy (not excluding his own). Such was the origin of *De Revolutionibus*.

Long years of gigantic, solitary endeavors were spent by Copernicus on the detailed examination of the celestial mechanism presented in his chief work. The amount of energy used for this purpose was much greater than that spent on the meditations preceding the writing of the *Commentariolus*, although it did not require so much concentration of mind and imagination as the creation of the heliocentric system itself. Reflections on the second period of Copernicus' life brought some historians of astronomy to "a sad feeling of deep regret" on account of the "tragedy of his wasted work." They considered it as wasted, because Copernicus (as we already know) remained all his life long a faithful adherent of the "axiom of Plato," which was based rather on metaphysical than physical premises. To build up his new model of the world, Copernicus was compelled therefore to employ the same geometrical means as those used by the creators of the Ptolemaic system;

with this difference, of course, that he did not furtively introduce their "seemingly uniform movements." The celestial mechanism explained in *De Revolutionibus* consisted of circles and circlets, which, like the wheels in a clock, moved with uniform velocity. But not very long after Copernicus' death, it was proved by John Kepler that the planets did not move according to this scheme. Kepler therefore rejected the "axiom of Plato" and substituted instead his famous "Three Laws." The first and the most important of them (published in 1609) affirms that the orbit of each planet is an eclipse having the sun in one focus. The ingenious clock, on the construction of which Copernicus had spent thirty years of intense work, had stopped after two-thirds of the century.

But can we for that reason speak of the "wasted work" of the greater part of Copernicus' life? Certainly not. Had Copernicus been satisfied with the general outline of his heliocentric theory, had he written (and published) only the *Commentariolus*, his fate would have been similar to that of the ancient astronomers (Heraclides of Pontos and Aristarchos of Samos), who two thousand years before him had supposed the earth might be moving. Their ideas, considered fantastic and unbelievable by their contemporaries and successors, were quoted only as astronomical curiosities, contradicting reality. The history of the Copernican system during the sixteenth and seventeenth centuries shows that he might have been in the same danger. This was what Copernicus feared and tried to prevent by writing his famous dedicatory letter to Paul III. Yet, the very thing he feared actually happened; his ideas were proclaimed not only absurd but heretical. There was left only a small group of scientists, who dared to share and admit them. And what did convince those few believers? Nothing but the fact that the astronomical tables based on the new system of Copernicus were much nearer to the movements in the sky than those of his predecessors.

The observations and calculations of the latter part of Copernicus' life, which gave us *De Revolutionibus*, were therefore not "wasted." It is true that the ingenious geometrical constructions, used in it to explain celestial motions, were not maintained permanently in science. They were destroyed by the same Kepler, who in an autograph note on his copy of Copernicus' book called it "rich in innumerable treasures of wisdom" (*innumeras sapientiae opes complexus*). Kepler's own astronomical knowledge grew out of those "treasures of wisdom." Although born only in 1571, he became a direct pupil of Copernicus, thanks to the *De Revolutionibus*. We have no reason to pity "the tragedy" of the master, because his student succeeded in the further simplification of the heliocentric system. The fact that Copernicus' gigantic work brought new important scientific results even seventy years later, proved rather that it had not been "wasted."

It is the usual phenomenon in the history of human thought that immortal discoveries do not appear at first in the same shape in which they are preserved later in science. This is the essence of progress in our knowledge of nature, which is built by contributions of individuals as well as whole generations, and which is becoming more and more precise and many-sided. "From the beginning of the world Wisdom has been growing gradually and even now its growth is not yet completed," are the somewhat naïve but true words of Roger Bacon, written in the thirteenth century. Our contemporary conceptions of the universe naturally differ not only from those of Copernicus, but also from those of Kepler, Galileo, Newton, Laplace. The great modern *Almagest*, Copernicus' dream, is not yet and probably never will be finished. This does not alter the fact that the whole magnificent structure of our contemporary astronomy was founded on the work of Copernicus.

Copernicus is "the father of modern astronomy." "There is no figure in astronomical history, which may more appropriately claim the admiration of mankind through all time than that of Copernicus." With these words of the great American astronomer, Simon Newcomb, we may close our chapter on Copernicus and on the important part he played in the development of our knowledge of the starry heavens.

Translated from the Polish by Dr. M. L.

A. FRYCZ MODRZEWSKI
guiding an untutored peasant
(From steel engraving by Henryk Redlich)

V

A. FRYCZ MODRZEWSKI

The "New Dealer" of Sixteenth Century Poland

1503-72

by

OSCAR HALECKI

THE year 1543, insignificant in Poland's political history, is a landmark in the development of Polish culture. It was then that Copernicus, on his deathbed, saw the first copy of his book, which was to change man's conception of the universe. And in the same year three outstanding authors published each his first contribution to Polish literature, inaugurating its golden age.

It is typical of the nation's chief concern in the sixteenth century that two of them were political writers, and it illustrates the intimate contact of their country with the great trends of European thought that both, writing in Latin, were deeply influenced by the Renaissance and Reformation movements. Of the two, Andrzej Frycz of Modrzewo, usually called Modrzewski, is far superior to Stanisław Orzechowski, as a thinker as well as a character. He is also superior to the third, the Polish poet and essayist, Mikołaj (Nicholas) Rey; and even, generally speaking, to his whole generation, brilliant as it was.

Superior to, but not independent of it. Thanks to his far-reaching, liberal ideas, chiefly in politics, but also in the social, educational and religious fields, Frycz Modrzewski belongs not only to Poland, but to Europe and to mankind. His whole outlook was, however, a product of the extraordinary cultural progress which after a thorough preparation in the fourteenth and

51

fifteenth centuries, was achieved in the Poland of the last two Jagellonians.

Both of these remarkable rulers, Sigismund I and Sigismund Augustus, were kings of Poland when Modrzewski started his public career. For the latter, quite exceptionally, had been elected and crowned in his father's lifetime and was taking an increasingly important part in the political and cultural life of the country. Both were truly Renaissance monarchs and in addition to a comprehensive diplomatic action which successfully maintained Poland's position as a great power, they promoted Polish humanism by their personal interest in, and their inspiring patronage of, all kinds of cultural development, focused at their splendid court.

There was, however, a striking difference between the old King who almost forty years earlier had ascended to the throne in mature age, and his and Queen Bona Sforza's sole heir, the thrilling hope of a younger generation. Not only was Sigismund I chiefly interested in the fine arts, and Sigismund Augustus rather in literature, being himself, if not a writer, an excellent speaker and an enthusiastic collector of books, but while the father had always been of an essentially conservative mind, extremely cautious in political and decidedly opposed to religious reforms, his son, the last of the Jagiellonians, was fully aware of the urgent necessity of political reforms and keenly interested in religious questions. Therefore his leadership was impatiently expected by a large group of people who, being much more than a political party in the Diet, were advocating and preparing a reform movement in both directions although formally they only claimed a rigid "execution" of the existing laws. Influencing their program, there was a much smaller circle which worked it out in theory, on a philosophical and moral basis, and with a wide outlook towards the future. To that intellectual elite belonged Modrzewski, the most cultivated and gifted writer and the most audacious reformer of them all.

Like most of his friends, he came from that extremely numerous gentry—about one tenth of the whole population—which gave to the country not only its warriors and politicians, including the ancestors of so many wealthy families of the aristocracy, but also a large majority of the intellectual leaders in every sphere of human progress. The position of Modrzewski's own family, which originally used the inconspicuous name of Frycz—Fricius in the Latinized form—was very modest. However, when he later attacked the privileges of the gentry, he could point out, as he did, that he was not of plebeian extraction himself. As in the case of the Copernicus family, that of Frycz Modrzewski came from that old Polish province of Silesia which politically had been separated from the Kingdom in the fourteenth century, but had never entirely severed its cultural ties with Poland and especially in its Eastern part had a mostly Polish-speaking population. From there the writer's grandfather moved to the neighboring region of Greater Poland, where he and his son were officials of the bishops of Cuyavia in their residential town of Wolborz.

When Frycz Modrzewski published his first pamphlet, he was forty, having been born in 1503. At the age of eleven he was sent to school at Kraków and had a carefully directed education. He was later on not only a student and bachelor of arts of the Jagiellonian University of Kraków, then more than a hundred years old and still a brilliant center of humanistic culture, with international reputation; but afterwards, in the thirties of the sixteenth century, he also had an opportunity of studying and traveling for several years in Germany and in France. He owed this opportunity to his connection with the powerful Łaski family, which then played a leading part in Polish diplomacy and culture, and entertained friendly relations with Erasmus of Rotterdam. One of them, the future Protestant reformer Jan Łaski, well known also in the church history of England, contributed no less to Modrzewski's first contact and lasting sympathy with the Reformation than Melanchthon himself, whom he met at Wittenberg.

When he returned home, his appointment as Royal Secretary, in 1540, seemed to be the first step of a promising political career. Immediately before and after the death of Sigismund I, between 1547 and 1549, he participated in important diplomatic missions, chiefly to the Hapsburgs, accompanying another member of the Łaski family, and the future cardinal and promoter of the Catholic restoration in Poland, Stanisław Hosius. But in his intercourse with the most distinguished personalities of his time, in his own country and abroad, at the Polish or at the imperial court, in Denmark or Prussia, Bohemia or Holland, he never was directed by personal political ambitions; he only utilized these contacts for propagating his ideas of social justice and for discussion of controversial religious problems.

It is extremely illuminating to note what subject first attracted his attention and never ceased to interest him almost passionately. Superficially considered, it might seem a question of detail, but Modrzewski was perfectly right in treating it as a test case and as a starting point for his systematic campaign for a great principle. There was in Poland and almost everywhere in his contemporary world, a striking inequality in the legal position of the various classes of society, especially as between nobles and peasants. And for a country so proud of its liberal constitution and so anxious to safeguard a status of full equality among all the nobles, rich or poor, it was particularly disgraceful that the whole peasant population, while less cruelly treated than in many other countries, was still kept in a position of inferiority, even before the law, to say nothing of social standing.

Without at once claiming complete equal rights for everybody, which he knew was impossible to put into practice, Modrzewski strongly protested against what seemed to him the most obvious wrong: it was the tremendous social discrimination in the punishment of murder. According to an ancient law, anybody who had killed a noble had to pay 120 marks and serve a jail sentence of one year and six weeks; while for killing a peasant, one had to pay ten marks only. The difference became still more shocking and even inhuman, since an offender who was unable to pay the fine for the murder of a noble, was remanded to prison for life or simply sentenced to death, which commonly happened to peasants prosecuted for murder. Deeply convinced that human life should be protected with the utmost vigor, without regard for social rank, Modrzewski wanted any murder punished by a death sentence, even in the case of a peasant killed by a noble. He was for severity in the interest of public order and safety, but before the court of law everybody in his opinion was to be absolutely equal.

Such was the topic of his first pamphlet, which he addressed in 1543 to Sigismund Augustus himself, taking advantage of his secretarial office. Realizing, however, that under the Polish constitution the matter could not possibly be decided by royal authority alone, he published, in 1545 and 1546, three similar "orations" to the members of the Senate and to the Knighthood, to the Church of Poland, and finally to the whole nation which he wanted to persuade. And he did not stop nor feel discouraged when this series of eloquent appeals remained unsuccessful. He could have expected it, for the very principle he was fighting for was so far in advance of contemporary public opinion all over Europe that the famous French political writer, Jean Bodin, when discussing the same subject of legal equality thirty years later, blamed Modrzewski for his "absurd" and impracticable request. This Polish crusader of social justice and precursor of the French author of *The Republic* continued to make this "absurd" request, and still more convincingly presented his case in his own standard work of a similar general scope. But before publishing it, Modrzewski had prepared himself for such a synthesis by attacking two other preliminary or introductory questions.

One of them, submitted to the Senate in 1545, almost simultaneously with his above-mentioned favorite thesis, was another protest against social discrimination, this time in favor of the townsmen who by a recently confirmed law were prohibited from owning rural property. The following year, once more addressing the king, the clergy and the nation as a whole, he turned for the first time to religious matters, recommending most urgently that a Polish delegation be sent to the Council of Trent to promote a reform of the Church. Here again he raised a problem which was to absorb his mind even longer than any constitutional, political or social issue. In doing so he was influenced not only by his experiences and observations abroad, but also by exciting discussions then conducted within a small group—almost a club—of Polish reformers with strong Protestant sympathies. Joining them, Modrzewski still hoped that all the religious controversies could be settled, without any rupture or division, by way of concessions agreed to by the Roman Church. This opinion was shared by many other Poles and he did not abandon it even after having published two minor tracts, in favor of lay communion in both kinds, and against the celibacy of the clergy. Both printed in 1549, one in Prague, the other in Antwerp, they were to be annexed to some of the later editions of Modrzewski's masterpiece, the commentaries *De Republica Emendanda,* first published in Kraków in 1551.

It is to this really epoch-making work that he owes his fame. Even if he had not written anything but that unique book, he would remain one of the glories of Polish civilization, inseparable from the tradition of a century which saw at its height both the political power and the first cultural flowering of his country. It was at the same time one of Poland's greatest contributions to European thought and political theory, to the ideas of ethics in public life, of justice, tolerance and peace. That such a statement is not exaggerated, may be seen from the interest that Modrzewski's treatise evoked in foreign countries. It was not without reason that he published it first in Latin, to be brought out in a Polish translation only after his death. Written in the international language of his time, a language so well known to all his cultivated fellow-countrymen, the book was soon reprinted at Basle in 1554 and again, together with the author's other writings, in 1559. In the same city, which then was such an important center of Renaissance and Reformation culture, there appeared in 1557 a German translation, which was soon followed by one in French, which was mentioned in Modrzewski's later publications; and a manuscript has since been discovered in Vienna, containing a part of a Spanish translation. How can we explain such a general, immediate, and far-reaching interest in the publication of an almost unknown Polish writer, at a moment of history when Europe certainly was not lacking in outstanding contributions to the discussion of similar problems? By way of answer let us look at the backgrounds of Modrzewski's *Republic.*

In the Middle Ages the Polish State had always been called a kingdom: "Regnum Poloniae." From the sixteenth century on it was called a Republic, although until the partitions at the end of the eighteenth century it never ceased to be ruled by kings. This astonishing change in the terminology can be explained by two reasons, both being closely connected with Modrzewski's political ideas.

First of all, the Latin name of *Respublica,* like its Polish translation *Rzeczpospolita,* has nothing to do with any specific form of government, either monarchic or republican; it was simply the ancient name of any state, one may even say of any orderly human society. Its adoption in Poland is therefore nothing but a proof of a particularly strong influence of ancient tradition in a country which enthusiastically participated in the Renaissance movement and where the Latin language still was in common use, both in public life and in literature. As already noted, Modrzewski too was decidedly under that influence, and when attempting to give a definition of the "Republic" in the very first pages of his book, he took it from Aristotle, the author he quotes most frequently and with whose treatise on Politics and Ethics he was of course well acquainted through Latin translation. His description of the State is also based partly upon Cicero, equally well known to Modrzewski, as were many other Roman authors, including the greatest poets.

But Modrzewski was not strictly confined to his classic models. He went much further than they did in adopting the precise, literal meaning of the word *Respublica,* and still more that of the Polish *Rzeczpospolita,* which is nothing but "common thing" or rather "common good" and should be translated into English not by "Republic" but by "Commonwealth." When, for instance, in 1569, still in Modrzewski's lifetime, the Kingdom of Poland and the Grand Duchy of Lithuania were brought closer together in an organic union, the federation was officially called "the common *Rzeczpospolita,*" which exactly corresponds to the modern British idea of a Commonwealth of Nations.

Considered from this viewpoint, the "Republic" was for Modrzewski, more than for any ancient writer, a predominantly moral conception, a problem of ethics. Therefore, when he devoted the first three parts of his treatise successively to morals, to laws and to war, he not only put the morals first, but made this "book" of his commentaries twice as long as the others, thus emphasizing the fact that in order to have a well-governed republic, morals were even more important than written laws. This moral basis of his whole political theory made his work congenial with the Polish tradition, as expressed in the famous charter of 1413, which proclaimed the *mysterium caritatis* to be the foundation of political life, and was two years later expounded in a treatise submitted to the Council of Constance by Poland's first political writer, the Rector of Kraków University, Paweł Włodkowic. But for that very reason Modrzewski's ideas were entirely different from the current Renaissance conception which, departing also from ancient thought, eventually separated politics from ethics. Machiavelli's idea of the State and of its best possible ruler was not unknown in Poland, where the Italian-born queen Bona Sforza, so influential in the later years of her husband's reign, tried to practice it. But there it met with overwhelming opposition and failed to change the existing constitution even with respect to one desirable element, the strengthening of the executive power.

The Poles were extremely anxious that their king should have nothing in common with a Roman *imperator* or with a modern *principe* (prince). Looking back to ancient Rome, they were not so much fascinated by strong imperial authority, supported by Roman law, as they were by the idea of republican liberty under the institution, for instance, of the *tribuni plebis*, with which Modrzewski compared the deputies to the Polish Diet. It is true that before discussing the role of Parliament, and especially of the Senate, he wrote a long chapter on the King. But he began by recalling that the Polish kings, elected and not hereditary, even in the Jagiellonian period, were not allowed to govern according to their own will, but had their power strictly limited by public consent and by law. Such a constitution seemed to him greatly preferable to the situation in other countries, where the kings could impose taxes and even declare war by their personal decision and therefore might become "odious tyrants." Just like any other person, the monarch should be subordinated to moral principles, and Modrzewski describes at length all the qualities which he ought to possess: marked culture, especially by reading; rigid self-control; love of his country and care for common welfare more than for his own convenience; generosity, courage, and so on.

There are of course in this scheme some platitudes, dictated by the ancient ideal of virtue; but when he speaks of the rules of justice which the king should observe, Modrzewski at once brings in his favorite idea of social equality and then outlines his whole program of a social order founded on justice and charity.

What he presents is by no means the remote vision of an Utopia. He was opposed to communism and even to any confusing suppression of the differences between the various classes of society. He considered all social classes as equally valuable and necessary, and therefore strongly condemned pride and violence in their mutual relations, and more particularly the prejudice that there must be a natural opposition between people of different birth: between the peasant's and the nobleman's blood. And in a special paragraph on Humanity toward those who were in a position of serfdom, Modrzewski not only urged kind and human treatment: he most emphatically defended the right of the peasant to own the land he cultivated, which no lord should dare to take away from him, while the peasant should be entirely free to leave it whenever he wished. Hence it appears that what Modrzewski really advocated was the total abolition of serfdom.

While advocating these and similar ideas of progress, Modrzewski not only moves the reader by his eloquence, but also suggests to him practical measures with a view of their realization. One of these suggestions, supported by examples taken from ancient Greece, was to recommend the appointment of special officials entrusted with the delicate task of supervising morals in order to stop abuses, to fight laziness and to protect the poor. It seems doubtful whether such a tutorial control could have been possibly organized, but Modrzewski was certainly right in looking for some way to prevent Polish liberty from degenerating into anarchy, and the examples he adduced to illustrate the necessity of the proposed reform show once more his deep human interest in all those he believed to be victims of injustice or to be handicapped in the existing social order, whom he wanted to assist not merely by alms, but by moral support, protection and direction.

Moreover, he was fully aware that this could not be done merely by official intervention or constitutional reforms, but that the problem had to be tackled in a more fundamental manner, namely, by education. A special chapter on education is to be found at the very beginning of his treatise, inserted between his introductory considerations on moral progress and the chapter dealing with royal authority. Here he speaks chiefly of the earliest education of children in their family circle, and he returns to the question of how to educate the children of the ruling class before discussing the treatment of the peasants. In addition, there is at the end of his book a whole section devoted entirely to the school problem.

Here Modrzewski takes occasion to express his genuine enthusiasm for learning and education, and for those who are responsible for progress in these fields: first for the scholars, the philosophers, as he calls them, claiming for them an even higher consideration in the Republic than for the King, and then for the teachers whose profession he regards as the most beautiful and indispensable in society. Recalling ancient as well as Christian traditions of cultural patronage, he requests the Church, both the bishops and the monasteries, to assist students and to observe strictly the old Polish law reserving a certain number of higher ecclesiastical offices to candidates possessing a doctor's degree. And speaking of similar obligations of the State authorities, he enters even into such details as the salaries of the teaching staff.

Modrzewski's truly progressive ideas on education, based upon a real understanding of any kind of intellectual effort and of its dignity, partly influenced by the general trends of the Renaissance period, partly, like many of his suggestions, in advance of his time, were certainly not less valuable because they were scattered in various parts of his book. For similar reasons, because many legal questions had been touched upon in the first of its sections, the second one, more systematically dealing with the laws of the Republic, could not entirely avoid some repetitions. But what the author repeated here was worth remembering: it was once more his leading principle of impartial equality in the treatment of criminals, regardless of their social position.

He himself refers to his four earlier pamphlets, where he first had raised the question of punishing by death any murder, whether committed by a noble or a peasant. Going now still further, Modrzewski points out that if there should be any discrimination in trial, it is the nobles, the rich, and those holding high office who should be treated more severely, because they have more reasons to abstain from crime. He has also some new things to say on still another problem of general interest. While advocating a rather harsh repression of any real wrong or violence, he becomes fairly indulgent when discussing what in Roman law used to be called a *crimen laesae maiestatis* (lese majesty). Opposed as he is to any kind of anarchy, he recognizes that there ought to be strong repression of sedition or treachery, but does not think that the right of free criticism, even regarding the person of the king, ought to be limited. Rulers who are not prepared to tolerate freedom of speech, should govern, he says, over "dumb animals" and not over intelligent men. What he wants in the nation's internal life is harmony of both authority and liberty, of duties and rights.

Turning to what we may call today international relations, Modrzewski discusses only the problem of war. Considering it from two different viewpoints, he first deals with the basic question of international morality. As Paweł Włodkowic had done at the Council of Constance, he examined the conditions of a just war and, differing from his scholastical predecessor only in method of his reasoning, arrived at similar conclusions, in agreement with both the Christian tradition and his own humanitarian outlook. After giving a moving description of all the horrors and dreadful consequences of war, he quotes not without sympathy the opinions of those who want war outlawed completely and who strongly believe that going to war is a crime in any case. Modrzewski himself does not go so far; he admits the right and even the duty to defend the Republic against aggression. Yet he not only condemns wars for mere glory and conquest but even advocates that if a real wrong has been done to the country, a serious attempt should be made to obtain the necessary readjustment without recourse to arms. Only if and when peaceful means have failed, should there be reason for a war.

Speaking of such unavoidable wars, Modrzewski was chiefly thinking of Poland's defense against the frequent Tartar invasions into her southeastern borderlands. For that reason frequent discussions in the Diet and the whole contemporary political literature considered the necessity of creating a permanent army or at least a frontier guard of the highest possible quality, and of providing the financial means for that purpose. It was therefore natural that Modrzewski should include this urgent problem in his program of reforming the Republic. His solution was not an original one: he was only developing a scheme drafted about forty years earlier by one of the Łaskis (chancellor and then primate of Poland under Sigismund I), with a view of establishing an adequate public treasury by a very radical taxation system. But here appears once more Modrzewski's constant care for the poorer classes of society, one of his main arguments being the fact that under such a system the distribution of financial burdens would be much more equitable. And he did not fail to emphasize the fact that the poor are affected much more by the consequences of war than those responsible for declaring it.

According to its title, Modrzewski's *Republic* was to contain five "books" or main sections. But only three of them appeared in the Kraków edition of 1551, the fourth and fifth having been withdrawn during the printing. There was no special reason for not publishing the last one, which dealt, as mentioned above, with the school problem. The whole difficulty arose in connection with Book Four, devoted to the Church. Even when read in manuscript it raised such criticism, chiefly from the Polish clergy, that it seemed advisable to stop at the end of the third part; and when in 1554 all five parts appeared at Basle, the author felt obliged to add an apology for his treatment of ecclesiastical matters. Because of his conviction that other parts of his comprehensive reform program might have a better chance of favorable attention and in order that it might reach the largest possible public, including all the Catholics, the author was willing to make a compromise by temporarily omitting the most controversial section.

Modrzewski's first ideas on the reform of the Church were neither original nor radical. In addition to the questions of lay communion in both kinds and of the clergy's celibacy, already discussed in his earlier pamphlets, he simply advocated the demands of a fairly large part of Polish public opinion for the use of the vernacular in liturgy and the suppression of part or all of the various taxes paid to the Holy See. Like many of his contemporaries, Modrzewski hoped that a general Council would not only approve such a program, but would also appease the whole Reformation movement. And when, in conformity with his earlier suggestions, the Diet of 1553 decided to send Polish representatives to the Council of Trent, the King attached him to the delegation as its secretary.

The reopening of the Council was postponed, and instead of leaving for Trent, Modrzewski started in his own country an assiduous propaganda of his religious ideas. At the beginning he was so strongly convinced of the possibility of having them accepted by the Roman Church that he dedicated one of his new tracts on Church reform to Pope Paul IV himself. Very soon, however, he plunged into dogmatic discussions with Catholics and Protestants. Publishing one pamphlet after another, he entirely abandoned the political and social problems which once had been his chief concern, with the one exception of the question of punishing murder, to which he returned for the last time in 1557. What interested him now almost exclusively was the conciliation of the different religious opinions which under Sigismund Augustus spread so rapidly over the whole country, and he did not hesitate to write on the most difficult theological problems, for instance, those of original sin, free will, divine Providence and predestination.

Modrzewski's personal views were growing more and more radical, and for that reason he wanted to satisfy even the most extreme sects questioning the dogma of Holy Trinity. Of course, he soon had to realize that no Council gathered under the control of the Holy See could possibly be expected to accept any compromise on questions of this sort; therefore, beginning in 1565, in the publication of a new series of pamphlets, called *Sylvae*, which recommended a mutual agreement among all the religious denominations, he invited the King to organize a national Council with the participation of all sects. Sigismund Augustus never ceased to be interested in the liberal ideas of the gifted writer and encouraged him to work to arouse a spirit of better understanding between the heterogeneous opinions. But the King had already decided to accept the decisions of the Council of Trent, and the hopeless confusion amidst the Polish Protestants and Antitrinitarians only confirmed him in his conviction that Poland, without persecuting anybody for his religious creed, should remain a Catholic country, faithful to her tradition. And the same conviction was shared by an increasing majority even of those who at first had been in sympathy with the Reformation movement, but now were spontaneously returning to the Roman Church.

Modrzewski's unionistic conceptions did not satisfy anybody, neither the Catholics nor even the Protestants. Having sacrificed his political career to his religious convictions, he eventually lost even the modest office at Wolborz which he had occupied many years, in succession to his father and his grandfather. It was an office dependent on the bishops of Cuyavia; and although one of them, when himself influenced by Protestant teaching, granted him his protection, it proved impossible later on even for him to keep in Church office an open adversary of Rome. Therefore, during the last years of his life, Modrzewski had neither an official position nor even a permanent home, and until his death in 1572 lived with various friends, ceasing to exercise the great influence of his earlier period of political and literary activity.

Realistic though he had been in almost all his other proposed reforms, he proved rather utopian in hoping to co-ordinate the various trends of the Reformation period. But he deserves unbounded admiration for his absolute unselfishness and the deep seriousness of his religious convictions, and for his broad-minded tolerance in a period of religious wars and oppression almost everywhere in Europe. Although the unionistic conferences which he lived to see in Poland remained limited to the three Protestant Churches which in 1570 concluded the *Consensus Sandomiriensis* and to another effort which brought together at Raków most of the Antitrinitarians, the practical freedom of worship which existed under Sigismund Augustus was legally ratified in 1573, one year after the death of the King and his former secretary, in the famous decree of the Warsaw Confederation guaranteeing general peace among those who differ in religion.[1] Men like Modrzewski had contributed much to make sixteenth-century Poland an island of religious liberty and a haven for all those persecuted in other countries.

---

[1] The text of the decree was as follows: "Although in our Commonwealth there are considerable differences of conviction with regard to Christian religion, nevertheless, being desirous of avoiding harmful conflicts among our people on that account, such as we clearly see in other countries, we hereby jointly pledge ourselves and our successors, under solemn oath, with our honesty, our honor and our conscience, that even though we may have different religious convictions, we shall maintain peaceful relationships and shall not shed blood for differences in faith or in church practices." (See Stephen P. Mizwa, *The Spirit of Polish Culture*, New York, 1940, p. 10.)

But what of the results of his endeavors to promote constitutional and social reforms in the Republic? The question is all the more important, as in this respect Modrzewski's writings were particularly illuminating, his ideas inspiring and his position outstanding. Outstanding, but fortunately not isolated. His influence on public opinion was considerable, and as to the necessity of "amending the Republic," especially in view of the expected interregnum, there was a general agreement among political leaders of the country, including the King himself. Modrzewski had, moreover, the great merit of presenting in a remarkable literary form a clear outline and a comprehensive synthesis of what others felt only vaguely concerning Poland's needs in his own time and for generations to come.

This is particularly true with respect to his main principle, that the Republic ought to be founded on a moral basis, on the "virtue" of its citizens, a principle which in the following centuries became almost a slogan, used and abused in many political discussions. As a matter of fact, Poland's decline, which began a hundred years after Modrzewski, resulted from a moral crisis rather than from any tangible shortcomings of her constitution. Most of these shortcomings could have been avoided, if all the practical suggestions of the great reformer had been followed. Fortunately, at least some of them had a decided influence on the constitutional development of Poland both in his lifetime, when the King himself joined the "execution" movement, and in the difficult years after his death. For example, Jan Zamoyski, who directed Poland's destinies during the first two "interregna" and then as chief collaborator of King Stephen Batory, seemed to apply the policies advocated by Modrzewski, both as a *tribunus plebis* defending freedom and democracy, and as a high official opposing anarchy and favoring the strengthening, when necessary, of the executive. The same might be said of his care for education and for justice as expressed in the creation of a Supreme Court.

Sometimes Modrzewski's most distinguished contemporaries accepted even his most advanced ideas, including, for instance, his theory of a just war. Poland's great military leader, the "hetman" Jan Tarnowski, a friend of the writer, who mentioned him more than once in his works, expressed a similar opinion when he said in his treatise on strategy that any war of aggression was in opposition to reason and to God. Yet there was in Modrzewski's conception of state and society an idea particularly hard to propagate, not only in his country and in his time, but in any country at any time: that of social equality between nobles and peasants, the rich and the poor. It is regrettable that very little was done in that direction and that, on the contrary, the condition of the peasants, instead of improving, was to deteriorate even more in the future. Nevertheless his appeal was not entirely made in vain; it was received with sympathy at least by individuals, especially by some idealistic groups among the Antitrinitarians, and was taken up by the end of the century by the greatest Catholic preacher of Poland, Father Piotr Skarga.

In this case, as in many others, a spiritual tie united the greatest men of Poland's golden age. And as there was at the same time an intimate intellectual communion between their country and the whole realm of Christian and Latin civilization, the problems raised far in the east of Europe by a leading political writer and reformer were almost without exception of equal interest for the western nations which printed, translated and carefully read his books.

Thus, for instance, in the seventeenth century a man as famous as Hugo Grotius was among the assiduous readers of the commentaries *De Republica Emandanda*. It is hardly possible to ascertain how strong their influence might have been in other countries, but it could have been only salutary, and for that reason it is worth while to recall the contribution which Poland made through Modrzewski to social progress and the contemporary culture of Europe.

JAN KOCHANOWSKI

(From painting by Jan Matejko—presented by the painter to the
Polish Academy)

VI

JAN KOCHANOWSKI
"The Founder of Polish Poetry"

1530-84

O mnie Moskwa i będą wiedzieć Tatarowie
I, różnego mieszkańcy świata, Anglikowie.
— Kochanowski, *Odes*, II, 24.

(Of me the Muscovites shall know, and the Tatars;
and the English, denizens of a world apart.)

by

GEORGE R. NOYES

JAN KOCHANOWSKI was the founder of Polish poetry and the greatest of all Polish poets up to the time of Mickiewicz. His work is representative of his age, but like that of all great poets it has permanent charm and beauty.

Poland reached its greatest political power in the fifteenth century. In the following century it retained its former boundaries and advanced immensely in civilization, sharing in the great intellectual movements of the time—the Reformation and the Renaissance. The former spread to Poland from the West, broadening the intellectual life of the Polish gentry, and giving them a keener interest in public affairs. But it had little influence on Polish poetry; it affected Kochanowski scarcely at all. Kochanowski was through and through a man of the Renaissance. This movement, beginning in Italy in the fifteenth century, soon penetrated into Poland. It was based on the study of Roman and Greek literature and art from the point of view of artistic form; it was thus essentially, though not outspokenly, pagan, even though its adherents might be sincere members of the Catholic Church. The *humanists,* as the followers of the "new learning" were called, were concerned with man's life on this earth, not with his future after death. They strove to create, and did create, a new literature and a new art based on the study of classical antiquity.

Renaissance ideals soon won favor with the Polish gentry, but they had small influence on the University of Kraków, which still devoted its main attention to theology. Hence it declined. Bright Polish lads went by hundreds to Italy, there to study Latin and Greek literature. One of them, the Polish youth whose foreign training brought the most brilliant results, was Jan Kochanowski.

The main outlines of Kochanowski's career are known, but the details are often uncertain, so that any brief narrative of his life must needs make positive statements on some disputed points. He was born in 1530 at Sycyna, a village about a hundred miles northeast of Kraków; his family were well-to-do gentry of literary tastes. In 1544 he went to the University of Kraków, where he remained till 1547. After an interval of three years during which he is lost to sight, he studied for some months during 1551-52 at the University of Królewiec (Königsberg), then the center of the Polish Protestant movement. In 1552 he went to Italy, where he attended the University of Padua and became a leader among the Polish students there. For somewhat less than a year during 1555-56 he was again at Królewiec, then made a second journey to Italy, but was called home in 1557 by the death of his mother. Late in 1557 or early in 1558 he again went to Italy, whence he proceeded to France, where he traveled for some months. In 1559 he returned permanently to Poland.

These years of foreign study and travel formed Kochanowski's intellect and his tastes and settled the whole character of his literary work. He was an apt student of Latin and Greek and, as is shown by two works of his latest years, he always retained an interest in technical scholarship. But he was primarily a poet, not a philologist. He read widely in Latin and Greek authors and steeped himself in their spirit. And, what was the highest accomplishment for a literary humanist, he learned to write Latin verse with skill and taste. Latin was Kochanowski's first literary language; it was a natural means of expression for him and he cultivated it all his life. He surpassed his Polish predecessors in Latin verse; and, when he began to write Polish, he followed Latin ideals of style. His Polish poems are full of references to ancient writers and of thoughts and turns of phrase borrowed from them. He is not seeking to display his learning; rather the learning has become as much a part of him as are his own emotions.

Kochanowski likewise studied Italian and probably also French. He admired Petrarch, the great Italian writer of sonnets, and in his own poems he was occasionally influenced by his phrasing. He wrote three of his own *Trifles* in sonnet form, and in two of them he adopted a rhyme scheme that is French, not Italian. But in general Kochanowski's debt to Italian and French literature is very small compared to that which he owed to his Greek and Roman masters. Yet we must make one reservation. In France Ronsard and his fellow poets of the *Pléiade* were successfully striving to create a literature that should be French in language but classic in spirit; there was a similar though much less important movement in Italy. Kochanowski in one of his Latin elegies expresses fervent admiration for Ronsard and his practice. So it is natural to conclude that he was stimulated by French and Italian examples to break away from the procedure of Polish scholarly poets previous to his own time and to do most of his work in his own language. His surviving poems include about 16,700 verses in Polish and about 7000 in Latin. His task in creating a new Polish literary style was made easier by the fact that, unlike Ronsard, he did not have to combat a great medieval literary tradition.

Kochanowski's earliest known poems are Latin elegies, modeled on Propertius and Tibullus and written in Padua; they were published, together with later work of the same sort, only in 1584. Some of them are addressed to a certain Lydia, apparently the name that he gave to an Italian courtesan. Even if, as is possible, these elegies contain no autobiographic details, it is certain that up to his marriage in 1575 Kochanowski was no ascetic. He loved wine and women as well as song and scholarship.

Kochanowski probably began to write Polish verse while still in Italy, but none of his surviving poems in his own language can be referred with certainty to a date earlier than his return to Poland in 1559. After that return he led for many years the life of a courtier and man of society, dependent on King Zygmunt August and on various patrons. For publishing his poems he cared little; most of his work circulated in manuscript according to the custom of the day; there was no large reading public that would support an author by purchasing his books. Kochanowski was not poor, for in 1559 he received half of the family estate of Czarnolas, but he had no immediate desire to settle on his lands and live in rustic simplicity. His wit, his social gifts, and his literary genius assured him success in the highest circles of Poland. A graceful poem would bring a gift of money; more important, his talents won for him sinecure positions that yielded a steady income. To the King he dedicated his poem *The Satyr,* and for a time he seems to have been one of the royal secretaries. But his most important patron was Piotr Myszkowski, Vice Chancellor of Poland, later Bishop, first of Płock, then of Kraków, whom he repeatedly addresses in terms of affectionate gratitude that suggest those used by Horace to Maecenas. To Myszkowski he owed his appointment in 1564 as provost of Poznań Cathedral, and in 1566 as priest at Zwoleń, near his own estate. Kochanowski did not discharge the duties of either post; the custom of the period permitted the appointment of unmarried laymen to church benefices merely for the sake of their income. He held these offices until 1574 and 1575, respectively; they may explain why he so long deferred marriage.

Of Kochanowski's bachelor existence we get a vivid picture in his Polish *Trifles (Fraszki)* and in his Latin *Foricœnia (Dinners Away From Home).* These are epigrams, varying in length from a single couplet to thirty-six verses; in 1584 the poet gathered and published them. His Polish collection includes 294 epigrams, of which fifty-seven are translations from the Latin or Greek. The *Trifles* and *Foricœnia* are dinner-table verse, intended to add to the mirth over the wine cups; they show Kochanowski as the boon companion of the highest dignitaries in Poland, both lay and spiritual. A *trifle* must be witty and entertaining: it might be a graceful love song; it might be a noble epitaph on a distinguished man; it might be a homespun anecdote, coarse and even obscene. The following quatrain is in his best vein:

Gentle lady, fair and kind,
In thy face I verses find:
If they sometime win success,
Thee, not me, they then must bless.

In another *trifle* the poet comments on his own work:

I write in the same fashion that I live:
My rhymes are drunken, for I love to drink.
I like a revel and I like a jest,
Sometimes a woman: such things fill my verse.
And why pretend? The priest who strives to teach
Me moderation, hides a devil within.

For these pithy poems Kochanowski felt special tenderness,
terming them:

My priceless *trifles*, full of many a charm,
Wherein I lay the secrets of my soul.

And when he printed them he refused to listen to a friend's suggestion that he omit such as would cause offense. He evidently
wished to publish a motley miscellany similar to the *Greek An-
thology* or the *Epigrams* of Martial, collections from which he
had translated many of the *trifles*. He defends himself in an epigram
addressed to Michael Firlej, Wojewoda of Kraków:

If in my pages there be something said
That is unfit to read before a maid,
Forgive me, Michael, for a poet can,
Despite loose verses, be a worthy man.

And in truth Kochanowski was "a worthy man," a solid citizen with definite opinions on public questions, albeit his views
were not particularly sagacious nor even independent. Though he
"loved to drink," he was no drunkard; in fact he wrote a prose
tract, *That Drunkenness is a Vile Thing, Unworthy of Man*, and
some verses to the same effect. More important, a whole series of
occasional poems, beginning in 1561 and continuing throughout
his life, bear witness to his public spirit. Only the most significant
can be mentioned.

Two pieces, *Harmony* (1562 or 1563: 158 verses) and *The Satyr* (1563: 452 verses), relate to internal conditions in Poland. The first is a squib on the well-worn theme of political and religious dissensions, but is directed particularly against the Protestants. Harmony, personified, lectures the clergy for their luxury and sloth; lectures the laymen likewise for their luxury and their loss of martial spirit, but above all for their rash intrusion into spiritual concerns: "They have begun to preach themselves and have taught their wives to do so: hence now everybody preaches and nobody listens." The Poles should refer their religious differences to the Council of Trent, then sitting. The advice was nothing new; such had been the verdict of the *Sejm* of 1555.

The Satyr is a similar but more entertaining document. By felling the forests in order to gain wealth the Poles have driven from his haunts a wise satyr or "wild man," who proceeds to admonish them for their sins. His counsel is much the same as that of Kochanowski's patron Myszkowski, in an address to the *Sejm* of 1563. "In helmets hens brood," he laments, "or carters use them for measuring oats when they feed their horses for the night." Hence the Tatars, Muscovites, Swedes, and Germans assail or threaten from all sides the once valiant "Republic," as the Polish kingdom was called. Thus Kochanowski shows himself merely an adept at refurbishing the political commonplaces of the period.

In 1567 Kochanowski accompanied the King in a bloodless demonstration of the Polish armies against the Muscovites. He commemorates his one military experience in an ode beginning: "O night of unwonted beauty, gaze on us brightly amid these forests, where like bees we stand on watch around our lord, keeping alive our fires till morn."

The finest of Kochanowski's political poems is *The Standard* (296 verses), inspired by the feudal homage rendered to Zygmunt August on July 19, 1569, by Albert II of Prussia. To the vassal a banner was handed as a sign of royal favor. This banner (in imitation of Homer, for the actual banner bore only a coat of arms) Kochanowski represents as embroidered with scenes from the history of the Poles and of other Slavic peoples. After the ceremony the King muses on the union of Poland and Lithuania that had been concluded a few days earlier. Kochanowski ends his poem:

By union, King, thou shalt cast down thy foes
And settle thy Republic in firm peace
And strong security. And for thy name
Thou shalt gain honor that shall never end.

At a moment of triumph Kochanowski had spoken with exultation. But in his prose tract *Omens* he is doubtful of the future of Poland after the death of Zygmunt August. When the King died in 1572 he took a vivid interest in the elections that followed. He sided first with Henri de Valois; then, when Henri returned to France, he supported in a rather inept speech the candidacy of the Archduke Ernst, the son of the Emperor Maximilian II. But when Stefan Batory won the throne Kochanowski became his warm admirer; possibly he was influenced by his patron Jan Zamoyski, the greatest statesman of Poland.

Meanwhile, aside from the *Trifles*, Kochanowski had continued his work in lyric poetry, both in Latin and in Polish. But while in his youth he had leaned heavily on Propertius and Tibullus, he later was more devoted to Horace. Horace inspired his Latin *Lyricorum Libellus* and most of his Polish *Pieśni* (*Odes* or *Songs*); in fact many of the Polish odes are translations or close imitations of Horace.

Kochanowski is the first author of love poetry in Poland worthy of mention. But nothing is known of the ladies for whom, in classic, pagan style, he declares his affection in his later elegies, the love poems in the *Trifles*, and his Horatian odes. Presumably some of them, like their Roman prototypes, were of doubtful reputation.

Despite his gay life, Kochanowski was a man of sincerely religious temperament. His longest work, begun before 1571 and published in 1578, is a translation of the Psalms into Polish rhymed stanzas. In English there is not even a mediocre metrical version of the Psalms; Kochanowski succeeded where English poets, including Milton, have failed. He produced a masterpiece, although it was a paraphrase, not a literal translation. "Only with Kochanowski's *Psalter* did the Polish language become capable of the poetic expression of powerful feelings, such as stir the soul of man. . . . The book also marks an epoch in the history of Polish verse and of the Polish stanza" (Chrzanowski). In the sixteenth and seventeenth centuries this *Psalter* had by far the widest circulation of all Kochanowski's works. At present, as a whole, it has passed out of common use, although individual psalms from it remain popular; some of them, in a version modernized by F. Karpiński, are still sung in church. A striking evidence of the poet's affection for the *Psalter* is the fact that of his original religious poems three are in the spirit of the Psalms and were obviously inspired by them.

Weary of court life and its dissipation, Kochanowski at some time before 1575 retired to Czarnolas, there to make his permanent home. In 1575 he married Dorota Podlodowska, the beautiful and well-educated daughter of a noble of distinction. It is pleasant to assume, though absolute proof is lacking, that some of his love lyrics were addressed to her. In one delightful song he invites "Hanna" to his estate: "The very walls call for you and with kindly thoughts await you." In another he rises to courtly phrasing that is reminiscent of Petrarch, not of the Roman poets:

> Paradise is where she sits, and where'er she passes
> Lilies white and roses fair bloom amid the grasses;
> Lovely trees to give her joy shed their generous shade
> And forbid the sun to scorch that most gentle maid.

Kochanowski was now a country gentleman, cultivating his lands and cultivating letters as well. His years of retirement produced his most important original poems, those by which he is best known today.

Kochanowski's longest original work in Polish is his drama, *The Dismissal of the Grecian Envoys* (606 verses), which was performed January 12, 1578, on the occasion of the marriage of Jan Zamoyski to Krystyna Radziwiłł. It tells of the coming of Ulysses and Menelaus to Troy, as envoys demanding the return of Helen, carried away from her home by Paris. Antenor, the wise councilor, supports their petition, but Paris and less prudent advisers prevail over the Trojan assembly, which in its disorder suggests a Polish *Sejm*. The envoys are dismissed and threaten vengeance; Cassandra the prophetess foretells the fall of Troy. At the close of the drama comes the news that the Greek troops have already landed for the attack.

Kochanowski's tragedy has neither hero nor heroine about whom the action might center; it is a series of dramatic pictures rather than a true drama. The speeches depict character well: Paris is an unprincipled, attractive young gallant; Helen a woman who, while attached to her captor, condemns herself for yielding to him; Antenor and Cassandra are equally distinct figures. But there is no development of character, no gradual revealing of a complicated personality under the stress of emotion. Kochanowski partially atones for his lack of dramatic talent by the sustained dignity of his style, which is polished and reserved, animated by a truly classic spirit. The three choral odes are among his finest lyrics. *The Dismissal of the Grecian Envoys* is the single original Renaissance tragedy in Polish; no work of comparable merit appeared until the nineteenth century.

Kochanowski's true genius was as a lyric poet. And two lyric sequences of his later years are, one the most Polish, the other the most personal of all his works. These are *St. John's Eve* and the *Laments*.

On the eve of the festival of St. John the Baptist (June 24) the village folk in some portions of Poland still dance around bonfires and sing folk songs. To this ancient rite Kochanowski devoted a series of lyrics; the date of the work is uncertain, but probably not earlier than 1571. In its form and its general character *St. John's Eve* owes nothing to any classical source; after four stanzas that describe the scene the poet's twelve maidens sing their songs as girls in Poland sang them. These songs, though they contain a classical story and classical allusions and reminiscences that startle us on the lips of village maidens, are not translations or imitations of any Greek or Latin originals, and they usually express the feelings of the different girls rather than those of the poet himself. In general type they are probably of the same sort that were once sung on the meadows of Czarnolas. Kochanowski cares nothing for detailed truth of atmosphere, nor does he even try to be faithful to the spirit of the folk song. Yet he is sincere; he has been touched by the beauty of a popular custom and he thinks it worthy of treatment in the style that he has developed by his study of classical antiquity. He gives a charming picture of Polish village life, a life of comfort and abundance, of simple pleasures and wholesome mirth.

Near the close of 1579 Kochanowski lost his second daughter, Ursula, a child of thirty months. To her memory he devoted a series of nineteen *Laments* that is the masterpiece of all Polish poetry earlier than Mickiewicz. The *Laments* have the usual classical atmosphere of the Renaissance, but they are full of realistic touches and of personal affection tinged with Christian faith. In the first the poet summons all the mourners of the world to help him express his grief; in the second he exclaims that, had he chosen to write verses for children, far better had they been cradle songs for the living rather than dirges for the dead. In *Laments III-VIII* he tells of Ursula's charming nature, her talents, her death, her burial, the desolation that she has left behind her. In *Laments IX-XI* his sorrow passes into despair and doubt, for which his learning can offer no solace. From this despair he partially recovers in *Laments XII-XIII*, which resume the tone of *Laments III-VIII*. *Laments XIV-XIX* describe how the father seeks and finds consolation. His search is at first vain, for it is in the world of ancient paganism, but in *Lament XVII* he turns to the Christian God for comfort. *Lament XVIII* is in spirit a psalm, a prayer to God for mercy. And God grants his prayer. *Lament XIX* is a vision of Ursula, happy in her heavenly home. The poet's mother appears to him, bearing the little girl in her arms—

> . . . just as she used to run
> To me at dawn to say her morning prayer,
> In her white nightgown, with her curling hair
> Framing her rosy face, her eyes about
> To laugh, like flowers only halfway out.[1]

The mother utters words of Christian consolation, conceived, one must admit, in a somewhat Stoic spirit that shows Kochanowski to be still more a philosopher than a mystic. But Christian faith affords him the relief that pagan ethics has refused.

For readers today *Lament VII* is the gem of the series. In it Kochanowski, laying aside his classical allusions, gives an immediate picture of the sorrow wrought in his home:

[1] Translated by D. P. Radin.

Sad trinkets of my little daughter, dresses
   That touched her like caresses,
Why do you draw my mournful eyes? To borrow
   A newer weight of sorrow?
No longer will you clothe her form, to fold her
   Around, and wrap her, hold her.
A hard, unwaking sleep has overpowered
   Her limbs, and now the flowered
Cool muslin and the ribbon snoods are bootless,
   The gilded girdles fruitless.
My little girl, 't was to a bed far other
   That one day thy poor mother
Had thought to lead thee, and this simple dower
   Suits not the bridal hour;
A tiny shroud and gown of her own sewing
   She gives thee at thy going.
Thy father brings a clod of earth, a somber
   Pillow for thy last slumber.
And so a single casket, scant of measure,
   Locks thee and all thy treasure.[2]

Thus in his last years Kochanowski was a devoted husband and father. Besides Ursula, he lost his daughter Hannah in her childhood. Four daughters grew to maturity; a posthumous son died in infancy. He himself died, stricken by apoplexy during a visit to Lublin, on August 22, 1584.

In his ideas on public affairs Kochanowski was merely an average conservative Pole of his generation, satisfied with the laws and the social order of Poland as he found them. Of the glaring social inequality and injustice in his country he had no word to say; in his works he barely mentions the existence of the peasants. His only suggestion for reform is a return to the good old times, when there was no luxury but much concord and martial spirit.

In religion, however, Kochanowski was by no means typical of his age and his nation. He was the intimate friend of Catholic prelates, held ecclesiastical benefices, and at least in his later years was always regarded as a true son of the Church. Yet his silences are eloquent. From his specifically religious poems no reader could determine whether he was a Catholic, a Protestant, or a Jew.

[2] Translated by D. P. Radin.

The words *Jesus* and *Christ* do not occur in his works. Not once does he mention the Trinity, the Holy Ghost, the Virgin Mary (unless an allusion to the old Polish hymn in her honor be counted), or any saint of the Church. He never mentions the sacraments or any specifically Catholic doctrine, except for an allusion to "the saints" in *Lament XVI* and a passing reference to Purgatory in *Lament X*, four times after a similar reference to Charon—he may have had no more lively faith in the one than in the other. Neither does he mention or quote (except once—see below) from any book of the New Testament, even when, as in the *Laments*, use of the Gospels would seem imperative. Except for the Psalms, Daniel (from the "additions" to which book he versified the story of Susanna), and a mention of Noah, he makes no use of the Old Testament. In one of his *Trifles* he sneers at "heretics" who scorn ceremonies yet are nevertheless greedy and ambitious; but the sneer is of no more account than his raillery at Catholic priests and monks of bad character. He evidently disliked the Protestants merely as bringers-in of discord, disturbers of the Polish national tradition; in the doctrinal differences between Catholics and Protestants he was not interested.

On the other hand Kochanowski constantly asserts his faith in an almighty, all-wise, all-merciful God, who loves men and is accessible to prayer. Such is the faith of the Psalmist. He also believes in immortality, but is led to his belief in it more by reasoning than by faith; there must be a future life, he argues, in order to correct the injustices of this world. In *Lament X* he implies a belief in pre-existence, a classical rather than a Christian doctrine, though many devout Christians have accepted it. Thus in regard to dogma Kochanowski adopted an attitude akin to that of many Western humanists, chief among them Erasmus. Nor was he any more a mystic than a theologian. Only once does he speak of revelation. In *Omens* a priest mentions "the highest prophet" (Christ) and quotes, in reference to Polish discord, from Matthew and Luke: "Every kingdom divided against itself is brought to desolation." The priest further reminds us that "God has revealed his will to us through the prophets and through his Son." This is not quite conclusive, for the priest may be speaking in character, not uttering Kochanowski's own convictions. It is noteworthy that even this priest bases his general argument on Cicero, not on the Bible.

Kochanowski then, like many pious and thoughtful men in our own time, far fewer in his, was a Catholic only officially; he remained true to the church of his fathers, but cared little or nothing for its doctrines and ceremonies. His attitude may be compared to that of a deist of the eighteenth century; Kochanowski might have found Rousseau's Savoyard Vicar a rather congenial spirit. Only in the *Laments,* under the stress of personal sorrow, does he adopt a definitely Christian attitude, finding in faith a solace that philosophy cannot give.

Whatever his convictions, Kochanowski was, as the Polish critics reiterate, "a poet by the grace of God." But he was not a poet of strong passions or of an exuberant imagination that early demanded expression. Mickiewicz was only thirty-five when he completed *Pan Tadeusz* and then laid aside poetic composition. Other great romantic poets, both in Poland and in England, did their best work when even younger. Kochanowski at thirty-five was just beginning his career; he wrote his *Laments* when he was fifty. He composed first in Latin, striving to attain the concise elegance of his Roman models, and then transferred his hard-won skill to Polish. He was a man of learning, and in his poems he made free use of that learning. Yet, though he addressed primarily a small circle of cultivated aristocrats, his poems gained the warm admiration of the entire educated population of Poland. He was a pioneer in Polish poetic expression; his genius ripened slowly, becoming more independent as the years passed by. Polish ideals of poetic style have changed since his day; much of what he wrote now seems stiff, mechanical, crude in its rhymes, even prosaic. Yet his best poems, with their reserve, poise, self-mastery, have an enduring charm, a charm that for some readers even of today surpasses that of the exuberantly imaginative work of Mickiewicz and his successors.

Finally, the personality of Kochanowski will continue to attract every generation of Poles. Through all his life, to use his own words, he "sang for himself and for the Muses." Though deeply indebted to patrons, he was not servile; he had self-respect and the respect of others. He was a student of great literature, a lover of beauty and a creator of it. He passed his last years as the leader of Polish letters, realizing his ideal of cultivated moderation and surrounded by the affection of his family and of his nation.

PIOTR SKARGA

(From painting by Jan Matejko)

VII

PIOTR SKARGA

Great Preacher and Champion of Catholic Renaissance

1536-1612

by

Stanisław Windakiewicz

PIOTR SKARGA, the greatest Polish preacher, a member of the Society of Jesus, in his time newly introduced to Poland, had like every monk a quiet, composed life, devoid of unusual events. He was born in 1536 in Grojec Mazowiecki into a family of towns-people, completed his university education at Kraków and made himself known as a preacher in the Church of Our Lady of the Snow, in Lwów. In 1568 he went to Rome and entered the Jesuit novitiate. After his return to Poland he held the office of vice-rector, then rector, of the College of Wilno, and from 1584 was superior of the Jesuit House of St. Barbara at Kraków. In 1588 he became preacher at the court of King Sigismund III and held this appointment until his death. He died in 1612 and was buried in St. Peter's Church in Kraków.

The important event which molded Skarga's personality was his stay in Rome, where he became fervently attached to the Catholic faith and was imbued with blind admiration for the papacy. The Tombs of the Apostles constituted for him objects of deepest ecstasy. He met saintly men all around him. At that time St. Pius V was pope, St. Francis Borgia general of the Society of Jesus, and Skarga began his novitiate immediately after the death of the saintly Polish youth St. Stanislaus Kostka, when his cult began to flourish. Skarga's associates were all meritorious Jesuit scholars and future Indian missionaries. Skarga did not close his eyes to what was happening around him. He studied the Holy City's social life and the politics of the Papal court, paying less attention to historical monuments, though by no means indifferent to them, especially if they were connected with the history of the church. The second formative event in Skarga's life was his close relationship with the great king and great soldier Stefan Batory, and with one of the ablest and wisest of Polish chancellors, Jan Zamoyski. After the conquest of Livonia he received from them the order to organize Jesuit colleges in Polock and Riga. This connected him with the great events in Poland, kindled in him active patriotism and a desire for action, and from then on petty endeavors lost attraction in his eyes; he became a purposive and steadfast propagator of Catholicism in Poland.

One more event occurred later in his life, which had no connection with his will and intelligence but which moved his heart and contributed to the development of his emotional qualities. After his appointment at the court he became closely attached to Sigismund III, surrounded Sigismund's little son, Ladislas IV, with deep affection, and regarded the family affairs and interests of the Vasa dynasty as almost his own. The Vasa dynasty found in Skarga a strong support and it was partly thanks to him that it was established in Poland. It is the boundless worship for that family that lends him his proper historical profile. He was an ardent royalist and adherent of the Vasa dynasty.

Skarga was above all a man of action and an energetic organizer. He transformed the Wilno college into an academy,[1] founded houses and colleges wherever he happened to be and collected funds for Jesuit institutions in other cities. Transferred to Kraków, at that time Poland's largest city, he was struck by the indifference of the authorities (universal in the sixteenth century) toward the misery of the lower classes and the immense influx of beggars. Skarga founded, on the Roman model, the Brotherhood of Mercy for those ashamed to beg and brought the beggars within the strong bounds of the St. Lazarus Brotherhood. The experience gained in Rome helped him in establishing his position at Kraków. The new institutions immediately struck roots and brought forth

[1] College in this historical sense was a secondary school, and the academy a higher institution of learning.—*Ed.*

new branches. Particularly the Brotherhood of Mercy proved very fruitful. A pawnshop or bank for the poor, *Mons Pietatis*, again on the Italian model, was organized under its auspices, followed by the *St. Nicholas' Chest* for endowing poor girls. Thanks to Skarga Kraków became the generating cell of social institutions in Poland and the perspicacity of his motives was so great that some of these institutions have survived to our days. Reflecting upon this action of the preacher we must regret that old Poland had no more men like Skarga.

But these were Skarga's subsidiary activities. The main object of his activity was the lifting of the religious life to a higher level and as far as possible the restoration of religious unity in Poland. That Poland remained Catholic is to a considerable extent due to him. He was an outstanding champion of the renaissance of Catholicism in Poland and in Europe. He found himself in a country considerably confused by the Reformation and various sects. He wished to restore religious life in the families and wrote the *Lives of the Saints*. The work is of no particular literary value, but gives the lives of the saints for all the days of the year and covers the whole range of the subject, its worth being enhanced by the fact that Poland had until then no survey of this kind. The abundant and frequently very interesting historical material of various countries and ages is provided with numerous moral instructions and warnings as to purity of faith and orthodoxy. For the turbulent heads of the sixteenth century it was the very book that was needed. It became extremely widely read, won the love of Polish families and even today it retains some of its popularity in Polish homes. Having thus laid the foundation for further action, the zealous monk exerted all his powers to break the influence of the Reformation in Poland. He wrote numerous pamphlets and polemic tracts, at first in Latin and subsequently exclusively in Polish, and strained his energies to find the best historical, theological, moral and political arguments to overcome the dissenters. He combated the Lithuanian Calvinists, the Confederation of Dissenters, the Unitarians of Little Poland and the Greek Orthodox writers, in his zeal to bring about church unity. The pamphlet written and rewritten, *About the Unity of the Divine Church* (1577, 1590) can be regarded as the best exposition of the program of his activities

in this direction. Skarga published also a separate historical opuscule, *Annual History of the Church*, adapted from Baronius
(1603), in order to prove that all heresies are old and unnecessary
inventions. Today these writings have no great significance for us,
except perhaps as a record of the religious disruption of Poland
during Skarga's time. Contemporaneously, however, his pamphlets
had great popularity and influence. They stirred up discussions,
evoked arguments, gibes, attacks and conversions, until in the
course of time, long after Skarga's death, the religious disruption
of Poland subsided and the whole controversy passed into oblivion.
Nevertheless one of those pamphlets has a certain importance for
the present time. It is an account of the proceedings of The Synod
of Brześć (1596), in which Skarga participated. It concerns the
union of the Latin Church with the Greek, the development of
which has been disturbed by the partitions and until now has not
been fully explained and assuaged.

But at the bottom of his heart Skarga was neither a social
worker nor a controversialist. These activities were only manifes-
tations of his active nature. Essentially he was a speaker and
preacher. He was endowed by nature with this wonderful gift,
that by his voice, eloquence, carriage, self-confidence and the
shrewdness of his arguments he carried people away, "held human
hearts in his hand, magnetized, and turned them wherever he
liked," as Father Birkowski said at his funeral. He commanded
the Polish language with the greatest ease and did not permit any
foreign elements, with the exception of Latin, to influence his
vocabulary, though he knew several foreign languages, particularly
Italian and German. This circumstance is not without bearing on
Polish literature, for it proves that the Polish language attained
in Skarga's mouth true maturity. He revealed the Polish language
in all its natural purity, strength, richness and sense of individuality. In the sixteenth century, a time of political controversies
of all sorts, it was Skarga who, amid so many famous parliamentary orators, achieved widest popularity. (Today it is difficult to
evaluate him as an orator. His voice has long since been stilled.)
There remain only two printed collections of sermons published
by himself: *Sunday Sermons* (1595) and *Sermons of the Seven
Sacraments* (1600), together about two hundred sermons which

should be studied to grasp something of the qualities of his rhetoric. We know that the famous Polish scholar, Jan Śniadecki, though a mathematician and astronomer, read Skarga's works with great enjoyment. In his sermons Skarga was neither a critic of morals nor a sagacious moralist, but the purely ecclesiastical catechizer needed at that time of disturbing religious controversies. His sermons are characterized by the great authority of the teacher of religion and guardian of orthodoxy, and consequently are somewhat polemical. They appealed to the masses, for they felt that the man behind the spoken word was a thinking, wise, educated, pure, inflexible character, a man of extraordinary piety, an ascetic, convinced of the truth of his word and a sincere believer in what he said. In addition, he was affable, tender-hearted, sensitive to human misery, attentive to his listeners, absorbed in the problem he was dealing with, as well as a shrewd psychologist, knowing when and what to say. Lovers of the Polish language even today read him with pleasure. He had three important qualities of a great preacher: a strong character, thorough education, and sweeping oratory.

But it was not in his church sermons that Skarga fully expressed himself. As court preacher he had sometimes to raise his voice in connection with court events and state occasions, not infrequently in praise of great successes of Polish arms. Extant are his sermons at the funeral of Queen Anne, the first wife of Sigismund III; of that of Anne the Jagellon, Stefan Batory's widow; on the occasion of Zamoyski's victory over Moldavia; Chodkiewicz's Kircholm victory over the Swedes; and the conquest of Smolensk. The most fervent of these sermons is the one in gratitude to the Lord of Hosts for the Kircholm victory. He also published in connection with the events of 1597 *Sermons Before the Diet*. We do not know whether they were actually delivered or put into circulation as a political pamphlet in the form of sermons. *Sermons Before the Diet* is a collection of sermons prepared for the eight consecutive Sundays of the weeks of the Diet's duration. With one, "On the Monarchy," Skarga had much trouble, for it was taken as proof that he advocated absolutist power and wished to limit the freedom of *szlachta* (petty nobility). All are beautiful, inspired, and present interesting problems suitable to serve as introduction to the proper proceedings

of the Diet. He discussed in them above all, like orators everywhere, questions concerning human gatherings in general, but he
was not afraid to tackle burning contemporary problems and
concluded with an almost critical view of the internal conditions
prevailing in Poland. The subject matter of all the sermons is conceived boldly, with prudence, by an experienced orator and active
politician. By the second sermon in this series, "On Love of the
Motherland," Poles are deeply moved even today. Here full expression is found of a pure and noble mind loving his country
in the manner of a soldier ready to give his life for the Motherland. For Skarga had something of the soldier's spirit, as is revealed
by a beautiful pamphlet of his, *Divine Service for Soldiers* (1606).
In the "Motherland" sermon he enumerates the advantages and
honors which everybody receives from his country, and demands
that, continuously thinking of it, everyone should sacrifice himself
for it and serve it disinterestedly. No one in the sixteenth century
defined these conceptions so clearly and convincingly. This gives
Skarga an exceptional position in the history of Polish patriotism.

Skarga limited his activity mainly to Poland and is of importance above all in internal Polish history. But as a Jesuit educated
in Rome he was strongly interested in Catholic missions in India,
Japan, and Brazil, and followed attentively the growth and success
of Catholicism in Europe. He became particularly interested in
England and could not get over the break of the Anglican Church
with Rome. Witnessing the success of his own apostleship in
Poland he was anxious for a similar development in favor of
Catholicism in England. The circumstances of his life enabled him
to become acquainted with four English exiles, chiefly Jesuits:
James Bosgrave, Robert Abercomly, Nicholas Sanders and Henry
Garnet. Thanks to this acquaintance he became interested in the
history of Catholicism in medieval England and included about
twenty biographies of English saints in his Polish *Lives of the
Saints*. The persecution of Catholics during the reign of Queen
Elizabeth was particularly painful to him. He translated into Polish
and published in Wilno in 1584 the Latin pamphlet by Edmund
Campion dealing with these questions, *Rationes Decem Redditae
Academicis Angliae.* From then on he continuously followed the
history of Catholicism in England, and to acquaint the Poles with

it, he added to later editions of his *Lives of the Saints* articles on "The Martyrs of England" (Sir Thomas More and John Fisher), "The Martyrdom of Mary, Queen of Scots," and "The Martyrdom of Henry Garnet." Church politician that he was, he was mainly concerned with English Catholicism and, writing about it, he was strengthening himself and others in religious fervor. This is in conformity with the chief characteristic of his activity as champion of Catholic renaissance in Europe.

Piotr Skarga was a great Pole, but his fame is confined to Poland, more specifically to Catholic Poland, and to catholicism in general.

He came at a time when Polish political thinkers and writers had said all they had to say about political and social reforms, when lay arguments had reached the saturation point and a new approach was needed to carry conviction. While Frycz Modrzewski and others had spoken in the name of reason and social justice, in the name of a better morrow in this vale of tears, Piotr Skarga, the monk, priest, and preacher, raised his voice in the name of God and religion and eternal verities as he understood them. His voice was the voice of a Polish Jeremiah calling upon his contemporaries to repent and reform before it was too late. Bent in modesty, his shoulders stooping under the might of self-mortification, this historian, theologian, writer of beautiful Polish prose, silver-tongued orator, preacher and prophet awakened the conscience of the nation, showed it its sinful ways and prophesied the downfall of Poland unless its citizens followed the straight and narrow path and thought more of their duties and responsibilities than of their rights and privileges. One passage in his sermon on lack of internal unity will never lose its prophetic significance, from which any nation at any time may take heed:

"There shall come a foreign enemy and taking advantage of your disunity, shall say unto you: 'Your hearts are divided, now you perish.' And this disunity shall bring unto you slavery that will bury your liberties and turn them into mockery. You will lose your language and your nation, and the scattered remnants of that nation so old and in other lands renowned shall be absorbed by another hostile to you peoples, of which alas! written annals tell us so many tragic stories. You shall not only be ruled by lords not of your blood and your choice, but you shall be without your country and your kingdom: aimless vagabonds, destitute and despised wherever you go, pushed and kicked and jostled you shall be where once you commanded respect. Your enemies you shall serve as hewers of wood and drawers of water, while you yourselves go naked and suffer hunger and thirst, and upon your necks they shall place iron yokes of great weight and unspeakable humiliation."

By daring to be unpopular, Skarga achieved greatness. His admonitions may well serve as commandments to any self-governing people likely to become soft or to relax its eternal vigilance.

Translated from the Polish by Dr. Ludwik Krzyżanowski.

JAN ZAMOYSKI

(From a contemporary painting of unknown authorship—in the Gallery
degli Uffizi in Florence, Italy)

VIII

JAN ZAMOYSKI
Statesman, Soldier, Educator

1542-1605

by

STANISŁAW ŁEMPICKI

JAN ZAMOYSKI, the chancellor and "hetman" or marshal of the Polish army during the reign of two successive kings (Stefan Batory and Sigismund III of the Swedish Vasa dynasty), was a "self-made" man and one of the most important and influential Poles of the second half of the sixteenth century.

He was born in 1542, in a small border castle called *Skokówka,* on the southeastern frontier of the Polish Republic. His was a Polish squire's modest home. His mother (nee Herburt) came of a family of Polish knights who were constantly defending their country's frontiers against Turks and Tartars. His father, Stanislaus, a commander of the Royal Court troops, spent his life fighting with pagan foes. This never-tiring knight had only a little learning, but wanted to furnish his only son with the best possible education, as conceived by his epoch. These were the times of Renaissance and humanism; new ideas were coming to Poland from everywhere, from Italy, France and Germany, and Poland's young men were leaving home in large numbers for the foreign universities.

Jan Zamoyski studied extensively in the three countries mentioned above. In France he was a student at the *Sorbonne* and the *Collège Royal;* in Germany, in the famous Academy of Strassburg and in Italy at the University of Padua. He was among the best students in law and humanities. At Padua he became the beloved disciple of the great philologist Charles Sigonio, and a friend of many Italian scholars. Even as a student he wrote and published a book, *De Senatu Romano*, which is still valued by experts on ancient Rome and its institutions.

Thanks to his abilities, his seriousness and his pleasing personality he gained a widespread popularity among Paduan students belonging to all nationalities near by. As a result of their esteem, this young Pole of twenty-one, this son of the far off northern Sarmatia—thus was Poland called in those days—was acclaimed by the students of the University of Padua as their Rector for the year 1563. Leaving this post of honor after a year of successful stewardship, he was supplied with high recommendations to the Polish king by the Senate of Venice, and the university erected a memorial tablet with the following, still existing, inscription:

"Dedicated by the Lawyers' University of Padua, to Jan Sarius Zamoyski, son of Stanislaus, starosta [sheriff] of Belz and commander of the royal troops, a Pole, Rector of this University, full of merit."

It seemed that Zamoyski, on his return to Poland, would begin his career as a distinguished scholar, writing learned books about the life and institutions of ancient peoples. Even when he became the royal secretary, he immediately started to work in the state's archives, which he put into order by indexing and cataloguing their material.

But Poland's eventful life of that time soon disclosed in the young lawyer and scholar the temperament of a great politician, and the unusual happenings in his country made him forget his studies in a maelstrom of other interests and tasks.

King Sigismund Augustus, the last of the famous Jagiellonian dynasty, died in 1572, without leaving an heir. Suddenly the state found itself in a peculiar situation, which threatened anarchy and disorder. The nation was free to choose a new sovereign. Representatives of the most distinguished dynasties in Europe were busy trying to secure the Polish crown and the vast realm belonging to it.

A struggle between the different parts of Poland, and among the great nobles and the masses of the country gentry, all wishing to influence the course of the election, began immediately.

Zamoyski, the disciple of Padua and of his master Sigonio, the admirer of the traditions of the Roman republic, the observer of the struggles between patricians and plebeians, remembering the part played by the Roman tribunes in the old days, contemplated the situation in his country from the point of view of a scholar deeply interested in ancient Rome. He saw certain similarities between Poland and Rome, between Polish senators and nobles on one hand and Roman patricians on the other. The vast masses of the gentry of the country were to him identical with the Roman plebeians. They were also faced by the predominance of the great nobles. Zamoyski understood that his should be the role of a people's tribune, like that of one of the Gracchi in ancient Rome.

He therefore put himself at the head of the country gentry, whose great body he managed to captivate by his enthusiasm and his power of conviction, and to subjugate by his brilliant oratory and his scholarship. He really became the people's tribune, embodying the ideas of ancient Rome. Thanks to him the gentry's doctrine of freedom and their view upon the king's election became definite and stabilized. It is a fact that it was he, Zamoyski, who created the theory of the so-called *viritim* election, a theory which maintained that every member of the Polish gentry had a right to vote *personally* at the place of election and to choose his own king.

As a leader of the gentry, Zamoyski had a hand in the election of the French candidate, Henry of Valois, because he hated the Germans and the Habsburgs. Zamoyski, among others, dictated the conditions under which the new king was to gain access to the throne, and helped to formulate the principles of the gentry's liberty, which every successive king was to confirm from that time on.

Together with a splendid ambassadorial train, he soon left for Paris in order to bring King Henry to Poland. There he gained the praise of both the French world of politics and of culture. French writers dedicated their works to him.

During this journey Zamoyski did not forget his scholarly past and his cultural mission. He planned a rejuvenescence of the old Polish Jagiellonian University at Kraków, and therefore tried

to persuade French and Italian scholars to come to Poland. King
Henry was won over by him to further this plan. The speech,
full of historical and classical erudition, which he wrote to greet
the king-elect, was published in Paris and translated into many
languages.

King Henry's escape from Poland in 1574, made in order to
secure the French crown after the death of his brother, Charles IX,
not only deeply offended the Poles, but also seems to have shaken
Zamoyski's popularity, for a time at least. The gentry, however,
did not lose their faith in their young, enthusiastic, and energetic
leader. Before and during the second election, he was very active
again, fighting against the great nobles and the Habsburg candidate and having his hand in the election of one of the greatest of
Polish kings, Stefan Batory, the palatine of Transylvania. It was
Zamoyski who supplied the masses of the gentry with the watchword of a "Piast" for a king, i.e., a Polish candidate, and as a
result the last member of the Jagiellonian dynasty, Princess Anne,
was elected queen, while Stefan Batory, by becoming her husband,
was the king of Poland.

After Batory ascended the Polish throne, a change took place
in Jan Zamoyski's way of thinking, which led to the most inspiring period of his life. The powerful personality of Batory influenced and attracted him immensely. He conceived a great admiration for the firm character of the king, who was full of ambitious
plans for his country, among them that of curbing the willfulness
of the gentry, whom he tried to force to respect his will. Zamoyski
became Batory's most devoted and confidential friend. Though he
had been protector and legislator of the gentry's freedom, and
their tribune, he began to perceive the weakness of a too radical
democracy.

From a Gracchus he turned into one of those wise Roman
senators, about whom he used to write once upon a time, whom
the tribunes could hardly excel in their steadfast watch and care
for the well-being of their country. The strong arm of Zamoyski,
the chancellor, was a faithful and fearless instrument of the king's
will, and his voice was forever raised in defense of the king's
policy at all the sessions of the Parliament. The influence of Batory,
a great warrior in those times, awakened in Zamoyski, the poli-

tician and statesman, the spirit of his forefathers from the Republic's borderlands and made of him a warrior and a great military leader. His deeds of valor in the course of Batory's struggles with Russia, particularly the heroic siege of Pskov during the disastrous winter of 1581-82, made his name glorious everywhere. Later on, he conducted several campaigns and won victories as a marshal of the Polish army during the reign of King Sigismund III.

Zamoyski was undoubtedly a highly ambitious man, dreaming of glory and personal power, as all strong individualities of the Renaissance era did. The king made Zamoyski his chancellor and commander-in-chief of the whole armed force of the realm; he bestowed upon him valuable offices, distinctions, and vast estates. Zamoyski also became the king's kinsman, by marrying his niece. But these ties were nothing compared to the deep devotion which he felt for his king, a devotion which was to last "until death do us part." These two men, the Hungarian and the Pole, the king and his subject, both pupils of the University of Padua, were united by such a complete mutual harmony of soul and thought, that it is often very difficult to separate their ideas or plans realized at that time, by distinctly pointing out which were the king's and which the spiritual property of the chancellor. They conducted wars together, they reformed the state, reorganized the judicature and the army, together they fought—not always successfully—the overbearing pride of the Polish magnates and the willfulness of the gentry.

A new period began in the life and in the activities of this great Pole after the death of King Stefan Batory, which plunged Zamoyski into deep mourning. All of his opponents combined against him, who had recently been so powerful. But Zamoyski was victorious once more. He still had a great many partisans among the Poles and again managed to frustrate the Habsburg candidature and to support the election of the national candidate, the Swedish prince Sigismund of the Vasa dynasty, whose mother, a Polish Jagiellonian princess, was the sister both of the late King Sigismund Augustus and of Queen Anne, Batory's wife.

But the chancellor and marshal was soon to receive a blow which touched him to the quick. His enemies did not give up the fight. They managed to get the king, whom Zamoyski elected, under their influence. Sigismund the Third kept himself aloof from the chancellor. This young sovereign was very much like the Spanish Habsburgs: silent, uncommunicative, proud and a slave of court etiquette. An ardent Catholic and a friend of the Germans, an eccentric character, he was more of an artist, a painter, a musician and even an alchemist, than a statesman or a warrior. What a difference between him and the Jagiellonian kings or Batory! The well-being of his dynasty was more important to him than that of Poland. He tried to regain Sweden and the Swedish crown, even at the cost of sacrificing Poland to the Habsburgs. The court faction, closely surrounding the king, gained new strength now and proceeded with its struggle against Zamoyski more consistently than ever.

The chancellor, whose life was a prolongation of Batory's great ideas, was sorely touched in his personal pride; but he was like one of those heroic senators of old Rome, whose highest incentive had been the welfare of the Republic. He disclosed the king's machinations and secret intrigues with Sweden and the Habsburgs; he reproached the king for neglecting Polish state affairs and for furthering his own private good. He went too far perhaps. Putting himself at the head of the gentry again, he did not hesitate to accuse the king openly before the nation at the Parliament session in 1592, and to force him to apologize and to abjure his intrigues with the Habsburgs. All this made the gulf between the court and the chancellor and leader of the army still wider and deeper.

Zamoyski began to understand that watching and counteracting was all he could do now, that his former influence upon the course of the policy of the Polish state was definitely gone from him. It was then that he returned to the pursuits of his youth, never quite forgotten, not even during the most busy years, full of politics and wars. He was fond of repeating those characteristic words: *Patavium virum me fecit* (Padua made a man of me).

But Zamoyski did not return to his scholarly researches on the political systems of the ancient states and on Roman culture. He wrote and published accounts of his own exploits, and ventured upon a more important task, similar to that of some statesmen and warriors of the classic era, like his beloved Julius Caesar, namely, the writing of a history. He outlined the course of Batory's great war with Moscow, he tackled the history of Poland from the death of the last Jagiełło till the most recent times. His favorite secretary, a capable historian, Reinhold Heidenstein, filled in those outlines and changed them into extensive historical works, written in beautiful Latin, which retain their value up to the present. They remained for months at a time—the chancellor and his collaborator—in the splendid residence of the former at Zamość, surrounded by books and source materials, and wrote together such works as *Commentaries on the Moscow War*, and *Twenty-two Books on Polish Affairs, from the death of Sigismund Augustus onward*. These works, though published under the name of Heidenstein, properly belong to Zamoyski, whose recollections and historical reflections gave them birth.

The chancellor's personal achievements in the field of writing form only a part of his merits as a promoter of culture. Our attention should be especially called to his activities as a patron, conducted on an imposing, truly European scale. His patronage over all fields of cultural achievement won for him the name of a "Polish Medici."

II

Zamoyski was one of the greatest patrons of culture in the old Republic of Poland. The broad scope of these activities and interests of his is equaled in sixteenth-century Poland only by that of Piotr Tomicki, the famous bishop of Kraków, and by that of the unhappy Polish king, Stanislaus Augustus Poniatowski, in the era of Poland's partitions in the eighteenth century.

Zamoyski, lord of an immense fortune, was a model master of his own estates and those which he held from the king. With the help of Italian architects, he built his residential town of Zamość in the Chełm district, a masterpiece of Renaissance art whose model was Padua. This town, like Kraków, gives us even today a tangible impression of the Polish Renaissance and is eloquent testimony of Poland's glorious past.

But Zamość was not the only town built by Zamoyski. Other towns and villages, besides castles and fortresses, were founded by him, thanks to which the empty spaces of Polish Podolia and the Ukraine, where Tartar hordes had so recently fought with the Polish knights of the Border, became colonized and were given back to a peaceful population.

The estates belonging to him consisted of 17,480 square kilometers, with 23 towns and 816 villages in their area. This vast expanse, in the last years of the chancellor's life especially, achieved a most vigorous development, full of bustling activity. It possessed a model administration. Zamoyski induced colonists from all parts of Poland to settle here. Artisans and tradesmen of all nations, Ruthenians, Greeks, Armenians and Jews, were free to carry on their pursuits and enjoyed many special privileges. Agriculture and trade in agricultural products were on a very high plane. The breeding of domestic animals (oxen, sheep, etc.), fishing, and apiculture, received special attention. Such branches of agricultural industries as brewing and the miller's trade, were highly developed, as were forestry (sawmills, the production of ashes, pitch, and nitrate of potassium), iron, glass, and cloth industries, furriery and the tanner's trade. Material well-being was accompanied by an increase of learning. Many churches and schools were to be found upon the immense area of the Zamoyski estates, with numerous missionaries, priests and teachers.

The glory and apex of Zamoyski's achievements in the field of spiritual culture are his Academy, founded by him at Zamość in 1595, and the cultural influence of his court in that town.

The Zamoyski Academy was really an university, founded and maintained by a private man, an astonishing and unique enterprise in Europe even in the times of the Renaissance.

This accomplishment was the result of long years of persistent work. The chancellor had wished at first to reform and renew the state university in Kraków. Later on, he thought (together with King Batory) of founding a second university, *Collegium Regium*, following the example of the *Collége Royal* in Paris. He planned to have there Europe's greatest scholars: Italians, Frenchmen, Germans and Spaniards, learned philosophers, Latinists, Hellenists, and Hebrew specialists; lawyers, physicians, natural scientists, and theologians. At this time (1577-78) Zamoyski sent invitations and messengers to the most prominent scholars of the world, till this magnificent and truly royal plan began to be talked about in all southern and western countries. In the name of the king, he promised to the candidates rich salaries and a comfortable life. But this plan was too ambitious and far-reaching to be fulfilled. Bold as Zamoyski's cultural projects were, they were doubly bold in that era of religious reformation.

After many further efforts the chancellor ultimately decided to found a private academy at his own Zamość. Its academic privileges were granted by the pope and by the Polish king, its existence was securely based upon an endowment out of his own estates. He erected a splendid building, provided it with all necessary equipment, and gave it Polish professors and a rich library, the nucleus of today's well-known Zamoyski Library in Warsaw. He even saw to it that it had a large and well-equipped academic printing office. The plans for this Academy, its privileges, statutes and curricula, were those of Zamoyski himself, the work of his creative and youthful enthusiasm and inspiration. But he did not wish it to be a complete university, though it was to have the right to present the entire course of studies ordinarily given in universities of that period. What Zamoyski wanted to do was to establish an educational institution for the vast masses of the Polish gentry, to imbue them with the new, humanist spirit, and train them for duties of citizenship and leadership in their country. His own ideals and objectives, acquired and worked out in the course of his life, were the foundation of this desire. It was to be "a citizens' school" (scola civilis), and he hoped that those who were trained there would be true Polish gentlemen in the noblest and best sense of the word.

The Zamoyski Academy pursued its course of splendid development up to the chancellor's death in 1605, and even later, into the lifetime of his son Thomas (a chancellor too) who was its first alumnus. It had a remarkable influence upon the Eastern districts of the Republic, not only upon Poles, but also Ruthenians and Lithuanians who stood in the greatest need of assimilating the culture of the West.

The happiest and best moments of Zamoyski's life were dedicated to the Academy, called by him his dearest daughter, whom he loved no less than he did his only son. He paid special attention to the pupils, whom he used to visit and ask questions concerning the subjects they studied. It was he, one might almost say, who compiled their textbooks. Very characteristic of his devotion to this school is the fact that he ordered the students' written tasks sent him to his camp, while he was away on a military expedition. There he would look them over, correct them like a most careful teacher, and send them back with his own annotations. This was his most agreeable task, on a night spent in camp between two battles, when everybody was asleep except the sentinels at the entrance to his tent.

The court of the chancellor at Zamość was closely connected with the Academy and served as a center of the literary elite from 1586 to 1605. The chancellor's personality became its focusing point. He was surrounded by professors of the Academy, by learned philologists, historians, poets, theologians, lawyers, printers and publishers. The representatives of the plastic arts, such as architects, painters, sculptors, engravers and even some musicians, formed an outer circle of this learned society. One could see here Germans, Italians, Englishmen, Greeks. Thanks to the chancellor's initiative, the publishing activities at Zamość achieved splendid results. The professors and the literary men from the court vied with each other in this work. Studies in law (particularly Polish law), historical and poetic works, appeared at frequent intervals. Besides, there appeared a number of *editiones principes* (first editions) of extremely rare publications from the field of philology. Among them were manuscripts of hitherto unknown Greek and Latin works, sought for by special messengers in Greece or in the Rumanian and Moldavian territories. The chancellor himself sponsored such researches. These Polish publications were afterwards sent out to other European countries (including famous book-markets of Germany), to the delight of admiring foreigners.

The court at Zamość formed a means of communication between the cultural movements of Western Europe and Poland and the farther districts of the East. People continually came to the chancellor's court with tidings from other countries. The chancellor himself kept up an immense correspondence with many celebrities among European writers of this period. An Italian, Father Convallis, lectured on theology at Zamość; a Scotsman, Doctor Bruce, was a specialist in Roman law. A Paduan, Bernardo

Morando, erected the buildings at Zamość. Some of the professors of the Academy went abroad to complete their studies: the physicians Ursinius (Niedźwiecki) and Birkowski to Padua; the renowned Polish lawyer, Dresner, to Bourges and then to Padua. At the beginning of the year 1600 the entire university in Padua, and particularly its medical department, carried on a learned discussion with the Zamoyski Academy on the existence and therapy of the so-called "elf-lock," then universally considered a serious malady. Distinguished guests were also often welcomed by the chancellor's court. The renowned Dutch humanist George Douza stopped at the court on his return from Greece, where he had tried to locate old Hellenistic manuscripts. A Roman dignitary, Bonifazio Vanozzi, also visited Zamość and admired the Academy, the library, and the Greek and Armenian manuscripts. The school theater where the students performed classic plays was observed by him with particular interest. Every foreigner staying at Zamość felt that the chancellor's court had a direct contact with the world's culture.

This Polish statesman and leader was a patron not only in the realm of Poland. His name was familiar to all members of the cosmopolitan society of scholars. He had corresponding friends, distinguished clients and scholarly acquaintances everywhere. He wrote to them, and received from them erudite letters, and dedications of works couched in terms of admiration. Jan Zamoyski exchanged letters with the Italians, Charles Sigonio and Paolo Manuzio, with the famous philologist Marcus Anthony Muret (Muretus). The great philologist and philosopher from Louvain, Justus Lipsius, was eager for his letters and his favors. Justus Scaliger, a monarch among contemporary scholars, sent Zamoyski his Arabian dictionary for the latter's son. Among the great number of the chancellor's literary friends, we find the celebrated French historian de Thou, the distinguished philologist Isaac Casaubon, the English humanists Thomas Segethus and Roger Ascham, and the creator of international law, Hugo Grotius. Zamoyski had also many friends among the Italian physicians of that time, such as Gabriel Fallopio, Fabricius ab Aquapendente, Mercurialis, and Saxonia. Some of them were induced by him to come to lecture in Kraków or at Zamość, others exchanged letters with him. And there were German scholars from Helmstädt, Leipzig and other cities, with the Greek specialist John Chessel, a professor in Helmstädt, at their head. They dedicated their works to Zamoyski as long as he lived, and after his death they rendered him homage in a series of famous elegiac publications. Matthew Dresser, a historian of Leipzig, praised the chancellor in his treatises and the German humanists Melissus Rhodoman, Diepholdius, Taubman, Peparinus, etc., extolled his virtues both in verse and in prose.

The erudite letters of the Polish chancellor, written in beautiful Latin, circulated throughout Europe. For example, the chancellor sought some of Cicero's works, lost in England or known in fragments only, as he wished to publish them with the co-operation of his professors at Zamość. He ordered the researches to be conducted in the English libraries and copies to be made at his own expense. He even thought of asking the English king's support in this matter.

The foreign scholars and literary men were not the only ones to remain in constant touch with our chancellor. Foreign artists worked for him, both in Poland and abroad. Tintoretto the Younger, of Rome, painted pictures for the collegiate church at Zamość. His palace and its courtyard were ornamented with sculptures by the Florentine, Santi Gucci. Giacomo Lauro and Cavaliero, both Romans, did beautiful engravings, representing the military exploits of Batory and Zamoyski. Artists from Germany and Flanders also executed his orders. The chancellor was interested not only in architecture, religious paintings, sculpture and portraits, but also in engravings, medals, artistic monography, weaving, and tapestries.

The entire world of Polish scholars and artists sought Zamoyski's patronage and eagerly thronged his court. Many an important scholarly enterprise, many a distinguished literary work, came into being thanks to his initiative or active support. Zamoyski had habits of economy and disliked spending money recklessly, but as a patron of culture he was very liberal. A scholar himself at the beginning of his career, he always felt like a grateful son toward knowledge and art, not forgetting what he owed to them: his life's splendid success. He always felt happiest in the society of scholars, literary men and artists, whether at a convivial table or at a literary symposium.

Zamoyski's declining years were spent in cultural pursuits, but his name was still a terror to Poland's foes, particularly to those in the East, the Turks and Tartars. Whenever his country needed him he answered the call. His campaign in Rumania and Moldavia in the years 1594-1600 forms a chivalrous epic, often sung by contemporary poets. But the last campaign of his life, when he defended Livland against the Swedish invasion (1601-1602), is most touching. Hardly back from the Moldavian expedition, tired to death by its hardships, he had been called upon to fight against the Swedes. Brave soldier that he was, a faithful servant of the Republic, the old leader hurried immediately to Livland, though he could have easily found an excuse to stay away from this war, started by King Sigismund III for his own private dynastic purposes, as Zamoyski well knew. Amidst untold hardships during the winter, with no financial help, handicapped by want and the ill will of his troops, he conducted this truly heroic war so successfully that he regained Livland and advanced to the frontiers of Esthonia. But the strength of this indomitable man was exhausted at last. He laid down his command and returned to Poland.

Soon afterward he died, on June 8, 1605, a victim of this war's hardships and of his sense of duty towards his country.

Zamoyski was neither an idealist nor a saint without any human weaknesses or faults. He was a live and complete human being. Some of his contemporaries accused him of being ambitious and eager for power, for wealth, even of miserliness. They said that he was impetuous and proud in his dealings with his inferiors, perhaps even overbearing and vain. But faultless people do not exist in this world of ours, and saints are not always makers of history. Zamoyski inherited some of his faults from his forbears and acquired others from his environment.

But his merits were far greater than his faults. He was a wise statesman, able to foresee the future; he knew what was good for the Polish state and ceaselessly endeavored to strengthen the bases of its power. He desired to achieve harmony between the three factors then governing Poland: the king, the nobility, and the gentry. He wanted to make Poland immune to any influence of foreign states, and to educate his fellow countrymen. The expansion of Poland's frontiers was not so important to him as their security and the peace and continuity of Polish life.

A medal, coined in the sixteenth century and dedicated to Jan Zamoyski, is still in existence. Zamoyski's likeness is encircled by two wreaths: one of oak leaves and the other of laurel, symbolizing his merits as a warrior and as a promoter of peace and civilization. Around it is the legend UTRAQUE CIVIS, which means that both these garlands were won by his merits as a great citizen of Poland.

Translated from the Polish by Dr. Krystyna Michalik.

JAN SOBIESKI

(From a contemporary steel engraving by L. Stephani—in National
Museum in Kraków)

IX

JAN SOBIESKI

"The Savior of Vienna and Western European Civilization"

1624-96

by

FRANK NOWAK

JAN SOBIESKI, King of Poland from 1674 to 1696, was the younger son of James Sobieski, the distinguished Castellan of Kraków, and Theophila Daniłłowiczówna, the grand-daughter of the remarkable statesman and brilliant Hetman Stanislas Żółkiewski. He was born in the castle of Olesko on the family estates in the eastern part of Poland on August 17, 1624. His mother, a highly patriotic and heroic figure, never allowed her boys, Marek and Jan, to forget the glorious traditions of their ancestors in defending the frontiers of Poland against Cossacks, Tartars and Turks.

The boys received their education at the University of Kraków, and in 1646 made the grand tour of Europe, visiting France, Holland, Italy, Germany, and England. They returned to Poland in July 1648, after the death of their father and while their mother was besieged in the fortress of Zamość by Bogdan Chmielnicki, leader of the Cossacks. In 1651 the boys served in the army and took part in the famous battle of Beresteczko. In the next year Marek was killed in the battle of Batoh and Jan remained to avenge the losses suffered at the hands of the Cossacks, Turks, and Tartars, by three distinguished families, Żółkiewski, Daniłłowicz and Sobieski.

During the years 1654 to 1660 Poland experienced one of the darkest periods in her history. Overwhelmed by invaders coming from every side, Cossacks, Muscovites, Tartars, Transylvanians, Germans, and Swedes, and wrecked by court intrigues and civil strife at home, the country was on the verge of collapse. King John Casimir and his Queen Louise Marie fled to Silesia, while the Swedish King Charles Gustavus proclaimed himself ruler of Poland, and received the submission of the *Pospolite Ruszenie* [1] and the allegiance of numerous aristocratic families, such as the Radziwills of Lithuania, who opposed their own king. During this period of great confusion young Sobieski found it difficult to orient himself and committed the worst blunder of his whole career. After fighting the Muscovites and Tartars at Ochmatov in 1655, he changed sides and served the King of Sweden for six months. In March 1656, realizing that the King of Sweden, who claimed to have come as a "liberator," was conquering and oppressing the nation, Sobieski returned to his proper allegiance, joined the heroic army of Stefan Czarniecki and in July helped drive the Swedes out of Warsaw. His military activities in defense of Poland now carried him to East Prussia and the siege of Toruń. After this very creditable campaign against the Swedes he co-operated with the Hetmans Lubomirski and Potocki in driving the Muscovites and Cossacks out of the country and took an active part in the victory over Sheremetiev at Cudnowo in 1660.

During these troublous times Sobieski gained valuable military experience, and was also drawn into the court intrigues of Queen Louise Marie, the ambitious French wife of John Casimir, who sought to perpetuate her power in Poland, and with the assistance of Louis XIV sought to place a French candidate on the Polish throne. She gained the reluctant support of Sobieski for her schemes through the influence of her protégée, another ambitious and calculating French woman named Marie Casimira d'Arquien, with whom Sobieski fell madly in love despite her marriage to Jan Zamoyski,[2] and whom he married May 18, 1665, upon the death of her first husband. Meanwhile the projected *coup d'état* of the queen in 1661 brought on a civil war in which Jerzy Lubo-

---

[1] *Pospolite Ruszenie* was the general mobilization of the country gentry, or petty nobility, in times of danger. This military service was based on a long tradition and on the assumption that every landed proprietor was to serve his country without any pay, but only in defensive war within the country.—*Ed.*

[2] Grandson of the famous chancellor.—*Ed.*

mirski, Marshal of the Crown, played the part of a Polish Cromwell in opposing the unconstitutional action of the royal family. Sobieski, unwillingly for his part, was dragged into the civil war and given the offices and honors of which Lubomirski had been deprived. The civil war ended in 1666 and in the following year its principal actors, Queen Louise Marie and Jerzy Lubomirski, both died.

Henceforth, during the remainder of the reign of John Casimir and throughout that of King Michael Wiśniowiecki, Sobieski was the outstanding patriot in Poland and upon his shoulders fell the task of defending the country even at times when the King and the Polish Diet gave him no support whatsoever. In 1667 he defeated the Tartars at Podhajce and in 1672, in a remarkable campaign lasting seventeen days, with a mere handful of men crushed an overwhelming army of Tartars. This campaign, fought in unorthodox fashion and demanding the utmost daring on the part of the leader, established the European reputation of Sobieski as a military genius. But the defeat of the Tartars brought upon Poland the whole Turkish army. Once more Sobieski repeated his brilliant feat of the preceding year by a resounding victory over the Turks at Chocim on November 11, 1673. Learning of the death of King Michael, who had died on the eve of the Battle of Chocim, Sobieski returned to Warsaw to support the candidacy of the French general, the Great Condé, who in his estimation would be qualified to defend Poland, but Sobieski himself was elected king in 1674. Postponing all coronation ceremonies until he had finished with the Turks, Sobieski at once returned to the battlefield and in a spectacular campaign not only defended Lwów, but forced the Turks to sign the Treaty of Żórawno, which wiped out the disgrace suffered by Poland in the shameful treaty of Buczacz signed by King Michael. After this long series of remarkable military victories the king returned for the coronation ceremonies on February 2, 1676. In foreign policy Sobieski sided with Louis XIV in the Hapsburg-Bourbon Wars, but in March 1683 definitely broke with France and signed an offensive-defensive alliance with Emperor Leopold of Austria, directed against the Turk. At the siege of Vienna, September 12, 1683, he not only saved the city but so decisively crushed the Ottoman forces that he was hailed as the Defender of Christendom, while the Turk never again regained sufficient power to menace Western Civilization. Throughout the rest of his reign Sobieski continued to regard himself as the champion of Christendom against the Turk and made every effort to drive the Turk completely out of Europe. Had his neighbors, Austria and Russia, given him the co-operation which he had a right to expect, he would have been completely successful in his plans. At any rate Austria reaped the fruits of his campaigns in 1699. He died on June 17, 1696. By his wife "Marysienka" [3] he had three sons named James, Alexander and Constantine, and a daughter named Theresa.

In 1933 the representatives of European countries gathered in the city of Vienna to celebrate the two hundred and fiftieth anniversary of the great victory of King Jan Sobieski over the Moslem forces of Kara Mustapha before the walls of Vienna in 1683. This epoch-making victory, which frustrated the last great effort of Islam to conquer Europe, put an end to the expansion of the Moslem world, enabled Europe to take the offensive against her most dreaded foe, and ultimately gave rise to the so-called Eastern Question, the problem of disposing of the remains of the "sick man of Europe," as the Turkish state was called. For this achievement contemporary opinion hailed Jan Sobieski as "savior of Christianity and Western civilization," and ever since that memorable day popes, emperors, kings, and princes have vied with one another in doing honor to the name of Sobieski, in order to associate themselves with the victor at Vienna, because they recognized the value of his achievement or because they hoped to gain some of the glory themselves. Even Louis XIV, relentless enemy of the house of Hapsburg and friend of the Turk who had done everything in his power to prevent the Christian victory, was temporarily overshadowed by the King of Poland and made haste to congratulate him upon his success. Humbler folk compared Jan Sobieski with Charles Martel, and the siege of Vienna to the Battle of Tours in 732.

Two hundred and fifty years have not dimmed the glory of

---

[3] Diminutive in Polish for Maria (Marie Casimira d'Arquien). Sobieski's own correspondence abounds in this pet name, which was accepted in Polish historical literature.—*Ed.*

Sobieski or wiped out the significance of his service to Western civilization. To be sure, even in our own day certain writers, influenced by political considerations, have attempted to minimize the achievements of Sobieski, as did the Emperor Leopold of Austria, to lessen the debt to Poland. But no superficial rationalizing or distortion of facts can alter the historic truth that "Sobieski earned the hundredfold gratitude of Austria for Poland for all time."

The services rendered by Jan Sobieski to Poland were no less significant than his brilliant leadership in what has been called the "last crusade of Christendom" against the infidel; but his role in Polish history can be properly appreciated only when sketched against the background of the Polish scene.

On the outer fringe or frontier of civilization, Poland was for centuries regarded as the farthermost outpost of Western civilization and she faithfully performed her mission as defender of the West from the inroads of Muscovite, Cossack, Tartar, and Turk coming from the East. Not only did she defend the culture of the West but she extended the frontier of civilization far to the eastward.

In the middle of the seventeenth century, however, Poland was so sapped of her vitality by foreign wars and internal social and political troubles that she was unable to hold back the invaders who poured into the country from all four points of the compass. While fighting the Cossacks of Bogdan Chmielnicki and the Muscovites in the east, she was attacked by the King of Sweden and his allies, the Elector of Brandenburg and the ruler of Transylvania from other directions. In a few months Charles Gustavus, who sought to emulate the military success of Gustavus Adolphus in the Thirty Years' War, was master of Poland, and the King of Poland had to take refuge in Silesia. The country was saved from annihilation or at least partition at this time by a supreme effort of national will inspired by the "miracle of Częstochowa." This monastery, ably defended by the Monk Kordecki and the national hero Stefan Czarniecki, became a rallying point for all the patriotic forces in the nation. Assisted by a timely attack upon Sweden by the King of Denmark and by a small contingent from the Emperor, the Poles drove the Swedes headlong out of the country by 1659, and concentrated their efforts upon the war with the Cossacks and Muscovites, which lasted until 1667.

The effect of this twenty years of continuous warfare on Polish soil from 1648 until 1667 was to leave the country in a condition of exhaustion, depopulation, and ruin comparable to the situation in the German states of the Empire following the Thirty Years' War. Industry, trade, and commerce were at a standstill; cities declined, prices rose, and the people generally were impoverished.

The social and political consequences of the wars of the "Deluge," as described by Sienkiewicz, were no less deplorable. The morale of the nation was shaken. The people seemed to have lost much of their former vitality and were so badly demoralized that they had scarcely enough energy left to defend themselves. The middle class, small as it was, practically disappeared and even the *szlachta*, or gentry, became so impovished that they sought the protection of wealthy nobles or magnates who purchased votes in this way for the purpose of controlling the Diet or even of disrupting it for purely selfish interests. Democracy in Poland was giving way to an oligarchy of aristocratic families which sought to control the king and to reduce him to the position of a helpless puppet.

With the election as king in 1669 of Michael Wiśniowiecki, the most incompetent sovereign that ever sat upon a throne, it seemed that Poland was doomed. Her social, economic, and political structure was further undermined by mutiny in the army, intrigues for the deposition of the king, and threats of civil war. While King Michael neglected the national interest and thought only of keeping himself on the throne by catering to the prejudices of the *szlachta* and their vaunted "golden liberty," the defense of the country fell squarely upon the shoulders of Jan Sobieski who held the offices of Marshal and Hetman (commander in chief).

Opposed by both King and Diet, who refused him subsidies for organizing the defense of the frontiers, Sobieski at his own expense recruited a small force which repelled the Cossack and Tartar invasions and saved the country from disaster. Yet this opposition to the Hetman and his increasing responsibilities stimulated and developed the best qualities of patriotism and the military genius of Sobieski who, with a mere handful of troops, repeatedly defeated overwhelming hosts of Cossacks (1667), Tartars (1672), and Turks (1673).

It is not surprising that after this series of remarkable victories in the field, Jan Sobieski was elected King of Poland upon the death of King Michael in 1674. He was the one man who could save Poland from disaster in this crisis. Without waiting for the coronation ceremonies, he returned to the battle line, checked the advance of the Turkish invaders, and forced upon the Sultan the Treaty of Żórawno in 1676, wiping out the disgraceful Treaty of Buczacz signed by his predecessor.

No one has ever seriously questioned the military genius of King Jan, but there has been criticism of his ability as a statesman. It is alleged that he was of too honest, trusting, and religious a nature to achieve any measure of success in international diplomacy and there is some truth in this charge. Machiavellian diplomacy was not his strong point. He believed in a united Christendom as a possibility and placed great faith in the sanctity of treaties which he carried out to the letter despite the perfidy of his so-called allies, Austria, Russia, and Brandenburg. Yet his policies show statesmanship of a high order.

In domestic affairs Sobieski clearly saw the need of reforming the Polish constitution, tried to strengthen the monarchy by making it hereditary, and made every effort to establish a regular army that would be adequate for the defense of the state. However, none of these objectives was attained because of the suspicion and the opposition of the *szlachta* and the interference of neighboring states which desired a weak Poland.

In foreign policy he co-operated with Louis XIV until 1683, maintained peace with the Turks, and with French and Swedish assistance sought to reconquer East Prussia for Poland. In 1683, however, he went to the assistance of the House of Hapsburg, signed an offensive-defensive alliance with the Emperor Leopold, and returned to his favorite project of a Christian league against the Turks.

In view of the recent attempt of certain German writers to disparage the services of Sobieski and Poland at the siege of Vienna by asserting that Poland had no choice in taking the course which she did, that Sobieski was only in nominal command of the Christian forces while the actual commander was Charles of Lorraine, that the Poles were compensated for their services by the Emperor although they failed to furnish the stipulated number of soldiers, that the Polish army was slow in arriving in Vienna, and finally that the heaviest fighting fell to the German forces, it might be well to consider the facts in some detail.

The treaty of alliance between Poland and Austria signed on March 31, 1683, provided for a joint war against the Turk. The Emperor agreed to recruit an army of 60,000 men, while Poland was to furnish 40,000. If the Sultan should besiege Kraków in Poland or Vienna in Austria the allies were to come to each other's aid with all their available forces, not including, of course, soldiers performing garrison duty or engaged in attaining secondary objectives.

It is to be noted that Sobieski signed this alliance with full knowledge that Poland was not directly threatened, for it was common knowledge that the army of four hundred thousand Turks was preparing to march on Vienna and not against Kraków. His action in coming to the aid of Leopold was therefore a generous deed of Christian chivalry. Even if Vienna had fallen, it is certainly conceivable that Poland might have defended herself successfully, as she had done again and again in the past.

To say that the Emperor had reimbursed Poland for her services verges on the ludicrous. Leopold promised a subsidy of 200,000 Talars or 1,200,000 złotys, which he paid in June, but the Polish diet voted taxes amounting to 18,000,000 złotys to cover the expenses of the war.

For the defense of his own territories Leopold was able to recruit an army of only 40,000 instead of the 60,000 demanded by the terms of the treaty of alliance. The princes of the Empire arrived with 30,000 men, while Poland mobilized an army of 45,000 men, of whom 37,000 took an active part in the campaign on the Danube and in Hungary. In addition, Poland sent 20,000 Cossacks into Moldavia. While the Emperor failed to furnish the stipulated quota of soldiers in defense of his own country, Poland put into the field an army far greater than she had promised.

The great expense entailed by the necessity of tripling the

peace-time strength of Poland, prevented recruiting for the army
until May, yet in the month of July the Polish forces already completed their concentration at Lwów according to plan. From Lwów
King Jan intended to move into Moldavia and Hungary when he
learned of the imminent danger of Vienna and issued a new order
on July 17, for a new concentration of all Polish forces at Kraków.
In the first week of August, only three months after recruiting
had begun in Poland, concentration of the army at Kraków was
completed, and on August 11 the army started for Vienna. The
speed of mobilization of the Polish army broke all records for
that age and won the commendation of all military men including
the German officers.

By September 5, 1683, the Polish army reached Stetteldorf
on the Danube, a distance of 500 kilometers from Kraków. To
accomplish this record-breaking maneuver, Sobieski marched his
men at the average rate of 20 kilometers per day, an unheard of
speed for that age.

Since Leopold had requested that a part of the Polish forces,
namely, the Lithuanian contingent of 10,000 men, be sent directly
into Hungary, only 25,000 soldiers of the regular army, exclusive
of volunteers, arrived at Vienna, where they joined the Christian
host consisting of from 18,000 to 20,000 imperial troops and from
27,000 to 30,000 men sent by the princes of the Empire. Thus the
Christian forces totaled about 70,000 to 75,000 men.

The question of leadership was settled by the treaty of Alliance of March 31, 1683, which stated that in the event of a union
of all the armies, that sovereign should be in supreme command
who was present with his army. When Leopold called upon King
Jan personally to lead his army before Vienna, he by that very act
placed command in the hands of the Polish king. Besides, the
reputation of Sobieski as a military leader in conquering the Turks
was well known and no one doubted that he was to be in command. Charles of Lorraine, the Imperial General, in his correspondence with Sobieski always assumed that he was writing to his
superior officer. For instance, in a letter dated August 21, 1683,
he addressed Sobieski in these terms, *"Deo auspice, Vestra Maie-
state duce."*

Nor can it be said that this leadership was merely honorary

or formal, for Sobieski made all military decisions regarding the
plan of the battle. He decided the point at which the Danube
was to be crossed, determined on the direction of the attack, personally reconnoitered the terrain on which the fighting was to take
place, determined the disposition of the troops, and finally made
changes in the plan of attack when he discovered that he had
been badly informed regarding the nature of the terrain before
the walls of Vienna.

Since the Poles were veteran soldiers with considerable experience in fighting the Turks they were ordered to advance over
the most difficult terrain and encountered the heaviest fighting.
Under the personal command of Sobieski the Polish Hussars descended the neighboring hills and charged the main mass of the
Turkish army in the camp of the Vezir. Driving the enemy before
them, they pushed on to the bridgeheads of the Wien River,
which were ways of escape for the Turkish forces and hence
were most strongly defended. Prince John of Anhalt, the envoy
of the Elector of Brandenburg, who was with the German armies
during the attack, without qualification reported to his master
that the charge of the Polish Hussars decided the battle.

A vivid account of the victory was sent to Queen "Marysienka" by Sobieski himself in a letter dated September 13 and
headed, "In the tents of the Vizier." "God be forever blessed!
He has given our nation the victory; He has given it such a triumph as no past centuries ever saw. All the artillery, the whole
Moslem camp, all its uncountable riches have fallen into our
hands. The approaches to the town, the neighboring fields, are
covered with the infidel dead, and the remainder is in flight, and
stricken with panic. . . ."

In 1684 Sobieski joined the Christian League against the Turks
and to the end of his reign continued the struggle with the infidel.
His campaigns in Moldavia, though less successful than his earlier
triumphs, enabled Austria and Russia to reap the fruits of his work
in the later Treaty of Carlovitz (1699).

The greatness of Sobieski consisted in his ability to arouse,
revitalize, and lead the Polish nation on to further triumphs at a
time when the people were demoralized and exhausted by the
twenty years of continual warfare (1648-67) of the period known

as "The Deluge." His successors on the throne down to the partitions of the eighteenth century failed to check the decline of the Polish state and did not preserve it from destruction.

In the gloomy years that followed the partition of Poland by Russia, Prussia, and Austria, the achievements of Sobieski brought hope and encouragement to a nation struggling against desperate odds to achieve its independence.

X

STANISŁAW KONARSKI
"Preceptor of Poland"

1700-73

by

WILLIAM J. ROSE

THOSE who serve their country best are not always best known to posterity. We need not be surprised if the Poles who deserved most of their nation in pre- and post-Partition days seemed a century later to have been eclipsed by those with more spectacular achievements. There were three of them—Konarski, Staszic and Kołłątaj. Of these the first may fairly be called the greatest, both for his vision and his achievements. He saw things other folk did not see, and he saw farther than they did. With him from thought to action was only a step, and he never despaired of the ultimate triumph of right.

Konarski was born in the central area of Poland, not far from Kielce, in the year 1700; and he lived to be seventy-three. This span of three score and ten years was one of the most momentous in history. All around was change—in political thought and action, in manners and customs, in science and in business. As a boy he must have heard of the transformations the Tsar Peter was work-ing in the still oriental Russia. As a mature man he watched Fred-erick transform the position of Prussia from one of negligibility to one of power on the continent. Those same years saw the Turks driven at last from south Russia and from Hungary. They saw too the mighty realms of Canada and India opened up to European influences; and at the end the preparations for the making of the great Republic of the New World.

STANISŁAW KONARSKI

(From a painting *ca.* 1750 of unknown authorship—preserved in the
Piarist Fathers' College in Rakowice)

No less startling changes were at hand in the field of science. The future statesman was at school while Newton and Leibniz were straightening out the laws of our universe, achievements which put mathematics and physics in the forefront of all search for knowledge. Before he died Buffon and his French colleagues had opened up the field of natural history, and laid the course for geological and biological inquiry on which we are still traveling. As a schoolboy Konarski knew nothing of what a laboratory or an experiment was; but he lived to introduce them both to their rightful place in all higher schools of Poland. But all this affected life as well as learning. What had been a world of arts and crafts in the early eighteenth century had largely become one of factories before its end. Instead of man power one now had horsepower—as measured by the steam engine. In a modest way the machine age was already at hand.

Finally there was already abroad a new spirit—felt powerfully first in England and France, that was to express itself in criticism and inquiry. Men know it now as Rationalism or the Enlightenment. Appearing in politics, it spread to religion; and was soon calling in question not only traditional ideas but even state and church themselves. Everywhere the trend was toward secularization, whether of concepts or of institutions. By this is meant that men ceased to say that this or that was "sacred" or "revealed" truth, but subjected everything to the tests of reason.

Into this progressive and turbulent era Konarski entered as a student. Sent with his brothers to the school of the Piarist Fathers in Piotrków, he did good work and in due course decided to become a member of that notable teaching Order. Showing marked ability in his higher studies in the capital, Warsaw, he was selected to go to Rome in 1725 for graduate work. Here he had the good fortune to find one of the liveliest groups of teachers in any Catholic institution of that day. He was introduced to mathematics, and became a tutor in that field. The "newer" philosophy, as it was called, was freely discussed; and Konarski decided to go further before returning home, and see and hear what was worth while in Paris itself.

Here learning had been just given a new impetus by the appearance of a great book by no less a mind than Montesquieu himself. In touch with a host of strangers and eager for knowledge, the young Polish priest must have added a wealth of secular knowledge to his store; and he returned to the land of the Vistula destined to be the man who would do more than any other to introduce there the new science, the new pedagogy, and another method and ideal for public administration. We shall see how stern this task was, how bitter the opposition, and how great the obstacles.

For eight years after his return to Warsaw in 1731 Konarski was occupied with matters that had nothing to do with his chosen vocation of teaching. Valuable if bitter lessons were his lot during that time. But in 1740 his chance came, when he was commissioned to found in the capital a College for Sons of the Gentry.[1] It was to follow lines already tried and proved in other lands, and to mark the first step in breaking with traditional scholarship. For fourteen years this enterprise was his major concern. To carry it out, he had to bring about a reformation of the whole Polish province of the Piarist Order—after he had been chosen as Governor. In no other way could he be sure of suitably trained teachers for his Warsaw college and similar institutions.

At fifty-five he could turn seriously to the hardest task of his career. Poland's public life was crippled by the long-prevailing principle of unanimity in legislative and executive counsels, a system which made it possible for any single member of the Diet by his "free veto"[2] to block and even wreck any project of legislation he did not fancy. This practice of "exploding the Diet" had been hedged about with sanctity for a century, and was indeed a Goliath for any David to attack. But Konarski went wisely to work, first studying the whole issue, and then proposing a remedy. We shall see how the evil was thrust upon him right after his return from the first visit to France; and though he had to wait thirty full years before he could strike, he struck home then. By a miracle he succeeded in his project. His last years were spent only in consolidating the positions thus won.

No wonder the King had a medal made for the Piarist leader, with the short but meaty Latin inscription "To Him Who Dared

---

[1] "*Collegium Nobilium.*"
[2] The so-called "*Liberum Veto.*"

To Be Wise"! And if the two great reforms for which Poland has Konarski to thank did not avail to hinder the Partitions, they at least did something of high value. They laid the groundwork for a social and spiritual solidarity in the Polish nation that neither force nor the wiles of imperial politicians availed to dissolve. Though the fabric of the state was lost, the unity of the social order was saved.

TRIAL AND ERROR

Six years of communion with the learned men of Europe's two capitals of that day were behind Konarski when he returned to Warsaw in 1731, doubtless a marked man. Even before he went abroad his abilities had drawn the attention of the court. His uncle was Bishop of Poznań, he was blood kin of the powerful Tarło family. Now he could claim to have some acquaintance with the culture of other peoples, and he might easily have been a little self-confident. In his own field he was a master, fitted both to teach and to command. The larger question was puzzling him: had he fitted himself to serve his country in a time of special need? Apparently he was not yet ready. His mind was ripe, but his character was still plastic.

The year 1732 was an unhappy one. For fifteen years the interference of Poland's neighbors—especially Russia—in her internal affairs had been growing. One party looked on this with tolerance, hoping in spite of it to strengthen the administration. The other, known as the Patriots, was bitterly opposed to such intrigues. With a Saxon dynasty on the throne, whose interests were rather in Dresden than in Warsaw, it seemed as though no leadership could come from above. Because of the opposition of the parties, and of the vicious "Free Veto" practice already referred to, no leading that was wholesome could come from parliament. This was the discovery Konarski made when he was asked by acquaintances to find for a price some member who would disrupt the Diet of 1732, in order to halt action. It was a mean task, which he looked back on afterwards with distaste; but it is well that he was drawn into it, for he saw with his own eyes the cheapness and depravity of politics at the time.

Fortunately he had been for months at work on a historical

study, the purpose of which was to assemble and print in a series of volumes all the laws of the land from the Middle Ages down. This showed him how different things had been, and how degenerate they were now. The contrast registered with him, though he did not as yet speak his mind. However, in a series of letters he did brand the easy tolerance shown by his fellows toward foreign counselors:

> Nothing is more fatal than foreign factions robed in the guise of friendship. . . . He is mad who thinks that Germans or Russians are more concerned for Poland's good than we ourselves!

Before the Diet of 1733 could meet King Augustus died, and the uncertainties of an interregnum followed. During the time of choosing a successor the Primate was Viceroy, but the evils of intrigue at home and abroad were worse than ever. Better a Pole than an outsider as sovereign, was the watchword of many who hoped for the return of the exiled Stanisław Leszczyński, whose daughter was now Queen of France. This end could only be achieved if the Court of France would exert its influence; and though the son of the deceased king was elected in his place, a group of patriots resolved to send an embassy to Paris to try and rouse French intervention and unseat him. Of this mission Father Konarski was made secretary, doubtless in part because he knew the facts, the language and not a few of the people involved. Again he was to suffer dark disillusionment. After seeing how unprincipled his own fellows were in regard to matters of state, he was to learn the same of the diplomats. He soon saw that France was looking out first, last, and always, for her own good, and a long and bitter year away left him glad to return home—resolved now to take up at once his true life work.

THE COLLEGIUM NOBILIUM

For generations the most popular and efficient educational agency in Europe had been the Jesuit Fathers. They gave special attention to what we should call High Schools, and for obvious reasons their pupils came chiefly from the various grades of the nobility. Wherever the Catholic Church prevailed in the religious struggle, the Jesuits had earned the gratitude of all and they meant to keep their supremacy. Yet their very strength in the sixteenth century was a weakness in the seventeenth, for their rules allowed of no improvements. Mankind was advancing, while they stood still. There were serious flaws in their pedagogy. All their teaching was in Latin, and this very medium was degenerating into rhetorical, bombastic wordiness. They did nothing for the now live and growing national tongues, in which a dynamic literature was being born, in France, Germany or Poland. By the same token they functioned openly as an international body, and went out of their way to avoid any inculcation of civic loyalties. Their spirit was cosmopolitan, and the last thing they knew how to do was to build up the tottering fabric of national virtues in Poland. The historian Józef Łukaszewicz (1799-1873) gave an admirable summary, when he said that: "They aimed at training youths for the monastery rather than for the state. They were imbued with the thought that on earth we have no abiding city. . . . The change came in the land when Konarski's schools taught both piety and a love of country, making the boy into a useful citizen."

When the Piarist Father began his task of founding the new College for Sons of the Gentry in Warsaw he knew well enough that there was a long and uphill fight ahead. The Jesuits were so entrenched in the affections of the nation as to be almost immune from assault. They would resent the new project the more keenly because their rivals, the Piarists, had been commissioned by the Church to work rather among the poor and in the elementary school field. Thus any effort to secure moral and material support for such an enterprise, or even to get pupils to start it, was bound to meet with opposition. And so it turned out.

The enrollment during the first year was only ten, but three years later it was twenty-nine. Temporary quarters were obtained in the existing Warsaw College in the heart of the old town, and these served for more than a decade. With only 1500 ducats to start on, Konarski leased the adjoining garden, and in 1743 the cornerstone was laid with pomp and ceremony for the new building, destined to be the first modern school structure in Poland. From the start the Founder had planned to keep himself in the background as much as possible; and it was fortunate that he could pick from among his colleagues a few men with ideas and hopes about education that were almost his own. One of them, Father Wiśniewski, became the head of the new science department, and brought from abroad the first laboratory apparatus to be used in the country. Another, Father Orłowski, became the vice principal; and succeeded so well as a friend and guide of students that Konarski himself was free from all anxiety as to the internal working of the new institution. This was the more necessary, since in 1742 he was elected Governor of the Piarist Order for Poland, and so had duties of a wider nature that took up much time.

Apart from getting a home for his little school and the right kind of teachers to guide it, he saw from the start the other essential need—that of a new brand of textbooks. It is notable that in this respect the Piarists initiated a new era in education, insisting as they did for the first time on students owning and using their own books in their studies. Two new books seemed to Konarski indispensable, a modernized Latin Grammar instead of the now antiquated Alvarez, and a new manual on language and speech in general. He produced the former at once, basing it largely on the ideas set forth by the famous Czech pedagogue Comenius (Komensky), and putting the Polish equivalents beside the Latin words in the early word lists. The manual, entitled *The Correction of Our Speech*, set the school leaders of Poland by the ears. It was simply revolutionary. All the fine talk, amounting in speech to what the worst baroque was in architecture, all the grandiose rhetoric, above everything the habits of eulogy and apotheosis in which he himself had been brought up, were thrown overboard. In the new age language was to be strictly and solely a medium of expression for ideas. These latter were the essential thing; they were the end in view, while speech was only the means.

Both in this daring book and in a sequel published over twenty years later the Polish reformer was following lines that had been clearly worked out in France: notably by Boileau whose dictum might have served as a motto for both: "*Avant donc que d'écrire, apprenez à penser!*" For generations there had been too much talk and too little thinking in public life in Poland. Konarski wanted an end of it. Hence his resolve to escape the sins of too many educationalists, notably those of the Jesuits of his day, and to relate everything done in his school to the life the boys would be expected to live afterwards. Many of them would become leaders, and needed to be competent orators. But the vital thing for them was to have something to say. Here as always knowledge would mean power. Nothing would be feared more by Poland's enemies than a generation of young men coming on, whose eyes were opened to the realities of the workaday world.

Yet life in the new school was not all drudgery. Provision was made for out-of-door exercise, for games and riding. So downright was the Founder in his decision in this regard, and so doubtful as to the virtues of the home-life of his day, that he discouraged long vacations spent at home. A summer pavilion was provided for the school on the banks of the Vistula, and enough diversion assured to make the hot months a time of both pleasure and profit for all. One other thing. In keeping with the trends in France, Konarski introduced dramatics into the school curriculum as a direct means of self-expression and development. One of the first objects to appear on the new grounds was a temporary theater, in which at regular intervals amateur theatricals were staged. Some of them were adaptations from the French; some original Polish pieces; some too, in time, in the French original. For Konarski meant no reflection on the supreme value of Latin as a tongue to be learned when he introduced French as a second living language, whose mastery was to be part of the education of all cultured citizens. This was only another example of his emphasis on utility as the first objective of pedagogy.

Hard times, serious political unrest in the land, and the ill-health of the Founder all helped to delay the completion of the school building. In 1747 Konarski had to leave Poland altogether for a year to seek rest and a cure in France. Funds were hard to get, and it was only by dint of faith in the cause that its promoters held on. The tide turned the next year, when the royal favor was secured for the enterprise. What helped most were generous gifts from the Tarlo and other families, and from 1750 things went rapidly forward. It was Father Orłowski who carried on the task, for his superior was absent in Rome on a vital mission. With two of his colleagues he was trying for a special Order from Benedict XIV, which would make possible a complete reorganization of the Piarist group in Poland. Only by a miracle did he get the personal interview necessary, but it sufficed. The result was a transformation of the methods and ideals of the body of men who were to win through in all they sought to accomplish, forcing the hand of their fellows—not excepting the Jesuits—until a new day broke in educational policies in the land.

Full of joy must have been to Konarski the great day in 1754 when the notables of the capital and the nation gathered to see the new College dedicated, and to listen to the Inaugural of the honored Founder. Curiously enough there was not a word in it about learning as the end of school discipline, but only about character-building. Only a good man, said Konarski, can be a good citizen. The place of books, and the love of books, the place of friendships, and the part played by mental discipline were given special attention. The relation of the parent to the work of the institution was made clear. As no building before it, the *Collegium Nobilium* was consecrated to the service of the nation. With its full quota of sixty students, its future looked assured. One part of the Founder's dream of helping his country was thus realized.

EFFECTIVE COUNSELS

The time had come when the Piarist leader could no longer ignore the growing threat to the existence of the Commonwealth from the evils of the "Free Veto." [3] What he had seen in 1732 stuck in his memory, and was stirred afresh by events in 1744 that could only make every patriot blush with shame. The issue

---

[3] The "free veto" or "*liberum veto*," which was undoubtedly the greatest single contributing factor from within to the downfall of the old Poland, is a classical example of pure democracy; of liberty ultimately reduced to absurdity. From the time of Casimir the Great, who was the last absolute sovereign of Poland, there gradually grew from precedent to precedent a peculiar concept of "freedom" of the landed gentry ("*szlachta*") giving rise through custom to the idea of legislative unanimity. If one deputy out of a hundred or more said "no," the act of legislature could not be made binding. In other words, one deputy could veto any act of the entire Diet or Parliament and dissolve or "explode" it at his own free will. To compel one to submit to the majority decision was regarded as tyranny. At first the majority was successful in persuading the minority of one or more not to use that dreadful privilege. Not until 1639 (in this case Jerzy Lubomirski) was there anyone found to abuse his privilege. Another abuse occurred in 1652, by Władysław Siciński. From 1652 on this abuse of personal and political freedom used to occur quite frequently until "*liberum veto*" was abolished in 1791, in the 3rd of May Constitution.—*Ed.*

had to be faced, and with his sound understanding of what ought to be done Konarski chose at once the scientific approach. He would diagnose the case in a detailed way, and would publish his findings. This would mean an appeal to public opinion, and the ensuing controversy would sift out those who stood with him from the advocates of the old order.

Evidence has come to light that during his rest cure in France the Father was already busy with his pen; in any case he showed certain of his friends a document dealing with the problem as early as 1749. But the whole educational enterprise, together with the necessity of carrying out a reform of the Order, was too pressing to allow of launching the plan for national reconstruction at that moment. Even after the College was completed Konarski still hesitated—no one today can see why. Not until 1760 did the first of four little volumes, which were to set the whole nation agog, appear under the title *On the Means of Effective Counsels*. Few books have ever made such a furore, and rarely has a work been so conceived to strike at and kill a public menace.

It was published anonymously, but everyone knew that only one man in the land could be the author. The first volume sufficed to show once and for all that the unanimity principle in parliament and the Veto that made it operative were neither legally nor morally defensible; that they were "idols" which people had come to worship blindly, and to their own undoing. The best parts of it were a sort of mirror in which the gentry saw themselves as others saw them; and the sight made them writhe.

"What can be done with a nation," the Grand Vizier had exclaimed in 1743, "where in order to get anything done you must get 30,000 heads under one cap!" This was only a sample of the way representatives of other European powers had come to despair of getting public affairs in Poland put on a stable footing. Some were sorry, others rejoiced, since precisely this helplessness gave them a chance to do their own nefarious business. Professor Konopczyński has put together in a single paragraph the record of misfortunes to the state covering a hundred years—from 1654 to the appearance of *Effective Counsels*. In at least a dozen major crises, involving relations with Sweden, Russia, Prussia, and the Turks, the hand of government was paralyzed—because some knave or fool held the power of stopping action. Poland had become the laughingstock of Europe. The tragedy was that those responsible for the fact did not know it, or rather would not know it, until Konarski told them, hewing to the line and letting the chips fall where they would. Once for all the fine boast was exploded that "Poland stands even by misgovernment!"

In Volume Two came the promise of constructive proposals, beginning with a study of the sources of anarchy and showing that since one never gets all those concerned to agree about anything, the only wisdom is to let the majority rule. Not this, but the Veto is the true way of tyranny. Volume Three continued the argument, telling in order the instances of "exploded" Diets, with their dire results for the state. Concluding, Volume Four reviewed the examples of such lands as Rome, England, and the Republic of Venice, to show the good results that obtained where the majority principle was in use. Nowhere poetry, and not much of relief in the whole work; but everywhere grim logic and the truth as every observer who was not afraid of his own shadow could see it.

The stir in the land was enormous during the three years in which the work appeared; but the time was ripe and the results were not in doubt.

Here too, just as in the matter of the schools, Konarski triumphed. No Diet was "exploded" after the appearance of Volume Three in 1762. What is more, the Piarist Father, in an age when the rest of Europe was crying out for liberties, when a Rousseau was praising the Free Veto, not only called his nation to discipline and renunciation of liberties, but won his case with them.

It was then time to retire. Yet not even the closing decade of Konarski's life was one of idleness or peace. There was writing to be done, notably a book on *The Religion of Good Fellows*, in which he turned on those about him who had been carried away by Voltaire and others; who thought that honor was a substitute for the altar, and the salon the successor of the Church. Just as thirty years before he had stood out against the obscurantists in the Church who were afraid of French letters and philosophy, so now he faced in the other direction, demanding for reason its true place in life and thought. Yet he was not to escape so easily, for the Papal Nuncio was of the sort who regarded all progressive action as dangerous to the faith, and charges were lodged in Rome against Konarski and the Piarist Order as a whole. Accused of corrupting the youth, as Socrates had been long before him, and of undermining the Catholic faith in the land, Konarski was compelled to act. The result, after much toil and trouble, was confusion for the Nuncio, and a vindication of all the Reformer had done.

Honored by the King, as recounted above, made a member of the Thursday Circle that dined weekly at the Palace, Konarski could feel that recognition had come to him at last. His modest quarters were the center of constant visits from every side, his circle of friends waxed every year. What impresses us most is that he bore no grudges; and before the end he had won over most of those who had treated him worst. Among others the Jesuits too, who obtained permission to conduct the impressive funeral services, did not spare themselves in eulogizing the departed leader.

For the student of Konarski's life and work three qualities stand out above many others, of which the Polish nation will be forever proud: industry, courage and wisdom. By the first is meant his boundless energy and capacity for work. By the last, his practical prudence and skill in doing what needed to be done. Finding himself in a world where action was needed (but wise action) more than anything else, Konarski left philosophy and poetry to others. Not that he was not at home in both, for he left proof enough of capabilities on those lines; but they were secondary matters. The main task was to rescue the Commonwealth, and to put it in such a position that no one could either ignore or make mock of it for the future.

Consider one single thing—the journeys the man made. Not only at home, across the broad plains of the Vistula land, but far abroad: to distant Rome, to no less distant Paris. All this again and again, and in an age when travel was not only slow but wearying, at times even dangerous. Few men of his time, either in the service of State or Church could have traveled more. And all the time he was at work. Wearing out body and spirit, making extreme demands on his powers—all for the cause on which he had set his heart. As for his courage, it could never have carried him where it did had it not been a compound of faith and stern resolve such as too few men possess. One thinks of the perils faced in earlier times by a St. Paul, or those encountered in our day by a Sven Hedin—they have certainly not been greater. Only a vision of a better future for his nation, only profound optimism as to the better qualities of his fellow countrymen coupled with a firm faith in the will of the All Highest could have carried him safe to his desired goal.

Nevertheless his own prudence and skill were his surest warrant of success. "The wisest of all the Poles," he has rightly been called, and the epithet would be hard to gainsay. Keeping his head among the clouds, he also kept his feet on solid earth. An idealist, yes, but a practical idealist. One of those figures that removes the reproach so often leveled at the Polish people, that they could not manage their own affairs. And so, both for what he achieved and for what he hoped to achieve, both as a thinker and a man of action, above all as a builder of his nation, the Piarist Father, Stanisław Konarski, belongs in the Gallery of Poland's Immortals.

TADEUSZ KOŚCIUSZKO

(From one of the best known oil portraits by J. Grassi—original in the
collection of J. Josi in Amsterdam)

XI

TADEUSZ KOŚCIUSZKO

Polish National Hero and American Revolutionary War Patriot

1746-1817

Hope, for a season, bade the world farewell,
And freedom shrieked—as Kościuszko fell.
—Thomas Campbell

by

STEPHEN P. MIZWA

COMMANDER-IN-CHIEF of the Polish armed forces in the final struggle before the last partition of Poland in 1795, a Polish national hero and the American Revolutionary War patriot, Tadeusz Kościuszko was born in the village of Mereczowszczyzna near Brest-Litovsk, on the twelfth day of February, 1746. He came of an old Polish family, with patents of nobility, though relatively poor, that eight or nine generations back had had White Russian and Lithuanian antecedents.

SCHOOL DAYS

Tadeusz Kościuszko was born into a family of four children, two girls and two boys, of whom he was the youngest. Following the custom of his social class, he was kept and taught at home till the age of nine, whereupon he was sent to a private school of the Piarist Fathers. Here he remained till he was fourteen. There was nothing unusual about his childhood: he was just a normal child, well brought up, perhaps of greater ability than the average, with strong moral background and a keen sense of social adaptation. That he was well prepared for school—and his mother deserves most of the credit—may be inferred from the fact that in this school he was taught Latin, natural philosophy, one modern language beside Polish (namely, French, possibly a little German), and history and mathematics. Geometry, trigonometry and drawing attracted his especial attention.

From the age of fourteen to nineteen he was at home again—reviewing, expanding, thinking over what he had learned at school. It was at this time that he was making his plans for his future career. As he was the younger of the two brothers and therefore, according to traditional procedure, was to take his share of the family estate in cash—his father having died when he, Tadeusz, was only twelve—he was to leave home and seek his fortune elsewhere. He made up his mind to be a soldier.

The career of a soldier appealed to young Kościuszko as the best channel of service to his country and the cause of freedom. This he had learned as a schoolboy of twelve from a story about Timoleon the Corinthian (410-336 B.C.), as portrayed by Cornelius Nepos in his famous biographies. Timoleon, who was Kościuszko's beloved hero from childhood even to old age, had freed his native land from tyrannical oppression and then had fought for the freedom of Syracuse. Having decided to be a soldier, Kościuszko wanted to prepare himself thoroughly. At nineteen (in 1765) he was successful in being admitted to the Corps of Cadets of the newly opened Royal Military School [1] in Warsaw. In this military academy, which was known as a school of patriotism and offered a general liberal education, Kościuszko studied for three years and began his specialization in military engineering and the art of fortification. He grew in mental stature, was graduated as one of the head scholars, attracted the personal attention and interest of the King, and a year after graduation (in 1769) was one of four recipients of the King's scholarships to

---

[1] This school was established by the last King of Poland, Stanisław August Poniatowski, in 1765. Prince Adam Kazimierz Czartoryski, the father of Prince Adam Czartoryski (see Chapter XIV), helped to organize the school, prepared a program of studies and was later on its commandant. Kościuszko studied under him and it was due to the benevolent intercession of this scion of the leading Polish family that the Polish and American hero was able to enter as matriculant No. 79 out of the limited corps of 80. (Monica M. Gardner, Kościuszko—a Biography, London, 1920, pp. 26-30. *Polski Słownik Biograficzny, Adam Kazimierz Czartoryski*, Vol. IV, pp. 249-257.)

continue his studies in military engineering in France. In the meanwhile, between graduation and departure for foreign supplementary studies, he was retained by the Royal Military School as instructor, with the rank of captain. He studied in France until 1774—possibly in the school of engineering and artillery in Mézières or in the *École Militaire* of Paris.

Kościuszko's struggle with financial difficulties began here. His share of the family estate was small, since it was heavily mortgaged and his elder brother (Józef), who remained at home, proved a spendthrift; the installment he received was soon spent and the King's stipend proved more of an honor than a dependable aid. Meanwhile the first partition of Poland took place in 1772, and the royal subsidy ceased entirely. He went home in 1774, but found the conditions depressing—both in the old homestead and in the country. His first reported love, at twenty-nine, for a Ludwika Sosnowska, daughter of a provincial governor, was frustrated by her ambitious father. The romance and the tragedy of mutual love between two young people, the allegedly intercepted elopement and a scheming rich rival (Prince Józef Lubomirski), make a familiar though eternally interesting story. Suffice it to say that it was not a happy ending, the young people did not live happily ever after, the rival won out and Kościuszko never married.

IN SERVICE OF FREE AMERICA

What was it that brought Kościuszko to America? What was the single motivating factor, if any?

Neither materialistic nor legendary interpretation answers this question satisfactorily. Undoubtedly a combination of many factors was responsible for his decision to come to America: a disrupted home, the unfortunate situation of his country, disappointment in love, the pull of Polish tradition at its best to support the cause of freedom wherever it may be at stake, and the influence on his imagination of Timoleon, the hero of his formative years. The New World might also have attracted him.

All stories to the contrary notwithstanding, there is absolutely no authentic record to show exactly when and how he came to America. This we know from documentary evidence: he borrowed eighty ducats [2] from his brother-in-law, Piotr Estko (who married Kościuszko's sister Anna); left Poland some time after October 10, 1775, possibly toward the end of October; took a barge down the Vistula River to Danzig, the cheapest means of transportation then available, traveling thence by boat to France. He bore no letters of recommendation from Silas Deane or Benjamin Franklin to the commander-in-chief or influential people in America. He arrived at Philadelphia in the latter part of August, 1776, and on August 30 he presented his Memorial to Congress, stating his readiness to serve in the American cause. Upon recommendation of the Military Committee, Congress appointed him Colonel of Engineers on October 18, and in that rank he served until the end of the Revolutionary War.

To the cause of American independence Kościuszko contributed three things: scientific knowledge of military engineering, most desirable traits of character, and an unalloyed and unwavering enthusiasm for the cause of freedom. His contribution found most effective expression at Saratoga, at West Point and with the Army of the South.

Upon his appointment as Colonel of Engineers, Kościuszko's first important assignment was with the Army of the North under General Horatio Gates, who entrusted him with the task of devising a plan for the defense of Saratoga, in order to check the advance of the enemy from the North. Kościuszko selected Bemis Heights and strengthened the position with redoubts "from the hill to the river." The enemy was enveloped in the Valley of Saratoga. The Americans were victorious, Burgoyne capitulated (Oct. 17, 1777), and hope again sprang up in the hearts of the patriots. The leading European powers recognized our independence. The Battle of Saratoga, one of the famous battles of the world, proved decisive.

It would be futile to try to give a definite evaluation of Kościuszko's share in the victory at Saratoga. There were many coordinating factors, yet American historians admit that his engi-

---

[2] There is a possibility he may have received a small subsidy from Prince Czartoryski, his former commandant at the military school in Warsaw, whom he met by chance just before his departure for America; but besides confused oral testimony given years later by eyewitnesses "who knew him when" there is no trustworthy evidence of this fact.

neering skill made a noteworthy contribution to this victory. Even such an historian as Professor Channing, who was not at all generous in recognizing foreign talent, except that of Von Steuben, admits that "whatever credit there may be would seem to belong to Gates and to his engineer, Kościuszko, the Polander." [3] Woodrow Wilson in his *History of the American People*, says: "It was the gallant Polish patriot, Tadeusz Kosciuszko, who had shown General Gates how to intrench himself upon Bemis Heights." [4] General Gates was among the first to acknowledge this when he unselfishly invited Kościuszko to participate in the flow of congratulations by the observation that "the hills and woods were the greatest strategists which a young Polish engineer knew how to select with skill for my camp."

The fortification of the Heights of West Point was Kościuszko's next task. It was perhaps his most important task in America and upon which he was engaged from March, 1778 until August, 1780.

In a communication to General Putnam, the Commander at West Point, Washington underlined the "importance of the Hudson River . . . and the necessity of defending it." [5]

Upon receipt of this communication from Washington, feverish activities commenced. Lieutenant Colonel Radière was engaged

---

[3] Edward Channing, *History of the United States*, Vol. III, p. 268.
[4] Vol. II, p. 282.
[5]   "Head-Quarters, 2nd December, 1777
"Dear Sir: The importance of the Hudson River in the present contest, and the necessity of defending it, are subjects which have been so frequently and fully discussed, and are so well understood, that it is unnecessary to enlarge upon them. These facts at once appear, when it is considered that it runs through a whole State; that it is the only passage by which the enemy from New York, or any part of our coast, can ever hope to co-operate with an army from Canada; that the possession of it is indispensably essential to preserve the communication between the Eastern, Middle and Southern States; and further, that upon its security, in a great measure, depend our chief supplies of flour for the subsistence of such forces as we may have occasion for, in the course of the war. . . . These facts are familiar to all; they are familiar to you. I therefore request you, in the most urgent terms, to turn your most serious and active attention to this infinitely important object. Seize the present opportunity and employ your whole force and all the means in your power for erecting and completing, as far as it shall be possible, such works and constructions as may be necessary to defend and secure the river against any future attempts of the enemy." (Edward C. Boynton, *History of West Point and Its Military Importance During the American Revolution*, New York, D. Van Nostrand, 1863, pp. 49-51.)

as engineer. "But," writes Brigadier General Parsons (temporarily in command of West Point) to Washington, on March 7, 1778, "Lieutenant-Colonel Radière, finding it impossible to complete the Fort and other defences intended at this post, in such a manner as to render them effectual early in the spring, and not choosing to hazard his reputation on works erected on a different scale . . . has desired leave to wait on Your Excellency and Congress, which I have granted him." [6]

It was under these conditions that Kościuszko came to West Point on March 26, 1778. Upon his arrival, writes Captain Boynton, "operations were at once resumed, and pushed forward with great vigor." Not quite three weeks later (April 13, 1778), General McDougall, the new commander of West Point, reported: "Mr. Kosciuszko is esteemed by those who have attended the works at West Point to have more practice than Colonel Radière, and his manner of treating the people is more acceptable than that of the latter, which induced General Parsons and Governor Clinton to desire that the former may be continued at West Point." [7]

"Until 1778," writes George Bancroft, the historian, "West Point was a solitude, nearly inaccessible; now it was covered by fortresses with numerous redoubts, constructed chiefly under the direction of Kosciuszko as engineer, and so connected as to form one system of defense, which was believed to be impregnable." [8]

It was at West Point that Kościuszko's traits of character, besides his technical knowledge, found expression; and among these were sympathy and charity. He had about 2,500 men working under him. They were not always a congenial group of people, were not well-clothed and well-fed, and did not work in harmony under all conditions. But he treated them with the consideration and sympathetic understanding that always characterized his dealings with his fellow men. A quiet and a modest man, he spent his spare moments by working in his little garden, thus intermingling diversion with meditation. "Kosciuszko's Garden," which can be seen at West Point even today, has become a part of the lore

[6] Boynton, *op. cit.*, p. 61.
[7] *Writings of Washington*, ed. by Jared Sparks, Vol. V, p. 311.
[8] George Bancroft, *The History of the United States of America*, Vol. V, p. 432.

of the Corps of Cadets.[9] His frugal life made it possible for him to save something even out of his meager allowance. It was discovered that he used his savings to buy food for the English prisoners.

Upon specific request of General Gates,[10] in the latter part of August 1780, Kościuszko was appointed Chief Engineer of the Army of the South. General Horatio Gates had always held Kościuszko in high esteem, and numerous letters from Kościuszko to Gates show that the Pole had an unbounded admiration for his commanding general. When General Gates was given the command of the Southern Army, it was natural that Kościuszko should be his first choice. However, on his way South, Gates was defeated at Camden, North Carolina (August 16, 1780), while Kościuszko was in Philadelphia en route South, and the command of the Southern Army passed to General Nathaniel Greene.

Kościuszko remained with the Army of the South, under General Greene, until the end of the war. His chief functions were to survey the whole field of operations, indicate strategic points, determine possible sources of food and water supply, and to devise means for rapid transportation of troops and provisions —especially in the crossing of streams and rivers. Those were his functions as chief engineer in a campaign conducted in marshy

[9] "It was here, when in its rude state, that the Polish soldier and patriot sat in deep contemplation on the loves of his youth, and the ills his country had to suffer. It would be a grateful sight to him if he could visit it now, and find that a band of youthful soldiers had, as it were, consecrated the whole military grounds to his fame." (Samuel L. Knapp, *Tales of the Garden of Kosciuszko*, New York, West and Trow, 1834, p. 6.)

"The small but historic rock garden, southward of Battery Knox and under the walls of Cullum Hall, is still called Kosciuszko's Garden, after the beloved Polish patriot, General Thaddeus Kosciuszko, who was called to this country to supervise the work on the fortifications at West Point during the days of the Revolution. This garden was his favorite retreat, and it is largely the work of his own hands." (Kendall Banning, *West Point Today*, New York and London, Funk and Wagnalls Co., 1937, p. 226.)

[10] In the private collection of letters to, from, or about Kościuszko, which belonged to the late Dr. Alexander Kahanowicz, there is a letter from General Gates to George Washington, dated June 21, 1780, which makes this request: "I could wish your Excellency would somewhat Brighten the Scene, by indulging me in my request to obtain Colonel Kosciuszko for my Chief Engineer. His services with me in the Campaign of 77 and the High Opinion I entertain of His Talents, and His Honour, induce me to be thus importunate with your Excellency, to let me have the Colonel for my Chief Engineer." Published privately by Dr. Kahanowicz in a catalogue: *Memorial Exhibition*, which exhibition was held at Anderson Galleries, New York in May and June, 1926.

and reptile-infested regions and frequently among impassable swamps. When the campaign changed into guerrilla warfare, as was very often the case, Kościuszko disregarded his rank and fought with the rest as a common soldier.

The following excerpts from correspondence [11] mentioning Kościuszko throw light on his participation in the Southern Campaign.

Greene to Washington.

"Camp upon the Pedee, December 29, 1780:

"I was apprehensive on my first arrival that the country around Charlotte was too much exhausted to afford substance for the army at that place for any considerable time. Upon a little further inquiry I was fully convinced and immediately dispatched Col. Kosciuszko to look out for a position upon the Pedee that would afford a healthy camp and provisions in plenty. His report was favorable and I immediately put the army under marching orders."

Greene to Governor Burke of North Carolina.

"August 12, 1781:

". . . I will send to your assistance Colonel Kosciuszko, our Principal Engineer, who is a master of his profession and will afford you every aid you can wish."

After the War and upon recommendation of the Commander in Chief and the Secretary of War, on October 13, 1783, Congress passed the following resolution:

"RESOLVED, that the Secretary of War transmit to Colonel Kosciuszko the brevet commission of Brigadier General and signify to that officer that Congress entertain an high sense of his long, faithful and meritorious services."

POLISH NATIONAL HERO

Upon his return to Poland in the fall of 1784 Kościuszko settled temporarily on his paternal estate—pondering upon the success of the American Revolution and trying to see what lessons learned in America could be applied to the Polish crisis. In re-

[11] *Op. cit., Memorial Exhibition.*

turn for what he had contributed to the New World, he brought back from America a deepened love of freedom and democracy and the consciousness that even an undisciplined and ragged citizen army, if fired with zeal for a sacred cause, can win victories against a powerful nation.

Poland was then passing through a period of turmoil and of frantic efforts to effect internal reforms—resulting in the adoption of the Constitution of May 3, 1791. It was a magnificent document, embodying liberal and far-reaching reforms. Adopted in the midst of national rejoicing, many of the old abuses were swept away, the system of elective kings was abolished, constitutional and hereditary monarchy (to insure continuity and strengthen the central government) was established, burghers were granted equal rights with nobility, and the condition of the peasants was ameliorated.

In the meanwhile, the Polish army was expanded by Act of the Diet, and on October 1, 1789, Kościuszko was given the commission of Major-General. The wide reputation he enjoyed and the experience he brought from America put him in the forefront among those qualified for military leadership.

But the constitutional reforms that were expected to give Poland a new lease on life, brought about her undoing. A liberal form of government could not be tolerated in the midst of unlimited autocracies. In 1792 Catherine of Russia declared war on Poland and Prussia disavowed her treaty with Poland (made only in 1790), and although the Poles fought valiantly under the youthful leadership of Prince Joseph Poniatowski, the King's nephew, they were defeated by a numerically superior enemy after three months of struggle. The remnants of the Polish army were scattered throughout the country and rendered powerless. Kościuszko emerged with personal prestige, but the only thing he could do was to tender his resignation. In 1793 the second partition of Poland took place; this time only between Russia and Prussia. Of the former kingdom of Poland that in the middle of the seventeenth century stretched from the Baltic to the Black Sea and far into the east, only a small inland portion remained around Warsaw and Lublin. Despoiled, weakened physically and morally, her political leaders silenced and the moving spirits of constitutional reform in exile, Poland now looked to the American Revolutionary War patriot as perhaps the only man who could arouse the nation and organize an armed uprising. He was a symbol of the democratic Poland that was trying to rise above the hardened substrata of political weaknesses and faulty social structure. By the qualities of his character and his service in the cause of freedom in the New World, Kościuszko had risen from humble origin into his position of general esteem.

Tadeusz Kościuszko answered the call. History in retrospect may dub him "a hero of defeat," but those who call themselves Poles cling to his tradition, which has become a vital part of national heritage. Not by what he failed to do but by what he tried to do and the way he tried to do it has he been judged by the subconscious standards by which national heroes are measured. His first steps were as revolutionary as the whole scheme of armed uprising was daring. He chose Kraków, the ancient capital of Poland, as his starting point and called upon the masses of burghers and peasants to win their social equality by the defense of their country. Up to that time Poland was divided, generally speaking, into a class of landed nobility—magnates and petty gentry—who won and enjoyed their extensive privileges on the ground that they were the only defenders of their country, and the peasant masses, hewers of wood and tillers of the soil, who were never called upon to bear arms and therefore were preordained to be underprivileged. Taking advantage of the temporary absence of Russian troops in Kraków, on March 24, 1794, Kościuszko proclaimed insurrection in the market square, took oath of office as commander-in-chief with unlimited powers which he swore to use only for the benefit of all, and ordered general mobilization of all men fit to bear arms, including the peasants. The Constitution of the Third of May only ameliorated their condition. Now, by the revolutionary edict of their leader, Polish peasants were to establish their claims to equal rights by sharing equally with the nobles the hard task of defending their country.

Peasants from all around, armed with scythes, as these were the only implements they had and knew how to use, flocked under the banner of Kościuszko by the thousands. The first test came on the field of Racławice, where, on April 4, this valiant peasant army attacked Russian artillery, captured its guns and won their first victory. One of these lowly-born, Bartos Głowacki, so distinguished himself that he, together with Racławice, passed into song and picture and into the lore of Polish valor. Racławice is not only a cornerstone on which rests the national esteem of Kościuszko as one of the great sons of Poland, but also a milestone in the arduous path of social progress and a starting point that opened for the untutored masses of Polish peasants the vista of equal opportunities through equal responsibilities. The struggle for them is not over, but it began in the baptism of fire and blood on the battlefield of Racławice under the inspired and inspiring leadership of Kościuszko. As one Polish historian aptly put it: "The blood shed at Racławice fertilized the Polish soil for the undying crop of national life throughout a hundred years of captivity." [12]

Inspired by the victorious peasant army, another "imperfectly emancipated class," the burghers or townsmen rallied to the colors of the national leader. The citizens of Warsaw, led by a shoemaker named Kiliński, drove the Russian troops out of the capital and thereby effected the union of the nation both territorially and spiritually. But the Polish patriots, though not lacking in valor and leadership, were greatly outnumbered and were poorly equipped. Though they harassed the enemy on and behind the line of battle, they were doomed to defeat. Prussia and Austria joined the forces of Russia, and thus tipped the scale against the Poles. Twice-partitioned Poland could not win out against the combination of three powers. After several minor victories and defeats and the magnificent and successful defense of Warsaw under the personal command of Kościuszko against the siege of combined forces of Russia and Prussia that lasted from July 13 to September 6, the battle at Maciejowice (on October 10) decided the issue. Kościuszko was gravely wounded, carried away as prisoner of

[12] Roman Dyboski, *Outlines of Polish History* (London, George Allen and Unwin, 1925), p. 151.

Alexander Świętochowski, in his monumental two-volume work, *Polish Peasants (Historia Chłopów Polskich)*, speaks of Kościuszko as "a great and wise man by virtue of intellect and heart, faultlessly noble, the most genuine of Poles, the purest of patriots, the noblest of democrats, with whom no one else can be placed on the same level in his love of and friendship for the common man—who really undertook an unequal struggle with the enemy under the motto of freedom for the whole nation, including the peasants."

war into Russia, and the insurrection collapsed. The third and
final partition followed in 1795; as in the case of the first partition,
it was between Russia, Prussia, and Austria.

It was this fall from horseback at Maciejowice that Thomas
Campbell immortalized in his *Pleasures of Hope:*

> Hope, for a season, bade the world farewell,
> And freedom shrieked—as Kosciuszko fell.

Kościuszko fell at Maciejowice, but with him did not fall the
hope of Poland reborn; and the legend that he was supposed to
have exclaimed *Finis Poloniae!* (End of Poland!), was a fabrica-
tion of the nineteenth century and came from the Prussian sources
of subtle propaganda. The Kościuszko insurrection collapsed at
Maciejowice, but it was the victory at Racławice that nurtured
hope through the nineteenth century—and again today.

IN PRISON AND EXILE

Even if the uprising seemed foolhardy when there was little
hope of its success before it started, from the point of view of
long-range historic forces it was successful, though it failed. In
this paradox one should seek the criterion of evaluation of Kościuszko's leadership. The country was utterly unprepared in a
military sense and the uprising broke out prematurely under
pressure of events. Besides, the burden of civil administration, the
mobilization of resources as well as of men, and the commanding
of a citizen army composed of raw recruits against three regular
armies was a task that no man could fulfill. Historians occasionally
suggest that Kościuszko was not a genius as civil administrator,
economic planner and military leader, and the occasion demanded
three geniuses in one. Perhaps he was not, yet he performed wonders. By virtue of his character and the burning love of his country
he evoked such a feeling of patriotism and spiritual discipline in
his citizen army as were seldom seen before. In the defense of
Warsaw and in the battle of Maciejowice his burghers and peasants stood their ground—and when the supreme test came, each
man died where he stood at his post, only after he had fired his
last round of ammunition or broke his scythe. "Freedom," "Coun-

try," "Kościuszko," were their watchwords—and these watchwords were passed on from generation to generation.

Gravely wounded, unconscious, his body covered with blood, Kościuszko was carried from the field of battle by Russian soldiers on an improvised stretcher. Held temporarily in a local manor house, where he regained consciousness the following morning, he was transported in a roundabout way that took two months, to the Peter-Paul fortress in St. Petersburg. After a few months of confinement as a rebel, and not as a vanquished enemy, the Empress Catherine had him removed to the Orlov palace as a more suitable place for his physically shattered condition. Here an English doctor, named Rogerson, attended him, since his wounds, unskillfully tended by the Russian surgeons, remained unhealed. Here he was permitted some freedom of movement, and an adequate supply of food which he was allowed to share with Polish prisoners in the fortress, and thus two years passed till November, 1796, when the Empress died and her son, Paul I, ascended the throne.

Although of violent temper and unpredictable, Paul had his moments of basic human sympathy. Accompanied by his son, the Grand Duke Alexander, he visited Kościuszko several times, was apparently deeply impressed by the simplicity and dignity of his "rebel" prisoner's bearing, and finally set him free. Kościuszko was showered with imperial gifts, some of which he took under compulsion, but got rid of as soon as he could. It was characteristic of Kościuszko that he accepted freedom only on the condition that the other leading Polish prisoners and about 12,000 other Poles in Russian prisons were also set free.

Still suffering from his wounds, broken in body and in spirit, Kościuszko's first plan when set free was to come to America, by way of Sweden and England. Accompanied by his lifelong friend, his adjutant in the uprising and fellow-prisoner—poet, statesman, political and social reformer—Julian Ursyn Niemcewicz, he set out on the tedious journey through the snowdrifts of Finland. When he reached Sweden and western civilization he was acclaimed as "one of the greatest men of our century," and leading citizens vied with each other to pay him homage. Upon his arrival in London (in July 1797) the *Gentleman's Magazine* announced: "Kosciuszko, the hero of freedom, is here." Another round of honors, which he tried to avoid whenever possible, began. His fame preceded him and tokens of admiration and esteem followed. Individuals and civic groups presented him with gifts—including a sword of honor from the Wig Club in London and a service set of silver from the city of Bristol, whence he sailed for America after a fortnight's stay in London. As he was carried on board the ship there was a triumphal procession of his English well-wishers, against whom, only twenty years before, he had fought on the American soil.

When he arrived at Philadelphia after nearly two months on the stormy Atlantic, having been nearly shipwrecked, the free citizens of Philadelphia unhitched the horses from his carriage and drew the carriage themselves to the quarters prepared for him on Fourth Street. In greeting the delegation, he said: "I look upon America as my second country, and I feel myself too happy when I return to her." Washington wrote him (August 31, 1797) from Mount Vernon, welcoming him "to the land whose liberties you have been so instrumental in establishing," and assured him that "no one has a higher respect and veneration for your character than I have." All his American friends, former generals and comrades-in-arms, welcomed him home and asked him to stay with them and rest.

In Philadelphia he met Thomas Jefferson, and their friendship developed into mutual admiration. In a letter to General Gates (February 21, 1798) Jefferson wrote of Kościuszko: "He is as pure a son of liberty as I have ever known, and of that liberty which is to go to all, and not to the few and rich alone."

In the turmoil and disturbances that followed in the wake of the French Revolution, Kościuszko thought there was a chance to do something for Poland and hurriedly left America, incognito, in the first days of May 1798. But before his final farewell he left a document with his friend, Thomas Jefferson, that will forever be a tribute to the heart of Kościuszko. It was his last will and testament (dated May 5, 1798), whereby he bequeathed his American property for the purpose of "purchasing Negroes from among his [Jefferson's] own or any others and giving them liberty in my name, in giving them an education in trades or otherwise and in having them instructed for their new condition in the duties of morality which may make them good neighbors, good fathers or mothers . . . and in whatsoever may make them happy and useful."

Social conditions at the time would have made it extremely difficult to carry out Kościuszko's will in all its implications, and his own poverty later on forced him to supersede this magnanimous gesture by more practical testaments, but we have reasons to believe that his first will expressed a genuine desire to ameliorate the condition of the colored people in America, as he was anxious to emancipate the peasants of Poland.

As his final gift to America, and at the request of General William R. Davie, then envoy of the United States to France, Kościuszko prepared in the year 1800, *Manoeuvres of Horse Artillery*, which was translated from the French by Colonel Jonathan Williams and published in 1808 by Campbell and Mitchell of New York. In recommending the manuscript for publication, General Davie wrote to the United States Military Philosophical Society of West Point: "The publication would be of great importance to our country. It is perhaps the only treatise on this subject in the world." At any rate it was the first effective system for the organization of the American Artillery. In his *Historical Sketch of the Organization, Administration, Material and Tactics of Artillery, United States Army* (published in 1884), Lieutenant Birkheimer states: "War [of 1812] was declared without the Government having at its disposal any system of manoeuvres for the artillery except that of Kosciuszko." For that reason Kościuszko is sometimes called, not without foundation, "the Father of the American Artillery."

Kościuszko's declining years were as unhappy as his youth was sad and full of disappointments. The entire Polish nation still regarded him as their spiritual leader ("*Naczelnik Narodu*") and hoped that somehow he might make a lucky move on the chessboard of power politics, as the game was then cynically played, among others, by Napoleon I and the Tsar Alexander I. Both tried to use his prestige among the Poles in order to organize Polish legions one against the other. But Kościuszko saw through their schemes and countered each move to secure his moral support, with the demand of a definite guarantee of complete independence of Poland with the restoration of territories belonging to the country before partitions. He did not oppose the various moves that different groups of Poles made to secure either from the Corsican Napoleon or the Russian Alexander, some advantage or semblance of independence. He was realistic enough to know that something for the time being was better than nothing at all; but he suffered spiritual torments when he saw that his compatriots spilled their blood in the Napoleonic legions for not much more than empty promises.

From 1798 till 1801 he remained in Paris, where he moved among the diplomats, renewing old acquaintances, making new contacts—all the while working for the Polish cause. Here he befriended Peter Joseph Zeltner, the envoy of the new Helvetian (Swiss) Republic at Paris. In 1801 he retired to the country estate of Peter Zeltner in Berville, near Fontainebleau, and here he remained as a guest of his Swiss friend till May 1815. During the Congress of Vienna the Tsar Alexander of Russia asked Kościuszko to come to Vienna immediately, as the Tsar had some important plan to reveal to him. In the belief that something really important had developed, Kościuszko went to Vienna only to be again disappointed. The plan was to create a Lilliputian "Kingdom of Poland," which for fifteen years had been known as the "Congress Kingdom." Alexander only wanted Kościuszko's moral support because of the latter's prestige in the nation, and for that support was willing to bestow on the Polish national hero some such empty honor as Viceroy. Kościuszko declined the honor and started back for France.

On his way through Switzerland he stopped at Soleure to visit Francis Zeltner, his Berville host's brother, and the two took such a liking to each other that Kościuszko remained there for the rest of his numbered days. He died in Soleure on October 15, 1817.

Of his meager means, his simple tastes and his charitable inclinations that befriended all the paupers, the poor and the sick in the village of Soleure, it is impossible to treat here. Suffice it to say that to his last day he remained faithful to his ideals of democracy and a true friend of the poor and the underprivileged.

His heart was buried in Rapperswill, free Switzerland, until

Poland became free again; and his body was laid to rest on the Wawel Hill in Kraków among Polish kings and a few other great men of Poland.

CONCLUSION

As a military leader, statesman and diplomatist, Kościuszko was not the genius of the century. In fact, many Poles before him and after him towered above his intellectual capacity, political dexterity, and organizational ability. His people know all that and yet he remains the beloved national hero of Poland. He possessed traits of character and homespun virtues which, in national esteem, raised him above mere genius. While Pułaski was a typical representative of the old Poland, a noble knight of a nation that was dubbed "Knight Among Nations," of a nation of warriors on horseback—Kościuszko was the forerunner of a new, democratic Poland, a country of common men, of burghers and peasants.

Not only to the Poles of Poland, but also to the four or five million Poles and Americans of Polish descent or extraction, Kościuszko is a source of pride, a hero and a symbol: a source of pride, because he was a democrat of the New World variety; a hero, because he forever made it possible for the growing generations of Polish-Americans to feel that they have not come empty-handed to the blessings of American freedom, that while that freedom was being won by those whose ancestors came in the Mayflower, there was Kościuszko helping them; a symbol, of the link between their new country, the United States of America, and the country of their grandfathers, Poland.

XII

CASIMIR PUŁASKI
"The Father of American Cavalry"

1747-79

by

HELENA WANICZEK

IN AN epoch which saw an enormous increase in militarism throughout Europe, Prussia and Russia emerged by the side of Austria as new and rapacious powers in eastern Europe. It was then that Poland, tired with almost century-long defense of her frontiers, yearned for peace and lapsed into disarmament. Among her other political weaknesses at the time was the fact that Poland was a Republic, under elective kings, with the power of kings hamstrung by the privileges of the nobles. When, on October 5, 1763, King Augustus III died and interregnum occurred, one of the candidates for the exalted office was Stanisław August Poniatowski ("The Last King of Poland"), the favorite of so-called Catherine the Great of Russia.

Under the pressure of the Russian army, the election of the unpopular Poniatowski was forcibly procured; but when that king showed too much zeal for political reform, the Russian Ambassador, Prince Repnin, forced the magnates and nobles to oppose him and they applied to Catherine to have their privileges guaranteed by her. When voices were raised in the *Sejm* (Diet), protesting against the interference of the ambassador, he gave orders that four of its most courageous members should be deported to Siberia.

These unparalleled outrages on the part of Russia revealed the sad truth that Poland's independence was endangered. It was

CASIMIR PUŁASKI

(From a steel engraving by J. Hopwood, based on an authentic oil
portrait by J. Oleszkiewicz in National Museum in Kraków)

already too late for reform; the time had come to take arms and to meet violence with force.

The king did not venture to take any action, fearing to lose his crown; neither did the *Sejm* show any activity, for it was terrorized by thirty thousand Russian soldiers; nor could the entirely inadequate Polish army, badly armed and unused to warfare, venture now to act. The only answer to the Russian outrages at this juncture would be a national uprising, especially of the middle and lower ranks of the nobility, and the plan of a conspiracy was prepared by Józef Pułaski, prefect (*starosta*) of the district of Warka, aided by Bishop Adam Krasiński. On January 29, 1768, the insurrection was proclaimed at Bar, an out-of-the-way village in Podolia, and on March 4, Józef Pułaski stood at the head of a military organization whose battle cry was "*pro fide et libertate.*" Hence this insurrection is known as the Confederation of Bar.

In this preparatory work Józef Pułaski found ready help in his sons, Franciszek, Antoni and, foremost of all, in Kazimierz,[1] whose heroic life and death are gratefully recorded in the history of the struggle for independence both of his native country and of the country he was later to serve, America.

Casimir was born on March 4, 1747, at Winiary, in the province of Podolia. There is considerable difference of opinion concerning details of his boyhood life and military training. His father, although a member of the nobility (he was connected with the princely house of Czartoryski) and a jurist of ability, had led a quiet, retired life and apparently brought up his sons in accordance with the country squire tradition. We know that the boy Casimir was taken as a page to the court of Prince Charles of Courland at Mitau. There, in 1763, he was to suffer privation during the hard times when the castle was besieged by the Russians, and probably his aversion to Muscovy dated from that period. Although he had received no formal military education, from the very beginning of the insurrection he opposed the enemy bravely and skillfully in the skirmishes at Starokonstantynów and at Chmielnik; later, when besieged by a much more numerous Russian army in the convent at Berdyczów, he repelled attacks

---

[1] Best known in the Anglicized form of Casimir.—*Ed.*

and bombardments, and, when his garrison ran short of ammunition, used nails, buttons and broken glass. At last, on June 13,
1768, he, together with his followers, fell into the hands of the
Russians, and they were taken to the prison camp at Polonne.
There he heard the tragic news of the dispersion of the rest of
the confederates, and of the massacre of the Polish nobles by
Ruthenian peasants, instigated by the Russians. He heard that his
father and brothers had fled across the Dniester to Moldavia, and,
thinking that all was now lost, he made a formal written renunciation of the confederacy. But as soon as he found himself at his
father's side, near Hotin, hearing the glad news of the uprising in
Kraków, he revoked his "renunciation" and, together with his
brothers, took up arms again. He was in charge of the armed positions at Zwaniec and at Okopy św. Trójcy (the Holy Trinity
trenches) on the Dniester, whence raids could be made upon the
Russians.

Casimir was attacked in the Holy Trinity Trenches by an
army of four thousand; when the outcome became hopeless, he
led out by night two hundred of his companions and passed with
them across the swollen Dniester to Bukowina. Through the snow-
covered Carpathians he reached Kraków. In the meantime, however, his father had died in the Tartar prison, his brother Anthony
had been taken prisoner by the Russians and he himself was un
justly suspected by his political enemies as a man entertaining
ambitious designs. After joining his brother Francis, Casimir once
more started an offensive; he supported the confederates at Sanok,
from Przemyśl made an unsuccessful attack on Lwów, and then
moved to Lithuania to stir up an uprising there. In a short time
all western Lithuania was afire—but the political leaders in Lithuania did not know how to profit by Pułaski's assistance and only
wasted the military force which he had created.

Together with his brother, Pułaski continued his activities in
Mazovia, where at Ostrołęka, the nobles, moved by patriotic
zeal, elected Casimir as their marshal. The newly created marshal
swore "to fight the country's enemies with all his strength" and
"to persist faithfully and obstinately in this struggle until the Republic internally and externally is at peace."

When the plan of occupying Warsaw failed, the Pułaskis

were once more summoned to Lithuania by confederates there. But Casimir was defeated at Orzechowo and Włodawa by General Suvorov and Colonel Roenn, and there, in a terrible scene of carnage, Francis Pułaski was killed. With a handful of men, Casimir escaped over the Hungarian frontier.

Not discouraged by that last failure, in September, 1770, he occupied the Convent at Częstochowa to establish there a base for his future operations in what was proving to be guerrilla warfare. That gave him his revenge. An army of three thousand men, under Drewitz's command, approached the Jasna Góra Monastery on December 31. They expected an easy victory and abundant booty. Pułaski, in command of the confederates, had prepared in an experienced way for the defense. At the risk of his life he led an attack against the enemy, and on January 9, 1771, after a desperate fight, he finally repulsed the main attack. This was followed by an ignominious retreat of the Russian troops.

This glorious defense of Częstochowa, the second in the nation's history, could not, however, save Poland. The situation of the Bar confederates was growing more and more desperate. Though the Częstochowa, Tyniec and Lanckorona fortresses bravely withstood the attacks, yet there could be no hope for the deliverance of the rest of the country. A handful of soldiers, brave, but poorly equipped, could not defeat the regular army of Russia.

Hatred against King Stanisław August Poniatowski was redoubled. A noble, Stanisław Strawiński by name, approached Pułaski with a plan to carry off the king. As a soldier, Pułaski undoubtedly had an aversion to the vacillating king who gave a bad example of cowardice to his people, but he was not in favor of abduction—at any rate, the king was not to be hurt. It was thought that in case of the king's abdication there would be candidates for the throne who would help Poland with men and money, and that a new king would follow a more resolute policy of freeing Poland from Russian influences.

On the evening of November 3, 1771, Strawiński made an attempt to abduct the king, but failed. This attempt raised a feeling of ill will against "anarchical" Poland in Europe; the "regicides" were generally condemned and Pułaski was counted as one of them. Though he had not taken part in the attempt, he was pronounced a criminal. Again at Częstochowa he prepared for his supreme effort. Suddenly, on April 19, 1772, the news came that Austria had joined with Prussia and Russia to partition Poland. The situation was desperate; to save his companions from useless bloodshed, Pułaski gave up the struggle and on May 31 went to Silesia.

From that moment commenced the heroic exile of the leader of the confederates. Under constant threat of being delivered to the Russians, he had to move from place to place; he stayed near Dresden for some time, then moved to Strasbourg and finally settled in Paris. It was chiefly against him that Polish opinion now turned. He was regarded as the principal cause of the appalling bloodshed and of the ill-timed action which had precipitated the catastrophe of the partitions.

The king gained sympathy, as the victim of rebellious subjects. Pułaski was accused, on the same grounds as Strawiński, of an attempt on the king. In his defense he wrote a public proclamation; it had not been he, who had committed the crime—so he defended himself—nor had he instigated it. But his defense was in vain. Some of those who had first drafted the act of dethronement now sat in the High Criminal Court, and on September 2, 1773, they passed sentence of death on the "regicide."

It happened that at that moment the Turks were victorious over the Russians. Pułaski, the "criminal" sentenced to death, collected all the forces still at his disposal and all his own resources, to renew the fight for his country from the Balkans. With a handful of newly-enlisted officers, he came to the camp of the Grand Vizier at the very moment of the final defeat of the Turks. Robbed of his arms and of money and valuable papers, he managed to get away from Rodosto to Smyrna, and thence went by sea to Marseilles.

Those were his worst days; he was penniless and almost starving. There were moments when he thought of suicide. He wrote to Prince Radziwiłł in September, 1775: "Education received in early days prevents me from raising my own hand against myself; but the prolonged hours of this torture do not bring the desired end to my life." Before financial help came he was cast into prison for debt, to lie among the lowest criminals. From this torment he was saved, partly by his relatives and friends and partly by the French government. The French felt in some measure responsible for Poland's misfortunes; and at the same time, they wished to give assistance to America in her fight for independence. On hearing that Silas Deane and Benjamin Franklin were recruiting volunteers, Pułaski awakened from the inertia of dejection. The war against the English in America appealed to him; it was the English, through their anti-French policy, who had encouraged the powers to partition Poland. Recommended by the French government and by Rulhier, a well-known historian, Pułaski met Franklin in Paris in the spring of 1777, and from him he received a favorable introduction to Washington. Following is Benjamin Franklin's letter to George Washington dated at Paris, May 29, 1777:

Count Pulaski of Poland, an officer famous throughout Europe for his bravery and conduct in defence of the liberties of his country against the three great invading powers of Russia, Austria and Prussia, will have the honor of delivering this into your Excellency's hands. The Court here have encouraged and promoted his voyage, from an opinion that he may be highly useful to our servcie. Mr. Deane has written so fully concerning him, that I need not enlarge; and I only add my wishes, that he may find in our armies under your Excellency, occasions of distinguishing himself.

Pułaski landed at Boston [2] about the end of July, at the time when fierce fighting was going on on the Hudson River and on the shores of Lake Champlain. He started a new life on American soil. Hopelessly depressed not long before, he now wished, with a new hope in his heart, to offer his military experience to George Washington. His written words are the best proof of his desire to take a prominent place among the volunteers. He thus formulated his desires:

I wish to receive under my command a detachment of cavalry volunteers, and to hold such rank as would authorize me to command a whole division if I deserve it. . . . I should like to receive a position in which I would be under orders only from the commander-in-chief.

---

[2] Some historians give Salem, Massachusetts, as the place of landing.—*Ed.*

If this is impossible, I would ask to share the hardships of war with the Marquis de Lafayette, and to execute the commander-in-chief's orders as the subordinate of the Marquis. The chief thing for which I ask is to be near the enemy, to have the opportunity to earn the name of a good officer. I had under my command in Poland in various battles, 18,000 men; attacks and sieges which I commanded allow me to count myself among those who have acquired experience in war. You should not slight such men; I have come from Europe in the hope that I may be accepted in the ranks of those worthy citizens who fight for their country and for independence.

Washington had by that time already been besieged by all kinds of titled Europeans, who included besides outstanding men, not a few ex-petty officers who wanted to be generals, and his enthusiasm for foreign officers was somewhat dampened. But, as in the case of Kościuszko, who had come the year before, he was willing to give Pułaski a fair chance. Washington's recommendation of Pułaski to the President of Congress, dated August 28, 1777, reads:

Having endeavored, at the solicitation of the Count de Pulaski, to think of some mode for employing him in our service, there is none occurs to me liable to so few inconveniences and exceptions, as the giving him the command of the horse . . . a man of real capacity, experience and knowledge in that service, might be extremely useful. The Count appears by his recommendations, to have sustained no inconsiderable military character in his own country; and as the principal attention in Poland has been for some time past paid to the Cavalry, it is to be presumed this gentleman is not unacquainted with it. I submit it to Congress how far it may be eligible to confer the appointment I have mentioned upon him.

While waiting for his formal appointment by Congress, Pułaski was invited by George Washington to serve on his staff as a volunteer officer. In this temporary capacity he passed through his first baptism of blood on the American continent in the Battle of Brandywine on September 11, 1777.

This battle and the part Pułaski played therein have been briefly described as follows:

Learning that the British forces were approaching, General Washington moved his army to meet the advance.

General Wayne was stationed at Chadd's Ford to oppose any crossing there. General Sullivan was on the right of the line. General Greene was in reserve.

The plan of the British was admirable, and was based upon time-worn battle tactics which had proved successful and which consisted of making a feint with part of the forces in front, whilst a strong force made a turning movement and attacked the enemy in flank.

General Knyphausen attacked Chadd's Ford as a feint and thus occupied the full attention of the American forces. General Cornwallis, meanwhile, who had been able to secure a competent guide, made a circuitous march in secret of eighteen miles to the left, attacked the American right and threw them into the utmost confusion. General Greene came to the rescue, having marched his force, it is said, five miles in less than fifty minutes and thus succeeded in staying the complete rout of the army.

General Wayne, seeing that the right had been broken, was forced to retreat in disorder. But through the efforts of Lafayette, another volunteer officer on Washington's Staff, the fugitives were finally checked at a deep stream by the American troops, stationed there by Lafayette.

Pułaski here saw his first service and exposed himself to great danger by riding close to the British lines and reconnoitering their position. At a critical moment, with Washington's permission, he gathered together Washington's bodyguard and made an unexpected charge on the British which stayed their advance.

Later, he was the first to detect the approach of the British in such force as to menace Washington himself, and part of his command near Warren Tavern.

Washington was engaged when Pułaski rode up and he was told that Washington could not be disturbed. Pułaski insisted, however, on seeing him and reporting the near presence of the British forces. Colonel Alexander Hamilton, who understood French, suggested that Pułaski may have mistaken British troops for American troops but Pułaski, with great heat, insisted that his report was accurate, and this afterwards proved to be true and it was through his intelligence and activity that further disaster was prevented.[3]

As a result of Pułaski's praiseworthy conduct in the Battle of Brandywine, Congress awarded him a commission on September 15, 1777, as Brigadier General in command of the entire cavalry of the American forces.

Within a few weeks Washington started an offensive and

[3] William W. Gordon in *The Georgia Historical Quarterly* for October 1929, Vol. XIII, No. 3.—*Ed.*

attacked the enemy near Germantown.[4] Unfortunately, by sheer accident, victory slipped from his grasp almost at the last moment and he gave orders to retreat under the protection of the cavalry. At the council of war, when all the generals were for ceasing military operations for the winter, the young general moved that operations should be continued, but his motion was not accepted, and the army went into winter quarters at Valley Forge. Pułaski was stationed at Trenton. He realized then that his heavily armed cavalry was considered by the Americans only as an auxiliary support for infantry, not capable of independent operations. He had some difficulties too, with his subordinates, especially one Moylan, who, having been Washington's aide-de-camp before, hardly cared now to submit himself to the orders of so young a general.

At Trenton Pułaski was ordered to join his forces with those of Wayne, when the latter crossed the Delaware River and was attacked by the British at Haddonfield, New Jersey. General Wayne succeeded in eluding the attack and withdrew under the protection of Pułaski's cavalry.

Many analogies might have been drawn between the guerrilla warfare of the Confederates of Bar and the American war, yet Pułaski, an enthusiastic and fiery soldier, could not fit himself to the ways of these rather phlegmatic men, and the language difficulties widened the breach. Discouraged, he gave up his command of cavalry and received from Congress permission to recruit a separate unit, composed of both cavalry and infantry, while retaining the rank of Brigadier General. Washington supported Pułaski's request to Congress to be allowed to raise an independent corps of 68 horse, armed with lances, and 200 foot as light infantry.[5]

In accordance with the formal resolution passed by Congress

---

[4] The Battle of Germantown took place October 3, 1777.—*Ed.*

[5] In a letter embodying this recommendation to Congress, dated March 14, 1778, Washington wrote: "I have only to add that the Count's valor and active zeal on all occasions have done him great honor."

That Washington had complete confidence in Pułaski, despite the latter's difficulties with his subordinates, may be concluded from a letter he wrote on the same day to Governor Livingston, to wit: "I am pleased with the favorable account which you give to Count Pulaski's conduct while at Trenton. He is a gentleman of great activity and unquestionable bravery and only wants a fuller knowledge of our language and customs to make him a valuable officer."—*Ed.*

on March 28, 1778, Pułaski was authorized to have the command of an independent corps of horse and foot, to be raised in such a way as the Commander-in-Chief might approve.[6]

Pułaski chose Michael Kowacz, Major Jules de Montfort and his relative, Zieliński, for instructors of cavalry. The Moravian Sisters of Bethlehem, Pennsylvania, presented him with a crimson banner, from which he never afterwards parted. It is now preserved in the collection of the Historical Society in Baltimore.[7]

In the middle of September, Pułaski's "legion" was ready; in October, at Little Egg Harbor, New Jersey, the first encounter with the enemy took place. Pułaski was dispatched there to drive off the British and he accomplished this with his infantry.[8] Then he spent part of the following Winter of 1778-79 with General Washington at Morristown and trained his cavalry near Washington's headquarters.

On February 2, 1779, Pułaski was ordered to join General Lincoln, who was in command of the Southern Army stationed in Georgia and South Carolina. At first he expected to take command of a larger detachment than before, and to be under the direct command of Lincoln. Instead of proceeding south immediately, Pułaski was delayed, probably by enlarging his force through recruiting, for he was still in Annapolis, Maryland, as late as April 10. In the meanwhile events occurred in quick succession. The British had captured Savannah (December 29, 1778) and from that vantage point threatened Augusta, Georgia and Charleston, South Carolina. Lincoln was at Augusta to ward off a possible attack by General Prevost (who was in command at Savannah); Moultrie was at Black Swamp, South Carolina, to watch the enemy's movements there; and Pułaski was already on his way

---

[6] "On April 13, 1778, a recruiting station was opened at Mrs. Ross' house in Baltimore and recruiting continued through the months of April, May, June and July, 1778, resulting in the forming of an independent corps of three companies of horse, armed with lances, and three companies of infantry, a total of 330, all recruited in Baltimore but of which 28 were from Pennsylvania. The character of the recruits and the size of the legion was approved by General Washington, who accepted it for service." (William W. Gordon, *op. cit.*)—*Ed.*

[7] This banner was made famous by the beautiful poem written by Longfellow in 1825 under the title of "Hymn of the Moravian Nuns of Bethlehem—at the Consecration of Pulaski's Banner."—*Ed.*

[8] Some historians believe that the British withdrew without putting up any resistance.—*Ed.*

southward as General Prevost crossed the Savannah River with
the intention of capturing Charleston. General Moultrie put up a
stiff resistance to Prevost's forces, but before Lincoln could bring
assistance Charleston was in serious danger. Pułaski arrived in the
nick of time, having reached Charleston on May 11 (1779), the
very day that Prevost crossed the Ashley River and demanded
that the City Fathers surrender the city. Pułaski made an immediate attack on Prevost's forces and pushed them back in great
disorder. Colonel Kowacz, second in command of Pułaski's
Legion, was killed; between forty and fifty men in the Legion
fell; Pułaski himself displayed great bravery and fought personal
combats with members of the enemy's cavalry. Charleston was
saved.

Military operations were suspended during the summer
months. The silent guns made Pułaski nervous. Besides, as a soldier and not a businessman, the constant demands of Congress
for careful accounts exasperated him. On August 19, he sent to
Congress a letter full of regret and bitterness: ". . . enthusiastic
zeal for a noble cause and for a life in America, and disregard
for death made me enlist in your ranks, and I flattered myself that
I should work to your satisfaction and earn your approval. It
must be my fate, that nothing but honor, to which I have ever
been faithful, makes me continue in this service; but I am disheartened by ungenerous treatment." He even suggested that he
would cover all the expenses of the Legion from his own resources, as soon as he received a payment, which he awaited, of
10,000 gold livres. "Be just, gentlemen," he added, "and think
that as I could not bow before the powers of Europe I came
here to sacrifice everything for the independence of America. I
wish to live in a free country, and before I settle down here I
wish to fight for that country's freedom. The campaign will start
soon; maybe I shall still have opportunity to prove that I am a
friend to your cause, though I have not been lucky enough to
commend myself to some persons."

The opportunity came sooner than he expected; in September Count d'Estaing, the French admiral, planned together
with Lincoln a movement for the recapture of Savannah. Pułaski
with his Legion was to attack British outposts and to effect junc-

ture with the French troops on the coast. This he did most successfully, having joined Count d'Estaing on September 15. On
September 16 the eager Frenchman called upon Prevost to surrender, in the name of the French king, but without result.[9] Without fully realizing the strength of the British forces, the American troops started the bombardment of the city. After some preliminary skirmishes the attack was minutely prepared to take the
city by assault on the morning of October 9. General Huger was
to attack the left side of the eastern fortifications, and the three
French columns were to strike at the center and the right of the
British lines. D'Estaing was to lead the third column to the main
attack and Pułaski was to follow him with his cavalry. At the
moment when the French admiral reached the redoubt, brave
Maitland rushed out of the fortress against him. The British turned
withering fire on the attacking troops and d'Estaing fell wounded.
Pułaski rushed forward to take command in the place of d'Estaing,
and to raise the spirits of the soldiers by the example of his own
courage, but he soon fell from his horse, hit by grapeshot.[10]

The attack failed. Pułaski died, in great agony, on board the
Wasp, on October 11. The most skillful surgeons of the French
fleet could not save his life, for gangrene had set in. His body was

---

[9] General Prevost cunningly asked for a truce, which was granted, to consider such a serious proposition. In the meanwhile he received reinforcements.—*Ed.*

[10] Accounts of eyewitnesses vary somewhat as to details, which may be
expected under the circumstances, but all who saw Pułaski fall bear witness to his
splendid conduct and great bravery. Perhaps the best account is given by another
Pole, one of Pułaski's officers in the Legion, Major Rogowski (in Jones' *History
of Georgia*, Vol. II, p. 402):

"For half an hour the guns roared and blood flowed abundantly. Seeing an
opening between the enemy's works, Pulaski resolved, with his Legion and a
small detachment of Georgia cavalry, to charge through, enter the city, confuse
the enemy, and cheer the inhabitants with good tidings. General Lincoln approved the daring plan. Imploring the help of the Almighty, Pulaski shouted to
his men 'Forward,' and we, two hundred strong, rode at full speed after him, the
earth resounding under the hoofs of our chargers. For the first two minutes
all went well. We sped like Knights into the peril. Just, however, as we passed
the gap between the two batteries, a cross fire, like a pouring shower, confused
our ranks. I looked around. Oh! sad moment, ever to be remembered. Pulaski
lies prostrate on the ground. I leaped towards him, thinking possibly his wound
was not dangerous, but a CANISTER SHOT had pierced his thigh, and the blood was
also flowing from his breast, probably from a second wound. Falling on my
knees, I tried to raise him. He said in a faint voice: 'Jesus! Maria! Joseph!'
Further, I knew not, for at that moment a musket ball, grazing my scalp, blinded
me with blood, and I fell to the ground in a state of insensibility."—*Ed.*

consigned to the watery grave, and only after the arrival of the *Wasp* at Charleston did a solemn and symbolic funeral service take place.

The tragic death of this Polish and American hero did not erase his deeds from the memory of future generations, either in the old world or the new. Pułaski could not save Poland from partition, but by his undaunted courage, shown in twenty battles, attacks, defenses and raids, as well as by the unceasing zeal with which he incited thousands of others, he contributed to the preservation of the Polish spirit. He was the man who, with Kościuszko, inculcated in the younger generation a strong faith in the restoration of Polish independence.

The heritage that Pułaski left to the Americans was a noble one. His legion earned Washington's approval and was a model for the formation of others in subsequent campaigns. The cavalry which he organized became the nucleus for future squadrons; and Pułaski has been rightly called the "Father of American cavalry."

In acknowledgment of his merits, Congress voted, as early as 1779, that a monument be erected to his memory, and this was done in Washington in 1910. At Savannah, a monument to him was erected in 1853, the cornerstone having been laid by Lafayette as early as 1825.[11] In such manner did the Americans honor the memory of this soldier of Liberty, the undaunted warrior who sacrificed his life in the cause of American independence.

[11] There is hardly a state in the Union that does not have a county or town, street or square, monument or tablet, school or highway named in grateful memory of General Pułaski.—*Ed.*

Translated from the Polish by Maria Traciłowska-Mężnicka.

STANISŁAW STASZIC

(From a lithograph by W. Walkiewicz, based on a contemporary portrait
of unknown authorship in the National Museum in Kraków)

XIII

STANISŁAW STASZIC
Scientist and Social Crusader

1755-1826

by

WILLIAM J. ROSE

THE year of the Lisbon earthquake, the year of Braddock's expedition, which first brought George Washington into prominence, saw the birth of a lad who was to leave behind him in the history of his nation what can only be called a trailing cloud of glory. Stanisław Staszic was born in November, 1755, in the little town of Schneidemuehl (Piła in Polish), to be found just outside the Polish frontier (before September 1, 1939), in the open plains of German Pomerania. None of those interested in the event could possibly surmise what the boy was to become for his people in a time of bitter crisis; the more so as he was not even of gentle birth. This fact would be of no consequence today, but it was then; and was symptomatic of much that was to happen later to stir the young patriot to battle with more than one social injustice.

Youngest of the family, he was destined by his parents for the priesthood, and actually followed their wishes though he never served the Church in the ordinary way. Other interests prevailed, no less vital to him—those of social betterment for his fellows and those of science. Curiously enough it was the spectacle of improper exploitation of the common people by the local County Lieutenant (*Starosta*), that seems to have opened his eyes while yet a youth to the needs for reform. He saw lands being taken from the small farmer to add to the size of the big estates, and he never forgot it. Nor can there be any doubt that something like a shadow lay over his whole life, so that he was rarely known to mix in society. Living for him was not a matter for laughter or play. Toil was predestined for him, toil in the service of others, notably of his nation. What Czarniecki had said a century earlier was true now of Staszic:

> Not from salt nor from the soil was my soul born,
> But from that which made me suffer, and made me mourn!

"Father Staszic," says Professor Chrzanowski, "was one of the loveliest figures produced by Poland in all her history. One of the noblest hearts that ever beat on Polish soil, he counts among the worthiest of her sons—fitted to take his place along with Skarga and Konarski. Like Skarga in his flaming patriotism, he resembled Konarski in his wisdom, and still more in his will power. In the breadth and richness of his learning as well as in his feverish love of the same, no one had ever equalled him in the land up to his day, and few since. He belonged to the first men of learning of his time, not only of Poland but even of Europe. He made his own the dictum of the Roman Terence: 'A man I am; and I count as my business all that is human!' "

I

Sent abroad to study at sixteen, he was first in Leipzig, then in Goettingen, and finally in Paris. From the start his interests turned to physics and the exact sciences. This fact made the French capital a spiritual home for him; for were not the greatest lights of the time assembled there? The Encyclopedists—D'Alembert, Buffon, Daubenton, and others—were his teachers, and the spirit of the Enlightenment pervaded the land. Before long Staszic had singled out geology as his specialty, and he pursued it in part by scientific expeditions in the Alps and Apennines. Years later he was to make special use of these experiences in his own Polish Carpathians. He was also to translate Buffon's *Epoch of Nature* into his mother tongue; and a copy of the second edition of this work, dated 1805, is a prized possession of the writer of this sketch.

In the year of Konarski's death Staszic returned home. He found the land and people in deep depression. A year earlier the first Partition had been forced on the nation, a token of worse things to come. Clearly political disaster was ahead. The one hope was to save what could be rescued of the cultural and spiritual heritage of Poland. Almost at once the young scientist set to work. At first anonymously, through the medium of two striking books, and then openly as a ripe man he led the campaign of cultural advance that saved the nation when the state was lost.

Most of us know of the efforts of Prussia in Bismarck's time and later to deprive the Poles of their speech and civic rights. The truth is that much the same thing was tried a century earlier, and it was to save the nation from such a fate that a group of men founded in Warsaw in 1800 the "Society of Lovers of Science." They represented the best brains of the land, and its warmest hearts. Headed by Bishop Albertrandi, they included the Potocki brothers whom Konarski's school had trained, the poet Karpiński, the lexicographer Linde, the scientist Śniadecki, the great preacher Woronicz, and Staszic himself. During the first years meetings were held in the Library of the Piarist College for Gentlemen, but from 1807 onward they moved to quarters provided by Staszic in the Street of the Canons. Sixteen years later they found a home in the fine new building at the top of that street in the Kraków Faubourg, since known as the Staszic Palace. Today it is the home of the Mianowski Foundation—the Carnegie Foundation of Poland.

From its beginning until his death Staszic was a member of this Society, and for seventeen years its president. He was re-elected for his scholarship and for his leading in social reconstruction. An address of honor was presented to him when the Palace was dedicated in 1823. Two years later he welcomed to Warsaw the renowned Danish sculptor Thorwaldsen, who came to set up his monument of Copernicus in front of the Staszic Palace. Meantime he had set a notable example to his compatriots, by willing in 1824 all his accumulated property to his tenants, who thenceforth held their lands freehold.

Before long he himself passed on. From the modest suite of rooms he had occupied even though he ranked as equal in the land with Cabinet Ministers, his body was borne out for the whole city to acclaim. The man who had avoided every kind of demonstration in his life was given a funeral such as would honor a king. Even his sternest critics were silent before the now prostrate form. First by his colleagues, then from the city limits by the students, the coffin was carried out through the Old Town, and laid to rest in the tiny church in Bielany. There the simple gravestone may be seen today.

II

Few men have ever been so much at variance with the rank and file of his own generation as was Stanisław Staszic. Too many of his contemporaries were unworthy of all he tried to do for them, too few understood him and his purposes. Curiously enough there is as yet no proper life story of the man in existence. When it is written it will tell us more of the world he lived in than of the man himself.

Returned from abroad, and unusually well equipped to serve his country, he could not find a place in which to begin. It seemed as if he was not wanted. The truth was that then no one who was not of gentle birth was likely to be acceptable in the public services of Poland. The boy had seen in his home town the workings of this class snobbishness; the young man was now to feel their bitterness in his own person. Nor did the best efforts he could make result at once in an opening. Then he had the fortune to make the acquaintance of the school inspector for Lithuania, Joseph Wybicki, who was later to become famous as a legionary in Lombardy and as author of the immortal hymn, "Poland's Power Is Not Yet Broken!"

Notable as a public servant, Wybicki had the ear of Chancellor Zamoyski, and told him of the young aspirant eager for a chance to serve his nation. The upshot was a post as tutor to the Chancellor's son, Alexander, which took him right across the republic to the ancient seat of Zamość. Teaching only one subject, Polish literature and history, to his pupil, Staszic was also engaged to teach French in the Academy founded long before by the great Chancellor Jan Zamoyski; and it was here that he met as a pupil the poet Koźmian. About this time the young professor fulfilled the desire of his mother, and was ordained to the priest-hood of the Church. When offered a parish by his benefactor, he declined, preferring to give his time to teaching and study. For this he was criticized at the time, and even today he has been charged—wrongly enough if one looks at his later life—with hav-ing been untrue to the Faith. As a matter of fact few men have ever preserved to the end a simpler and surer faith in God than Staszic. The only difference was that he did not choose to give his life to the routine of parish work.

What attracted him in Zamość was the opportunity afforded by the splendid library. He loved books, and lived with them throughout his busy life. But he loved them as a source of knowl-edge that would make it easier for him to be of use to his day and generation. It was the state of the republic that disturbed him most. Things were moving from bad to worse, with Russian in-terference in the east and Prussian intrigue from the west. Perhaps what hurt him most was the inability of his own countrymen either to think clearly or to act. No wonder then that he broke into print, and published anonymously in 1785 *Remarks on the Life of Jan Zamoyski;* of which it has been truly said that the right title should be: *Remarks on the Condition of Poland.* Five years later a second work appeared, *Warnings to Poland*, a mes-sage with two major ideas—the radicalism of Rousseau and a warm devotion to his people and their welfare.

A thrill went through the commonwealth, as men read these tracts. The mantle of Konarski had fallen on Staszic. The new works could be set alongside *Effective Counsels.* All the fire and vigor, all the power of painting vivid pictures which had made the Piarist Father Stanisław Konarski famous were found again a generation later. Nor was the response slow in appearing. A score of pamphlets were published as comments on or answers to the *Remarks,* and the interest aroused did more than can ever be told to make the work of the Four Year Diet a success, and to pave the way for the Constitution of the Third of May, (1791). What had been a dangerous quietism and even apathy was trans-formed into a will to action. Building on what Konarski and others had done, Staszic at an early age made a signal contribu-tion to the national well being.

Trained in the best thought of the eighteenth century concerning the social order, Staszic really was ahead of his time—he belongs rather to the following century. He envisioned a nation or people as a living organism, "a single spiritual entity, of which the citizens are members." That he was a lover of individual freedom cannot be doubted. He held firmly to the views set forth long before his time by a Modrzewski that the business of the state is to be the servant of mankind, not a tyrant; but he was as far as Konarski from glorifying "golden liberty"—that shibboleth of Polish history. To him the truth was something different. "No one is born to servitude, but every man is born to obedience!"

Knowing his people so well, and sensing the importance of stability in a time of upheavals in Europe, Staszic disagreed with Kościuszko on the one occasion when they met. He preferred constitutional monarchy as the best form of government, while the national hero was out and out for a republic. This disagreement did not spoil their friendship, however; and to the end they were of the same mind on at least one vital matter—a deep mistrust of Napoleon Bonaparte and all his ambitious plans for Europe.

Two demands loom largest in what Staszic wrote and felt at this time. He wanted the serfs of the land set free, and he was resolute in challenging men to action for the deliverance of the land from subjection to the three empires that had swallowed her up. For the peasant he urged personal and economic freedom of the kind that would make it possible for him to own his bit of land and his home, and thus have a feeling of proprietorship and responsibility. As yet he would not advocate the franchise, for how could unlettered folk vote to any good effect? His own example set long afterwards showed how much in earnest he was about this in the darkest moment of his nation's history. "Where the farmer is a slave," he said, "the gentry will be subject to foreigners."

His challenge to the national leaders to do something about delivering the land was only an echo of Konarski's "*Nil desperandum!*" of decades earlier. In his own words he put it, and those words have become an immortal heritage: "Even a great nation may fall, but only a worthless one can perish!"

Nothing finer was ever said than that.

Without knowing it the young patriot was expressing the new spirit that was sweeping Europe. Rationalism was to make way for Romanticism, Voltaire was to yield to Rousseau. Staszic was reared in the spirit of science, but there was in him also the element of passion, even of mysticism. With Patrick Henry he could cry "Give me Liberty or give me Death!" Already there is an adumbration of the gospel soon to be proclaimed by Mickiewicz and others, and called in time, "Messianism"—the conviction that in the Divine economy there is a sure place for every people, and that sooner or later that place will be given to each. In a word, Staszic had not only a head, but also a heart. The one meditated, the other beat—only for his nation.

III

In 1790 the young tutor accompanied the Chancellor on a mission abroad. They made their way via Vienna to Italy, where a long stay was made. Thanks to his position as secretary, Staszic got to know the most important people in church and state in Rome and many other cities. Returning through Switzerland, they broke the journey for some time in Vienna; so that by now he knew by heart most of western Europe. A year passed in this way—a welcome change from the routine of a provincial town and an opportunity to discuss people and events.

Another year passed, and then a shock—the sudden death of the Chancellor, which left the family without its trusted head. As soon as was convenient the widow arranged that her elder son should succeed to all the property except that in the part of Austrian-Poland. This she took for her own use, and with her younger son resolved to end her days in the Austrian capital. As the trusted friend of the family, Father Staszic was asked to accompany her. This time he was away for five years.

Before leaving Zamość he had come to know a very notable fellow countryman, Joseph Czartoryski, who had been made Lieutenant of Lithuania when Poniatowski became King of Poland. In this high official and loyal citizen the younger man found a counselor in respect to matters that seemed vital to both. Czartoryski had long since felt that Poland would never be a power unless something was done to improve her industry. It was already clear that agriculture alone could not hold a nation together, and in the West the Machine Age had begun to make itself felt. Among his experiments must be noted the bringing of Sèvres experts in chinaware production to Poland, and the founding of the famous Korzec factory, whose wares in time became famous in Europe, and are sought after today as almost priceless treasures. Contacts with Czartoryski only strengthened the feeling of Staszic that this kind of thing was what Poland had most need of. The time was at hand when he would make his own modest contribution.

Countess Zamoyska died in 1797. Staszic was free. During twenty years he had saved something, and by fortunate investment he had brought together a small fortune. Returning now to Poland, he settled on a farm, meaning thus to work out some of his ideas in his own way.

"To dwell among my own people" was the famous ambition of John Bright. The Polish crusader for a happier countryside for his people was ahead of the English statesman. But he did not mean to live the life of a hermit, to seek escape from the unkindliness of the age. Rather did he address himself forthwith to the hardest of tasks, viz., to rebuild in his neighborhood the ways of living of that most conservative and stubbornest of mortals, the peasant. To this enterprise he was soon to add other interests, among them the Society in Warsaw, of which the reader has already heard. Finally a study, amounting to a survey of the natural resources of Poland, was to be based for the first time on scientific principles. There remained, of course, literary activities, but of those we can say little here.

During 1804 and 1805 Staszic made his two expeditions through the uplands of southern Poland, intent on appraising the mineral and other wealth likely to be hidden there. During this time the first blast furnaces using coke for the refining of iron ore were set up just across the Prussian frontier in Upper Silesia. Nothing was surer than that something similar was in the surveyor's mind for the lands adjoining, under Russian rule. He published his findings the next year, but it was not till after the Congress of Vienna ten years later that as Commissioner for Industry and Commerce he could get constructively to work. The result was the reorganization and expansion of what had been very primitive beginnings in the Dombrova area, the taking for the first time of lead from the Olkusz pits, and the founding of six zinc mills. Finds of copper were registered. Two veins of silver, discovered in 1820, furnished metal for the first ten-zloty pieces to be struck. Most important of all, the now growing production of iron was put on the most modern lines, with great advantage to all concerned. It was this sort of thing that won for Staszic the name of the Founder of Polish Mining.

In the field of public service his efforts were no less untiring. Paying little attention to who was for the time being political master of the country, he went about his way building the cultural ramparts of the Poland-to-be. The home and the school were then as ever the instruments of social solidarity that offered sure returns. During a single decade the number of elementary schools in the Warsaw district was raised to 1200—this at a time when eastern Europe as yet knew little or nothing of popular education. For Staszic vocational schools seemed even of greater importance. This child of French Rationalism could still write: "Sciences are only empty inventions, are nought but hollow evidence of brains, unless they are set and applied to the uses of the people."

This conviction led him into a curious altercation that became known throughout the land. Learning that a certain Abraham Stern, a townsman in his own district of Hrubieszów, had been the author of a number of clever inventions, Staszic sent for him and made his acquaintance. He then set about giving him an opportunity for further education, and a place to continue his work. As soon as wider circles got to know that inventions of Stern's were in use in the land, and doing valuable service, Staszic proposed that he be invited to become a member of the Society of Lovers of Science. Sharp opposition made itself felt, as the new candidate was not a Christian. The issue was a clear one, but the spirit of Staszic would stand no nonsense. He announced that he would resign from the Society if racial prejudice was made one of its principles. He won his point. Perhaps on this account Professor Dickstein has called him "the conscience of his nation."

IV

We have noted that Staszic agreed with Kościuszko in not trusting the good will of Bonaparte. This very fact was now to get him into no small trouble with his fellow countrymen. Most of the nation thought that the man who had won the Peace of Tilsit from Prussia in 1807 would rehabilitate Poland, on the ruins of other empires, if necessary. The creation of the Duchy of Warsaw seemed to be the first step, and the victories won by Poniatowski over the Austrians only served to strengthen the loyalties of all to the French cause. Staszic accepted office in the provisional administration, and found new responsibilities added when in 1809 he became President of the Society. But the whole scene changed when Napoleon's armies were driven from Moscow in the terrible winter of 1812. All hopes of a better future as guaranteed by the French Emperor were dashed to the ground; and the man who had always felt that the Polish and Russian peoples ought to hold together could see in what happened a vindication of his view.

Naturally he counted on something like equality and mutual co-operation as the basis of relations, but not even this sufficed to reconcile his fellows. Nor did it help that the eminent and patriotic Adam Czartoryski held the same view. The sentiments of the nation were with Napoleon and with the Polish hero Joseph Poniatowski, who gave his life in the Battle of the Nations in 1813. Such times of crisis are disruptive even of the closest ties, and the catastrophe for Poland reached unheard-of dimensions. It cast a shadow over the life of Father Staszic and in a way he never recovered from it. Two pamphlets record his feelings; one, *On Equilibrium in Europe,* came out immediately after the retreat from Moscow, the other, *New Warnings for Poland,* after the Congress of Viennna, which consummated the Fourth Partition of the land.

As head of the Department of Industry and Commerce in the succeeding regime Staszic labored abundantly to realize his dreams of a strong Poland; but the reactionary turn given to things by the Grand Prince Constantine in spite of Tsar Alexander's promises created such an atmosphere of mistrust and ill will in the land as to paralyze all constructive efforts. Only at home, in his own small community, could he hope to see realized a part of his dream; and here came into being the Hrubieszów Agricultural Society.

This organization was really a farmer's co-operative, the aim of which was to promote better tillage of the soil, better handling of produce and profits, and even the cultural improvement of its members. A limit of about forty acres per farm was set for the members, and poorly handled property was to be taken from careless owners to be given to more deserving ones. A community bank, a community school, and co-operative stores were a part of the enterprise, which was made economically sound by the fact that the promoter gave his own estate as the nucleus of the new scheme. To secure the project a rescript was obtained from the Tsar in person in June 1822, so that the community could claim to enjoy imperial patronage.

Unfortunately the splendid example of reconstruction thus set found little favor, and was not copied by a single other estate owner in the land. It existed for over a generation, only to succumb in time to intrigue from without. Obviously such communities were a serious obstacle to all the Russian plans for assimilation, and had to be abolished sooner or later. Meantime Staszic had brought on himself the ill will of a Polish colleague, Franciszek Lubecki, an able and ambitious man who became Minister of Finance in 1821. No less a patriot than Staszic, he was vain of his personal influence, and he used his relations with the Grand Prince to get control of the State Mining Interests—the apple of Staszic's eye. Worse was to follow. More and more the real designs of the Tsarist regime began to manifest themselves, and the rise of new leaders made the prospects of co-operation between ruler and ruled darker each year. Staszic could do nothing, so he withdrew, a more or less disillusioned man.

The death of Tsar Alexander toward the end of the year 1825 was a hard blow to the Polish leader. Believing in the good will of that potentate toward all Russia's subject peoples, Staszic hoped to the last for things which were slipping out of sight. He was doubtless too optimistic, too trusting where love for his people was in question. In any case even he now felt that his hopes were delusions; and his own end was probably hastened by this fact. It came early in the new year.

One day before it, the poet Koźmian, his one-time pupil, visited him. To Koźmian Staszic commended his village Society in eloquent terms. "Keep in mind, watch and care for my Hrubie-szów Association. I know your way of thinking and your integrity. You have stood for the villagers in your writings; defend and pro-tect that institution both from interference by government and from abuses on the part of those whom I put in charge of it. Let it flourish. Its consequences will be useful and significant for the land. This I charge you, as you love your country!"

By his own directions his funeral was to be as simple as had been his manner of life. Even as a Cabinet Minister he had eschewed all show or extravagance. He would choose the cheap-est seats in the top gallery of the theater, and the students about him would always hold a place for him if he came late. It is told of him that on one occasion he had driven out of town in a shabby carriage with one horse, and the local customs official (who was somewhat the worse for liquor) had refused to admit him on his return. No explanations availed until someone came along who knew him and rescued him from detention. The official was sent to jail for some months, but when he came out and visited the Minister to beg his pardon, he was recompensed by Staszic for the time he had lost. Always accustomed to the most modest dwellings in this world, he preferred a simple coffin as his last resting place. He would die as a simple Christian; "for before God," he said, "we are all equal."

Like most great men, Father Staszic had his foibles, and some of these have been magnified into faults. He has been accused of miserliness, because he did not do enough for his own kith and kin. The answer is simply that he saw things in a larger way, and gave all he was and had to the nation. By this alone, even if he had done nothing else, he won his place in the gallery of Poland's immortals.

PRINCE ADAM CZARTORYSKI

(From a steel engraving by Léopold Massard, a French artist)

XIV

PRINCE ADAM CZARTORYSKI
Statesman, Soldier, Diplomatist

1770-1861

by

MARCELI HANDELSMAN

ADAM JERZY CZARTORYSKI, born in Warsaw on January 14, 1770, was the son of Prince Adam Kazimierz and Izabella (nee Fleming) Czartoryski. From his earliest childhood he received a most careful training and the best instruction obtainable, especially along lines of history, political science, classics, mathematics and modern languages. In his youth he showed a special gift for drawing, painting, and writing poetry, and besides Polish spoke fluently Latin, French, English and German, in time also mastering Russian and Italian. Very industrious, though not always concentrated in any particular direction, he kept on expanding the boundaries of his knowledge and interests—not neglecting such arts and social amenities as fencing, shooting, horseback riding and dancing, required by the code of his social position. Always a conscientious and indefatigable worker, from his earliest youth he had the inner urge to keep on improving himself intellectually and morally, and to that urge he remained faithful to the end of his life.

His father regarded travel as an indispensable part of good education. Therefore, in 1786, he sent the young student prince to Germany where he became acquainted with Goethe, among other men of letters. Later on his mother took him to France, Switzerland, Holland, England, and Scotland. For a while he studied at the University of Edinburgh. In England he painstakingly observed the functions of local self-government, listened to Parliamentary debates, visited farms and factories, and met leading English writers and painters. These early travels in England enabled him to formulate for the rest of his life certain policies of liberal Toryism, and to make friendships which proved valuable in 1814 and after.

Prince Adam returned to Poland in the spring of 1791, in time to witness the historic event of the promulgation of the Constitution of the third of May. Moved by the patriotic fervor that reigned in his family, in 1792 he joined the Polish Army as a volunteer and distinguished himself for personal bravery in a short-lived but disastrous campaign against the Russians. After this episode, which left him deeply devoted to Kościuszko, he went again to Vienna and to London, and was outside the country when the Kościuszko Insurrection of 1794 broke out.[1]

During the Kościuszko Insurrection the town of Puławy, where the Czartoryskis had a famous palace, was pillaged and the family estates in provinces seized by Russia were confiscated by the Russian Government. Trying to save at least some of these estates, the Czartoryski family decided to send their two sons, Adam and Constantine, to the Court of St. Petersburg. After considerable internal struggle young Prince Adam decided to sacrifice his personal scruples for the sake of his family and, together with his brother, left for Russia at the end of January, 1795.

It was the Twelfth of May, 1795 [says Prince Adam in his *Memoirs*][2] when my brother and I arrived at St. Petersburg. In

[1] There is a difference of opinion as to where young Czartoryski was during the Kościuszko Insurrection. In Prince Czartoryski's own memoirs there is a break from 1787 to May 12, 1795. To fill the gap, the editor of the English edition of the Memoirs, Adam Gielgud, gives the following version (Vol. I, pp. 53-4): "In 1793, he again went to England and entered into close relations with nearly all the politicians of note in that country. It was while he was still staying there in 1794 that the Kosciuszko Insurrection broke out. Directly he heard the news, he hurried back, to join the insurgents, but was stopped at Brussels and put in arrest under orders from the Austrian Government. Meanwhile the insurrection was suppressed, and the third partition of Poland took place. Soon after the Prince rejoined his parents at Vienna, where the Emperor Francis intervened with the Empress Catherine of Russia to cancel the confiscation of the estates of the Czartoryski family, ordered by her in consequence of their participation in the insurrection. The Empress insisted, as a condition of entering into negotiations on this subject, that the two young princes [i.e., Adam and his brother Constantine] should go to St. Petersburg to enter the Russian service, and after much deliberation at a family council this condition was accepted."—*Ed.*

[2] Vol. I, p. 55.—*Ed.*

order to form an idea of our feelings on entering that city, it is necessary to know the principles in which we were brought up. Our education had been entirely Polish and Republican [i.e. liberal]. The love of our country, of its glories, its institutions, and its liberties had been inculcated into us by our studies, and by everything we had seen or heard around us. I should add that this feeling, which penetrated the whole of our moral nature, was accompanied by an invincible aversion to all who had contributed to the ruin of the fatherland which we so much loved.

This twofold sentiment of love and hatred dominated me so entirely, that I could not meet a Russian either in Poland or elsewhere without feeling a rush of blood to the head—without blushing or turning white with anger—for every Russian seemed to me an author of the misfortune of my country.

My first task was promptly to replace on a satisfactory footing the affairs of my father. Three-fourths of his fortune, all consisting of land situated in the provinces seized by Russia, had been sequestrated. These estates were mortgaged to a considerable extent, so that not only my father's own property, but also that of a great number of our countrymen, was in question. The representation made in my father's favor by the Court of Vienna had had no result. Catherine was provoked by the patriotism of my father and mother, and their sympathy with the Kosciuszko Insurrection. "Let their two sons come to me," she said, "and then we will see." She wished to keep us as hostages.

The high life of the Court, full of gaieties but likewise of dangers, intrigues and stratagems, did not deaden his longing for the homeland nor his deep sorrow caused, as he expressed it, "by the sad position in which we were placed." He and his brother at the court of his country's enemy, while Kościuszko and his comrades were in Russian prisons and Polish patriots were heading the Polish legions in Italy!

Into that melancholy life there peeped for a moment an unexpected ray of hope in the spring of 1796 when the grandson of Empress Catherine II, the Grand Duke Alexander, formed with young Prince Adam Czartoryski what appeared to be a deep friendship. The Grand Duke denounced the policy of force followed by his unscrupulous grandmother; he seemed to be an enthusiast for freedom and favored Poland. In that friendship Adam Czartoryski found the purpose of his life's work and hoped that by his sojourn in St. Petersburg he could really do something for Poland and the Poles. His heart was on fire and his head was swarming with ideas. No wonder. Only yesterday, an exile from Poland, he was trembling before the Empress Catherine as he pleaded for the favor of restoring to his parents their confiscated estates. Today he was so close to the Grand Duke Alexander (whose age was eighteen), possibly the future Czar of Russia, that the latter, in utmost secrecy, asked him to prepare a State Manifesto to be promulgated in case the Grand Duke should suddenly be called upon to be the ruler of Russia. The Manifesto was prepared, though it never saw the light of day; Poland was to be free, and everybody was to be happy.[3]

The illusion was short-lived. The Empress Catherine died in November, 1796; and Paul, her son, and not Alexander, her grandson, succeeded to the throne. To be sure, Paul released Polish prisoners from Russian jails, but did not change the system. A new era of repressions commenced. All trembled before the uncertainties of the future, not excluding the Grand Duke Alexander and his friends.

[3] Prince Czartoryski (in his *Memoirs*, Vol. I, p. 110-13) reports on his first intimate discussion with the Grand Duke Alexander as follows:

"The Grand Duke asked me to come to him to the Tauris Palace for a walk in the garden. . . . I am sorry I did not take note of the exact date, for that day had a decisive influence on a great part of my life and on the destinies of my country. . . . Our conversation then led to a mutual friendship. . . . The Grand Duke told me that he had felt it necessary to let us know what he really thought. He added that he did not in any way share the ideas and doctrines of the Cabinet and the Court, and that he was far from approving the policy and conduct of his grandmother, whose principles he condemned. He had wished for the success of Poland in her glorious struggle and had deplored her fall. Kosciuszko, he said, was in his eyes a man who was great by his virtues and the cause which he had defended, which was the cause of humanity and of justice. He added that he detested despotism everywhere, no matter in what form it was exercised; that he loved liberty, to which all men had a right.

"I was deeply moved, and could hardly believe my ears. That a Russian Prince, Catherine's successor, her grandson and her favorite child, whom she would have wished to see reigning after her instead of her son, and of whom it was said that he would continue her reign, should disavow and detest his grandmother's principles—should repel the odious policy of Russia—should be a passionate lover of Justice and liberty—should pity Poland and wish to see her happy—seemed incredible. And that such noble ideas and great virtues should be able to grow and flourish in such an atmosphere and with such surroundings, was surely little less than a miracle.

"My attachment to him was boundless, and the feeling with which he inspired me at that moment lasted even after the illusions which had given birth to it successively disappeared."—*Ed.*

One of the first blows was directed against Prince Adam. At first the Emperor threatened to send him to Siberia, then changed his mind and nominated him Envoy to Sardinia (August 12, 1799). Whether an exile in Siberia or an Envoy to Sardinia, it apparently made no difference to the new potentate. Prince Adam had to leave Russia immediately to proceed to his destination. He could not even visit his parents.

The Emperor Paul was murdered in 1801 and the Grand Duke Alexander succeeded him—the liberal, Western-minded Alexander who five years back had planned to make Poland free and everybody happy. The New Czar forthwith recalled Prince Czartoryski from Sardinia. Apparently bigger things were in store for him. He returned to St. Petersburg in July, 1801. Although the changes wrought looked favorable, and he was received cordially, he hesitated to accept new appointments, honors and duties that would collide with his conception of responsibilities as a Pole.

But compromise was necessary. He was willing to accept appointments that would give him an opportunity, directly or indirectly, to plug away at the "Polish Question." In 1802 he became Vice Minister and in 1804 Minister of Foreign Affairs; and in 1803 he was appointed Inspector of Schools in eight western provinces of Russia, a position including the control of the University of Wilno, which he held till 1824.

Raised to such a high position in Russia in spite of himself, frequently called upon to give his counsel on important government decisions, Prince Adam Czartoryski became convinced that by faithful service to Russia he could render really important service to his country, Poland, and his compatriots. He was grateful to the Emperor for the liberation of Poles from Siberia, for the restitution of their properties and for the intervention of the Emperor in behalf of Poles even under Austrian regime. During his incumbency as Minister of Foreign Affairs, Czartoryski constantly argued—in personal conferences with the Emperor Alexander, in written memoranda, in the Council of State—that the peace of the world should be based on Russian-English understanding and on the recognition of Napoleonic France. He regarded Austria and still more Prussia as the greatest enemies of

Russia. Their rights to independent existence should be recognized, but no further concessions given them. Germany should be organized beyond these two states. The integrity of Turkey should be respected, but the Slavonic nations of the Balkans should enjoy autonomy under Russian benevolent protectorate. Russia's relations toward a restored Poland, united with her under the rule of the King-Emperor, should be the criterion of the whole system's sincerity. Unfortunately other counsels in the Court of St. Petersburg prevailed.

The turning point came in 1805 when Russia was heading toward war with Napoleon, in spite of Czartoryski's counsels and warnings. Instead of trying to win the Poles for a war against Prussia, Alexander went to Berlin with his Minister of Foreign Affairs and there forced him to sign a treaty of friendship with the Prussians. This treaty gave nothing either to Russia or to Poland. From Berlin they hastened to Austerlitz, to witness a defeat. When they returned to St. Petersburg the Emperor, who could do no wrong, put the blame on his Minister, and the latter merely tendered his resignation, which was not accepted until the following year.

Though Minister of Foreign Affairs no longer, Prince Adam Czartoryski kept on trying to solve the Polish question, somehow, with the aid and within the sphere of influence of Russia. Now he would approach the problem from one end, then from another, but all his efforts were of no avail. In November, 1806, he tried to instigate the Polish nobility in Lithuania against Napoleon, but Alexander opposed this movement. In April, 1807, he tried to incite the Poles of Warsaw against Napoleon—while urging that Alexander proclaim himself King of Poland—but this, too, was fruitless.

In the meanwhile events moved swiftly, beyond his control, in an unexpected direction: the reconstruction of a part of Poland, with Warsaw as a nucleus, under a Saxon king but without the name of Poland.[4] Warsaw was then attracting Poles from the

---

[4] The so-called Duchy of Warsaw, a temporary arrangement (1807-15), was established by the Treaty of Tilsit in 1807 by Napoleon. It consisted of territories seized by Prussia in the second and third partitions of Poland and was enlarged in 1809 by a part of Austrian Poland. Frederick Augustus, the Saxon King, was the reigning Duke.—*Ed.*

other two sections of partitioned Poland and practically the entire population was ready to serve under Napoleon. Prince Adam alone, suspected in St. Petersburg and not trusted in Warsaw, was outside this national movement. Suddenly, in January, 1811, the Emperor Alexander called upon him to try to win the Poles and their army against Napoleon, but it was hopeless. In 1812 the Poles rose against Russia under the nominal leadership of his own father, Prince Adam Kazimierz Czartoryski, and all the plans of Prince Adam the younger were broken.

When in December, 1812, the Warsaw leaders of the Polish movement were convinced that Napoleon would lose, they advanced the proposition to the Emperor Alexander that the Duchy of Warsaw be joined to Russia as an autonomous state, under Russian hegemony but with a separate Polish Constitution. They called upon Prince Adam to serve as intermediary in these negotiations. He did so, and awaited a reply. In the meanwhile Russian armed forces were occupying the Duchy of Warsaw and the country was groaning under the occupation. Prince Adam interceded with the Emperor for his country but nothing came out of it. Then he went to France and to England, and pleaded with the Allies, advancing the plan of uniting the eight Polish northeastern provinces under Russia to the Duchy of Warsaw as an autonomous Polish state. He renewed his old friendships and made new contacts; became acquainted with new statesmen, warmed up the English a little and saw through Talleyrand. Though he found himself between the devil of the growing Russian enmity and the deep blue sea of indifference of the West, he did not lay down his arms in the fight for a better future for his country.

He was present at the Congress of Vienna (1814) to plead the cause of Poland. If there was ever an occasion to play both ends toward the middle, this was the one. The world has perhaps never seen a gathering of more clever diplomats playing the game of power politics. Prince Adam first represented the victorious Emperor Alexander in the difficult negotiations with the latter's adversary, Castlereagh of England, and his alleged allies: the wily Metternich and the brutal Prussians. Then in the same breath he had to plead the cause of Poland before the tribunal of western

Europe, against the annexationist arguments of the other Russian
plenipotentiaries. Finding himself in a deep conflict between the
Czar of Russia, who was to take Poland under his protection, on
one side and on the other side western Europe and England, that
was to guarantee Poland's relative independence and internal institutions, Prince Adam Czartoryski finally succeeded in the
realization of his program. On May 3, 1815, the Congress of
Vienna created the so-called Congress Kingdom of Poland—a
small, autonomous state, united with Russia under the rule of
Alexander, but having its own army; local self-government and
economic integrity were promised to the other parts of former
Poland.

Thereupon the Emperor Alexander delegated to Prince
Czartoryski the function of preparing the new Polish constitution, liberal in tone but with ample safeguards for the interests of
Russia. This done, Alexander put Czartoryski brutally aside, never
to be called back to any position of importance.

Thus were shattered forever Prince Adam Czartoryski's
idyllic dreams of youth, his hopes of young manhood, and his
works of mature statesmanship.

The first blow under the new order came when the Emperor
Alexander, instead of naming Tadeusz Kościuszko (the Polish
national patriot and American Revolutionary war hero) as commander in chief of the Polish Army and Czartoryski as viceroy,
nominated his own brother, Grand Duke Constantine, for the first
place and a servile general, Zajączek, for the second.

As conditions in the Congress Kingdom went from relatively good to bad, and then from bad to worse under the cruel
rule of Constantine, a half-crazed despot of unbridled temper,
Prince Czartoryski at first retired (in 1816) to the quiet of his
home to settle his long-neglected personal affairs, and then devoted
the rest of his life to the service of his country, in open disregard
of the interests of Russia. Although he still felt a lingering friendship for the person of Alexander, he knew that the interests of the
two countries could no longer be reconciled. He continued to believe that Alexander was still liberal-minded, but that he was weak
and vacillating and surrounded by advisers who were working not
for reconciliation but for the subordination of Poland to Russia.

His personal affairs were not sailing smoothly either. Not to mention the complicated material situation, his belated marriage also caused a crisis. For a long time he had sought the hand of Anna Sapieha, the daughter of another noble Polish family, but his mother objected. He finally married her (September 25, 1817), to the accompaniment of two duels with his rival, named Pac. This "scandal" left him with a wound and a considerable amount of undesirable publicity. But it also gave him an excuse for retiring from public life temporarily.

In retirement as a statesman, he retained for several years his position as Inspector (Curator) of Schools in the northeastern provinces. In that capacity, having selected the best Polish collaborators he could find (among them the celebrated Polish historian and educator, Tadeusz Czacki), Czartoryski worked in two general directions. From the very beginning he paid especial attention to the University of Wilno, in the selection of professors, in the preparation of the program of studies and in the solicitous care of its students. It was his burning desire to recreate in Wilno a real center of Polish studies so that it could radiate its influence into other parts of Poland—and perhaps into other kindred Slavonic nations. He felt that the best thing a nation like Poland in political bondage could do was to preserve its traditions and cultivate its cultural heritage. His second objective was to extend primary education to the masses, through the medium of Parochial Schools. It has been said that during the term of his office, in twenty odd years, he succeeded in "polonizing" the mixed population of these districts even to a larger extent than when Poland was independent.

Prince Czartoryski's interests in political problems continued and he kept himself thoroughly informed of all secret movements of his compatriots in Warsaw. Under one pretext or another (his own or his wife's health) he traveled through Germany, Switzerland, France, and Italy, trying to arouse such public opinion as might prove articulate with a view to bettering the existing conditions in the Congress Kingdom.

When Alexander died in 1825, under mysterious circumstances, Constantine, till then the virtual military dictator of Poland, found himself in personal opposition to the new Czar Nicholas I of Russia. The new situation gave Czartoryski full moral freedom of action. He became the moving spirit of legal opposition to Muscovite policies, of the defense of Polish youth—especially students—against force and injustice, and of the constitutional rights of the Poles against the brutal disregard of these rights by the Czarist regime. By 1830 Prince Czartoryski had gained the highest personal authority among Polish patriotic elements in Warsaw. This conservative statesman, imbued with the spirit of western liberalism, fought the cause of Poland with all the moral arguments at his command. His book, *Essai sur la Diplomatie* (published in France in August, 1830, under the pseudonym of Philhellen), contains his political philosophy. The world can survive, he argued, only if it lives in peace; and peace is possible only through an effective league of nations fully recognizing and guaranteeing to each member its national rights.

Although he would have preferred to see Poland restored to her full independence through peaceful means, together with a better international order, the oppressed Poles decided on direct action and in November, 1830, started an insurrection against Russia. Prince Czartoryski was against the uprising, but by virtue of his position felt duty-bound to urge the Administrative Council [5] to speedy action. Negotiations followed with Grand Duke Constantine who, in the meanwhile, left Warsaw. Consequently, the Administrative Council was abolished and a temporary government established. Placed at the head of that government, Prince Czartoryski tried to localize events and through negotiations, supported by the threat of such force as he might be able to gather, to gain the desired constitutional concessions from the Czar of Russia. But the plan miscarried. If the insurrection were to be successful, an army had to be raised, Austria neutralized, the support of France and England gained. He realized all that, but events called for a strong hand and he had no ambition to be a ruler, much less a dictator, which the situation demanded. He had the power to act but did not use it; he consulted his colleagues, whose counsels were divided. The Diet decided to dethrone the Russian Czar as King of Poland (January 25, 1831), and to or-

[5] The administrative branch of the Congress Kingdom of Poland, acting mostly in an advisory capacity.—*Ed.*

ganize a national government. Prince Czartoryski consented to serve as titular head of the government but passed on the authority that he himself might have exercised, at first to one general as commander in chief, then to another, though neither was fully competent to carry on the insurrection to a successful conclusion. The fact is that Poland was not fully prepared in a military way to wage a successful war against a big power. France and England declined to intervene, and the insurrection failed. On August 17, 1831, Prince Czartoryski left Warsaw, never to see his native land again. The Russian forces occupied Warsaw on September 6 and remained until the first World War.

Prince Czartoryski barely escaped with his life. Condemned to death by Russia, his estates confiscated, the great moral prestige he once had among his compatriots lost, he was burdened with the consciousness of sins of omission, and accusations of sins he had never committed followed him. He was held personally responsible for the failure of the November Insurrection. At first he sought asylum in England, then went to Paris in 1833, and there remained for the rest of his life.

Now began the third period of his life and work. First, in the Court of St. Petersburg as a hostage, as a friend and confidant of the Czarevitch, later Czar Alexander, as a Minister in the service of Russia with a hope of doing something for Poland in the court of his county's enemy. When that failed, came the second period: service in the Government he had helped create in Warsaw, and then open rebellion. That also failed. Now came the third period, that of exile and such work as could be done under the new conditions: all of Poland occupied by the three partitioning powers (the largest share under Russia), with some of the best brains of Poland also in exile, mostly in France.

Prince Adam Czartoryski was the original founder of a Polish Government in Exile [6] while the country was under total foreign domination. When he settled in Paris he purchased an old palace, Hôtel Lambert, and converted it into a center of Polish cultural and political activities. Cultivation of Polish cultural traditions

[6] The Polish Committee in France during the first World War, headed by Roman Dmowski and Ignace Jan Paderewski, as well as the Polish Government in Exile in Paris, Angers and London during the second World War that began in September 1939, are familiar to American readers.—*Ed.*

among the Polish *émigrés* in France as well as in other countries, with sporadic penetration into occupied territory, and political propaganda of the Polish Question among statesmen and peoples that would listen to him, were the two tasks to which he devoted his entire energy for the balance of his life. In fact the two functions merged into one channel with a double objective: to arouse public opinion everywhere to the sense of historic injustice that had been done to Poland and gain friends that would help restore her independence; and secondly, to prepare his compatriots in exile for active participation in whatever events that might present themselves to bring about restoration.

The Hôtel Lambert became a buzzing beehive of Polish patriotic, educational, and political activity. Here a school for Polish girls was housed, whence he directed a Polish Library and research center, a Historical-Literary Society (and various associations granting scholarships), a Literary Society of French Friends of Poland, fraternal benevolent organizations and offices of periodic and scientific publications. From that center emanated and radiated influences into occupied Poland, where Czartoryski had formed a network of secret organizations, and into every country where conflicts might arise and the Polish Question be given a hearing. While the national poet of Poland, Mickiewicz, prayed for "a war of nations" so that readjustments might be possible, Czartoryski was constantly on the lookout from the watchtower of his Hôtel Lambert for points of friction. Wherever he noticed sparks he was on the spot, so to speak, to present his Polish cause.

At first (until 1838) it seemed that a European conflict might start in Belgium, in Portugal, or in Spain, and in each of those countries he placed Polish officers in responsible positions. Then he turned to the Near East, to the Caucasus, where he thought he might join the Polish Question to the anti-Russian unrest. He also tried to bring about an Anglo-French alliance against Russia.

Prince Czartoryski's enthusiastic supporters went so far as to advocate proclaiming him King of the Poles in exile, which plans he disavowed before his collaborators in Poland. He undertook diplomatic plans, however, on a really gigantic scale. When Anglo-French alliance against Russia did not materialize, he renewed his erstwhile plan of organizing the Western Slavs, with

Poland as a nuclueus, under Turkish hegemony. Turkey's sovereignty and integrity in turn was to be guaranteed by western powers. This grandiose scheme was financed by contributions coming from Poland and through the generosity of Lord Dudley Stuart. With this financial support and the master plan in view, in 1841 he established in Constantinople an Eastern Agency which co-operated closely with his emissaries in Serbia, Bulgaria and Rumania. Later on a Western Agency was also established.

Czartoryski's activities were directed mainly against Russia, but he did not neglect possible conflict with Austria and foresaw the coming revolutionary storm. Its outburst in 1848 revived his hopes; he thought of organizing Polish legions in France, decided to make a hurried trip to Poland, but on his way he stopped in Berlin, whence he returned to Paris completely cured of his illusions. He lost faith in the possibility of Franco-Prussian-Polish war against Russia. Now he was building on the necessity of disrupting Austria; he wanted to create a strong Slavonic block but at the same time tried to reconcile Hungary with Slovaks, Rumanians and Serbs; he also restrained Southern Slavs from anti-Italian and anti-Magyar action. He succeeded in placing one of his Polish generals on the general staff of Sardinia, and at his behest Generals Dembiński and Bem [7] took command of the Hungarian armed forces under Kossuth.

In the same year, 1848, Prince Czartoryski extended his diplomatic activity into the Scandinavian north and, counting upon the possibility of Finnish uprising, visioned a defensive-offensive alliance against Russia between Poland on one hand and Sweden and Norway on the other.

Despite the disastrous results of the events of 1848-49, Prince Czartoryski continued his activity on the Bosphorus, even though on a smaller scale, in anticipation of a general European war. The so-called Crimean War came in 1853-54 and it seemed to open up new possibilities for the Poles. But they were new disappointments.

From 1857 new enterprises absorbed the attention of ever-active Prince Adam. He established a new publishing house in Paris,

---

[7] Gen. Bem so distinguished himself for personal valor that the Hungarians erected a monument in his honor in 1880.—*Ed.*

issued a periodical *News from Poland* (*Wiadomości Polskie*), which gave an excellent reflection of the situation in Poland, and through his new emissaries renewed old contacts with political organizations in the homeland and gradually strengthened these ties. He strongly counseled Polish leaders at home to promote and participate actively in the incipient plan for peasant emancipation in the northeastern provinces.

The year 1859 seemed again decisive in the general European situation. After the defeat of Austria and the triumph of Cavour a new International Congress was expected. Czartoryski pleaded with Napoleon III to raise the Polish Question at such a Congress and to remind the world that Prussia and Austria were not carrying out the provisions of the Treaty of Vienna with respect to Poland.

A year later Prince Czartoryski established in Paris under his own presidency a *Bureau des Affaires Polonaises*, which exerted considerable influence, through Havas, on the French, English and German press, and penetrated into Poland through its own correspondents. Through this medium, from exile, he passed on his last will and political testament to his fellow countrymen at home: to hold fast to peasant emancipation and social progress, and to hold high the standard of complete independence.

Having fought the good fight even though he lost most of the battles, Prince Adam Czartoryski passed on to his reward on July 15, 1861.

A great statesman of a Poland struggling to regain some form of independence, the unusual combination of a freethinker and Freemason, but at the same time a strongly believing Catholic, a man of deep erudition and of indefatigable industry, a strong believer in education both for classes and masses, Prince Adam Czartoryski may truly be regarded as one of the "heroes of defeat." He was a Polish patriot, yet destiny had reserved for him the paradoxical role of working for Poland through the devious path of working for and at the same time fighting Russia, Poland's enemy. He tried to serve two masters for the benefit of one, Poland.

That he did not always succeed, in fact, rarely if at all succeeded, we have seen from the brief sketch of his life. Other considerations besides his paradoxical dual role militated against the success of his policies. Although he had no personal ambitions for power or for wealth, and was always charitable in his disposition even toward his bitter political enemies, he was deeply conscious of the role he was to play on the stage of history because of his birth, training, natural calling and sense of duty. He was endowed with great intellect and uncommon political tact, could foresee distant objectives without losing sight of the immediate practical means at his disposal, but he lacked the ability to judge people, and to select and surround himself with men who would help him carry his visions through. His greatest contribution lay in this, that whether at home or abroad, in the capitals of his country's enemies or of friends, openly or secretly, at peace conferences or on the fields of battle, he always kept the "Polish Question" alive.

Condensed and translated from the Polish by Stephen P. Mizwa.

XV

JOACHIM LELEWEL
Historian and Teacher of Patriotism

1786-1861

by

IGNACY CHRZANOWSKI

JOACHIM LELEWEL, the most eminent Polish historian of all times, was the son of a Polish mother, Ewa Szeluta, and of a Polonized German father, Karl Laelhoeffel de Loewensprung (court surgeon to King Augustus III). Lelewel [1] was born in Warsaw on March 22, 1786. He received his secondary education at the Piarist Fathers' School in Warsaw (1801-4), and attended the University of Wilno (1804-8).

From his childhood he felt an irresistible inclination for history, and during his studies in Wilno he indulged in it with his whole soul. He was also particularly interested in so-called "auxiliary studies," especially in the critical investigations of historical sources, geography and numismatics.

Upon completion of his university work, he taught ancient history and geography for a short time at the Krzemieniec Lyceum, and from 1815 until 1818 was assistant professor of general history at the University of Wilno. From the spring of 1818 until the autumn of 1821, he lectured on bibliography at the University of Warsaw, and later, on general history. His university lectures in Wilno, as well as in Warsaw, won him great popularity among the students, which continued to increase, when, at the beginning of 1822, he once more started lecturing on general his-

---

[1] His German name was too complicated; he therefore changed it into a simplified Polish name: Lelewel.

JOACHIM LELEWEL
(From a contemporary lithograph done in Brussels)

tory at the University in Wilno. The best expression of the joy of the students on the return of their beloved professor is the poem by Mickiewicz, "To Joachim Lelewel." But their joy was of short duration; in August, 1824, Lelewel, Gołuchowski and two other professors were dismissed on the accusation of the Russian Governor, Novosiltsov, who thought that if the students, particularly those belonging to the organizations called the Philomats and the Philarets, "wanted to spread unreasonable Polish nationalism by means of learning," it was in large measure the work of Lelewel. Novosiltsov was perfectly right: Lelewel considered it not only as a point of honor and ambition, but his sacred duty, to pour patriotic feelings into the hearts of his young hearers. He returned to Warsaw, but could not think of returning to his lectures, in view of the policy of the Grand Duke Constantine, the Czarist Governor of the Congress Kingdom of Poland. To a man of Lelewel's character, however, it was impossible to think of renouncing his patriotic work. He continued to spread "unreasonable Polish nationalism" with the help of books, which were partly works of pure research, and partly popular accounts of great historical subjects. They followed each other as if poured forth from a veritable cornucopia.

He worked with the students privately in his own apartment, spreading among them, to the great indignation of the "classicists," the cult of Mickiewicz and the love of the national past and of liberty, in defense of which he exerted himself actively, in secret as a member of the Patriotic Society, and openly as a deputy to the Diet from the Żelechów District.

The Insurrection of 1830-31 broke out. Lelewel knew that it would come; he knew it from this young generation, which considered him an "infallible oracle," not only in matters of learning but also of politics. But a bitter disappointment followed. The great scholar turned out to be a poor politician. He was a member, at the same time, of the National Government and of the Patriotic Society, in spite of the obvious contradictions in views between those two bodies concerning the means to be employed in their fight for independence. No wonder he was accused of insincerity and opportunism. And his quarrelsome disposition, his stubbornness, presumption, and impetuosity, together with the boldness of his democratic and republican views, drew down upon him the most infamous calumnies.

After the suppression of the Insurrection, Lelewel settled in Paris among the Polish emigrants. But he did not give up politics. He was chosen President of the National Committee, but in this position, apart from issuing appeals to foreigners, he achieved nothing remarkable. On the contrary, by his behavior he only fomented "accursed squabbles," as the poet Mickiewicz calls them, among the unfortunate emigrants. And to tell the truth, the French Government, in banishing Lelewel as an "anarchist, a leader and instigator of revolutionary riot," did no injury to the Polish emigrants—but rather rendered a great service to Polish learning and to the Polish cause in general: because Lelewel settled in the capital of Belgium (which loved and adored him) where he could again devote himself exclusively to his labors of research. This he did in spite of the financial misery into which his personal pride, which did not allow him to accept any help whatever from his compatriots, had thrown him.

Here, in Brussels, appeared his two monumental works in French, which form the cornerstone of his world-wide fame as a scholar: *Numismatique du Moyen Age* and *Géographie du Moyen Age*, and another work in French which crowned his innumerable studies on Polish history and its sources: *Considérations sur l'État Politique de l'Ancienne Pologne et sur l'Histoire de son Peuple* (1844). This work, in the author's own Polish translation, appeared ten years later, with the title: *Remarks on the History of Poland and its People*.[2]

Also in Brussels Lelewel prepared for publication a work in four volumes, which was in the main a collection of his earlier studies: *Poland of the Middle Ages, or Observations on Polish National History*.[3] He did not live to see the complete edition of his works. He died on May 29, 1861, in Paris, where he had been brought three days before his death by two of his friends, presumably for the purpose of improving his health. His body was laid to rest provisionally in Paris, in the cemetery of Mont-

---

[2] *Uwagi nad Dziejami Polski i Ludu Jej.*

[3] *Polska Wieków Średnich czyli w Dziejach Narodowych Polskich Postrzeżenia* (1846-51).

martre, and on October 9, 1929, was transported to Wilno.

"If I have rendered any service to my country, it has been in no other field than that of learning." In saying this of himself, Lelewel told the truth. In the field of politics he was of no service to his country—and rather, did it an injury. But in the field of learning he rendered services which must be called immense, both as a research worker and as a teacher of the young generation and of the whole nation. As a research worker he indeed laid the foundation for modern Polish historiography. He was the first to apply strictly scholarly methods of criticism to historical sources (on principles unknown to his eighteenth-century predecessor Naruszewicz); he was also the first to understand properly the importance of "auxiliary studies" for the science of history, and in this province he made innumerable researches of great importance. He was the first who not only in theory, as had been done by Naruszewicz, but also in practice, treated the history of Poland as the history not merely of a state, but also of a nation, which means the history of the whole national civilization. He was the first to give a deeper meaning to the idea of historical pragmatism, searching for the true causes of the course of national events in the action of prominent and of less prominent individuals, and in physical factors (as had been done by Montesquieu), and above all in the particular national character and in the "spirit of the time." He was the first who, having understood this axiom, laid the basis for comparative researches in the history of different nations. He was the first to break with the chronicler's arrangement of historical narrative, grouping the events, not mechanically by years, but organically by their inward connections. He divided history into epochs, not according to dynasties or the reigns of particular sovereigns, but according to certain social, political, and intellectual tendencies.

All these research labors of Lelewel enabled him to create the first really scholarly survey of the whole of Poland's history in his work, *Remarks on the History of Poland and Her People*. This survey could, in its most general outlines, be summarized as follows: the golden age of the Polish nation was the pre-Christian era in which the "estate of workers on the land was equal with that of its defenders," that is to say, the peasants were equal with the gentry. The contest between those two estates for liberty and equality, and the later contest between the victorious gentry and nobility against the crown, constitute the essence of Polish history. During the whole of his life Lelewel dreamed of liberty, equality and fraternity, as of treasures lying deeply embedded in Polish national character. From the point of view of these dreams and of this belief, he appraised the history of his beloved country. As he considered every social injury to any class, that is, the deprivation of any of the classes of those treasures, as a crime against his country, so he considered it a great merit if at least a part of the nation was endowed with them. This is why he admired the so-called "democracy of the gentry," why he considered the period of its flourishing as the golden age of pre-Christian Poland.

But the democracy of the gentry "went astray," and this was thanks to the foreign spirit which slowly warped the national character. This foreign spirit spread, thanks to the "power of the Roman Court" and of the Jesuit Order, and to the foreign kings and the foreign fashions of the aristocracy.

These are the chief causes of the "moral decay" of Poland, which prepared the "fall of the country and its institutions" (with the efficient help of Poland's three predatory neighbors).

The *Remarks* of Lelewel had an immense influence on the later development of Polish historiography, and by the daring of their constructive treatment and the strength of the impression they produced, they were to be equaled only much later by a work written in a completely different spirit, *The History of Poland in Outline*, by Michael Bobrzyński (1877).

Lelewel was not only a great scholar, but was also a great national teacher, at the University as well as in his popular books. The best idea of the spirit in which he lectured can be conveyed by his lecture; *The Rescue of Poland in the Time of King Łokietek*,[4] read at the University of Wilno on June 29, 1822. From this lecture we can see that he really meant what he said in his book *The Science of History*,[5] that not only the ideal of the True but also that of the Good should be the guiding star of a

[4] *Ocalemie Polski za Króla Łokietka.*
[5] Historyka.

historian; and as the supreme spiritual good of a nation he considered patriotism and faithfulness to the national spirit, which does not exclude progress.

These two ideals were his leading motives when he wrote that popular book, which for a long time enjoyed a popularity not less than the *Historical Songs* [6] of Niemcewicz. The title of the first edition (1829) is: *The History of Poland Told in a Popular Way by Joachim Lelewel.* [7] Since 1843, when this schoolbook first appeared, the number of editions has reacheed fifteen; the last one appeared thirty years after the death of the author under the title: *The History of Poland Told by the Uncle to His Nephews.* [8]

Until the present day, we have had no other book on the history of independent Poland uniting popularity of style with such a high patriotic spirit (though free from infatuation) and with such universality; for although Lelewel concentrated his attention chiefly on political events, he also took into consideration other branches of civilization.

From this book of Lelewel's, the young generation as well as the old learned to know the past of Poland and the Polish national spirit, and learned how to love it. And this is his greatest merit, not only in the history of Polish learning, but in the general history of the Polish nation.

[6] *Śpiewy Historyczne.*
[7] *Dzieje Polski Joachim Lelewel Potocznym Sposobem Opowiedział.*
[8] *Dzieje Polski, które stryj synowcom swoim opowiedział.*
Translated from the Polish by Elizabeth Clark Reis.

XVI

ADAM MICKIEWICZ
"The National Poet of Poland"

1798-1855

by

Manfred Kridl

I

THE foreigner would doubtless find the conditions and circumstances surrounding the life and creative work of Adam Mickiewicz difficult to understand without a knowledge of the historical background of the period and of the vicissitudes of the Polish nation during that period. Mickiewicz was born on December 24, 1798, three years after the final partition of Poland, on territory taken over by Russia in the vicinity of Nowogródek, in the erstwhile Grand Duchy of Lithuania which was then in union with Poland. He stemmed from the moderately well-to-do country gentry, settled in this region for centuries. His childhood and boyhood were spent in that milieu which he was later to depict in the Polish epic *Pan Tadeusz*. In the very beginning of its rule over that part of Poland, Russia left certain liberties to the Poles and allowed some of the old autonomic institutions to continue. Hence, during the youth of Mickiewicz, Polish courts, Polish local self-government, and Polish schools still existed. Mickiewicz received his early education in the parochial secondary school at Nowogródek; upon the completion of this *gimnazjum*, he entered the University of Wilno, founded in 1579 by the Polish King, Stefan Batory, and reorganized in the early part of the nineteenth century, chiefly because of the efforts of Prince Adam Czartoryski.

ADAM MICKIEWICZ

(From a charcoal sketch done posthumously on the basis of known
likenesses, by L. Horowitz in Warsaw, 1873)

This University was at that time the best in Poland; it possessed all the university faculties and numbered among its professors such scholars of European repute as the astronomer Jan Śniadecki, the chemist and physician Jędrzej Śniadecki, as well as the historian Joachim Lelewel. Wilno, at that time the capital of a large section of Poland, was a city humming with activity, attracting to itself the gentry of the vicinity and possessing an extensive social life. The University was the center of a lively intellectual movement which radiated over the entire city and beyond, and which found partial expression in the impressive array of serious periodicals then appearing in Wilno.

Thus the young Mickiewicz encountered at the University conditions favorable to the development of his innate abilities. He studied in the humanistic faculty, devoting the major part of his time to Polish literature, ancient languages, and history. His studies were serious and deep, as is borne out by the fact that twenty years after the completion of his university work, followed by a difficult and stormy period in his life, he was able to accept the chair of Latin language and literature offered him by the University of Lausanne in Switzerland, and to teach these subjects with surprising knowledge of his field and with great success. The integrity of his university preparation is further evidenced by the fact that one year after his Lausanne appointment, he was able to take over the chair of Slavonic literature in the *Collège de France*.

The interests of the young Mickiewicz, however, were not confined to study. He plunged wholeheartedly into the activities of the student organization, the Philomats and the Philarets, which evolved from study club into a vast organization embracing various groups and various degrees of scientific and social endeavor. Their slogan was "Motherland, Study and Virtue," bespeaking a patriotic, intellectual and moral upbringing. Unfortunately, the activity of this society lasted but a few years. The Russian government came upon its trail and regarding its program as too menacing to the Russian state, dissolved it, arresting its outstanding members and sending them into the interior of Russia.

Mickiewicz attended the University of Wilno for four years (1815-19). He then left for a stay of several years in Kowno, as a secondary schoolteacher, without, however, severing his contact with Wilno and its intellectual movement and his beloved Society of Philomats. In 1824 he was arrested with other Philomats and, after a six months' imprisonment, was deported to Russia. It did not occur to him that he would never see his native land again.

The first epoch of the life of Mickiewicz came to an end. It was an exuberant life, rich, intense, beautiful, replete with work, friendship, poetic creativeness, and love—a love that was deep, ardent, even requited, but unhappy none the less because of the too great class difference between the poor student and his beloved, the daughter of a wealthy aristocratic house.

Already the powerful individuality of Mickiewicz had found its strongest expression in the realm of poetry. In the years 1822 and 1823 he published the first two slender volumes of his poetry. By virtue of these he was immediately recognized as the moving spirit of the contemporary poetic movement in Poland, the master and herald of romanticism, at first still moderate in tone, but in the second volume already extreme and revolutionary.

The poet's sojourn in Russia lasted four years. It was marked by a magnificent growth of poetic talent (to which the *Crimean Sonnets*, published in 1826, bear eloquent testimony) and by a closer acquaintance with official, literary, and underground, revolutionary Russia. Mickiewicz acquired a justifiable distaste for the Russia of the officialdom, but entered into friendly relations with the young Russian literati and revolutionists. But he was eager to go out into the world, desirous of becoming familiar with the culture of western Europe. In 1829 he left for the West, visited Bohemia, where he entered into relations with Czech men of letters, Germany, where he listened to the lectures of Hegel and was the guest of Goethe in Weimar, and finally cut across Switzerland to get to Rome. Here he underwent a religious crisis which was of great importance in his life and which found utterance in a series of exquisite religious lyrics.

It was in Rome also that he learned of the outbreak of the insurrection in Warsaw in November of 1830. Warsaw was then the capital of the so-called Congress Kingdom, set up at the Congress of Vienna in 1815 to supersede the erstwhile Duchy of Warsaw. The Kingdom was bound to Russia merely through a common ruler and was assured autonomy by treaty. Russia, however, paid no attention to treaties, maintaining an autocratic and irritating policy, which finally provoked the November uprising.

Anxious to take part in the uprising, Mickiewicz left Rome for the province of Poznań (then under Prussian domination), whence he intended to cross over into the Congress Kingdom. However, he arrived too late, for the insurrection was already on the wane. His repeated efforts to cross the frontier, moreover, came to nothing, as it was strongly guarded by the Prussians.

After the failure of the insurrection, Mickiewicz was compelled to share the fate of the many Polish emigrants, who in protest against the Russian policy of oppression, proceeded to France, to prepare there for a further struggle with the czarist regime. After a brief stop at Dresden, where, under the influence of Poland's misfortunes, one of his best works, the third part of *The Ancestors*, was written, the poet continued on his way to Paris. His life and that of his compatriots was not an easy one. The despair of defeat, the slight hopes of renewing the struggle in the face of the contemporaneous political situation in Europe, homesickness, the lack of security, material poverty—such were the conditions under which the Polish exiles in France lived. But Mickiewicz did not lose heart. His long sojourn in France, lasting almost to his death, with a one-year interval caused by his acceptance of the chair of Latin literature in Lausanne for the school year 1839-40, teemed with intensive, enthusiastic exertion in the domain of poetic creation and in that of social work and political activity. The realm of poetry gave rise to the masterpiece by Mickiewicz, *Pan Tadeusz* (in the years 1832-34), while his activity in other fields of endeavor assumes a different character in different periods. However, it is always animated by the same ideals: the identification of the Polish question with that of humanity itself, with that of liberty, equality, fraternity, lofty moral ideals, and the casting of the human soul into their mold. In 1832 the poet published a short work in prose entitled *The Books of the Polish Nation and of the Polish Pilgrims*, in which he proclaimed these very ideals erected upon the broad foundation of Christian love, mutual tolerance, and brotherly assistance. It is filled with indignation and an apostolic rage toward all lawlessness, oppression, and evil in the world. This work achieved a widespread renown in

Europe, was translated into a number of foreign languages and even found a lively echo in the celebrated *Paroles d'un Croyant* of De Lamennais. The articles Mickiewicz wrote for the contemporary periodical, *The Polish Pilgrim*, are similar in character. Later came the period during which Mickiewicz stressed moral education, propagating above all the development within each Pole of an inner moral strength which would permit him to cope with the tasks of the future. He then fell into a kind of mysticism, violated his own active nature, gave himself up to various "spiritual exercises," and to contemplation, and shut himself within a small circle of people who thought and felt similarly. His lectures in the *Collège de France* (1840-44), at first devoted exclusively to the subject of Slavonic literatures, contained first-rate syntheses and characterizations of the various periods and authors, and in general were on a level consistent with contemporary knowledge, but changed in character later, under the influence of this new spiritual state and, imbued with a marked moralizing element, proclaimed the poet's new ideas, which were to save Poland and humanity.

All this served to draw Mickiewicz away from his natural sphere of endeavor, i.e., poetry, in which he was without doubt strongest and most creative. As a matter of fact, he never did return to poetry, even when he had freed himself from mysticism, and had resumed his activity on a larger scale. He then began what the romantics termed "the translation of poetry into life." He engaged in this with the passion and enthusiasm characteristic of him, with a complete devotion to the cause, without becoming disheartened by obstacles. One of these beautiful moments in his life was the formation of a Polish legion in Italy in 1848. At the first news of the outbreak of the revolution in Italy, Mickiewicz proceeded to Rome to organize a Polish armed force, which, in the spirit of ancient Polish traditions, would through its struggle for the liberation of Italy, fight by the same token for the emancipation of Poland. Here indeed reality became transformed into lofty poetry. At the head of a group of young volunteers—enthusiasts all—Mickiewicz covered Italy from Rome to Milan, arousing admiration and lively interest wherever he went, delivering many speeches to the multitudes on the subject of liberty and the fraternity of peoples. The contemporary Italian testimony is unanimous in its assertion that there was something entrancing and fascinating in the figure, voice, unshakable faith and fire of the poet.

But the Italian expedition of Mickiewicz was more than a fantastic poem. Soon after his arrival in Milan, a Polish legion was organized, and, under the professional direction of Polish officers, took part in the brief Italian war.

Meanwhile, revolutionary events were occurring in France. Mickiewicz went to Paris to continue his work there for the cause of the revolution and of Poland. In company with a group of co-workers of various nationalities he founded the newspaper *La Tribune des Peuples*, and at the head of its editorial committee (a proof of the confidence and popularity he enjoyed in "republican" circles) he published well over one hundred articles dealing with a variety of timely subjects, inspired by one thought: the defense of the Republic and of those gains which the February Revolution had brought.

When reaction again set in over France, the *Tribune* was liquidated. But it was not given to Mickiewicz to rest for long. In the year 1855 the Crimean War broke out. The keen and ever alert spirit of the poet immediately sensed that where the fight went on against Russia there was room to unfurl the banner of the Polish cause. He went to Constantinople to organize a Polish legion with the Turkish army. Once again we see the incorporation of poetry into deed, but this time under conditions much more painful, much more difficult, than in Italy. Although the Polish military formation which sprang into being in Turkey could not, in the face of the known outcome of the war, attain its aim of transporting the scene of battle to Poland, it demonstrated to the world the unwavering determination of the Poles to fight for the liberation of their homeland at every opportunity.

This was the last great deed in the life of Adam Mickiewicz. Stricken by cholera, then raging in Constantinople, he died there on November 26, 1855, away from his native land and his beloved France. In time, his body was transported to Paris, where it remained until 1890, when it was conveyed amid great ceremony to Kraków, ancient seat of Polish Kings, and placed in the Wawel Castle among the tombs of the nation's greatest men. The French nation, in rendering homage to the meritorious deeds of the Polish poet and leader, who fought also for the French cause and who was one of the foremost poets of the world, erected in the *Place d'Alma* in Paris a monument to him by Bourdelle, the renowned sculptor and admirer of the works of Mickiewicz.

II

The creative genius of Mickiewicz began, as we have seen, to manifest itself very early. Disregarding the youthful specimens which he wrote in his student years, his first mature works are ballads and romances, included in his first volume of poetry (Wilno, 1822). It was a genre popular in the Europe of that day. It is true that in Poland many kinds of ballads had been written before Mickiewicz, but it was he who elevated them to the status of high poetic art. He drew his source material, in the manner of the poets of westen Europe, from folklore, replete with the fantastic and the supernatural. This material, poured into artistic forms, revealed certain basic traits of Mickiewicz's talent, viz., a plasticity of the poetic word, a rich imagination together with an amazing realism of detail, and a magnificent mastery of Polish meter. Some of his ballads are in no wise inferior in poetic value to analogous ballads of the German poets Schiller, Goethe, Uhland and others.

These poems, however, were not as great as the Polish poet's contribution in his second volume (1823). The latter contains two parts of *The Ancestors*, a drama in verse, whose title comes from the ancient folk rites celebrated in the province of Litwa on All Souls' Day with the intention of honoring the dead. These ceremonies were held in deserted chapels or in graveyards, and were accompanied by the "calling out" of the spirits of the departed and by the subsequent offering of food and drink to them. Such is the setting for one of the parts of *The Ancestors*. The skeleton of this drama, or rather dramatic poem, consists of three dramatized ballads, about children in purgatory, the wicked lord, and the inaccessible shepherdess. These ballads are thematically bound together by the conception of the necessity of suffering on earth, which alone opens the door to better worlds, a general idea which would not be particularly original, were it not presented in a novel and suggestive manner. Mickiewicz achieves this artistic suggestion by evoking an atmosphere of gravity, mystery, and horror in his presentation of the rite, by skillful contrasts in the introduction of his characters (first, innocent children, then the austere, merciless, country squire, and finally the virgin, deaf to the pleas of love and the young suicide's ghost), and by a plasticity of symbolism, by the rhythmic measures of the choruses, intermingled with the speeches of the acting figures, and mostly by his poetic language and verse.

The power of his poetic expression grows even stronger in the next part of the poem, which retains some of the adjuncts of the rite, but which is mainly devoted to the picture of a passionate, mad, truly romantic love, portrayed in a dialogue between the ghost of the young suicide and the simple country priest. The form of half-dream, half-vision, in which this moving confession is presented artistically justifies the entire fantasy and supernaturalness of those scenes, in which for the first time in Polish poetry the feeling of love was uttered with such force and truth of expression, with such ardent passion, with such a well-nigh metaphysical sublimity and in such deeply human accents.

His stay in Russia brought about a partial change in the poet's creativeness. He turned away for a while from the world of mystery, metaphysics, romantic spells and witchcraft to the charm and beauty of the outer world. His excursion to the Crimea inspired him to write a series of sonnets, which he published together with his erotic sonnets of the same period. In both types, and especially in the Crimean sonnets, certain traits of Mickiewicz's talent, evident in his earlier works, now came to light in all their luster and magnificence. These were an immense plasticity and precision of expression, an almost absolute control over poetic language, and an infallibility in the choice of attributes and phrases. To these may be added a splendid mastery of the difficult form of the sonnet, a compact composition, a precise rhythm, and effective final points. Virtually every Crimean sonnet is composed of two parts, closely bound together, constituting a compact whole. In the first part we usually have a fragment of majestic Crimean nature, drawn in general but expressive strokes, while against the background of this description emotion discreetly but suggestively appears in the two final tercets. There is no romantic sentimentality, verbosity, or carelessness in composition. Everything is compact, concentrated, precise, unique in expression. These are traits characterizing a masterpiece and the Crimean sonnets may undoubtedly be counted among masterpieces. Polish metrics and versification had never risen to such heights of originality and perfection.

But the sojourn in Russia also brought the poet other moods and reflections, which served as an inspiration for a very different long poem, somber and despairing, describing the fortunes of *Konrad Wallenrod*, told in the form of a Byronic poetic novel. This was a new tribute paid to the spirit of the times by Mickiewicz. The form of the poetic novel allowed a looseness of construction, overflowing sentimentality, lyrism, timely allusions, and digressions. *Konrad Wallenrod* abounds in all of these elements. Under the mask of a Teutonic Knight of the fourteenth century we see a modern man with his inner conflicts, moral experiences, spiritual storms, despair, and hopelessness. The fate of Wallenrod is tragic in the real sense of the word. Abducted by the Teutonic Knights from his native Lithuania, he lives long years in slavery with the sole thought of inflicting vengeance upon the enemies of his country. Compelled to hide his feelings, to pretend, and to mask his thoughts, he gains ever higher offices in the Order of the Teutonic Knights until he finally reaches the rank of Grand Master. He organizes a Teutonic expedition against Lithuania and deliberately directs the campaign in such a manner that he brings about a terrible defeat of the Order. He obtains his revenge, but is himself morally broken and dies a suicide. This schematic outline of the plot cannot, of course, give an adequate picture of the real problem of Wallenrod. His tragedy lies in the fact that he is forced by circumstances, by the horrible fate of his native land, to commit deeds which are simultaneously good and bad, good because they render service to his country, bad because they are performed with the aid of stratagem and treachery. Such in brief is his problem—a problem which condemns him to everlasting tortures and from which there is no escape save death. This narrative poem is permeated with an atmosphere of frenzied patriotism which demands absolute self-sacrifice and is despairing and hopeless. The poem devotes some very beautiful strophes to this emotional experience—strophes which to this day evoke in every Pole deep emotion. Its lyric portions are among the poem's most suggestive.

The wealth and versatility of the talent of Mickiewicz are astonishing. Proof of this may be found in his religious lyrics, written in Rome. They belong among the priceless pearls of Polish lyric art and would indubitably occupy an esteemed place in the lyric literature of the world were they—like all poetry—at all translatable. They are characterized by a special relationship to the Supreme Being, expressing a feeling of humility, insignificance and nothingness in the face of the might and immensity of God, a feeling of boundless joy and gratitude simply because He is, because He exists, because man can feel His presence within himself, because he can receive Him in "the little home of his spirit." There is an absence here of those reproaches, complaints, grievances, revolts, even pretensions as regards God which are so commonly found in other poets. The only grievance expressed in these lyrics is the grievance that man always crucifies God in his heart, constantly inflicting wounds and suffering upon Him by his "spite." The only reproach, complaint, and revolt are those directed against oneself, against man's presumptuousness, against his attempts at comprehending the Mystery. . . . One can easily imagine that this type of feeling and state of mind could not be expressed otherwise than in the simplest language and verse, and in the most spiritual and purest. It is indeed a lyric poetry that is ideally "pure" in the sense that it is concerned only with "pure" feelings, which are freed from all earthly fetters and require for their translation virtually no attributes from the outer world. There are few such lyric poems in world poetry. The religious lyrics of Mickiewicz represent this type in an admirable manner.

We already know the conditions in which Mickiewicz found himself in 1832 in Dresden and under the influence of which came into being the third part of *The Ancestors*. Here again we witness a different atmosphere as well as different problems. The atmosphere is somewhat reminiscent of *Wallenrod*, and especially of the earlier parts of *The Ancestors*; but the basic tone, or rather the basic tones, are different. In nine loosely connected scenes of the romantic drama (preceded by a Prologue), the poet encompassed in symbolic pictures and poetic epitomes the whole martyrology of Poland, the last act of which had just been enacted in the years 1830-31. In a group of realistic historical scenes he presented in turn the imprisonment of the Philomats within the walls of a convent in Wilno; the suffering of these young patriots, persecuted because of their work for "Motherland, Study and Virtue"; the unwilling and slighting attitude of the corrupted Polish upper classes who met in the "Warsaw Salon" to revolutionary patriotic activity and their submissiveness and loyalty towards the Russian government; finally, the activity in Wilno of the Russian satrap, Senator Novosiltsov, who had been in charge of the trial of the Philomats. Authentic features (names of places and of people, presentation of facts) are of course intermingled with poetic fantasy and are transmuted by this fantasy for purposes of artistic suggestion. It could not have been otherwise. But it is this transmutation which renders these images a poetic symbol by endowing them with distinctness, often with power and horror, at times with a grotesque or ironically derisive coloring.

This poetic symbol becomes strongly underlined and emphasized by a series of other scenes, which might be termed fantastic and prophetic. Good and evil spirits appear in them in a variety of shapes, deriving from a crude folk tradition, from the Middle Ages, or from the meditations of mystics. This entire celestial world assumes a direct and lively part in the actions of individuals, exerting an influence upon them and directing their course. The fusion of these two worlds is complete. The good spirits battle with the spirits of evil and failure for the souls of the heroes. Furthermore, the various characters of the drama have prophetic visions of their own fate or that of Poland. The main hero, Konrad, in a Promethean flight, challenges God to a combat, hurling at Him the accusation that He is not the Father of the world but its Czar, and demands of Him "government over souls" so that he may make his nation happy, "so that he might astonish the whole world by it." Without concluding this blasphemy, he loses consciousness; then occurs a unique scene of its kind, the exorcising of the "devil" from the possessed—strictly in conformity with medieval ritual. Finally, the closing scene reverts to the folk rite of the ancestors, a picture of a bloody vengeance wreaked upon the executioners of the Polish nation.

These diverse elements in the drama are fused not by definite realistic compositional ties but rather by the heat of a lyrism which penetrates the whole work and manifests itself in a very rich range of emotions and moods. The language and verse in which these emotions and moods are expressed fairly sparkle with the hues and radiance of the highest poetic art, especially in the scenes of the "Improvisation," of the dream visions, and in the description of the persecution of the Philomats. The many-sidedness and wide range of Mickiewicz's talent appeared here in the equally masterly command of the very varied poetic "techniques," the use of which was necessitated by the type of subject manner.

The creative work of Mickiewicz does not follow a calm even line of development; it develops rather in spurts, by bounds—ever revealing new phases of his talent, or rather, underscoring certain constant factors in his rich poetic nature.

In the same year (1832) which marked the appearance of the third part of *The Ancestors*, the poet commenced his last work, perhaps his greatest, which is at least the best known abroad and the most frequently translated. This was *Pan Tadeusz, or the Last Foray in Lithuania, a Tale of the Gentry, in Twelve Books in Verse*. According to concurring German, French, English, and Russian critical opinion, it is the only real modern epopee in world literature. It presents contemporary Polish society at the turning point of history in its entirety, at the time of Napoleon's Moscow expedition in the years 1811-12. This was an epoch familiar to the poet from childhood, an epoch in which were preserved in full the old types, customs and traditions—in a word, all the typical old Polish life. The epic idyll which Mickiewicz paints in his poem is a full picture of that life. It is composed of an entire series of scenes, figures, types, and affairs conducted among them—all against the background of splendid descriptions of nature and of the life of animals. Thus, the whole contemporary Polish world is contained within its range. The epic abilities of Mickiewicz, marked in some of his earlier works, are manifested here in augmented measure. The poet's ardent gaze, held in check by sobriety and moderation, sank into the details of this life, knew how to accentuate them, to unite them with each other, to combine them in interesting complications. Minuteness, precision, exactness, in brief, "epicness" reign here in a pure form. The wide epic stretch of narration, slow and staid in its tempo, the sunny humor with which the minor affairs and events are described, the life of these people against the background of a very beautiful nature, the life of this nature about them and within them—are other traits of this epopee. Not a little charm, dignity and ofttimes nobility are added by the thirteen-syllable verse, rhymed in pairs, "the Polish hexameter"—a form known, to be sure, in older Polish poetry but never till now used with such simplicity and craftsmanship.

One of the Polish critics called *Pan Tadeusz* "the immortalization of Polishness," [1] meaning the eternization in poetry of those traits of character and national custom which had evolved in the course of centuries. Indeed, in this respect *Pan Tadeusz* is undoubtedly a kind of historical document (of course with reservations as to poetization and symbolization). The figures peopling this poem are individuals standing in general on a rather high cultural and social level, attached to all that is Polish, hard working, enterprising, industrious, humane in their dealings with their subordinates, with highly developed family feelings, moderately religious, moderately liberal, with a sunny philosophy of life, moderately egoistic but capable of great sacrifices in matters concerning the common good, frequently quarrelsome and hypersensitive in private affairs but capable of solidarity in national affairs, born to "soldiering," gay, witty, fond of play without extravagances, rash and violent by nature but easily making peace after an outburst, accustomed to liberty and personal freedom and jealous of it in both private and public relationships. The historical epoch in which they lived naturally left its imprint upon them. It was the epoch of the Napoleonic wars, of endless changes of the map of Europe, and together with it, of Poland. It is small wonder then that the majority of the Polish nation bound its fate with that of Napoleon, who created the Polish Legions and the Duchy of Warsaw in 1807. This Napoleonic epopee likewise plays an important part in *Pan Tadeusz*. One of the main characters of the poem is the Napoleonic Emissary, who is anxious to organize an insurrection in Lithuania against

[1] *Unieśmiertelnienie Polskości.—Ed.*

Russia, before the advent of the Emperor's army. One of the most imposing and joyous scenes of the poem is the closing scene, when a detachment of Polish soldiers under the command of generals Dąbrowski and Kniaziewicz, famous in the Napoleonic Wars, encamp in a quiet Polish estate in a remote locality. This detachment is a section of the great army of Napoleon, advancing toward Moscow. The enthusiasm is general, faith in the victory of Napoleon and in the reconstruction of Poland is invincible, the young men speedily volunteer into the ranks; cheers, cries of joy, and the traditional polonaise on the lawn are an expression of the prevailing mood. The epic poem ends on this optimistic note of faith and hope, which, although not realized at that time, nevertheless has a symbolic meaning.

III

Adam Mickiewicz is, according to the consensus of Polish opinion, Poland's greatest poet and the one who is closest to the nation. He is regarded not only as a great poet artist but also as the nation's great teacher; in the trying period of its history he kept up the spirit of the nation, healing its suffering and instilling into it a faith in a better future; and in that period when Poland was forgotten and stricken from the roster of living nations, he made its name known all over the world and lifted the Polish banner high.

Indeed, the services rendered by Mickiewicz in behalf of Polish poetry cannot be overestimated. He can compare in this respect only with Jan Kochanowski, the founder of Polish poetry. But Mickiewicz surpasses Kochanowski by the range and wealth of his talent, by the scope and extent of his creative work, by his significance in European literature and by the influence which he gained. The fact that he was the leader of Polish romanticism and its actual creator need not of itself have such great importance, but he created both within romanticism and beyond its limits (mainly, indeed, beyond its limits) new, original, forms and new poetic themes. Whatever form he touched, ballad, poetic tale, or romantic drama, always or almost always developed under his pen into an original work, important in its poetic value and its social significance. He gave to Polish literature and, in part, to world literature a series of works which have a permanent value. These works place Polish literature on a high plane, especially among the Slavonic peoples, among whom the influence of Mickiewicz manifested itself to a very marked degree. Thanks above all to Mickiewicz, Polish literature entered the orbit of world literature.

Mickiewicz's influence in Poland has continued to this very day. In the realm of poetry this is apparent because of the adoration with which he is regarded by each succeeding generation of Polish poets, and the influence which he exerts upon their creative work. In the moral sphere, in the sphere of certain established feelings and attitudes, the spirit of Mickiewicz continues to hold sway over the nation. The attitude of Polish society toward official Russia was shaped in a large measure under the influence of his inspired pamphlet, published under the title of *Excerpt* as a supplement to the third part of *The Ancestors*. This influence endures likewise in other fields. He wrote and spoke much of Poland's role in Central Europe, of the "mission" which Poland was to fulfill, placed by the fate of history between the two mighty and equally hostile nations of Germans and Russians, and a great deal of what he said has remained in the national consciousness.

Mickiewicz the man is amazing in his inexhaustible store of spiritual energy, ever on the qui vive, by his wide horizons of outlook and emotions, not confined to the affairs of Poland alone but full of concern for humanity in general. He was devoid of even a shadow of chauvinism or nationalism, always uniting the cause of Poland with that of Humanity fighting for a better morrow, and rejecting all manner of separatism and egoism in relations among nations. This noble and lofty idealism, these ideas of love and fraternity proven and sealed by an entire lifetime, united to make the Polish poet an unfaltering herald of a better future world. And they constitute one of the many guarantees that such a world must come.

Translated from the Polish by Halina Chybowska.

JULIUSZ SŁOWACKI

(From a lithograph done by Sommer in Warsaw based on a contemporary
portrait of unknown authorship)

XVII

JULIUSZ SŁOWACKI
Poland's Bard of the "Golden Harp"

1809-49

by

ARTHUR PRUDDEN COLEMAN
and
MARION MOORE COLEMAN

JULIUSZ SŁOWACKI had to die, and his works had almost to die with him, before he began to be appreciated. In his lifetime he was chilled and starved and treated with a neglect so deliberate and universal as to smack of conspiracy. Only his colossal pride and an unconquerable "will to fame through poetry" sustained him and gave him the strength to play to the finish the role in which he saw himself cast.

Foresight of what his role was to be came to Słowacki early. It came when he was still a child, dreaming alone among the golden, wind-swept meadows of the Podolian-Volhynian border. He saw himself then as a knight, proud and undaunted, full of that "living spirit" which drives man forward and upward "toward the heights," and he determined then to play that role to the end, with words for his knightly lance and ideas his Pegasus.

For encouragement and support along his way Słowacki never had anything that came from his fellow human beings. He had only his "voices." A melody, unheard but intimately perceived, sustained him. He called it the music of a "golden harp."

The music of the harp pervaded Słowacki's life, as it was to pervade his poetry. He heard it in childhood as the voice of the Borderland, rising from the objects of daily experience: the picturesque huts of the Ruthenian peasantry, the oat fields with their "silvery tinkle," the murmuring pear trees and the larch-timbered cerkiew,[1] the graves of the ancestors dotting the steppe. Later he heard it as the voice of his country's guardian angel, a kind of magical "call to arms" in his nation's history.

In the music of the harp Słowacki early perceived a promise for his own life: through poetry, the golden music seemed to say, he would become immortal. He accepted the promise and neither then nor ever after doubted that it would be made good. Time did not weaken his faith nor neglect cause his confidence to wither. The golden voice sustained him and even when contempt was at its very height he still could say,

> Today you may resist: but still the future shall be mine,
> And mine the victory beyond the grave.

Słowacki prophesied correctly: his, "beyond the grave," the triumph was. Dying, he lived. His poetry was exhumed and a cult grew up around his name. Admiration mounted as new times came on and the verses which had been neglected in their author's lifetime were found to contain formulas adequate and farsighted. In Reborn Poland (1919-39) the triumph of the "golden harp" became complete: Słowacki was hailed as great in himself and great in an evolutionary sense. He was recognized as the link in Poland's literary tradition, which alone, of all the links, made from such isolated jewels as the classic Kochanowski and the modern Wyspiański and Żeromski a single, close-knit chain.

More than one formula has been invented in an effort to state precisely the reason for enshrining Słowacki among the Polish immortals. "The King of Fantasy," one calls him, who saw in *Spiritual Genesis* the whole structure of Athenian democracy in the pistils of a clover-blossom and the principle which dictated the Mayflower Compact in the delicate, butterfly blossoms of the pea vine. "The King of Realism," says another, who, in *The Grave of Agamemnon*, probed as a surgeon might do with his scalpel, the festering abscess of Romanticism and drained its poison

---

[1] Cerkiew is the word used in Polish to indicate a Russian church.

from Poland's blood. "The Master of Beautiful Language," says another, having in mind the gorgeous, untranslatable cadences of the Swiss sonnets. Others have called him "The Philosopher of Polish History," who tried to read an evolutionary significance in the broken Polish past, the Polish Shakespeare, the Polish Molière.

Each formula which tries to capture and define the essence of Słowacki's immortal qualities expresses a truth, yet none imprisons the whole truth about the many-sided poet. That cannot be done in a single word or formula: Słowacki's genius not only had many facets, but it fertilized many branches of his nation's literature. The reason Słowacki lives is the reason Shakespeare lives, and Homer. Like these, he was an instrument and through him, as through these, a culture found voice.

Słowacki sensed his peculiar mission himself, when he saw himself as the transmitter of the music of the "golden harp." To put it more plainly, he was the voice of Poland's whole, unique culture.

Polish culture is commonly regarded, by those who observe it only superficially, as Latin, and Latin alone. But it is "northern," too, as the pines and dunes of its Baltic periphery are "northern," and it contains, at the same time, a persistent "Greek" coloring which is derived from unbroken association with the eastern Mediterranean by way of the Dnieper and the south Russian steppe. The tree of Słowacki's poetry grew up at the base of Queen Bona's Hill, in a Borderland town where winds from the Baltic meet winds from the Mediterranean, where the heritage of Greece and Byzantium has its symbol in the Russian cross, that of Rome in the Latin. In his poetry were happily fused the "northern" Romanticism of the Baltic, the English and the Germans, with the "sunny clarity" of the classical tradition.

Let us see what made of the boy who was born at the crossroads the instrument of that culture.

Słowacki describes, in one of the cantos of his celebrated *Beniowski*, the kind of youth which alone, of all kinds, may justifiably be called beautiful. Beniowski's youth was not without its ups and downs, but it was beautiful nevertheless, for it fired the young breast; it did not let the nerves grow soft but hardened them, so that when they had to ring with pæans of enthusiasm they would not snap.

Słowacki's own youth was to Beniowski's as the life of a hothouse vine to that of some wild shrub of the steppe. There was no hardiness in it, no strictness or spiritual balance, no discipline. There was only softness and feminine coddling, for Słowacki was reared by women. He had an indulgent grandmother, two adoring elder stepsisters and a mother whose single outlet for her own emotional frustration lay in babying her son and setting him up as the center of her world.

Słowacki's youth had in it, also, a strain of disharmony, which arose from complex causes. His family, in the first place, was not like Adam Mickiewicz's or Joseph Conrad's, each in its respective way deeply rooted in the soil of the Borderland and heir of its best traditions. In the second place, the spiritual atmosphere which surrounded Słowacki in his growing years was not harmonious. Forces that were contradictory and mutually hostile tore through it like bolts of lightning, leaving loyalties of every kind, personal and national alike, tragically and irreconcilably split.

Słowacki was born in the Volhynian town of Krzemieniec, on September 4, 1809. Krzemieniec is not far from the imaginary line, which, according to geographers, marks the merging of southern steppe with northern forest. The region is famous in Poland's tradition as the cradle of heroes in the romantic Polish mold, of such men as Sobieski, Żółkiewski, Wiśniowiecki and other "watchdogs of the Cross."

Słowacki's family, though native to the Borderland, was not typical of what we think of as Borderland-Polish. His mother's people, the Januszewskis, were of Armenian origin. They were practical and realistic and fond of business, a branch of human activity traditionally shunned by the Pole of the Borderland. Słowacki's grandfather Januszewski was manager of the estates of the Lyceum of Krzemieniec.

The Słowacki side of the poet's family also displayed a trait which was not quite typical, in a marked talent for the literary and a decided bent toward bookishness, gifts which were not nearly so highly regarded on the frontier as more manly virtues.

Słowacki's grandfather, Jakób Słowacki, was a tutor in the court of Hetman Rzewuski at Podhorce, the great castle on the edge of the Volhynian plateau which was once the home of King John Sobieski. His father, Eusebius, was "literary." When no opportunity for formal education appeared he taught himself, mastering through assiduous self-instruction the languages and literatures of antiquity as well as those of his own time.

Eusebius Słowacki was thirty-six years old when, as a teacher of poetry and rhetoric in the Lyceum of Krzemieniec, he married sixteen-year-old Salomea Januszewska. He was not young, and unfortunately, he was not in good health, for tuberculosis, hereditary in his family, had already set its mark on him. But he was charged, even overcharged, with psychic energy. It was as if he knew life would soon end and that he must make the most of it while it lasted. He was ambitious for advancement and dissatisfied with Krzemieniec, famous though it was and becoming each year more famous. He was eager to go on to Wilno, the goal of every Polish professor in the early nineteenth century.

Juliusz was in his third year when his father's efforts for advancement were rewarded and he was appointed to a professorship in the University of Stefan Batory in Wilno. The little family moved at once from the provincial town to what was then the intellectual metropolis of the Polish realm. They remained there three years. Then Professor Słowacki died and the young mother had to take her black-eyed, curly-haired son back to Krzemieniec to the shelter of her own childhood's rooftree.

For four years Słowacki lived in the warmth and protection afforded by his devoted grandmother. Here he filled his mind with all the beauty and the sadness of the Borderland. He began to show signs during this time of aloofness to human society and of deep pessimism.

Słowacki's mother was not content to remain in Krzemieniec, either on her own account or for the sake of her son. Soon a chance of escape from the town's circumscribed existence appeared, when Dr. August Bècu, the Wilno professor who introduced smallpox inoculation into Litwa, asked her to marry him. Salomea's practical Armenian blood told her that here was an opportunity to make a career for herself as the mother of Dr. Bècu's two daughters and to provide for her own son, at the same time. She and Dr. Bècu were married in Krzemieniec on August 17, 1818.

Once again mother and son moved to Wilno. This time Salomea had the means and the position, as well as the native charm, to make herself a factor in Wilno life. Her home quickly became the meeting place of the university folk who liked to discuss books and plays, who enjoyed good music (Dr. Bècu was a fine musician) and witty conversation, and who were of a convivial disposition. Salomea's *salon* was soon known as the most popular literary rendezvous in Wilno.

Young Juliusz, the darling of his mother and the pet of his two stepsisters, moved in and out of the assorted company, a contemplative youth with proud, dark eyes. Sometimes he sang for his mother's guests, or recited for them.

Once, however, it is said, an incident occurred which crystallized in a dramatic manner a problem Słowacki was to face as long as his stepfather lived. Soon after the first poems of Adam Mickiewicz appeared, Dr. Bècu entertained his guests by holding them up to ridicule. Among Wilno Poles the act was hardly short of treason. Słowacki burst into tears and fled from the room.

Słowacki was by no means the only Pole who had to meet the issue of loyalty. Every Pole of his day was confronted with it in its national aspects. Słowacki's tragedy was that he had to take sides in his own home, either for or against a man who was a good husband to his mother and a good father to himself.

Dr. Bècu was a more or less self-made man. He had won his way to a high position in the University and he had his eye on the Rectorship. To win this crowning glory, and other rewards, he was willing to be a "yes man" for the Czar and even, it is said, to become an informer against the student societies when a purge was instituted in 1823. Though of French origin, Dr. Bècu was more "Russian," in the sense of being anti-Polish, than the Russians themselves, for he had the zeal and the thoroughness of a convert.

The un-Polishness of his home life hung over the sensitive Słowacki's spirit like a black pall. He saw his mother resolving the issue of loyalty by denying its existence, by turning frigidly away from incident or allusion which might raise it. Słowacki sensed that evasion was no solution, but he himself could find no other more satisfactory. He lived in an atmosphere utterly lacking in spiritual harmony. To escape it he drew more and more away from the world, into the narrow shell of his own small self.

Now and again from his lonely island Słowacki would thrust out a hand and grope toward normal human relationship. But a blight seemed to be in his very touch, for his only friend, Ludwik Spitznagel, a youth of the Werther pattern, committed suicide, while the girl he adored and believed he loved, Ludwika Śniadecka, refused to take him seriously and laughed at his pretensions.

It will be recalled that when Adam Mickiewicz was a student in Wilno (1815-19), and during all the next college generation as well (1820-24), the air of the university town was on fire with patriotic exaltation, and every Polish youth felt himself secretly enlisted in an army whose slogan was "Learning, Virtue, Father-land!" How different it was in Słowacki's day! When he entered the university in 1825, Mickiewicz himself was an exile in the heart of Russia and his friends were in far-off Orenburg. Patriotism had been silenced and reaction's dull shroud lay over all student activities. There was nothing in the air to tone up young Słowacki's spirits, as there had been in Mickiewicz's day, and nothing in the students' talk to make him feel he had a country to serve, or even a reason for living.

Słowacki had only his own secret reason for living. He had not forgotten the promise of his "golden harp"! Now pride slowly forged in his unhappy soul a steely determination to claim the promise. "To live, to suffer—and create, that is my road!" he wrote.

A trip to Odessa in 1826, the tragic death, soon afterward, of his friend Spitznagel, and a visit to his mother in Krzemieniec in 1829, provided Słowacki with literary materials and with the sharp spur of vivid experience. He began to find himself in writing.

When Słowacki finished his studies in Wilno, there was at first some thought of his mother's accompanying him to Warsaw, where he decided to seek a career. But the son, for all his devotion to his mother, was anxious to be free from her. He spent a little while with her in Krzemieniec, then in February 1829, at the age of twenty, bade farewell forever to the Hill of Queen Bona. Soon he was at the very other end of the Russian part of Poland, seeking to accommodate his searching spirit to the smug Polish capital.

Słowacki remained in Warsaw about two years, earning his living during that time by working in the Treasury Department, where Lubecki, the financial wizard of his day, was in charge. In Warsaw Słowacki renewed old ties with Edward Odyniec, the favorite lion of his mother's *salon* in Wilno, and published in Odyniec's journal *Melitele*, his own first drama, and a piece called *Hugo, a Tale of the German Knights*. The literary activity which engrossed Warsaw at this time had little effect on Słowacki; here as in Wilno the world outside his own imagined universe was distasteful. He hated the work that gave him his daily bread and thought of himself increasingly as a Byron, lonely, misunderstood, proud, too good for the common world. He "plunged even more zealously than in childhood into the land of dreams."

Dreams now reinforced the visions Słowacki had experienced in childhood. He felt a mounting sense of his own greatness and a certain knowledge that he would win fame through poetry. He was impelled to write and write, persistently and furiously, until he should discover a form and forge a style suitable to his genius.

Old themes recurred to Słowacki and chief among them was the familiar one of divided loyalty. Though the idea of treason had caused him no personal torture until his youth in Wilno, he had been conscious of the prevalence of disloyalty in human life from childhood. "Debatable strips," like the border region between the purely Polish lands on the one hand and the purely Russian on the other, are fruitful breeding places of every variety of Fifth Column. Słowacki had heard repeatedly how this lord or that, to avenge an insult, had fled to the Cossacks, or Muscovites, or even the Tatars and Turks, for allies against his own race. Treason fascinated him and he toyed with the theme persistently.

Out of his preoccupation with the dark theme came two important works during the Warsaw period. The two are the drama *Marya Stuart* and the verse narrative *Jan Bielecki*. In both of these the by-products proved to be of greater and more lasting importance than the theme which impelled Słowacki to write them or his manner of handling it.

With *Marya Stuart* Słowacki performed the great service of bringing an end to the classic tradition's monopoly of Polish dramatic literature, and of paving the way for the modern drama of character. Słowacki's Mary is a woman who, because of her "alien faith," feels herself betrayed on every side and who, for love of the adventurer Bothwell, herself betrays both husband and Church. As Słowacki paints her, Mary is good and bad, saintly and bedeviled, all at once, but a true and living woman. She stands as a milestone in Polish drama.

Jan Bielecki proved to be important for another reason. It acclimatized the Borderland, with its violent passions, its brilliant aspects, to Polish romantic literature in a form worthy of the "great tradition" in Polish letters. It is the story of a Polish lord of Podolia, Jan Bielecki, who, to avenge a wrong committed against him by his neighbor, the Lord of Brzezany, goes over to the Tatars and gets them to help him lead a bloody foray against his enemy. Interspersed throughout the tale, which Słowacki called "Polish" and "national," are descriptions of Border life: the drinking party of the magnates at Brzezany, the foray by night against Bielecki, the wedding of Bielecki, the masked ball, the tragic scene at the village church. Every element of "Słowacki country," that meeting place of East and West, North and South, is in the tale, save only the swift czajki [2] of the Dnieper Cossacks and the river rusałki,[3] and these were soon to have their day in another "Tale of Treason" called *The Viper*.

Słowacki had been in Warsaw only two years when the consequences of the national uprising which broke out in November 1830, forced him to leave his homeland. Shunning, as usual, all human entanglements, Słowacki was not involved in the act which precipitated the uprising nor in the conspiracies of the young patriots. He was evidently, at this time, a typical Byronic dilettante, thrilled by the idea of Corsairs and Laras, but paralyzed when a chance appeared to demonstrate the corsair spirit in action. Słowacki gave the uprising, however, two memorable songs: a "Hymn to the Virgin," in which he reworked Poland's famous

[2] Cossack canoes.
[3] Slavic river sprites.

medieval song, "Bogarodzica," and the "Song of the Rutheno-
Lithuanian Legion."

In the first spring of the uprising, 1831, Słowacki was
given an opportunity to serve his country. He left his post in
the Treasury Department for a mission to England on behalf of
the revolutionary National Government. He left Warsaw in
March, and never returned to the Polish capital or to any portion
of the Polish realm.

For the rest of his life Słowacki was a wanderer. He was
spared, through his mother's tender provision, the poverty which
normally dogs an exile, but he shared the exile's sense of rootless-
ness and loneliness. In Paris, to which he came after a short stay
in London, he wandered in and out of the places where his
fellow-exiles gathered, a proud, aloof, uncongenial spirit. If he
could have married a woman suited to his temperament, he might
have found a measure of spiritual peace at a fireside of his own,
but, though he had experiences of exaltation and delight in the
company of women from time to time—there was Kora Pinard,
the daughter of his publisher, in Paris, then Eglantine Pattey, the
daughter of his landlady in Geneva, later Marja Wodzińska,
whom Chopin loved, and finally Joanna Bobrowa, a "melancholy
Ukrainian beauty"—but Słowacki "loved weakly," and never with
his full soul. The wall of pride which in childhood he had begun
to erect around his inner self had grown so high and so forbidding
that now it kept affection out and the true Słowacki miserably
inside.

Pride was rendered the more defiant in Słowacki by an experience he had in Paris. This was the blow delivered by Adam
Mickiewicz, whom Słowacki called his "opposing deity" in *The
Forefathers* (*Dziady*), a work which appeared late in 1832 and
was eagerly read by all the Polish exiles. In it Mickiewicz portrayed
Słowacki's stepfather as all true Poles of Wilno saw him, as a
fawning sycophant of Czardom and an unprincipled opportunist.
Słowacki was wounded to the quick that anyone should publicly
depict in so evil a light his mother's husband and one who, after
all, had been a good father to himself. Feeling himself under the
accusing glances of his countrymen, Słowacki fled to Geneva.

Pride rescued Słowacki, as it always did. He resolved to

avenge his mother. He resolved also to make certain that the interpretation of Poland's history set forth by Mickiewicz should not remain the final one.

Słowacki began now to study history deeply and intensively and to review his own nation's long career, trying always to find in it some guiding principle. This led him to the source of all history, the human being, and he began to deepen his investigation of human motives. As the work proceeded, he grew more human himself: "I love the people more than I love the dry, dead bones of the past!" he flung at Mickiewicz, and to his mother he wrote, "In childhood I trained myself to be unlike people; not until this moment have I ever worked on myself to be like a human being."

In Geneva Słowacki began the trilogy of Polish history whose single finished segment, the drama *Kordian*, has fertilized Polish literature and provided it with a vocabulary to a degree no other single work from the same period has done save the one which inspired it, namely, Mickiewicz's drama of Gustav-Konrad in *The Forefathers*. [A comparable fertilization was to be performed in the early twentieth century by Wyspiański with his play *The Wedding* (*Wesele*).] The name Kordian, like the name Konrad, has come to stand for a type of individual, as the names Don Quixote, Hamlet, Don Juan and Werther stand for types. As Mickiewicz's Konrad is the Polish Prometheus, Słowacki's Kordian is Polish Romantic Youth, the type that is positively bursting with enthusiasm for the national cause—as Kordian was when he organized a plot to kill the Czar—but paralyzed and ineffective when action is required.

Kordian led Słowacki deep into the study of Polish history and personalities. The fruit of this study was a series of historical dramas and narratives in verse, some of them like *Balladyna*, fantastic evocations of a wholly legendary past, others, like *Mazepa* (which was in some respects a Polish *Othello*), new versions of old historic episodes. In one drama from this period, *Lilla Weneda*, Słowacki portrayed the earliest clash of hostile elements in Poland's history, the clash of the "earthy" with the "knightly," and introduced in striking manner the symbolism of the "golden harp."

Słowacki spent the final years of his life in Paris. Before he settled there, however, he culled bright flowers of poetry from a love idyll in the high valleys of the Swiss Alps and darker blossoms from an excursion to the Levant. A majestic poem, *The Father of the Plague-Stricken*, often compared to the sculptured figure of Niobe, or the awful Laocoön, arose from an experience Słowacki went through in the course of the latter journey, as he saw the father of a family watch all his children die, one by one, in a quarantine station at El-Arish on the border of Syria.

When Słowacki, only forty years old, died in 1849, there was but a handful of mourners at his grave and not a single member of his own family. His passing was hardly noticed. Only the poets Norwid and Zygmunt Krasiński, of his contemporaries, correctly estimated the loss his death meant to Polish letters. No one missed him very much as a person. It was not Słowacki's destiny to influence mankind through his personality: he did it, as he always knew he would, through his poetry.

When Słowacki lay buried in his grave *Anhelli* and *The King Spirit* (*Król-Duch*) remained, and both had that "certain power" of which blind Derwid spoke in *Lilla Weneda* when, with golden harp in hand, he faced the conqueror with confidence and pride. Both had in them something enduring, something "tempered, that would not snap under strain," which Słowacki yearned for in *The Grave of Agamemnon*.

For Słowacki had deepened by the time these works were written. The longer he wrestled with the inner secret of the universe, trying to find some way by which man's spiritual nature might soar, though burdened with a body, trying to probe the mystery of history's rise and fall, the more impressed he became by man's eternal willingness to struggle, the humbler he became before the appalling pageant of mankind. He longed to see the Polish *szlachta's* (gentry's) "golden freedom" become the property of all the Polish nation. Never making the mistake of believing a "drunken peasant" the equal of "a fair and noble knight," he yearned, nevertheless, to see the nobility which marked the knight pervade the whole of Polish society. Sensing Mickiewicz to be wrong in his belief that the Emigration could save the Polish nation, Słowacki offered in *Anhelli* a pattern of his own for the nation's salvation, the principle of voluntary sacrifice of a pure and spotless victim. He saw Polish history now, as he saw all history, indeed, as a series of episodes linked together in a magnificent unity by a great, moving force which from time to time makes itself felt in titanic personalities.

Through the works of his last, "great" period, Słowacki exerted a profound influence on the generation which matured in the late fifties of the nineteenth century, when he had himself been ten years in the grave. *Anhelli* and *The King Spirit*, the latter the principal vehicle of his theory of history, were in a sense the very blood that gave the nation life in the second great uprising of the century, which occurred in 1863. They helped the King Spirit rise, the "golden harp" resound.

In Reborn Poland (1919-39) Słowacki's triumph was complete: by his poetry he had won through to fame, and to higher regard among youth than his long more highly regarded contemporary, Mickiewicz. On September 4, 1939, when Słowacki had been dead for ninety years, on the one hundred and thirtieth anniversary of his birth, a gigantic celebration was to have taken place at the foot of Bona's Hill in Krzemieniec, "at the place where winds from two oceans cross."

The celebration never took place. Four days before it was to have occurred the Polish republic was invaded by the German army and the peaceful doings of mankind were abruptly stopped. We are told, however, that on the morning of September 3, while bombs dropped and the air crackled with the sound of guns, a speech we ourselves had prepared for the Słowacki celebration actually was sent out over the air by the Polish Radio! Słowacki was remembered until the very final moment of Reborn Poland's existence.

He was remembered beyond that moment: when exiles of the New Emigration began to cry out for books in Polish, from their camps in Scotland and throughout the British Isles, they demanded Słowacki, "because of the beauty of his language," as one soldier put it. Thus, in his nation's new exile and captivity, Słowacki achieved his utter triumph: he had not only entered the "poet's land" himself, but he had made it the common man's.

XVIII

FRYDERYK CHOPIN
"The Greatest and Most Polish of Polish Composers"

1810-49

by
ZDZISŁAW JACHIMECKI

AMONG the great men nurtured by Poland, Chopin occupies a truly unique position. His origin seemed not to have destined him for the role of one of the world's greatest representatives of Polish culture, since it sent him on life's journey with a French name. The career of musician was not thrust upon him by the atmosphere of his home nor by the friendships and associations of his childhood years. For Fryderyk Chopin was the son of parents who did not regard their modest inclination to music as a priceless gift of nature which might be expected to grow to some unusual proportions in their progeny.

Nicholas Chopin was a teacher of French in the home of the Skarbeks, owners of Żelazowa Wola (a few miles from Warsaw), when on February 22, 1810, a son was born to him and his wife Justyna, nee Krzyżanowska. The infant was baptized on April 23 with the names Fryderyk Franciszek. It is possible that he was named Fryderyk because that was the name of the younger Skarbek, pupil of Nicholas. The second name was given him by Nicholas Chopin in honor of the latter's own father. Old François Chopin was still living in 1810 in his native village of Marainville in the Vosges in Lorraine, whence the Chopin family of wheelwrights and vintners derived its origin.

The peasant hut had no doubt seemed too small to Nicholas Chopin. The distant world beckoned to him. As a youth of

FRYDERYK CHOPIN

(From an oil painting by Eugène Delacroix—in the Louvre Museum in
Paris)

seventeen he tore loose from the hearthstone of his home, crossed the frontier of France and wandered all the way to Warsaw. On foreign soil, he found employment very soon in a small tobacco factory owned by some French industrialists. This was sometime in 1788-89. A few years later the factory went bankrupt, and the young French emigrant found himself in the street. Pressed by necessity, in 1794[1] he joined the Polish national guard and in November of that year attained the rank of captain. Were it not for the fact that the division with which he served in the suburb of Warsaw known as Praga was relieved of duty on the tragic fifth of November, he would have sealed his expedition to Poland with a soldier's death. In spite of the tragedy that Poland suffered, Nicholas Chopin made up his mind to stay in the country of his adoption. He lacked higher education, but being resourceful and intelligent, he was able to teach others that which he himself knew best, namely the French language, also the German. In his new vocation he soon won the confidence of many important families. At first, he accepted the offer of the position of tutor in the house of Starostine Laczyńska. There, among his four pupils was fourteen-year-old Marie, the later Mme. Walewska, mistress of Napoleon and mother of his son, Count Alexander Colonna-Walewski. In 1802 Nicholas took a similar position in Żelazowa Wola. Here he met Justyna Krzyżanowska and married her in 1806. Three daughters, Ludwika (Mme. Jędrzejewiczowa), Izabella (Mme. Barcińska) and Emilia (who died in 1827 of tuberculosis), and Fryderyk, the only son, were the issue of that happy union.

In the year of Fryderyk's birth, Nicholas Chopin, through the support of influential friends, secured the post of teacher of French in the lower classes of the Warsaw Lyceum. In the fall of 1811 the Chopin family removed permanently to the capital. Kind to his family, honest and upright in all his relations, Nicholas Chopin apparently did not wish to let anyone know of his humble origin. He preferred to give Nancy, rather than some obscure mountain village in the Vosges, as the place from which he had come to Poland. Even his tombstone, standing to this day in the Powązki cemetery in Warsaw, names Nancy, the ancient capital

[1] In the uprising led by Kościuszko.—*Ed.*

of Stanisław Leszczyński, as his birthplace. For a good many years, with the objective of giving Chopin a purely Polish family tree and creating a legend that the name Chopin had had its origin in the old-Polish "Szopa," all search for Chopin's ancestors started in Nancy. This legend persisted until 1926 when a family tree, written in Nicholas Chopin's own hand in 1837 and attached to an application for a retirement pension, was discovered and published. In this document the old emigrant had to give authentic dates and, above all, the name of his place of birth, Marainville.[2]

Our best guide to an opinion concerning Nicholas Chopin's attitude toward his second fatherland is the diary of Fryderyk Skarbek in which the young man wrote of his teacher: "He was a good and upright man, who, having devoted himself to the education of Polish youth, never sought to change his pupils into Frenchmen and to imbue them with the ideas prevailing in France. Respecting the Poles and grateful to the land and the people among whom he had found hospitable reception and an adequate means of livelihood, he sincerely repaid his debt of gratitude by conscientiously training their descendants into useful citizens. By reason of his long stay in our country, by reason of his ties of friendship with Polish homes, but chiefly by reason of his marriage with a Polish woman and hence by bonds of marriage and family, he became truly a Pole. . . ."

One may conjecture variously as to the causes why Nicholas Chopin broke all the ties that bound him to his old fatherland and to his kin in France, but one comes to the conclusion that this was a very favorable factor in the spiritual development of Fryderyk. It saved him from falling into a state of divided national feeling. In the home of the teacher of French, one spoke with the children in Polish, and French was learned in lessons or in conversation with the pupils. The letters which in later years Nicholas Chopin wrote to his son were basically Polish, merely variegated with picturesque gallicisms. Thus from earliest childhood Fryderyk grew in a Polish atmosphere and felt himself

[2] This document, found accidentally among the materials of the National Archives sent back to Poland by Russia after the Treaty of Riga in 1921, was published together with a number of Fryderyk Chopin's letters by Stanisław Pereswiet-Sołtan.—*Author.*

unqualifiedly a Pole. He has given testimony of this in the hundreds of letters, written in Polish, which have come down to us.

The manner in which the little boy began his piano lessons was quite unusual. His first instruction was given him by his sister Ludwika, his senior by three years, although his mother qualified better for the task since, in the boarding school for boys of good family which she and her husband conducted in Warsaw, she combined the duties of housewife with those of piano instructor to some of the pupils. After approximately two years of this home instruction little Chopin was put into the hands of a professional teacher of the piano, a man already quite advanced in years, Wojciech Żywny (1756-1842). The information which we have concerning him is meager and contradictory. He was Czech by origin, but like many of his compatriots at that time he spoke German, took a great deal of snuff and imbibed freely. One of his pupils, Edward Koźmian, wrote of him later that "he was one of the worst teachers of music in Warsaw." Chopin, on the other hand, gave him a more flattering, though ambiguous tribute: "With Mr. Żywny even the biggest jackass would learn!" Although some contemporary Warsaw musicians, Edward Wolff for one, considered Żywny to be a violinist rather than a pianist, and although with the piano his influence upon Chopin could have been but slight, still the "kind old man" was able to point out to his pupil the best models for his development. "An enthusiastic devotee of John Sebastian Bach," Franz Liszt called Żywny in his fine monograph on Chopin published in 1852; adding, that in his long years of teaching, Żywny adhered strictly to the classical school.

At the first touch of the keys of the piano there must have been aroused in little Chopin an irresistible attraction to music, but specifically to piano music, music having its beginning and its outlet in this and no other instrument. On the other hand, the violin, and the flute, which his father played in his free moments, interested him not at all. The merely melodic possibilities of these instruments were not enough to satisfy his imagination in the realm of sound, an imagination the principal element of which was, to be sure, lyricism, but a lyricism resting on a foundation of rich harmony constituting the second element of his musical personality.

Little Fryderyk Chopinek, as he was nicknamed in Warsaw, having acquired a certain number of motifs, a certain repertoire of chords and passages, having possessed himself, in short, of a certain minimum of musical material, began to find his way to fulfilling the need of self-expression by means of sounds evoked from the piano. The spontaneity of his free improvisations and his ingenuity in constructing fantasies on themes familiar from hearing, aroused the admiration of young and old hearers alike. The seven-year-old composer was on the lips of everyone, as a phenomenon never before seen in Warsaw and reminding one of Mozart and Beethoven as children. Finally they began to write down his first efforts at composition (Żywny did this while the father of little Chopinek transcribed the notations), and toward the end of 1817 the music printing shop of the rector of the Church of the Virgin Mary in Nowe Miasto, The Reverend J. J. Cybulski, published the first musical composition bearing the name of Chopin. It was a Polonaise [3] for piano, dedicated to the daughter of the Skarbeks, young Countess Victoria of Żelazowa Wola.

In the January number of the *Pamiętnik Warszawski* (*Warsaw Memoir*) for the year 1818, there was a mention of this composition and several very flattering statements about the phenomenal child of the professor of the French language and literature. For long years, in the course of intensive work on the biography of Chopin, not a single copy of this work was known to Polish or foreign Chopinists. The accidental finding of the printed composition in 1926 enabled us to observe in this childish attempt certain characteristic elements of the composer's polonaise style, elements which persisted throughout the entire first phase of his polonaise production. An objective evaluation of this Polonaise in B flat major by contemporary musicians as well as by historians of music has placed and will continue to place it beside the polonaises of Michał Ogiński, Elsner, Kurpiński and Serwaczyński, Deszczyński and W. W. Wurfl. From the childhood period (in which, aside from his piano, Chopin had no instruction

[3] The title page read: *"Polonaise . . . faite par Fr. Chopin Musicien age de huit Ans."—Author.*

in the theory of music or composition), only a few works of the young musician have been preserved, these being the Polonaise of the year 1817, the B flat major, the Polonaise in A flat major for the name day of Żywny in April 1821, and the Polonaise in G sharp minor of the years 1822-24. There appeared also, in printed form, without the author's name, a military march dedicated by Chopin, in accordance with the wish of his elders, to the Russian governor, the Grand Duke Constantin.

There undoubtedly must have been a considerably greater number of these childhood compositions of the popular young pianist, but no one took care to preserve them in some place safe from destruction. Little Chopinek's drawing power was used for philanthropic purposes and he appeared at numerous affairs arranged by ladies of the aristocracy for the benefit of various humanitarian institutions. Juljan Ursyn Niemcewicz wrote a sketch on this theme entitled *Verkehry*, in which little Chopin, though not appearing in person, was the hero. On the occasion of the coming to Warsaw of the Empress-Mother, the nine-year-old Chopin was singled out for the honor of being presented to the Empress and was permitted to give her two of his polonaises.

"The open intelligence" of little Chopin absorbed with ease all that pertained to the general school curriculum. Exceedingly sensitive to all aesthetic stimuli, the child Chopin had a joyous disposition, which prompted him to play innocent tricks on his schoolmates and his elders. He had some drawing ability, made small-size portraits and caricatures, was an especially good mimic, and one of his vacation periods in the country (the summer of 1824 in Szafarnia) was spent in carrying on a gay correspondence, through the medium of a publication which he edited and which he called *Kurier Szafarski*. The Polish village in which he was born and to which he later had the opportunity to return, Żelazowa Wola or Szafarnia, in the county of Lipno, endowed the young soul of Chopin with the marvellous seed of folk music which was later to yield so rich a harvest in the form of his glorious mazurkas, the sound epic of the Polish people.

Amid the difficulties which beset his path in seeking to acquire the technique of composition, Chopin steered his own way. In 1823 he came upon K. A. Simon's manual of harmony, then newly published in Warsaw under the title *Krótka Nauka Poznania Harmonji czyli General-basu* (A short course in the knowledge of Harmony or of General-bass). But the benefits he could derive from this book were in no way commensurate with what swarmed in his mind, which he was able to embody in finished compositions. The Polonaise in G sharp minor is a good example of these powers of the youthful composer. The level of artistry and the range of pianistic possibilities in this work exceeded immeasurably everything which had been produced in Poland in the field of the polonaise. Only two earlier polonaises of Karl Maria von Weber may be named for the purpose of setting a criterion by which the value and historical position of the Polonaise in G sharp minor may be determined.

These few polonaises came to have an almost symbolic meaning in Chopin's creative work; they became the perfect expression of its complete polonism, they gave to its development the proper rhythm, a rhythm deriving directly and spontaneously from the Polish spirit.

But to increase the production—then already quite copious in Warsaw—of polonaises and to refine this genre in content and effectiveness was not the only thing which Chopin felt called upon to do at the age of fifteen. His prolific invention of themes and independent treatment of the keyboard appears in the Rondo in C minor composed in 1825, published in the same year by Brzezina's music store in Warsaw, and designated as the young composer's Opus 1.[4]

No contemporary would have dared to ascribe this composition to a fifteen-year-old student of the Warsaw Lyceum. Nor did Schumann suspect it when the Rondo came into his hands in 1832. He liked it very much and urged Klara Wieck, his future wife, a splendid pianist, to learn it.

Upon the youth of Chopin, illuminated by the golden glow of genius, now began to fall the sinister shadow of poor health.

[4] In the year of the appearance of this—officially the first—Chopin Opus, the *Allgemeine musikalische Zeitung*, published in Leipzig, carried news of the success the youthful pianist achieved in Warsaw when he played the allegro of the Concerto of Moscheles, in the following words: "Der junge talentvolle Chopin, der sich durch einen Reichtum musikalischer Ideen in seinen Phantasien auszeichnet und ganz Herr des Instrumentes ist, machte grossen Eindruck."— *Author.*

The portrait of Fryderyk, painted by Miroszewski, speaks for itself. It shows a very pale, highly anemic youth, with an asymmetrical face, a sharply hooked, protruding nose, and a very prominent Adam's apple. Frail and slight was Chopin's frame and his musculature showed obvious adynamia. In his fourteenth year he was fed with various pills and when he ran a temperature or had enlarged glands, leeches were put on his delicate throat. By 1826 he was coughing constantly, which, in view of the definite symptoms of tuberculosis in his youngest sister, Emilia, filled his parents with understandable fear for him and prompted them to go to the waters at Reinertz in German Silesia. Chopin's future on the score of health was not rosy. He "fell apart," as he put it, at the least cause, he sickened frequently, complained constantly of feeling cold, and by reason of faulty diagnosis, intentionally or unintentionally made by various physicians, and the wrong methods of treatment prevailing then, he became more and more susceptible and helpless before the onslaught of the disease which was to torment him for years and bring about his premature end.

In 1826 Chopin studied Józef Elsner's course in composition at *Szkoła Główna Muzyki* (the Main School of Music). A man to whom musical Warsaw owed much, a former director of the Opera, a productive if not a distinguished composer, but above all an energetic organizer of the city's musical life and a mature, conscientious teacher, Elsner was well able to direct Chopin's studies. He did not hamper him too much with academic formulas; he let him choose his way, confident that his genius would save him from the mistakes against which less gifted natures must constantly be warned. On the lists of students of his classes Elsner wrote beside Chopin's name notes which singled him out from all the others, notations such as: "uncommon ability," "musical genius."

The period of study with Elsner saw several larger works, whose creation was dictated by the normal course of conservatory studies. The first of this series was a set of variations in E major on the theme of a German-Swiss song known as *Der junge Schweizerbue*. Next perhaps was the *Rondeau à la Mazur*, published in 1836, which received the number of Opus 5—a composition bursting with verve, highly original, and characteristic in its folk color and dash. Chopin composed several more polonaises in those years, giving them an ever richer romantic content; yet, notwithstanding the high merit of these compositions (the Polonaise in B flat major entitled "Adieu," the D minor, later designated as Opus 71, No. 1, the B flat major, Opus 71, No. 2, and the Polonaise in G flat major), Chopin did not include them in his published works, with the result that they appeared only after his death at different times and in different editions. As an obligatory work Chopin wrote also a Sonata for Piano in C minor. He probably regarded it as the crowning achievement of his studies with Elsner, since he dedicated it to the master. The sonata was ready in 1828 and soon thereafter reached the hands of the Viennese publisher Haslinger, who, however, was unwilling to take the risk of publishing the long, serious-appearing work. Later Chopin lost faith in the value of the youthful composition and did not take the trouble to have it published. There is little in this sonata of the typical Chopin quality, melodiousness unhampered in its poetic flow. In the web of its text one feels a little compulsion; but the subtlety and refinement in the use of sound material are apparent in every beat, and the lush chromatics of the first portion, so emphatically characteristic of the epoch of romanticism in music, assumed in the theme forms very closely approaching those which Wagner used in his epochal music drama *Tristan und Isolde* (1857-59). In the elaboration of the composition Chopin did not adhere strictly to the "classic" sonata form which for two generations had served as the norm in the shaping of instrumental music (chamber and symphonic alike), but reached back for his models to the earlier epoch of the Viennese classicists, Haydn and Mozart. This form must have been the one best suited to Chopin's aesthetic sense, for he used it in two later piano sonatas (Op. 35 and 38).

Between his seventeenth and his twentieth year Chopin's production was abundant and varied. From his school years and from the short period following, we have the splendid *Krakowiak* (*Grand Rondeau de Concert*), Opus 14, for piano with orchestra accompaniment, published in 1834 as Opus 14; the Fantasia on the Theme of Polish Melodies, likewise for piano with orchestra accompaniment, Opus 13 (this contains a transcription of the song of Laura and Filon), next an original *Kołomyjka* (of which Kurpiński claimed to be the author), and a fiery Kujawiak; further, a trio published in 1833 as Opus 8; finally the brilliant Variations on the theme of the duettino *La ci darem la mano* from Mozart's opera *Don Giovanni*. In Robert Schumann it evoked a boundless admiration and a prophetic criticism, containing the memorable words: *Hut ab, ihr Herren, eine Genie!* An unequaled originality in creating new values out of all the factors of piano music, characterizes every page, every measure, of these compositions. What Paganini was to the violin, Chopin was to the piano, even in these youthful compositions. A true discoverer of sound colors hitherto unforeseen, a genius of harmony, inexhaustible in creating dissonances and modulations, a peerless etcher of *fioriture* and weaver of lacy designs of marvellous decorative value, a magician able to breathe into tonal arabesques the spirit and moods of the subtlest poetry of contemporary poets and to speak to the romantic imagination with unprecedented clearness, a genius whose appearance was destined to create an epoch in the history of music, Chopin might have said of himself in the words of Napoleon: "I am my own ancestor."

No other composer in the entire span of European musical history achieved at so early an age as Chopin such heights of perfection in works of such originality. One may say that Chopin was a unique experiment of nature, a miraculous mutation of musical genius whose destiny was to give new impulses to the ossifying forms of postclassical academicism. It is not difficult to point out how much common ground the music of Chopin has with that art which, coming from the Apennines to the cooler climate of the countries north of the Alps, became the music of all cultured Europe, almost without regard to state or national boundaries. The currents of that music have become so uniform, the banks so fixed and strong, the harmonic bed so smooth and polished and the material of the motives so molded, so stereotyped, that the first measures of "new" compositions foretold their entire course. Chopin, without breaking with the external laws of musical composition as dictated by the classic norms, became, as regards them, an exceedingly bold revolutionary; but his revolutionary deeds had in them a certain unearthiness and the charm of flowering youth.

Chopin's youth was not without the emotions necessary to spiritual development, emotions flowing out of the feelings of friendship and the still more tender moods of love. He frequently met with a group of talented young writers, such as Maurycy Mochnacki and Bohdan Zaleski; and after a few transitory student flirtations he fell seriously in love with a young and beautiful singer of the Warsaw Opera, Konstancja Gładkowska, to whom he directed the most moving passages of the compositions he was then creating.

Even if Chopin's production had been limited to those works which were created prior to the year 1830—the year the composer turned twenty—those works alone would have assured him a distinguished place in the history of music. For among them were, in the first place, the immortal *Études* of the two brilliant cycles known as Opus 10 and Opus 25. The two concertos were also ready, the earlier chronologically, F minor, Opus 21, and, following it by only a few months, the E minor, Opus 11. No wonder then, that a musician of this caliber, fully aware of the distance which separated the world of his art from the level of the musical needs of the average Warsovian, began to feel ill at ease and cramped on the native heath on which, to be sure, he shone with the brilliance of a star of the first magnitude, but with a melancholy sense of solitude.

Stronger and stronger grew the call of foreign soil where he had traveled in 1828 (Berlin) and 1829. His second journey had taken him to Vienna, where the fledgling graduate of the Warsaw Conservatory appeared in two public concerts. In the city of Haydn, Mozart, Beethoven and Schubert, the hitherto unknown youth from Poland achieved a great success both as pianist and composer. Upon his return home it became clear that further stay in his native country was not the thing for a musician of that stature, a musician unquestionably possessed of a mission to perform in the world. Chopin's family began to think more and more persistently of Fryderyk's departure for the wide arena of some great musical metropolis. First choice was given to London. The final year in Warsaw passed very quickly in intensive work of composition and in the arrangement of several concerts. The moment of departure arrived at last. Acclaimed in many panegyric verses, bidden an affectionate farewell by his family and friends, escorted beyond the gates of the city where a male chorus under the direction of Elsner rendered a cantata specially composed for the occasion by Chopin's old teacher (to words by Dnuszewski), Chopin set out into the world on November 2, 1830.

Four weeks later there reached him in Vienna the painful and at the same time joyous news of the outbreak of the insurrection and of the first triumphs of the Polish sword. The love which glowed in his heart was dimmed by the news, quickly spread in the Danubian capital, from the scenes of battle in Poland. The tragic news of the failure of the insurrection, which reached him during his few days' stay in Stuttgart, where he had gone after a very successful concert in Munich, dealt a crushing blow to Chopin's spirit. This was reflected in the compositions which Chopin created in those dreadful Stuttgart days. "If we could look at the very bottom of the causes which gave rise to certain compositions, we would learn dreadful things," said Schumann, who admitted that he himself "had to express in music what in any given moment moved him particularly in the world of political and literary events and human affairs." Of such dreadful things we learn from the "Revolutionary" *Étude* in C minor, from the Prelude in D minor, and from the heartrending epilogue of the Scherzo in B minor into which Chopin poured his anguish over the events in Poland. In those works Chopin attained the pinnacle of the sociological and ethical mission of the artist. Of all the commentators, the distinguished French musical essayist, Camille Bellaigue, expressed this most beautifully in his splendid sketch of the great virtuoso: "The heart of his nation beat in his breast. I know of no other musician who was a greater patriot than he. He was a Pole in far greater degree than any French-man was ever a Frenchman, any Italian an Italian, any German a German. He is a Pole, nothing but a Pole, and from that devastated, murdered country his music rises like its immortal soul. A soul melancholy and mournful, such as we hear in his ballads and nocturnes."

Toward the end of September, 1831, Chopin found himself

in Paris. He was to be there only in passing, according to his passport. He remained, however, for the entire second half of his life. He intended, and actually began here, to take lessons from the celebrated pianist Frederic Kalkbrenner, calculating correctly that for his projected debuts in Paris as concert pianist and composer the influence of the well-known Paris musician would be very useful to him. The period of preparation for the first Paris appearance was not long, for in February, 1832, Chopin won (after one concert) the universal acclaim of even the most reserved critics and the admiration of men possessed of intuition—which did not fail them. The weightiest voice of the musical circles of contemporary Paris, that of François Fetis, uttered the following judgment in the *Revue Musicale* for March, 1832: "Here is a young man who, following no models, has found, if not a complete renewal of piano music, then in any event a part of that which, for a long time, has been sought in vain, namely, a wealth of original thought examples of which are nowhere else in evidence. I see in M. Chopin's conceptions the promise of a renewal of forms which may in consequence exert a great influence on that part of music." Thus Chopin found himself at once in the circle of the greatest composers of his time residing then in Paris—Berlioz, Liszt, Mendelssohn, with all of whom he became united by bonds of lasting friendship. Presently he became acquainted with Mickiewicz and Słowacki. Acrid, sarcastic Heinrich Heine succumbed to the charm of his music and expressed great admiration for his compositions. In one of his famous Paris letters (in the series entitled *Lutetia*) Heine wrote in terms of the greatest enthusiasm of the great Polish musician: "Poland has given him the chivalry of her spirit and her historic pain, France her charm and grace, Germany her romantic depth; and Nature has endowed him with a graceful, slender, somewhat fragile figure, the noblest of hearts and genius. Yes, one must concede genius to Chopin in the fullest meaning of that word. Nothing can equal the ecstasy which he creates sitting at the piano, improvising. Then he is not a Pole, nor a Frenchman, nor a German, but gives witness of a much higher lineage; one recognizes then that he comes from the country of Mozart, Raphael, Goethe, that his true fatherland is the fairy kingdom of poesy. . . ."

But success in the concert hall and a composer's renown were not enough to assure to Chopin the means of even a modest subsistence. He had to harness himself to the hard and, above all, tedious treadmill of a piano teacher. He began to give lessons, well paid for those times, at twenty francs an hour. This gave him his living, even a fairly luxurious one, but it took him from the much more important work of composition. Thus, as compared with the rich productivity of the Warsaw period, the number of works composed in Paris was quite modest. An important cause of this slower tempo of production was the gradual deterioration of Chopin's health. His frail strength could not cope with the duties which fell upon him in Paris without serious impairment.

In the poetic study of Chopin's personality published by Emile Vuillermoz in 1927 under the title *La Vie Amoureuse de Chopin* occurs the following sentence: "It is an entirely certain thing that the basis of Chopin's temperament was eroticism in the etymological meaning whose noble character is distorted by a puritanical interpretation. This ardently feeling musician was incapable of writing so much as two notes without the whispered inspiration of love. His musical sense had an erotic tinge, just as other composers have a heroic, a tragic, a fantastic, mystic or pastoral sense. His music is the music of a lover. All his works have the rhythm of love, its sweetness, its tenderness, its passing doubts, its disquieting nostalgias and its constant beating of wings. His music is the divine fever of Eros, a fever whose every rise and fall found a faithful record in an arabesque arpeggio. This is the music of one enamoured of music. That is why its accents speak a universal language. Only the adoration of love can raise an artist to the heaven of the ideal where one may write masterpieces. . . ."

What were the sources of these erotic emotions of Chopin? After the fading of the dreams of which Konstancja Gładkowska was the object, after an episodic but doubtless highly exciting and exhausting relationship with Mme. Delfina Potocka, Chopin's heart was occupied for a longer while, in the years 1835-37, with the thought of permanent union with Marja Wodzińska, whom he had known since his childhood years in Warsaw. When this project failed, the composer, living in solitude in Paris, found a devoted friend and companion, who understood his artistic temperament, in the person of the famous novelist, Aurora Dudevant, who published her works under the pen name of George Sand. This relationship began in 1838 and was destined to last almost ten years, despite the considerable difference of temperaments and social and literary viewpoints which existed between the two. During the first months of this friendship Chopin's tenuous health became so much worse that a departure to a warmer climate seemed imperative. And so Chopin spent the winter of 1838-39 in the company of Mme. Sand and her children in Majorca, in Palma, and Valdemosa. Upon their return to Paris, Chopin took quarters very near his friend, spending the summers, for several years, in the novelist's country home in Nohant.

During his stay in Paris Chopin gave at least one concert each year, which brought him several thousand francs. The publication of his compositions, for which several firms competed, did not provide a sufficient income, though the fees paid him were quite high. Appearing much in high society, he played frequently in private circles of friends of his art, rather than for gain. He was not the type of the traveling virtuoso, bidding for the attention of audiences. Wholeheartedly devoted to the Polish cause, he was one of the leading personages among the Parisian *émigrés*, and never refused his help to needy compatriots.

In the second period of his creative work, in the years spent in France, Chopin gave up entirely composing for piano and orchestra and, aside from one piece of chamber music (the sonata for piano and violoncello, composed in 1847, and a number of songs), confined himself exclusively to works for piano alone. This was the result of the necessity of the greatest possible concentration in the use of the means needed for the realization of his musical concepts. Liszt observed very aptly: "The best proof of the fact that Chopin could have entrusted his conceptions, without difficulty, to an orchestra, is the ease with which the finest and the most important among them may be transcribed for orchestra. Thus if for the expression of his inspirations Chopin did not resort to the symphonic form, this was because he did not feel any compulsion to do so. He was motivated neither by false modesty nor by scorn but by a clear and sure consciousness that the forms chosen by him were the best suited to his inspiration.

And this consciousness is one of the truest marks of genius in all arts, particularly in music."

The repertoire of compositions with which he began his Paris appearances, came, as we know, from the Warsaw period. For a number of years he drew on this rich store without the need of satisfying the demands of publishers with new compositions. Hence the first few years of his stay abroad passed without more conspicuous fruits of composition. The retouching of the final edition, the transcription and orderly arrangement of a cycle of *Études* alone occupied the Master for the time being. Almost at the threshold of his Paris sojourn, as though to mute the nostalgia for his native land, Chopin created two Cycles of Mazurkas. Thereafter he published forty-one in all. In his portfolio, at the time of his death, there still remained eight, which with the permission of the composer's family, were published posthumously by Fontana. In this form, so beloved by him and to which he returned in the last weeks of life, to which he brought the warmest desire for understanding and, indeed, the deepest understanding of the spirit of Polish folk music, "Chopin took the eternally beating heart of the race in his hands and recreated it anew in the form of a perfect, universally understandable form of art, that which appears in the common people as a self-existent creative force unconfined by any discipline." These are the words in which Karol Szymanowski characterized the artistic mission of Chopin as creator of mazurkas. The mazurka brought to European music hitherto unknown elements of native rhythm and harmony, a harmony deriving its exotic qualities from the primitive but rich varied tonal factors of Polish musical folklore, whose "savage beauty" revealed to the composers of other nations the hitherto undiscovered possibilities of speaking in the tonal language of their own race. It is enough to cite the Norwegian Grieg and the Czech Smetana, who admitted frankly that without Chopin, and, above all, without his mazurkas, they could not have become "national" composers.

Two new forms appear in Chopin's production in the second period, namely: the ballade and the scherzo. Chopin was the first to bring the ballade to instrumental music from the genre of vocal art, which was its natural place. The author of the first comprehensive and scholarly monograph on Chopin, Frederick Niecks, placed them first among Chopin's compositions. "In no genre," says Niecks, "has Chopin created anything greater in respect to perfection of form, beauty and poetic quality than in the *Ballades;* here he has reached the culminating peak of his artistic power." The four *Ballades* of Chopin (Opus 23, G minor, Opus 38, F major, Opus 47, A flat major, and Opus 52, F minor) are musical analogues of the masterpieces of Polish romantic poetry of Mickiewicz and Słowacki. At their base lies a poetic program which of itself impresses the imagination of the listener.

The four scherzos of Chopin (Op. 20, 31, 39 and 54) likewise constitute the highest reaches of musical romanticism. To this form, taken from the symphonic cycle and made independent, Chopin assigned a paradoxical rôle in respect to its original character, which was dictated to the scherzo by the aesthetics of the classical period. We might compare the scherzos of Chopin with the poems of Byron in their fancy, their dramatic expression, romantic quality, contrast of moods and the enchanting grace characteristic of both.

The same spirit of romanticism, clothed in the most original concepts, fills the *Preludes* (twenty-four, comprised in Opus 28) of which some are short, like lightning, while others sing with the melancholy of rainy evenings or the sorrow and the longing of lonely hearts. The composer's nineteen *Nocturnes* "are among the most spiritual things imaginable in music," said Schumann. Close between the *Preludes* and the *Nocturnes* are the four *Impromptus,* the *Fantasia Impromptu,* the incomparable *Berceuse* (Opus 57) and the *Barcarolle* (Opus 60), so Italian in its melodic fluidity and attuned to the mystic ecstasy of Zygmunt Krasiński's *Before Dawn.* Of Chopin's shorter compositions, often containing suggestions of monumental content, the marks of a giant spirit, the second cycle of *Études* (Opus 25), and the fifteen *Waltzes* should be mentioned. They create almost a system, embracing within it all the spheres of emotional life and all the sectors of the social structure, and form the chapter entitled "*Salon.*" To those looking at Chopin's music from the angle of the waltzes, the brilliant maestro appeared primarily to be a salon composer; looking at it from the angle of the polonaises, one regards him as a master in the creation of pictures characterized by the chivalrous, knightly gesture, a musical painter of battle scenes, the singer of the triumphs and tragedies in the history of the nation. The six polonaises of the second period of Chopin's creation (C sharp minor, E flat, A major, C minor, F sharp minor and A flat major) and the *Fantasie Polonaise* constitute a kind of tone representation of Polish heroism. Though there has been no lack, in times past, of judgments expressing certain reservations on the subject of Chopin's mastery in the realm of great forms, none the less the composer's two sonatas of the Paris period (Opus 35, B flat minor and Opus 58, B minor) have withstood the test of time and even today, after so many changes of musical taste, stir profoundly. This alone, without considerations of a more factual nature, suffices to substantiate the opinion that in the realm of greater forms Chopin was equally gifted, equally brilliant as in the smaller forms.

Chopin's health began to decline definitely when he finished his thirty-fifth year. The lung disease which had been consuming his body for so long was slowly making impossible all creative work, all concert appearances, lessons and social life. Letters and short notes written in the years 1845-48, which have come down to us, show the flame of his vital energy growing weaker day by day. The blow which shook him most was the break with Mme. Sand in the winter of 1847-48. This break was imperative for both sides. It was preceded by the publication of Mme. Sand's novel, *Lucrecia Floriani* (1847), in which the author in quite transparent fashion made public her intimate misunderstandings with her friend of many years. Impelled by these sad experiences, Chopin decided to spend the spring and summer of 1848 in England. With the final remnants of his strength he played at public and private concerts in London, whence he later went to Scotland. There, in the vicinity of Edinburgh, a wealthy, very devoted friend, Miss Jane Stirling, offered the sick composer her hand in marriage in order to make his life's sad finale materially secure. But Chopin did not accept this sacrifice. Toward the end of 1848 he returned to Paris to finish the last months of his life. The winter and spring of 1848-49 passed in constant illness. He could no longer give lessons. Poverty began to oppress the artist who until so recently had lived in comfort and even luxury. Lack of income forced Chopin gradually to sell his more valuable possessions. The final solace of the period just preceding his death, the summer and fall of 1849, was the arrival of his deeply beloved sister, Ludwika Jedrzejewiczowa. A few weeks before his death, Chopin moved to a sunny apartment in the *Place Vendome*. Even then he still had hope that the change would bring about an improvement in his health. But the first days of October showed that the catastrophe was inevitable and very near. Death put an end to Chopin's suffering on October 17, 1849, at dawn. Two weeks later the embalmed remains of the Master were laid in a tomb in *Père Lachaise* Cemetery. The heart of the great composer, in accordance with his deathbed wish, was taken to Warsaw and built into the wall of the burial nave of the Church of the Holy Cross in Krakowskie Przedmieście.

The historic rôle of Chopin is defined by the absolute value of his music and by its undying vitality and the influence which his art has had upon the development of music in the succeeding years. Without question Chopin was, and is still, by his creation of supreme aesthetic values, one of the great benefactors of humanity, one of the great teachers of future generations on their quest of the ideal of beauty.

Translated from the Polish by Helena Stankiewicz Zand.

JAN MATEJKO

(From an oil portrait by Izydor Jabloński painted in 1873—in the
Matejko Museum in Kraków)

XIX

JAN MATEJKO

*"A Half-Blind Polish Painter Who Kept the Spirit of Inde-
pendence Alive by Depicting Glorious Episodes
of Poland's Past"*

1838-93

by

A POLISH SCHOLAR

"*Spiritus flat ubi vult*" (The Spirit breatheth where it will).
This Latin maxim has, in the course of centuries and generations,
repeatedly received confirmation, but its aptness has perhaps never
been demonstrated more convincingly than in the case of Matejko
and of Polish painting.

In the olden Poland of the monarchy, painting constituted a
cultural import from the various art centers of the world. The last
influx of artistic talent, in the latter half of the eighteenth century,
was centered in Warsaw around the throne and person of Stanisław August Poniatowski, King of Poland and brilliant patron of
the arts.

Poland's loss of its political independence brought Warsaw's
existence as the nation's capital to an end; the foreign artists returned to their native lands, while the handful of mediocre talents
educated by them, dispersed over the nation and took over the
teaching functions in schools of painting and sculpture, which, in
reality, formed only art faculties appended to the University in
Warsaw, the Academy in Wilno, and the Institute of Technology
in Kraków. These faculties, despite the conscientiousness of their
directors, barely vegetated. Small wonder, then, that one of the
keenest intellects of nineteenth-century Poland, the recipient of a

French Academy award for his *Causeries Florentines*, not only failed to foresee the formation of a truly Polish "school" of painting in the future development of art, but went so far as to deny to the Poles the ability and capacity to cultivate it in their own country.

"Plastic art in our country will ever remain but an exotic shrub, painstakingly nursed in the hothouse of dilettantism; it will never mature of itself into a fruit containing juices and seeds. Sons of the North, it is only in the richness of thought and of spirit that we may find a compensation for our deficiency in form and in nature, which are the elements conditioning the blossoming of plastic arts. *We are Slavs and can only be masters of the word.*"

Thus wrote Juljan Klaczko in 1857, only ten years before Matejko's exhibition in Paris, the art capital of the world, of his painting "The Sermon by Skarga," and not quite twenty years before he received a gold medal for his second great canvas, "Reytan."

Verily, no prophet has lived to see a pleasanter non-fulfillment of his own predictions!

Jan Alojzy Matejko, the eleventh of thirteen children of Franciszek Ksawery and Karolina (nee Rosberg) Matejko, first saw the light of day in Kraków, on July 28, 1838. We do not know much about his earliest childhood, orphaned as it was by the premature death of his mother. The little that we do know concerns the secondary but far-reaching fact that this constitutionally delicate child developed very slowly and did not begin to talk until the age of five. This handicap caused the child and later even the mature Matejko to experience great difficulty in formulating his thoughts. And it exerted a considerable influence on the evolution of Matejko's personality, forcing him to seek a different medium for the expression of his impressions and experiences. The boy's lively disposition and innate intelligence found such a medium in drawing. His early efforts did not extend beyond the primitive level of childish play and were restricted to a freehand copying of the illustrations contained in the books read by his older brothers and sisters. But here, too, a secondary factor entered into play: the most popular reading matter in the Polish homes of those years were the *Historical Songs* (*Spiewy Historyczne*) by Juljan Niemcewicz (a collection of poems rendering homage to outstanding personalities and events in Poland's history) and *Evenings 'Neath the Linden Tree* (*Wieczory pod Lipą*) by Lucjan Siemieński, a popular history of Poland. They awakened a predilection for history in the child and, as Matejko's intellect matured, this interest grew into a serious consideration and study of Poland's history, which in turn became the axis of the painter's entire artistic creativeness.

But this was not all. This copying of illustrations, at first only the playful occupation of a child, ripened, in the course of time, into the acquiring of factual knowledge, thanks to the influence exerted upon Matejko by his eldest brother, Franciszek. As an *amanuent*, that is, an aide of the Jagiellonian Library, and subsequently as instructor in the auxiliary historical sciences, sphragistics, chronology, and bibliography, the latter would systematically lend his little brother hand-illuminated parchment codices from the University library, such as the famous *Codex picturatus* by Balthazar Bem and the *Liber geneseos familiae Szydlowiciorum*, or the ancient chronicles of the sixteenth and seventeenth centuries, abounding in woodcuts and portraits, or the contemporary illustrated publications, such as the Bible, memoirs, travel books, histories of costume, etc. At the same time, the adolescent Matejko was exposed to the general atmosphere of Kraków and its national pantheon situated on the Acropolis of the Wawel hill, its cathedral, its statues and ashes of Polish kings, with war trophies hung about the altars as votive offerings—an atmosphere of the relics and memories of a great past, whose charm casts a spell even over foreigners. This learning process was supplemented by trips across the country; by visits to ruined castles, steeped in knightly legends, to monasteries and cloisters with their *argentarii* and reliquaries, to churches and their treasure-stores, to synagogues and chapels, cemeteries and belfries; and by conscientious study in museums and capitularies of liturgical manuscripts, of the royal or episcopal privilege grants dating from the Middle Ages with their decorative script and seals, oftentimes genuine toreutic masterpieces, from which Matejko's intuition could virtually resur-

rect the long dead generations. Matejko's furious studies through
the years acquainted him with all the great stylistic periods from
the Renaissance through the baroque and the rococo, gave him a
knowledge of the material background of bygone epochs, and
furnished him with an inexhaustible treasure-house of forms, which
his visions of the past rendered so suggestive that no Pole, even
if he be a historian, is able to imagine and see a Poland different
from that depicted by Matejko's brush. That Matejko did not
devote his life to archeology or confine himself to purely scientific
research may be ascribed to his vivid imagination and to his intense desire to invest the tragic fate of his nation with a plastic
shape.

But let us not run ahead of events. The boyish years of
Matejko were years filled with studies at school, and with drawing
and piano lessons which were given the lad by his father, a professional music master. The boy's difficulties with book learning,
however, increased, and his musical talent never exceeded medioc-
rity, while his passion for drawing began to reach for colors
with growing insistence and to manifest itself in surprisingly mature family portraits. His father, at first considering the profession of a painter with reluctance, finally agreed to remove the
boy from the *gimnazjum* or classical lyceum and to enroll him
for the school year 1853-54 in the art faculty of the Institute of
Technology.

Relieved of poring over grammars and henceforth rounding
out his general education by reading, Matejko in his new environment entered into a completely different atmosphere and formed
new spiritual ties. His parental home, very worthy and pious, did
not rise above the level of lower middle class needs, habits and
ambitions; family love and a restriction of life and existence to its
own hearth were its dominant characteristics. In the Institute of
Technology and particularly in the school of painting, the horizon
of Matejko's cultural interests widened immeasurably. Yearly ex-
hibits of the pupils' work, visited by a large number of Krakovians,
as well as occasional exhibitions of paintings from private galleries
and collections became an incentive to wholesome emulation and
evoked a fermentation in youthful minds and hearts. The flames
of awakened emotions and of an excited imagination were fanned

daily by Wojciech Korneli Stattler, instructor in drawing and painting, who was a Swiss but was enamored with Poland's past and her national traditions. In spite of certain misunderstandings and frictions with Stattler, Matejko gained a thorough knowledge of perspective and anatomy from his teacher, and thanks to his progress received a scholarship enabling him to continue his studies abroad.

Matejko's choice fell upon Munich as the nearest important art center, and the school year 1858-59 found him there. But he did not fare very well in this foreign land. His inadequate knowledge of the German language hampered social intercourse with his fellow students; and to make matters worse, he could come to no understanding with the class professor, Anschütz, whose instructions he did not comprehend and to whom he was unable to explain his artistic reasons and intentions. But his stay in Munich was spoiled mostly by his conviction that, having come to Mecca, he had failed to find Kaaba in it. Too serious for his age, reticent and introverted, he complained in letters to his Kraków friends of the disappointment he experienced. He was dissatisfied with the general direction of the Academy, headed by Wilhelm Kaulbach; he was dissatisfied with the teachers and with the class professor whose views on art differed from his own. For the young Matejko already had his own opinion on art. He recognized the rôle of the brush in the hand of the artist, he felt that a painting should be more than a canvas covered with paint and more than the product of a creative imagination, holding that it should also be a social function, generated by and forming part of life. This independent philosophy of art precluded the possibility of any understanding between Matejko and Professor Anschütz, but that did not prevent the young student from winning his first mark of honorable distinction: a bronze medal for the painting "The Poisoning of Queen Bona Sforza."

In the following school year, 1859-60, Matejko was a student of the Viennese Academy in the painting class of Professor Ruben. Yet Matejko was not destined to remain long in this school either. The final crystallization of the youth's highly original and powerful individuality revealed, in periods of stress, a stubborn, restive nature and brought about a situation whereby the artist, without even taking leave of his fellow students and professor, suddenly left Vienna before the year was out to return to his native Kraków and to his sole real master and teacher, Wit Stwosz, the fifteenth-century wood carver whose huge altar graces the Church of Saint Mary.

Having found himself again in the beloved and stimulating atmosphere of Kraków, Matejko embarked on an independent artistic life and, taking advantage of the materials accumulated in his portfolio, set to work on the truly monumental publication *Dress in Poland* (*Ubiory w Polsce*), which to this date has remained the standard Polish costumology. On ten oversize plates Matejko systematically gathered all the data pertaining to costumes worn by the Poles during the six centuries from 1200 through 1795. When one stops to consider that before Matejko could publish his costumology, he had to discover 684 figures on authentic dated statues, copy them, divide them into groups (the royal court, the clergy, the magnates, etc., down to the town wights and executioners), transfer the drawings to a lithographic stone, see to the presswork, provide each figure with a commentary, and finally meet the costs of printing, and when one reflects that all this was accomplished by a twenty-two-year-old youth, it is difficult not to marvel at his strong will, his competence and his industry. Matejko's industry was simply uncanny; it accounted for thousands of drawings and sketches, for 238 easel paintings, among them colossi such as the "Prussian Homage" or "Sobieski at Vienna," and finally for the personally executed pasteboards used in the polychromy of the 10,000-meter wall surface of Saint Mary's Church. Nothing conveys a more telling characterization of this inordinate capacity for work than the fact that Matejko's atelier contained but one chair, and a hard wooden one at that, so that the visitor might feel embarrassed by the lack of a seat for the host of the studio, and in order that the host himself might not become lazy by too frequent repose in a comfortable armchair.

As a result of his publication of *Dress in Poland*, forming but a by-product of his art work proper, Matejko immediately entered the ranks both of the rebuilders and the builders of modern Polish culture.

During his work on *Dress in Poland* the years 1863 and 1864, momentous for Matejko, drew near. These dates constitute a turning point in the artist's life; the first being concerned with national events which shook the soul of Matejko the Pole to its core, the second marking two personal experiences of Matejko the man and the artist which resulted in the apogee of his life. The tragic blow that fell upon Matejko in 1863 was, of course, the heroic but futile insurrection against the tyrannical rule of the Czar in the erstwhile "Congress Kingdom" called to life in 1815 by the Congress of Vienna.

Busy with his studies and wielding no weapon, Matejko could not even dream of personally taking part in the uprising; nevertheless, he was wholeheartedly in favor of armed combat with the invader and gave his active support to it, contributing his hard earned money toward the purchase of weapons which he courageously smuggled through the Russian lines and presented to the insurrectionists. But upon viewing the situation in the Polish camp, he was filled with doubt and despair by the scarcity of arms, equipment and provisions, by the lack of discipline on the part of the subordinates and by the absence of a plan of action on the part of the leaders. Returning home, he felt crushed in the first moments, then repented his sins, which, however, were for the most part not his own, and finally sought refuge in prayer. *Nil desperandum!* All was not yet lost since God was in his Heaven. This faith colored Matejko's mighty creative art and served as the content of his great historical compositions.

The first of these is a painting perhaps meaningless to the foreigner but offering an eloquent message to the Pole: the painting which portrays the King's jester, Stańczyk, who, while the court, with the King and Queen, are dancing, remains in a secluded chamber of the Wawel Castle, wringing his hands and meditating upon the military defeat sustained that very day on the Eastern frontier of his homeland. But the court fool's thoughts are not confined to the loss of the fortress of Smolensk in 1514. Through the eyes of Matejko (for the artist, having conferred his own facial traits upon Stańczyk, reveals himself in the other's form), through Matejko's mind, the court fool endeavors to learn how it could happen, that a populous and independent nation should fall a victim to inertia and, finally, to slavery. He feels the burning blush of shame and is also filled with dread of the future, a future foretold by the priest, Piotr Skarga,[1] in his *Sermons Delivered before the Sejm*. One must have suffered like the Poles to realize the full implications of Matejko's Skarga, whose hands uplifted as if in malediction and whose eyes, seeing into the future, are so expressive, so overpowering in their depth of feeling, that they leave a marked and lasting impression upon the beholder.

The other work, the "Sermon by Skarga," having been accorded the gold medal in Paris, immediately earned a favorable opinion for budding Polish painting. But to Matejko it gave fame and personal happiness, for it won him the heart and hand of Theodora Giebultowska, the sister of his boyhood friend. This love, the first and only one in his life, ecstatically passionate, and during the period of work on the "Sermon by Skarga" radiant and happy, refused to remain hidden even in a painting on so tragic a subject; and it invested the composition with an ineffable charm, for which we would look in vain in other paintings, formally as perfect or even more perfect. Happiness is experienced, if at all, but once in one's life. And so the year 1864 marks a peak in the artistic as well as the private life of Matejko. It is a peak upon which Matejko the painter will maintain himself for many years to come, but upon which Matejko the man will never stand again. Of his marriage, entered into November 21, 1864, one must say with Schiller: *"Der Wahn ist kurz, die Reu ist lang."* [2] And one might apply this equally well to Matejko's entire family life. The union, four times blessed by a child (Matejko had two sons and two daughters, none of whom are living), could not by its very nature ensure the artist's happiness; the chosen woman of his heart possessed great beauty, but she was not well and, suffering from a psychosis on the subject of completely unfounded jealousy, transformed Matejko's life into a veritable hell.

Matejko's personal unhappiness, however, brought forth advantageous results as far as his art and Polish painting are concerned. Deprived of the joy of a happy domestic life, he flung himself all the more vigorously into artistic creativeness. The

[1] See Chapter VII on Piotr Skarga by Professor Stanisław Windakiewicz.—*Ed.*
[2] Madness is short, the result thereof is long.—*Ed.*

"Sermon by Skarga" had not yet returned from its tour of foreign expositions, the prophetic words contained in it had not yet stopped vibrating in Polish hearts, but the canvas stretched out in Matejko's workshop was already peopled with new figures through whom the threats and predictions of Skarga received realization: a crowd of deputies to the *Sejm* at which—except for the lone Tadeusz Reytan—all agreed under duress to the partition of Poland among Russia, Prussia and Austria!

The painting "Reytan" (the abbreviated title by which this work is known in Polish painting), acquired for the Viennese Gallery by the Emperor Franz-Joseph, met with the highest acclaim in Paris. It was unanimously awarded the grand gold medal and its author received the additional honor of associate membership in the fine arts section (*Institut de France*) of the French Academy.

The reception accorded to Matejko's masterpiece in his own country, however, was quite a different story. The artist was accused of placing his native land in the pillory for all Europe to see. Nor was he spared by the prominent Polish novelist, Józef Ignacy Kraszewski, who wrote of him: "It is an ugly bird which defiles its own nest." This judgment wounded Matejko to the quick. And, indeed, how could it not hurt him for whom—as for Wyspiański—the day began and ended with Poland, who lived only in her and for her, whose dying words were the prayer: "Oh God, deliver my country." The indignation which greeted Matejko's masterpiece was a grievous blow to the artist and, perhaps, hastened the termination of his act of penance executed by means of paint and brush. Henceforth, Matejko's artistic production entered the period and the cycle of paintings strengthening the spirit and testifying that a nation with great peacetime and wartime feats to its credit has a right to its own life and sooner or later will find itself equal among equals in the family of civilized nations. The consciousness of this truth henceforward served as a beacon for Matejko's work and is the thread of Ariadne in the gigantic labyrinth of his creative art. The cycle of Matejko's great paintings comprises "Stańczyk" (1862), "The Sermon by Skarga" (1864), "Reytan" (1866), already briefly described, and the "Union of Lublin" (1869), "Batory at Pskov" (1871), "The

Battle of Grunwald" (1878), "The Battle of Varna" (1879),
"The Prussian Homage" (1882), "Sobieski at Vienna" (1883),
"The Battle of Racławice" (1888), "The Constitution of the
Third of May" (1891), and the unfinished canvas, "The Vows of
Jan Kazimierz in the Cathedral of Lwów" (1893), a painting
psychologically as compelling and perfect as the "Sermon by
Skarga" or "Batory at Pskov." While he was at work on this
composition Matejko lost consciousness and two days later
breathed his last.

We cannot, of course, discuss at length each of these huge
and masterfully conceived compositions and must content ourselves with the assertion that every one of them is not only a
first-rate work of art but also a civic and patriotic deed. That the
first three paintings of this cycle ("Stańczyk," "Skarga," and
"Reytan") should be characterized in this manner is in agreement
with what we have said of them above; as for the later ones, a
disclosure of Matejko's aim in painting them will suffice. Thus,
"The Union of Lublin," executed on the 300th anniversary of the
memorable Polish act of state, was to recall to the Poles and manifest to the world that it is possible for two neighboring nations—
despite the diversity of their interests—to make peace and arrive
at a mutual understanding without recourse to arms or to the
annexation of territory. The next painting, "Batory at Pskov,"
was the warning of *Fortuna variabilis!* cast in the direction of the
Czar in the period of the severest oppression of the Polish element
under the Russian occupation. "The Battle of Grunwald," on the
framework of which Matejko caused the inscription "*Si Deus
nobiscum, quis contranos*" to be placed, was Matejko's and the
nation's answer to the exterminatory policy of Bismarck. This
was supplemented by the most decorative of Matejko's works,
"Prussian Homage," which shows the world how in 1525 Prince
Hohenzollern pledged feudal loyalty to Poland in his own name
and in that of his successors. Matejko was next fired by the thought
of reminding the world that Poland acted as a bulwark of European civilization against the deluge of the wild hordes of Tartars
and Turks pressing from the East and bared her breast to protect
Christianity from paganism. And since even Rome forgot Poland's historical rôle, Matejko, scarcely earning enough to make

SOBIESKI AT VIENNA

"Veni, Vidi, Deus Vinxit"—"I came, I saw, but God conquered."

"Under the personal command of Sobieski himself the Polish Hussars descended the neighboring hills and charged the main mass of the Turkish army in the camp of the Vezir."

This huge canvas by Jan Matejko, 4.6 by 9 meters, shows the victorious Sobieski in the camp of the Vezir. Matejko offered this canvas to Pope Leo XIII, and it is still in the Vatican.

THE PRUSSIAN HOMAGE

by Jan Matejko

On a large canvas, 3.88 by 7.85 meters, Matejko portrays the historic moment on April 10, 1525, when Albrecht Hohenzollern of Prussia swore homage and fealty to the King of Poland (Sigismund I) in Kraków, the ancient capital.

both ends meet, presented Pope Leon XIII, in the name of the Polish nation, with one of his magnificent compositions, "Sobieski at Vienna." He chose the opportune moment of the persecution of the Uniates in the Polish eastern provinces, for the presentation of his gift. Matejko's concern was to keep the memory of Poland's gallant deed, the raising of the siege of Vienna, alive in the Vatican and in the conscience of the civilized world.

Thinking now of his own nation, by way of encouragement and admonition Matejko created his three last great paintings, a trilogy on the development of democracy in Poland. "The Battle of Racławice," the "Constitution of the Third of May," and the unfinished "Vows of Jan Kazimierz in the Cathedral of Lwów" all pertained to the concept of a peasant Poland. Matejko hinted at this in the "Union of Lublin," when he introduced a peasant into the assembly room of the *Sejm*, and caused him to be led by the hand of the prominent political writer Frycz Modrzewski.[3] He showed in the "Battle of Racławice" that the recognition of the peasant, freed from serfdom and endowed with a free will, in national life brings victory to the country; that this victory would have been complete and lasting had the Constitution of the Third of May concerned itself sincerely and more basically with the lot of the peasantry. And since the Constitution did not accomplish this, let the Poland of tomorrow—for all the strong spirits in Poland believed in its resurrection—recall and fulfill the promises that the king Jan Kazimierz made in his "Vows."

Is it necessary, after what has been said above, to write about the rôle Matejko played and still plays in the life of fettered Poland? Beginning with the University professors, whom Matejko surprised by his erudite knowledge of old Polish custom, and ending with the unlettered peasant dwelling under a thatched roof, Matejko was for all a teacher of Poland's past; feeling very deeply and imbuing his painted figures with deep emotions, he evoked corresponding emotions in the spectators; he taught sacrifice for the motherland; he tempered anew the souls that had been softened by servitude; he constantly portrayed instances of civic generosity, bravery, enthusiasm and heroism. All this was imparted to

[3] See illustration to the chapter on Frycz Modrzewski.—*Ed.*

the spectator by one glance at the pulsating canvas. It was the incarnation of a great tradition. If Poland, thrust into her grave against her will, did not succumb and refused to die, it is to the saber of Tadeusz Kościuszko, the lute of our three national bards, the songs of Chopin and the brush of Matejko that she owes her life. Sienkiewicz roused the nation from its dangerous lethargy by his renowned trilogy. Yet this trilogy could not have been conceived without the work of Matejko which preceded it. The genius of Matejko and of Sienkiewicz shook the nation to its very foundation, exerting a profound influence on such varied personalities as Stanisław Wyspiański, Paderewski, and Józef Piłsudski.

The artist's individuality left a singular imprint on the intellectual work of an entire generation and through its radiance engendered new fields of Polish cultural life. It awakened the liveliest general interest in the mores of bygone epochs and in the material background for these mores—architecture, interiors, dress, furniture, printing, illustrations. Thus a painter with barely an average education was able to become the great inspirer of a new realm of knowledge, as far as Poland was concerned, namely, the history of art. That the number of artistic monographs is increasing, that the conservation of relics, churches, etc., has profoundly affected Polish museum art, that we are learning to relate the life of today to the cultural production of the past, and finally that we are becoming more and more strongly convinced that ours is an individual, native culture—is due in large measure to Matejko.

While Matejko the artist was telling the heroic story of Poland, the life of Matejko the man and citizen was full of unhappiness, of failures and disappointments. The sole victory of this life was the founding of the first modern School of Fine Arts in Kraków. But this triumph, too, included its deeply felt defeat. Matejko dreamed of a national "school" of painting and erected only the walls of an institution of learning, the direction of which remained in his hands for nearly two decades. There was room only for second-rate imitators at the side of so powerful an individuality—a personality approaching Michael Angelo in its tragedy and Shakespeare in its drama. With the blindness characteristic of the gifted, he regarded his imitators as his successors.

He sincerely rejoiced in them and was sincerely deluded. The less submissive escaped from beneath his wings and found their way to other Academies to seek other means of scaling the heights of fame. Matejko was spared a fall from Olympus by a merciful death. Physically frail, suffering hunger all his life as the result of a prolonged illness (*ulcus ventriculi*), lashing his nerves with black coffee and nicotine, shattered by work, burned through by his emotions, Matejko expired almost suddenly on November 1, 1893.

The last tribute paid to Matejko by the nation was the solemn public funeral accorded him on November 7. The population of Kraków and all Poland, sobbing with the peals of the historic bell in the Wawel, and all nature itself participated in the burial ceremonies. It was a murky, cold, windy day. The flutter of black wings and of black flags beat a cruel accompaniment for the handful of ashes on its way to the family mausoleum in Rakowice. It was only with the strains of *Salve Regina* that his tortured soul found peace.

Translated from the Polish by Halina Chybowska.

XX

HELENA MODJESKA
Dramatic Artist—"Every Inch A Queen"

1840-1909

by

ERIC P. KELLY

ON THE thirteenth of August, in the year 1877, there appeared
before the footlights of the California Theater in San Francisco,
a Polish actress in the title rôle of *Adrienne Lecouvreur*. It was
not a widely heralded performance, nor had stage artists or car-
penters been at work preparing special scenery; indeed, they were
engaged in making sets for the great actress Rose Eytinge, who
was to appear shortly in a magnificent production of *Cleopatra*,
to be followed later by the theater's lessee, the famous John Mc-
Cullough in *Othello* and *Hamlet*. But a quite distinguished audience was nevertheless present, including many members of the
Polish colony [1] in California, many of them exiles from their na-

---

[1] One member of this Polish colony in California, Mr. Zbigniew Brodowski
(1853-1901), at one time American consul in Breslau, Germany, gives an interesting account of incidents leading to Helena Modjeska's first appearance on the
American stage—published in *Nowy Świat* (*The Polish Morning World*) in New
York, April 8, 1936:

"The recent dispatches about the burning down of the Baldwin Hotel and
Theatre evoke in my mind old memories when Mme. Helena Modjeska appeared
for the first time on the English stage in that very Theatre. There was then on
the Pacific coast a small group of Poles—in the majority shipwrecks of our
national epic—Captain Bielawski, Dr. Pawlicki, old Captain Korwin Piotrowski,
General Krzyżanowski, and others.

"Mme. Helena Modjeska's arrival in San Francisco brought a feeling of
unspeakable bliss to our old soldiers; they all strove to show her—'our lady,' as
they called Mme. Modjeska—the deepest admiration. Simultaneously with her
came a small Polish colony which stayed some time with Mr. and Mrs. Chłapowski at an orange farm in the vicinity of Los Angeles. Among them was also

250

HELENA MODJESKA

(From an oil portrait by an American painter, Frank Fowler, done in
1884, in the possession of the Juliusz Słowacki Theatre in Kraków)

tive land after the unsuccessful uprisings of 1831 and 1863; also some notables of the Golden West, a territorial ex-governor among

Henryk Sienkiewicz who took up residence with Julian Horsin in San Francisco. At that time he was a man of thirty, with a melancholy expression on his face, but with eyes so clever and bright with intelligence that in spite of himself he attracted attention. Nevertheless, when Horsin introduced him to me at the next opportunity: 'Mr. Henryk Sienkiewicz, author from Warsaw writing under the pseudonym of Litwos'—it never occurred to me that I saw before me the future intellectual giant, the author of the *Trilogy, Quo Vadis* and *The Knights of the Cross.*

"Another person who also associated with us was Edward S. Solomon, former governor of the Washington Territory, a colleague of Gen. Krzyżanowski from the Civil War. Krzyżanowski had obtained his rank by dispersing one wing of the enemy army by an excellent charge of his cavalry in the battle of Chattanooga. The governor became so fond of the Poles that he would come to see the General every evening and because Horsin somehow could not make himself understood in English, Solomon picked up some Polish, at least so much that he could bid in playing cards and converse with Horsin partly by speaking and partly in energetic sign language. In addition we were joined by a certain Captain Coon, a former Confederate officer. Judging by his nose and speech he was a Jew and his father's name was undoubtedly Kohn, but as a jack-of-all-trades in Gen. Krzyżanowski's affairs he showed much cunning and honest diligence. It was about him, or rather about the General, that Sienkiewicz said that a Polish squire whether at home or abroad always remains the same: he can't do anything without a Jew.

"'Our lady' required half a year to master the English language to such an extent that she could use it on the stage, her teacher being an American woman of Polish-Jewish extraction, with even a Polish name which has now slipped my memory. (Joe Tucholska—*Ed.*) She was a highly educated lady, with a strong sense of her Polish nationality, though she did not speak Polish, and a most devoted admirer of Mme. Modjeska.

"As soon as 'our lady' declared that she was ready to go on the stage, the Polish group, and particularly Krzyżanowski and Solomon, began to get busy. The Grand Opera House was the most outstanding theatre in San Francisco and its manager agreed to give Mme. Modjeska a rehearsal. We all went to that rehearsal, cock-sure of ourselves and ready to stone to death any one doubting the genius of 'our lady.' She entered the stage and began to speak. . . . Scarcely a few minutes had passed when the manager exclaimed rather loudly: 'She is no good!'—The blockhead did not realize the heavenly accent with which she was to charm millions, and in his stupidity considered it a defect!

"At such a verdict 'our lady' rushed crying behind the scenes,—'Gentlemen, what have you exposed me to!' were the only words which amid sighs came from her lips. We stood like stunned, like condemned to death. . . . Only Captain Piotrowski muttered under his nose: 'Oh, the rascal.'—The first to recover from the unpleasant impression was Gen. Krzyżanowski, who called out in his facetious voice.

"'But he's an ass, Madam, it is not for this blockhead to pass judgment on an artist like you.'

"In spite of that Modjeska was utterly discouraged by what she called her 'humiliation.' She did not even want to hear about a new rehearsal for which Solomon had already made preparations, and thus through the ignorance of that hapless manager we would have lost the fame with which the name of Poland was ringing all over the world immediately after Mme. Modjeska's first appear-

them. Henryk Sienkiewicz, the talented author of *Quo Vadis*, and the future creator of that glorious Polish *Trilogy*, also occupied a prominent seat, possibly a box, and was to dispatch a description of this performance to the *Warsaw Gazette* directly after the last curtain-fall.

And, before the evening was over, it was quite apparent that a new star had arisen in the American theatrical firmament. This Polish actress, now thirty-seven years of age, of medium height and delicate features, speaking the English language with an accent, had captured her audience from the very first moment of her appearance on the boards. The play, which had been assembled and put on without too much preparation, must have staggered in places; cues went wrong, lines were misplaced, and once the actress' veil caught fire from the footlights. But she put it out and went calmly on. And when the evening had come to a close, she followed the performance with a one word dispatch to her husband—"Victory."

The career of Helena Modjeska in America had begun.

ances, if it were not for old Captain Piotrowski, who, full of cunning, like a true Ulysses, said to her: 'Well, if one such knave was able to frighten you, certainly you are not a Polish woman.' By this he touched 'our lady's' most sensitive chord. Consequently she extended her hand to the Captain and said: 'Then, my friends, do with me what you like.'

"At that time the Baldwin Theatre was under the management of a once famous American actor, John McCullough, now an old man of seventy. He accepted the suggestion of a rehearsal but demanded that Mme. Modjeska play her role in Polish.

"And again a handful of us went to the Baldwin Theatre . . . with a heavy heart, for though we all trusted the genius of our artist, we did not have much confidence in the American's knowledge of art. For her rehearsal Mme. Modjeska chose the balcony scene from 'Romeo and Juliet.' She entered the stage 'every inch a queen' as the American press expressed it later—and all of a sudden a wonderful stream of our beloved language began to pour on us.

"To hear there, on the coast of the Pacific Ocean, from an American stage, the Polish language—was for us a moment of deepest emotion and the eyes of all of us filled with tears. Captain Piotrowski began to clear his throat so strangely that Sienkiewicz, sitting next to him, whispered some remark in his ear, and Gen. Krzyżanowski pretended that something had fallen in his eye. Suddenly McCullough, with silver hair streaming on his shoulders rushed from behind the scenes and bending his knee before Mme. Modjeska with the flexibility of youth, exclaimed in English: 'You are the greatest artist I have ever seen and I foretell you unusual triumps on our stage!' And he did not let her go from his theatre until she had signed with him a temporary contract for a certain number of appearances.

"Two or three weeks afterward Mme. Modjeska's first appearance took place and the poster read: 'Adrienne Lecouvreur'."—*Ed.*

It was a very opportune time that fate chose in which to introduce this tragedienne. The American stage, which had been struggling through its period of early growth, was now at the beginning of a period of exceptional brilliance, excelling that which had gone before and that which was to follow. The Polish actress had come into the American scene as an American in time to add to the talents with which the stage was becoming so rich, and to quicken it with the culture and art of a people who had cherished the drama for centuries. America had become enormously stage-conscious. Every little town had its theater or opera house, the logical successors of church and town-hall entertainment. In the cities elaborately furnished theaters had their gold-leaf finish, red plush, and dangling glass chandeliers. With their passion for "meetin's" and lectures, the American public had turned eagerly to the stage, and constituted, then as now, the best and largest audiences for any kind of dramatic presentation.

Great artists were already established or growing up in this new civilization who were also recognized as great in other parts of the world. Contemporary with Modjeska's career were actors and actresses of such genius as Edwin Booth, Joseph Jefferson, Julia Marlowe, and many, many others. Artists from abroad who were at one with the stars of the American stage included such brilliant personages as Sarah Bernhardt and Eleonora Duse. These, with such actors as Maude Adams and Otis Skinner, delighted the American public with the finest and most artistic entertainment the New World has ever known, and this over a period of more than thirty years.

Among these, then, came the new actress Helena Modjeska. Her name as a child was Helena Opid; her mother, having been married a second time, to Simon Benda of Kraków, brought her up with the children of the Benda family, sons and daughters of rich gifts in every variety of artistic talent, both for Poland and for America.

Helena was born October 12, 1840, in Kraków, some nine years after the tragic events of the Polish uprising of 1831, but almost from infancy the child was witness to violence and force in the Galician country subdued by Austria and made a part of that realm.

She grew up in the atmosphere of one of the most artistic and delightful cities in the world. Kraków is one of the few cities in which the culture of all ages is embodied in some lasting and living form. One is surrounded there by all the qualities that a cultured civilization has preserved. In the salons the talk is ever stimulating. The afternoon teas and evening meals are often prolonged for hours by interesting discussions among people who find intellectuality exciting and the flow of ideas fascinating. In the shapes of the buildings, the courts, the arches, the monuments, the interior of churches, one finds living thoughts in stone crowding upon the senses and demanding expression. Music, literature, art, ideas from every remote corner of the world, somehow find a forum there. The trumpet sings from the tower of Panna Maria church the song of the Heynal with its tragic note, that has a true quality of the everlasting about it. Goethe found a vision of Faust walking these Gothic streets seeking the philosophy of man's identity, the Elixir and the Stone that released the lonely soul from its enforced habitation. Anything is possible in Kraków, and everything has an inner life.

Out of this city and out of this life came the actress Modjeska. She was as intimately a part of it as the wood carvings of Wit Stwosz or the effigies in the Wawel Cathedral. "If there were no Rome, then Kraków would be Rome," so runs the proverb. She gained from it the dramatic symbolism of life. Life came to her as a thing of double significance, the outer with its manners and its customs and its dress, the inner with the hidden fire of emotion and soul. Her very country was like that. On the surface it bowed to the enforced mandates of its conquerors. In the heart it blazed with an undying fire that knew no quenching. She noted at an early age the power of compression and restraint, more potent than robust expression or exaggerated gesture. She went to the house of the artist Matejko and noted his infinite pains with the expressions of his subjects, and particularly their hands. It was said of her in her triumphal days on the American stage that she could impart a dramatic silence in a crowded theater, by the simple motion of her fingers in setting a book on a table or opening a letter. She watched people in their rounds of duty, saw them in all the poses of action and meditation; she practiced before a mirror the motions of their eyes, the swing of their bodies. The first play she saw, *The Daughter of the Regiment*, excited her so highly that she passed through a whole series of emotions and spent days in bed with a high fever.

Childhood passed into girlhood and youth. Her tutor, Gustaw Modrzejewski, a man twenty years older than herself, whom she later married, guided her through studies of music, art and literature. She read the Polish authors, Mickiewicz, Słowacki, Krasiński, and was thrilled at their expression of Polish national hopes, straightforwardly or in allegory. She read the foreign writers, Dickens, Scott, Bulwer Lytton, and George Sand. Byron she seems to have missed, but she worshiped Schiller, and had a bust of him in her room. In the meantime, her half brothers interested themselves in the stage. Felix Benda became a successful actor in their own theater in Kraków, and with his encouragement she set herself to learn passages out of plays and recited them to her tutor. One night when she was seventeen she saw a German actor, Fritz Devrient, in Shakespeare's *Hamlet*. The bust of Schiller was discarded and Shakespeare took his place in her heart. From that day until her death many years later she was an ardent disciple of the Shakespearean stage, and all her ambitions were directed toward the playing some day of Ophelia, Desdemona, or Juliet. Although the name of Modjeska is still linked in many minds with Camille and Adrienne, the Shakespearean rôles were her greatest desire. Those still living who saw her as Lady Macbeth will never forget her in that rôle.

At length she was married to her loving tutor. The name he gave her became, in modified form, that under which she won her fame. At the time that she was preparing for her first appearance in California, John McCullough's manager explained to her that the name Modrzejewska would not go with American audiences. It must be changed. And so she took the name Modjeska, by which thousands of Americans and English knew her. After her marriage, she lived with her husband in the little town of Bochnia in Poland, a town of ancient salt mines; and the result of an accident in the salt mines led to her first appearance on any stage. People had been hurt in the accident, money for relief was needed, and a quickly arranged benefit performance by talent in the town seemed the best way to get it. A play was arranged and given, and Modjeska appeared in it on a small stage, about ten feet deep, before scenery made out of wallpaper and canvas, with a curtain of red calico covered with silver paper stars. The benefit was a success. Modjeska apparently suffered pangs of stage-fright before the curtain rose, but once she was behind the footlights she was as cool and collected as if she had been brought up on the stage. It was a quality that marked her in all her career, a steadiness and assuredness that no mishaps behind scenes could shake.

From this year, 1861, to 1865 she played continuously in a little company in which her husband was the manager and director. It was actually a barnstorming company, for in their travels about Galicia they acted in almost every kind of building known to man. This was in a way a good preparation for her American career, for in earlier years there, and in later years of success, she never neglected small towns, and many a mining camp in California and Nevada added its plaudits to an actress who took life as she found it and seldom became temperamental over bad roads, drafty stages, poor lodging houses or cranky managers. In 1866 she went to Poznań, where the fame of her performances in Galicia had preceded her, and this helped to win the attention of Warsaw critics and theatrical managers. In these years of beginnings she played literally hundreds of parts, in classics, farces, and even operas. She was cast in a great variety of rôles, and once appeared as a man in a play given in a small Galician town. But changes had come about. A sad melancholy hung over the country, censorships had increased because of the uprising of 1863, and all plays were thoroughly scrutinized by officials lest some treasonable matter should reach the public. Then, too, she lost her little daughter Marylka by death, and this was followed shortly by the death of her husband.

From Poznań she went to the country's most important theater in Warsaw. Here she ran into something she had not met with to any extent before—professional jealousy on the part of other actors. Moreover, the life of a prima donna in Warsaw was no easy task under the Russians. She added to the complications of censorship and suspicion and intrigue by marrying Count

Charles Bozenta Chłapowski before her appearance in the Warsaw Imperial Theater in 1868. He was interested in a Kraków
newspaper, which, being outside the Russian portion of Poland,
could print articles in a much freer vein than could those in the
capital, and for this reason he was looked upon with considerable
suspicion. Modjeska herself became actively interested in this
paper, and as a result was constantly under the eye of the officials
while she was in the Polish capital.

Yet she was growing in fame. She visited theaters in Vienna
and Berlin, and was asked at one time to appear in Paris. Theatrical celebrities all over the continent came to know her, and she
gained much through friendship and associations with them. Her
Adrienne had become famous and she repeated it many times. She
was the center of an intellectual group which included the greatest writers and artists in Poland. Adulation poured in upon her
from all sides. As the wife of a count she mingled with the highest
groups in society. The De Reszke family became close friends, and
she even introduced the famous Jan on his first appearance before
the public. Editors, journalists, Moniuszko the famous musician,
Sienkiewicz the novelist, Anton Rubinstein the composer, and
many others were among the visitors at her Warsaw house. She
went to Berlin to see Madame Ristori in *Mary Stuart,* and the
great actress received her with enthusiasm in the house where she
was staying. She met in Warsaw a young American actor,
Maurice Neville, who was playing Hamlet (in English with
Polish support) according to Edwin Booth's conception of the
part. From his lips she first heard of Edwin Booth, little realizing
how much of her destiny was to be linked with that of the great
American actor.

But at the height of her career there came a series of stunning
blows: the death of her half brother Felix Benda; misunderstandings with the Russian censor; a farce produced in the crowded
theater, in which her life and that of her husband were satirized,
and a number of insulting insinuations were made. Compelled at
length by government officials to appear in plays that were not of
her choice and liking, she broke down in health and retired temporarily to private life. This was in 1875. And it was in the winter
of that year that the decision was made to leave a scene already

hopeless, and to emigrate to America with a few choice spirits to whom reports of the coming Centennial Exhibition in Philadelphia opened vistas of a land of great opportunity and happiness. Henryk Sienkiewicz himself was at the house when the decision was made. There was much discussion of different states, but California was agreed upon in the end, despite talk of jaguars and rattlesnakes. They should all at once begin life anew, raise coffee, castor oil beans, and pepper, live off wild game and wild cactus fruit, and possibly dig gold out of the earth, as it was said to exist everywhere beneath the soil in the Golden West.

The ranch upon which they settled in California did not prosper so well as they—and a company of intellectuals—had imagined. But Sienkiewicz was to find characters there among the Polish exiles for his great *Trilogy*, and Modjeska was to find a career that led to great heights. They all worked hard on the ranch, that is, the Count and his wife did. Some of the intellectuals found that tending cattle and milking cows was rather exhausting work. But the lady herself worked faithfully, and the hundred and one chores she had to perform did not dampen her enthusiasm. Something, however, did happen to cause her dismay, and hard work was no remedy for it. Their money ran out, and the ranch was "in the red."

Determined not to abandon the American experiment and return to censorships, she set herself out to recoup the family's fortunes. There came the visits to San Francisco, English lessons, visits to the manager of the San Francisco theater, and the first performance of *Adrienne Lecouvreur*. It was the mighty accomplishment of a huge task: the learning of a new language, the art of fluency of expression in it and the memorizing of plays. Yet she did this in a few months by the most unremitting labor and toil. When it came to playing Shakespeare in those early days, she occasionally lapsed into Polish, but the audiences thought not a whit of that. In a few weeks after her first appearance she was booked for a western trip in small towns. And then came a call to play in New York.

She opened with *Adrienne Lecouvreur* again; it was in the historic old Fifth Avenue Theater. As she remarked in her memoirs, *Adrienne* seemed to bring an element of confusion with it; in

San Francisco it was the burning of her veil, and in New York she carried a shoehorn in her hand in one act, thinking that it was a fan. In Boston, while leaving the stage she failed to notice a bar across the bottom of the door and fell full length over it. But none of these mishaps did the audience seem to mind. She carried them all with her in absolute absorption in the part. *Adrienne* was fairly successful; it introduced her to the powerful cultural group in New York, among them Richard Watson Gilder, editor of the *Century*, and his sister Jeanette Gilder, writer and critic. It brought her in touch as well with probably the greatest dramatic critic America has ever known, William Winter. This was in December, 1877. In January of the next year she appeared in *Camille*. This time there was no question of success. New York thronged to see her. The theater was sold out for a long time ahead, and the orchestra chairs had to be taken out to make room for those who wished to see and hear the new sensation.

As was the custom, she moved on to Philadelphia, and then to Boston. While she was playing at the old Boston Museum she met Henry Wadsworth Longfellow, with whom she began a lifelong friendship. With her son Ralph, she visited the poet's house in Cambridge and had luncheon there. She also met Oliver Wendell Holmes, Thomas Bailey Aldrich, James T. Fields, and Celia Thaxter, who wrote a poem in her honor. The Boston audiences of those days reminded her of the crowds in Warsaw, and when she came back to the hotel after her last performance, the streets were so crowded that the carriage could hardly move. All were anxious to see the Polish Countess. In Washington she met General Sherman, Roscoe Conkling, and General Grant. In Louisville she was entertained by "Marse" Henry Watterson. In St. Louis she had a pleasant chat with Eugene Field. The best of America had taken her up and admitted her to the best intellectual circles that the country knew. In each of these, and in fact in every circle, she was at home.

From *Adrienne* and *Camille* she went on to Shakespearean roles: as Rosalind in *As You Like It*, Viola in *Twelfth Night*, and above all, her tragic roles in *Hamlet*, *Macbeth* and *Othello*. By 1883 she was a recognized part of the American stage. Her husband had become an American, and she had changed her citizenship with him; and year by year for some twenty-five years she appeared during the theatrical season in different cities in the country, except, of course, in those periods in which she filled successful engagements in London, Warsaw, Kraków and Praha. A number of articles about her were printed in the leading American magazines: in *Scribners, Critic, Catholic World*, the old *Bostonian*, and others. An article in the *Century*, which Mr. Gilder edited, compared her with Sarah Bernhardt. The French actress, the critic said, had brilliancy, but with it the hardness and coldness of a diamond. Modjeska, in addition to her skill, possessed warmth and a sympathetic touch which never failed to grip her audiences. Even when she played parts that she hated, in the detestable (to her) *East Lynne*, which she called "Beast Lynne," and that of Odette, she was supreme.

She played a variety of parts, at first under Dion Boucicault's direction, later under Charles Frohman. All the Shakespearean roles were included, with Mary Stuart, Adrienne, Camille, Frou Frou and others. She played in Ibsen's *A Doll's House*, though at first seemingly without realization of what Ibsen's plays would mean to the stage. It is quite evident, too, that she gained enormously in her power to play the more tragic roles. For while at the beginning, as the *Century* critic pointed out, she was better liked as Rosalind and Viola, she later came to stir audiences as a tragedienne, and under this designation she finished her career on the stage. She was cast with the greatest actors of her day, Booth, Salvini, and the young Otis Skinner. Booth, Barret, and Modjeska, and later Booth, Salvini, and Modjeska were household words.

There was something in the glory of the stage in the eighties and nineties that warms the hearts even of this later generation of theater-goers. The American stage was then probably at its highest point of development. This actress of Polish blood, who became an American, was for twenty-five years and more a part of the American "star" system and also a part of what has now become a wonderful tradition. Audiences who saw these plays in such glorious theaters as, say, the Tabor Grand Theater in Denver, with its inlays and gold and chandelier of Paris Opera House style, its luxurious fittings, and marvelous curtain and orchestra, may well sigh today for the emotional and intellectual thrills of the theater of yesterday.

The groups that interested themselves in the theater were everywhere. In New York, for example, at the Gilder studio Modjeska met such people as John La Farge the artist, St. Gaudens the sculptor, Joe Jefferson the actor, and Walt Whitman the poet. When she returned in the middle eighties to Poland and England and France, she had interviews with the most famous people of that day, was entertained by the Prince of Wales and Tennyson, talked with Dvorak in Praha, was a guest of Paderewski, and visited with Joseph Hofmann. Everywhere she went, people of the highest cultural influence sought her out. In Ireland, because of a few words about her "oppressed country," the people swarmed about her in excitement and a riot was narrowly averted. A policeman was detailed to her by government order to see that she took her boat safely. In Warsaw, a group of youths, defying the government officials, offered her a bouquet tied with the Polish national colors, which caused seventeen of them to be expelled from school, and one suicide resulted. In Chicago a speech at the opening of the World's Fair was taken by Russian officials to be hostile toward their government, and her visit to Warsaw was decidedly unpleaasnt. But she went back to Kraków to help dedicate the magnificent theater there; and then, at the height of her career, and under the less aggressive Austrian government, she received, probably, the greatest ovation of her life.

Her life was so full of incident, her career so crowded with events, that her memoirs seem like many lives rather than one. Returning to America after her European triumphs, she went back to New York and the road and played everywhere to crowded houses. In the late nineties, she took up the role of Cleopatra in the Shakespeare play, and it is in this role that many people remember her today, together with Camille, Rosalind, and Desdemona. It is of interest that in her last performances as Cleopatra, her nephew Władysław Benda, the famous artist, then recently arrived from Vienna, made the sketches for all the stage designs and costumes.

In 1905 a testimonial performance was given her in New York, close to the time of her retirement. Some of those who took part were Louis James, Mrs. Patrick Campbell, Ada Rehan, James O'Neil, and many other famous artists. Mr. Stedman, the poet, made a speech after the second act of *Macbeth*, and a letter from Paderewski was read. For two years thereafter, she continued to give farewell performances in different cities, appearing mostly in *Macbeth* and *Mary Stuart*.

In 1909 she died in California and was buried in Kraków July 18, 1910. According to her own wishes she was buried in the city of her birth, and there visitors from America and from all Europe, in fact, brought flowers constantly. Like the great Polish writers and artists, Wyspiański, Sienkiewicz, Matejko, she did not live to see her country once more free. And though there is sadness in the truth that an actor's art dies with him, there is solace in this, that an eternal flame may be enkindled in one heart and spread itself throughout thousands of other hearts, and thus live on.

ZYGMUNT WRÓBLEWSKI

(From a woodcut published in the Warsaw scientific journal *Wszechświat*
for the year 1888, sketched by Bronisław Puc)

XXI-XXII

ZYGMUNT WRÓBLEWSKI

1845-88

and

KAROL OLSZEWSKI

1846-1915

"The Siamese Twins of Polish Science"

by

Tadeusz Estreicher

Of all the changes in science and technology which de
veloped in the last half-century, the widening of the range of
temperatures both upwards and downwards was not the least
important. Although a scientific scholar or a technician of fifty
years ago was able with great effort and on a small scale only
to obtain a temperature of 2000° C. or above, now he can obtain
much higher temperatures. The same was the case with low
temperatures. Fifty years ago nobody could go lower than Faraday
was able to do in the forties of the last century, that is, hardly
a temperature of 110° C. was obtained. If this limit was surpassed,
if the frigorific methods reached almost their possible limits of
273° C., it is due mainly to the work of two Polish scientists,
Karol Olszewski and Zygmunt Wróblewski.

The problem of obtaining lower temperatures is closely
connected with the liquefaction of gases; and the liquefaction of
the air and its constituents, oxygen and nitrogen, achieved by the

above-mentioned two scientists in 1883, was of decisive importance. This problem had interested scientists for a good many centuries; but it was not until the end of the eighteenth century that it was stated in a clear and scientific manner by Lavoisier, the famous French chemist. Since that time many experiments were undertaken, but without results, although they had been carried on by great scientists, among others by the great Faraday. They succeeded in liquefying many gases, but hydrogen, oxygen, nitrogen, carbon monoxide, nitric oxide and methane resisted even Faraday and they were recognized as permanent gases not to be liquefied. It is true that Faraday was of a different opinion and thought that all gases could be liquefied but that they must be sufficiently cooled, as the mere condensation of the gas even under the greatest pressure was not enough. But Faraday could not obtain a lower temperature than the 110° C. mentioned above.

A quarter of a century after Faraday, Andrews, an English physicist, carried on research with carbon dioxide, a gas easy to liquefy, and he generalized the results obtained by stating that every gas has a so-called critical temperature which is the limit between the liquid and the gaseous state; below this temperature even a not very high pressure is sufficient for the liquefaction of the gas; above this temperature not even the highest pressure can liquefy the gas. Viewed in this way, the negative results of Faraday's research prove that he worked in too high a temperature, or that the temperature of 110° C. although it may seem very low, is still higher than the critical temperatures of the constituents of the air. A field was left open for further research, which was carried on by numerous scientists in the seventies, above all Cailletet in France and Pictet in Switzerland. Their experiments, and especially those of the latter, were widely renowned; but only the work of Cailletet preserved its scientific value. He was not fortunate, either, in liquefying air and its constituents, but he was able at least to transform them for the fraction of a second into a state of mist, and mist is of course nothing but a spray of small drops. In this way the possibility of liquefying these gases was experimentally proved; public demonstrations of Cailletet's experiments excited general interest and hundreds of apparatuses of his system were sold for laboratories all over the world.

It was at this time that our two scientists appeared.

Zygmunt Wróblewski was born in Grodno on October 28, 1845. He attended the local secondary school, which he finished brilliantly, as attested by a silver medal. For further studies he went to the University of Kiev in Russia. But he could not study here very long; this was the year 1863, when Polish youth in the schools thought less of their books and more of taking arms in revolt against the Russian oppressor. And Wróblewski, too, did not neglect his national duty; but a few months after the outbreak of the insurrection, in July 1863, he was arrested and sentenced to exile in Siberia. In Tomsk he spent three years, was forced to earn his daily bread by hard manual labor, and was able to acquire knowledge only by the unsystematic study of popular handbooks and through self-education. In spite of all these difficulties and his feeble health, he worked to create by himself a new theory of electricity, which he intended to prove experimentally. At last, in 1869, on the basis of a general amnesty, he came back to Poland, but with impaired health and weakened eyesight. Nevertheless he made efforts to continue his studies in his beloved field of physics and mathematics. But his eyesight was so bad that he went to Berlin for a cure. After two operations and six months' stay in a dark room in the hospital, he at last was able to matriculate in the university there, still in danger of losing his eyesight. He was warned to refrain for a number of years from reading and writing.

Much strength of character was needed for work under such conditions. He diligently attended all lectures; first in Berlin and afterwards in Heidelberg, where he studied physics under Helmholtz. When the latter became professor of physics at the University of Berlin, Wróblewski followed him there. But the way of his career was by no means smooth: he had no money even to pay the university fees, to say nothing of expensive laboratory experiments. He offered his help as an assistant to different professors, and, at last, in the summer of 1872, obtained the post of assistant to Professor Jolly in Munich. As an assistant he was able to carry on his work without financial worries. Although he still was not allowed to read or write, he did such brilliant work that two years afterwards he received his doctor's degree with the highest distinction (*summa cum laude*) on the basis of a dissertation in the field of electricity.

In the same year he moved to Strassburg, as laboratory assistant to Professor Kundt, and in 1876 he was accepted as candidate for a lectureship on physics, on the basis of his paper on the diffusion of gases through absorbing substances. His sojourn in Strassburg, where he remained for four years, was important in that it enabled him to take better care of his health and to devote himself entirely to scientific research. In consequence, the scientific world began to value him more and more highly, until in the year 1878 he received a proposal from the Japanese government offering him the post of professor of physics at the University of Yeddo. Negotiations followed, but in the meanwhile an opportunity of returning to work in his own country was offered to Wróblewski. Stefan Kuczyński, professor of physics at the University of Kraków, was approaching the age at which professors generally retire; a successor to this post had to be found. The choice fell on Wróblewski. The Polish Academy of Sciences in Kraków granted him a research fellowship, in order to enable him to visit foreign laboratories and to become acquainted with their work and methods, which later on he might apply in organizing the Kraków laboratory.

Thanks to this fellowship, Wróblewski worked under Debray in the laboratory of the *École Normale Supérieure* in Paris; also in the laboratories in London, Oxford and Cambridge. Wherever he went he made personal contacts with eminent physicists. In Paris he wrote a paper on the chemical composition of carbon dioxide with water. For this work he had to use an apparatus exerting a very high pressure upon the gas; he bought for the purpose a compression pump made according to the model which at that time was being used by the French physicist Cailletet, who was then working on the liquefaction of the most resistant gases, above all of the constituents of the air. Although Cailletet's researches did not attain strictly positive results, they still proved that the possibility of liquefaction existed.

With this apparatus, and under the impression of Cailletet's experiments, Wróblewski returned to his country in 1882. In the University of Kraków, where he became professor of physics, he

KAROL OLSZEWSKI

(From a photograph preserved in the Institute of Inorganic Chemistry
at the University of Kraków)

met his colleague, the professor of chemisty, Karol Olszewski.

Karol Olszewski was born in Broniszów near Tarnów on January 29, 1846. His youth was no less difficult than that of Wróblewski, except that his travels had not been so extensive. The beginning of the year 1846 marked a sad period in Polish history; the Austrian government feared that the movements for freedom which broke out among the nations all over Europe would have an especial justification in Poland—oppressed as she was by the three partitioning powers—and so instigated the uneducated peasants to rise against the country gentry. The landowners were represented to them as their worst enemies and the movement for freedom as a tendency to oppress them. The Austrian Emperor and his German magistrates, on the other hand, were held up as the friends and defenders of the peasants. Orders were given to the magistrates to organize riots, and landowners were murdered by peasants thus deceived by the emissaries of Prince Metternich, the Chancellor of Austria. Among the murdered victims was Olszewski's father; his mother with her daughter and baby son Karol, only a few weeks old, escaped to Nowy Sącz, where Olszewski spent his childhood and entered the secondary school.

Then came the year 1863 when the whole patriotic youth of Poland arose in their struggle against Russia for the freedom of their country. Olszewski, seventeen years old, joined the movement, but before he left for the front, he was taken prisoner, together with the whole training camp, by the Austrian authorities. When at last he was released, it was too late to take part in the insurrection. So he came back to school, graduated from a *gimmazjum* at Tarnów, and in the year 1866 entered the University of Kraków. He was a very good student, not infrequently receiving from his professors such notes as "*diligentissime*" or "*summa cum diligentia.*" The unusually fine results of his studies recommended him to the special attention of his professor of chemistry, Czyrniański, who as early as 1869 appointed him his assistant. Olszewski, who by nature was endowed with great practical sense and ability in the construction of machinery, at once began to repair an old and damaged Natterer's compressor and with its help succeeded in liquefying and solidifying carbon dioxide, which afterwards was used for scientific purposes. It is true that this experiment was neither new nor difficult, but it was of great importance for Olszewski's further scientific career, since it made him acquainted with the technical methods of compressing gases and obtaining low temperatures.

With the paper containing these data he left in 1872 for Heidelberg, where he studied chemistry under Bunsen, physics under Kirchhoff and mineralogy under Blum. There, in August of the same year he received his doctor's degree, *"insigni cum laude."* During this short stay in Heidelberg he acquired a wider outlook upon new problems and new methods of research, and the influence of the great scientist Bunsen played no small part in the development of Olszewski's mind. He brought from Heidelberg some instruments which are still kept in the Kraków laboratory; there were only a few of them because he could not afford to buy many out of the small yearly sum of 600 florins (about $250) which he received from the Department of Chemistry.

Upon his return to Kraków he continued his former duties as assistant, then became a "docent" or instructor, and in 1876 was nominated as associate professor of analytical chemistry. His position, however, was not improved; he had no laboratory of his own and no grant of funds. At last, in 1885 he was granted the small sum of 200 florins (equivalent to about $83) yearly. It was due entirely to the benevolence and kindness of Professor Czyrniański, who at that time was director of the Institute of Chemistry, that Olszewski had facilities for scientific research.

Thus matters stood till the year 1882 when Wróblewski, the newly appointed professor of physics, arrived at Kraków with great enthusiasm for scientific research and information about modern problems in which the scientists of England, France and Germany were interested. The acquaintance of these two Polish scientists, and conversations about problems they had in common, soon led to plans of experimenting together on the liquefaction of the most resistant gases and above all the constituents of the air.

The chief obstacle which stood in the way of Cailletet's experiments was that he was not able to obtain a sufficiently low temperature which would be lower than the critical temperature of the gases under investigation. For cooling he used a liquefied gas called ethylene which boils at 104° C.; but this temperature is still a few degrees too high for the liquefaction of oxygen (119° C.). Olszewski suggested that by lowering the pressure upon the boiling ethylene with a pneumatic pump its boiling temperature would also be lowered. He constructed an apparatus for obtaining ethylene in large quantities, and another one for the purpose of boiling the liquid in a vacuum. The experiments carried on in the Chemical Institute proved the success of the method, and further research was transferred to the Physical Institute, where Cailletet's apparatus in a somewhat modified form was to be found, enabling the scientists more easily to cool and examine the liquefied gas.

The results of the co-operation of a chemist and a physicist were not long in forthcoming; two months after the beginning of the experiments they succeeded in liquefying oxygen, although in small quantities. Nevertheless this was great progress; the liquid could be kept as long as the tube was cooled and under high pressure, while in Cailletet's experiments only a fleeting mist for a fraction of a second could be seen. What was more, the conditions under which the liquefaction occurred could be measured and the necessary temperature and pressure exactly indicated. In short, this experiment was a broadening of the field of scientific research by the addition of a range of temperatures much lower than had been possible up to that time; it was also the beginning of further research on other gases, not yet liquefied, permitting the supposition that there was a still further possibility for the lowering of temperatures; and furthermore, it brought a deeper knowledge of the various properties of matter and of its reactions to these changed conditions.

April 9, 1883, the day when the news of the result was officially sent to the Academy of Sciences in Paris, is recognized as the date [1] of the liquefaction of oxygen, marking an epoch in the history of science.

---

[1] One may still meet the opinion, even in scientific literature, that air was liquefied for the first time by Cailletet and Pictet. I have explained above that these scientists by no means obtained air as a liquid. As a characteristic proof I quote a passage from the book *Air Liquide* by Claude, the greatest of the French

This sensational news was shortly afterwards followed by news of the liquefaction of nitrogen and carbon monoxide; later on of the solidification of carbon disulphide, ethyl alcohol and methyl alcohol, and other substances which had been known until then as liquids only.

But this co-operation so brilliantly begun, of chemist and physicist, who, it would seem, supplemented one another perfectly, was not to last long. The chief reason for this was that each of them possessed a strong personality and differed in temperament, which made relations between them difficult; each of them wanted to work in the same direction, but in a different way, and neither would make concessions and be subordinate to the other. About the middle of the year 1883 they parted, and from that time on each worked by himself. Wróblewski found himself in an easier position, since he had his own laboratory furnished with apparatus for this type of experiments; Olszewski was forced to buy everything with the small means which, with the greatest difficulty, Professor Czyrniański was able to supply from the subsidies he received for the necessities of the Chemical Institute. The Institute had at its disposal the sum of 1200 florins (about $500) a year, and out of this sum the costs of the new expensive apparatus had to be covered. But with economic management of the small amount, and Olszewski's ability in the construction of machinery, not only had the apparatus of Cailletet been purchased by the fall of that year, but an entirely new apparatus had been constructed by Olszewski on quite different lines, which in comparison with the previous one showed enormous progress.

In the years following, both scientists developed their activities separately and intensively, as if each of them wished to surpass the other. Both had the same end in view: to liquefy the lightest and most resistant of all gases then known, namely, hydrogen. Both used similar methods: they tried to cool hydrogen compressed to 100 or 200 atmospheres in order later to expand it,

workers in the field of the liquefaction of gases, who, being himself a Frenchman, would be favorably disposed toward the French scientists. He says:

"Le 9 avril, 1883, date mémorable, ils virent l'oxygène . . . se reunir en gouttelettes. . . . Quel enthousiasme pour les premiers expérimentateurs auxquels il était enfin donné de voir le fluide que nous respirons transformé en un liquide tranquille, limpide. . . ."—Author.

much as Cailletet had done before with oxygen. Through this sudden expansion of the gas a great, though very brief, lowering of temperature is obtained. This enabled Cailletet to transform oxygen into a state of mist for the fraction of a second. The experimenters reached similar results with hydrogen, which certainly was a great triumph, though rather a theoretical one, because in practice it did not lead to the obtaining of a liquid which, for instance, might be used for cooling other substances.

With this chief end always in view, they did not neglect other problems which came up as a result of the widening of the range of low temperatures for more than 100 degrees in the minus field; they investigated the behavior of other gases, their temperatures of boiling and solidification, their intensity in the liquid state, their electric and optic properties and others; they improved their apparatuses more and more and obtained constantly larger quantities of cooling liquids.

In the midst of this feverish work Wróblewski unexpectedly died, in April 1888. Late in the evening, when he was alone in the laboratory, designing a plan of a new apparatus, he accidentally knocked over a kerosene lamp which fell and broke to pieces, pouring upon him a stream of flaming liquid. Before he could run out into the courtyard, or the servants could hurry to extinguish the living torch, he had been so seriously burnt that after three weeks of terrible suffering he died, a martyr in the cause of science. His death aroused genuine grief both in Poland and in other countries, where during his long sojourns he had made many acquaintances with whom he kept in contact through his scientific activity. His name had become famous in the last few years of his life; his elections to the memberships of different scientific societies, such as the Academy of Sciences at Kraków, the Academy of Sciences at Vienna, the *Société de Physique et d'Histoire Naturelle* at Geneva, serve as a proof of the appreciation he enjoyed. He was also granted the money award of the Vienna Academy for the best research work in science during the three-year period of 1883-86.

Wróblewski's death had no influence on Olszewski's further activity, since for five years he had worked alone, perhaps even more effectively than Wróblewski. An able constructor, he built, in September 1883, as mentioned above, an entirely new apparatus in which much larger quantities of gas could be obtained. If in the first apparatus the quantity amounted to 10-20 cubic millimeters, in the new one about 20 cubic centimeters could be obtained, that is, a quantity one or two thousand times larger. What was more, a measuring instrument could be immersed for measuring the temperature in different conditions of pressure, or the liquid could be used as a cooling bath, etc., all of which greatly widened the range of experiments. He constantly published new treatises in different fields of physics and chemistry on low temperatures. His apparatus, which was of very ingenious construction, was comparatively simple, and it was easy, with its use, to demonstrate the liquefaction of oxygen or of air, even before a large assembly during university lectures. The liquefaction took place in a thick-walled glass tube, resistant to high pressure amounting to seventy atmospheres, and it could be observed even from a distance.

But these advantages had also their defects. The glass tube could not be large, as it would then have been less resistant to high pressure. In any case, exposing the glass tube to high pressure was a dangerous procedure and threatened explosion. This induced Olszewski to make further improvements. In 1889-90 he built an apparatus in which the glass tube was replaced by a resistant steel cylinder with a volume of about one-quarter of a liter. Thus the process of liquefaction itself was not visible, but this was of little importance, since the conditions of liquefaction were already well known. On the other hand one-fourth of a liter of liquid was obtained at one time, and could be poured into another receptacle below and used for further purposes, scientific or practical. As the process could be repeated again and again, and new quantities of one-fourth of a liter of the liquid obtained, the question of getting liquid oxygen or air in the quantities required was reduced to a fairly simple problem.

This apparatus constituted the greatest progress in the field of the liquefaction of gases and was a real sensation in the scientific world of those days. Other experimenters, such as Kamerlingh Onnes in Leyden, Holland, and James Dewar in London, imitated it when organizing their laboratories for research in low temperatures. Dewar, in particular, imitated Olszewski's apparatus and also repeated his experiments and showed them in public, thereby winning wide and great renown in England. Dewar became famous by repeating Olszewski's experiments, and was granted the Rumford Gold Medal in 1894 by the Royal Society in London. English scientists were aware of the injustice done to Olszewski by the distinction conferred on Dewar. Therefore Ramsay, the most prominent English chemist of those days, turned to Olszewski with the proposal of publishing in the English scientific journals the results of his entire research work, and thus defended his right of priority in the field of the liquefaction of gases and lower temperatures.

Olszewski accepted the proposal, and, with Ramsay's help, he published in *Nature*, for January 1895, a short article entitled: "On the Liquefaction of Gases—a Claim for Priority." A month later, there appeared in *The Philosophical Magazine* a larger report of the results of his research done in Kraków. A controversy with Dewar ensued, which ended in the successful establishment of Olszewski's claim in English opinion.

But Olszewski's name was to become still more famous in England. For at the same time (1894) Ramsay and another great physicist, Lord Rayleigh, made the unexpected and sensational discovery that air, a substance which was apparently so well known and had been so well explored, contained one more gas (whose existence nobody seemed to have suspected), a gas with quite unusual qualities which were not to be found in any other substance. This was the element called argon, the first of the group of inactive gases, of which five more were gradually discovered by Ramsay. Now problems for investigation from several different points of view arose. Ramsay tackled the chemical side of the problem, Lord Rayleigh the physical side; and for investigation concerning its spectroscopic properties and the conditions under which the gas could be liquefied, they turned for co-operation to the two best specialists of that time, Sir William Crookes and Olszewski. It was characteristic that instead of putting the problem of liquefaction of argon into the hands of their compatriot Dewar the two Great English scientists, Ramsay and Lord Rayleigh, entrusted it to Olszewski.

The discovery of argon was the sensation of the year; the

whole scientific world impatiently waited for the moment when the discoverers would officially publish the results of their research. This took place on January 31, 1895, at a solemn public meeting of the Royal Society which at least a thousand people attended, including all the most prominent English scientists and the great contemporary physicist, Lord Kelvin. Dewar was not invited.

The results of the research conducted on argon were reported by Ramsay, who recapitulated the experiments carried on by himself, Lord Rayleigh, Crookes and Olszewski. This last name, which had hardly been known to wider circles in England, now appeared in all the English newspapers and scientific journals, and attention was drawn to the controversy which was simultaneously being carried on in *Nature* concerning the claim for priority in the liquefaction of gases. Public opinion unreservedly took the part of Olszewski against Dewar.

In May 1895, two inventors, Hampson in England and Linde in Germany, quite independently of each other applied for patents for their apparatuses for the liquefaction of air. Their machines were based upon entirely new principles. Formerly, different cooling agents, becoming gradually stronger, had been used for refrigeration—that is to say, ice was used for cooling carbon dioxide, which was thus solidified and used in turn for liquefying ethylene, and the latter finally was used for liquefying oxygen and air. The newly patented method entirely dispensed with cooling agents; it made use of the fact that gas, compressed and expanded in an especially constructed apparatus, is by this very compression and expansion cooled.

The principle being simple and the experimental side not at all complicated, it was easy soon after the announcement of the new method to understand that it was to this and not to the former apparatus that the future of the technique of the liquefaction of gases belonged. Since all great laboratories for physical and chemical research had purchased the apparatus of Hampson and Linde, the Kraków Laboratory had also to be provided with the modern apparatus. Olszewski directed a note to the Ministry of Education in Vienna (Kraków at that time was under the government of Austria) in which he pleaded the necessity of granting a subsidy of 24,000 kronen (about $4500) for the new apparatus. The Austrian Ministry, unfavorably disposed toward Polish science, granted only 6000 kronen (about $1130) to be paid in six installments of 1000 kronen a year. On such a poor financial basis Olszewski set to work to change the equipment of the laboratory, purchasing apparatus and machines partly on credit and partly from his own private income. The writer of these words was at that time in Ramsay's laboratory in London, and saw there the installation of the Hampson machine and observed the first experiments. An enthusiastic letter describing this experience influenced Olszewski's decision to purchase that machine and not Linde's. Since I had become acquainted with the construction of the machine and its working I was able, upon my return to Kraków in the early part of the year 1900, to help with the new installation which was to be used in further experiments.

In the meantime Dewar, who had at his disposal the financial support of the Royal Institute in London, and for several years had had the new apparatus, successfully accomplished that which Wróblewski and Olszewski had set forth to achieve some years before; that is, he liquefied hydrogen in an apparatus similar to that of Hampson, the construction of which, however, he kept secret and never revealed. But Olszewski, and Travers in London, simultaneously but independently of each other, set out to build a hydrogen apparatus which would be so constructed that it could be cooled with liquid air before the liquefaction of the hydrogen. This is easy to write but difficult to accomplish technically; therefore Olszewski had to construct many models, more and more perfect, till after several years he built an apparatus which in its field is unrivaled.

Olszewski also devoted much time to the problem of liquefaction of helium, but always with discouraging results. He realized the difficulty: an apparatus must be built similar to the hydrogen apparatus, but smaller, since helium, then very expensive, was produced only in very small quantities from rare Scandinavian minerals. But for that a great deal of money was necessary, which the small university laboratory in Kraków could not afford. Kamerlingh Onnes of Holland was in a much easier position; he was able to get large quantities of helium, and in 1908 was the first scientist to carry through the liquefaction of helium. Olszewski till the end of his life never gave up the idea of building such an apparatus and constructed one at last in the years 1913 and 1914. He was not at all jealous of other scientists and freely offered advice to the well-known German physicist and chemist, Haber, who bought a hydrogen apparatus of Olszewski's construction from the mechanician of the University of Kraków for his own laboratory in the *Kaiser-Wilhelm-Institut* in Dahlem.

It would be impossible to enumerate here all the work accomplished by Olszewski in his chosen field; only that which was most important or most characteristic has been mentioned here. It may be added that he also built an apparatus in which any required temperature might be obtained continuously down to 190° C., to be used for practical purposes as well as for scientific research; a similar apparatus in which any required temperature down to 252° C. could be obtained by using liquid hydrogen; also an apparatus for separating the constituents of air by fractional distillation and many other apparatuses, some of which never became known because his feeble health did not allow him to complete all his work before he died.

In his youth Olszewski was very lively and agile; he was a sportsman, liked hunting and was one of the first cyclists in Kraków. After 1892, a long illness seriously weakened him. From that time on he lived in the laboratory building, which he very seldom left. He held examinations and classroom sessions in his lodgings and not at the university. Thus he was able to prolong his work for more than twenty years. But his strength diminished more and more and the final stroke was the outbreak of the Great War. Living conditions in Kraków grew more and more difficult; the echo of battles, ever more serious and nearer Kraków, disturbed him; he was much worried about the fate of his laboratory, which was turned into quarters for Austrian soldiers. All this had a bad influence on his mental and physical state, and he died on March 25, 1915. During his last night, alone in his lodgings (he was not married and had no relatives), he wrote down on a sheet of paper his wishes as to his funeral and his personal observations upon the symptoms of approaching death.

At first his death passed almost without any notice. Kraków was cut off from the world by the war fronts, and the news of his death was deafened by the peal of cannon and alarming war news. But the name of this scientist will never perish and the results of his research caused a revolution in science and industry. If today science has at its disposal temperatures amounting almost to 273° C.; if the industry of today produces liquid air in ton quantities for cooling purposes and as an explosive agent (oxyliquit) or as a reservoir of oxygen in condensed form; if today factories produce ammoniac and nitric acid out of nitrogen obtained through the distillation of liquid air; if great towns glitter at night with innumerable lights of neon advertisements (neon is also a product of the distillation of liquid air)—all these phenomena of modern life have their common source in an experiment insignificant in dimensions if measured according to the modern scale: the experiment noted in the annals of the history of science under the date of April 9, 1883, which was carried out at the University of Kraków by Olszewski and Wróblewski.

What is the contribution of each of them to their joint achievement? Whose is the greater part? Such questions may be met with even today. A number of years ago these questions were put far more frequently, when both scientists worked together and it was difficult to separate one from the other; when they separated they divided the scientific world into adherents of one or of the other. Today we may look upon these questions more dispassionately: one was a theoretical physicist and the other a practical chemist; they jointly solved an important problem, which up to that time had not been solved by the greatest scientists. That both were equal to their high aims, is proved by the great amount of research and experiments carried on by each independently of the other; but their common work gave the most valuable results.

Translated from the Polish by Jadwiga Zemanek Targoszowa.

XXIII

HENRYK SIENKIEWICZ
"The Patriot Novelist of Poland"

1846-1916

by

Monica M. Gardner

Henryk Sienkiewicz was born of a family of the Polish country gentry at Wola Okrzejska on May 5, 1846. He was educated in Warsaw. At school he excelled in Polish composition, but otherwise showed no distinction as a scholar, spending most of his time in reading with avidity the authors who most strongly influenced his future work, Dumas, Scott, Homer and Shakespeare. In 1866 he entered the University of Warsaw, where he studied medicine, history and philology. While there he wrote articles for the press, and when in 1870 he left the University it was to take up journalism. His first immature novel *In Vain* was published in 1872; but it was not until the publication in 1875 of the short tale *The Old Servant* and in 1876 of the long short story *Hania* that he was recognized as one of the most promising fictionists of the epoch.

In 1876 he left Poland for a journey in the United States, which played a decisive part in maturing his genius. While there he wrote his *Letters from a Journey in America* and the tale *Sketches in Charcoal*. Returning to Poland, he published the short stories that established his fame: *Janko the Musician, The Diary of a Poznań Tutor, For Bread, The Lighthouse Keeper, Tartar Captivity,* and *Bartek the Victorious* (1879-92). In 1881 his play *On One Card* was produced in Warsaw, but without success, for although Sienkiewicz wrote more than one drama he lacked the

HENRYK SIENKIEWICZ

(From an oil painting by Kazimierz Pochwalski, a pupil of Matejko and
later professor of painting in the Vienna Academy of Fine Arts)

qualities of a dramatist. In 1883-88 he brought out as a serial, in which form all his novels appeared before publication in book form, the trilogy which placed him in the first rank of the world's writers of historical romance: *With Fire and Sword, The Deluge, Pan Wołodyjowski*. Side by side with his novels he continued to write short stories, of which the most popular is the humorous tale *That Third Woman* (1888). The trilogy was followed by the psychological novel *Without Dogma* (1890-91), after the publication of which Sienkiewicz travelled in Africa. His *Letters from Africa* (1892) hold their place among the best Polish books of travel. In 1893-94 his second novel of contemporary life, *The Polaniecki Family*, inferior to its predecessors, appeared, after which Sienkiewicz returned to historical fiction, bringing out in 1895-96 the phenomenally popular romance *Quo Vadis?* and in 1897-1900 his last great book *The Knights of the Cross*. His intention of writing a second national trilogy was only carried out in its first part in *On the Field of Glory* (1903-4), and his novel on the revolution of 1905, *Whirlpools* (1909-10), was a failure. In 1905 he was awarded the Nobel Prize, the first Pole to receive that distinction. In 1910-11 he again produced a masterpiece in a story for children, *Through Forest and Jungle*. He was engaged upon a romance of the Napoleonic epoch, *The Legions*, when the Great War broke out. He laid aside his pen to devote himself wholly to the work of the Red Cross Fund which he inaugurated for the relief of the Polish victims of the war, in the midst of which he died at Vevey, Switzerland, on November 16, 1916.

Henryk Sienkiewicz is the greatest novelist that Poland has so far produced. No Polish writer of fiction before him, or as yet after him, has ever evoked with such dramatic power and wealth of color the most heroic and the most tragic episodes of a national history which, it has been truly said, abounds more than that of any other nation in matter for drama. The great patriotic purpose which underlay his writings raised him to a position that only Mickiewicz had occupied before him: that of the moral leader and spokesman of oppressed and dismembered Poland.

Sienkiewicz began his career as a writer in the years following

the failure of the Rising of 1863. The nation was then ground
down by a ruthless persecution of every national heritage. Her
faith, her language, her education were proscribed. On the other
hand, the catastrophe of the doomed insurrection had brought
about a reaction that took the form of Positivism, which the Polish
youth were embracing with an exaggerated ardor that bade fair
to destroy the national ideals they could learn by no normal
channel, and that threatened them with denationalization. It was
to counteract the moral and national danger to which he saw his
young compatriots exposed that Sienkiewicz wrote not only his
epic romances on the history of fallen Poland, but his novels on
contemporary matters.

Sienkiewicz first proved his genius with short stories, and the
best of these were written before the publication of the Trilogy.
The love of the Polish peasant inspired his earliest efforts in this
direction, which at the outset were impregnated with an irony
and a melancholy bordering on morbid sentimentality. In *Sketches
in Charcoal* compassion for the peasant is expressed with the crude-
ness of a young writer and as a young reformer. In *Janko the
Musician* it takes the form of the innate artistic yearnings of an
unconscious village genius whom the rougher clay of the peasants
around him put down as a half wit. The masterly little sketch
which the author calls by the peasant word for an angel strikes
the same note of profound pity for a peasant child; but its irony
is of a different nature. The orphan child whom the half-drunken
village women have bidden to seek protection of her guardian
angel, alone in the forest hears light steps in the snow, thinks they
are the angel's—and is face to face with a wolf. The fate of the
derelict Polish emigrant in the United States, decoyed thither by
a German swindler, is the tragedy of *For Bread;* and again Sienkiewicz's pen turns to the Polish wanderer in the New World in
the exquisite story of *The Lighthouse Keeper,* one of the pearls
of Polish literature. Here the sound of the tropical seas, the music
of Mickiewicz's verse and the yearning of the exile for his country
make an incomparable whole, free from the touch of morbidity
and exaggeration that is the blemish of the tales mentioned above.

Two of Sienkiewicz's first batch of stories were direct
weapons in the cause of Poland against Prussian tyranny, which

he was to take up on a greater scale in his *Knights of the Cross.*
In the *Diary of a Poznań Tutor* he leaves his peasant types for the
figure of a Polish schoolboy like hundreds of other Polish boys
who were victims of the brutality of the Prussian schoolmaster
in Sienkiewicz's day. The story was in reality intended to represent
the condition of the Polish pupil in the Russian schools, but as it
would have been impossible to print it in Russian Poland the
author substituted the Prussian for the Russian setting, the anti-
Polish methods of the Russian and Prussian governments in both
divisions of Poland being identical. Here Sienkiewicz weakens the
effect of what would have been a powerful study by a gratuitous
piling up of the agony. But his second tale of the Pan-Prussian
persecution of Poland, *Bartek the Victorious,* one of the happiest
blendings of humor and pathos in all Sienkiewicz's work, is marred
by no such tendency, and stands out as a plea against Prussian
methods which needs no comment. Among these early stories
there is one foreign to what was Sienkiewicz's style at the moment,
though he was to make it pre-eminently his own. *Tartar Captivity*
is a beautiful little sketch told in the form of the memoirs of a
Polish knight taken prisoner by the Moslem in the borderland
warfare that played so great a part in Polish history. It was the
test by which Sienkiewicz tried his power of writing historical
fiction before embarking on the huge enterprise of the Trilogy.
He continued to write short stories at intervals between bringing
out his novels. Among these may be mentioned *That Third
Woman* as a laughable comedy of Warsaw art student life in
which the chief female character, an actress, is founded on the
author's friendship with Modjeska, whom he met in the United
States. As Sienkiewicz had made a trial venture in a short historical
story before writing the Trilogy, so before taking for his theme
the early Christian epoch of *Quo Vadis?* he wrote the tale *Let
Us Follow Him,* in which his characters are the eyewitnesses of
the crucifixion of Christ.

The Trilogy is Sienkiewicz's greatest work. He took for its
subject a period in Polish history that approached cataclysm: the
Cossack rebellion in 1648, the Swedish conquest of Poland that
followed it, and the great Turkish and Tartar invasion which
swept upon Poland in 1672. It seemed as if no nation, torn by

war with foreign enemies and by internal treachery, could have
stood against such a tempest: yet Poland weathered it, so that the
Trilogy can end with as glorious a moment in the history of
Poland as the salvation of the Christian world by a Polish army
under Sobieski at Vienna. It was of set purpose that Sienkiewicz
chose these troubled years of the national history upon which to
build his book. He wished to point the moral, to fortify the souls
of his compatriots whose nation when he wrote the Trilogy had
passed through a more overwhelming catastrophe than any he
describes, and to inspire them with hope.

In the figures of the national heroes whom Sienkiewicz introduces into his pages his readers were shown what men could do to
save their country. He depicts, too, the treachery and dissensions
of her unworthy sons as a warning of the baseness that contributed
to bring Poland to her fall. He conjured up before the eyes of
those who had never known freedom a vision of their country
when she had held a proud position on the map of Europe. He
transported them from a dreary present and a seemingly hopeless
future into a stirring past. The refreshness and buoyancy of his
outlook, to which the morbid element apparent in his early work
had yielded forever, were of themselves a mental stimulus to his
fellow Poles, living as they were at that time under the abnormal
conditions of the conquered. Into this task he impressed the
gorgeous coloring and the splendid descriptive powers in which
he excelled. A romantic at heart, a realist in his methods, he made
the dead bones of history live before the reader's gaze. Behind all
this beat a tender and impassioned love for an adored nation that
bids her children suffer everything and forego all else in life to
serve her first. The Trilogy took the hearts of Sienkiewicz's compatriots by storm. The characters in the story became the personal
friends of every man and woman in the nation, and it is said to
be the first book after their New Testament and *Lives of the
Saints* that the Polish peasants were seen to read. This book renewed national faith. It was, says a Polish critic, more than a
book: it was a deed, and a deed that saved countless Polish souls
for Poland. The words with which Sienkiewicz closes it sums it
up. These books, he writes, were "written with no little labor—to
strengthen hearts."

Of the three parts of the Trilogy, the first book, *With Fire and Sword*, which is devoted to the Cossack Rising, is the finest from an artistic point of view. Its pictures of the borderlands, those countries sacred to Polish tradition, its magnificent painting of war, and the wild romantic atmosphere of the Cossack stronghold, stand out in unforgettable colors in the reader's memory. The second part, treating of the invasion of Poland by the Swedes and their subsequent defeat, *The Deluge*, suffers from excessive length, and as a whole is equal neither to its predecessor nor to its successor: but from a patriotic standpoint there are passages in this book that speak more eloquently to the anguish of the Pole whose country had been rent asunder than any other that Sienkiewicz penned. Only the son of a conquered race could have described with such tragic power the condition of Poland lying prostrate beneath the heel of the conquering Swede. Moreover, the miracle of Poland's deliverance, initiated by that favorite episode of Polish heroism, the repulse of the invader at Częstochowa, was of a nature to restore hope to the Polish heart—a hope that was justified two years after the novelist's death when Poland rose from the grave. The third part, *Pan Wołodyjowski* (or *Pan Michael*), is a simpler and more intimate story, its first volume a picture of the manners of the epoch, merging into a fascinating tale of the Christian outpost in the borderland steppes, with the undercurrent of Tartar love and revenge, culminating in the immortal glory of Jan Sobieski.

But the charm of these books does not lie exclusively in their splendid presentment of the drama of history. The great crises in the national history are the background to a multitude of characters, historical and fictitious, that make the Trilogy a multi-colored, restless panorama of life, always with that noblest of human passions, a profound patriotism, behind it. In each of the three books a national hero—Jeremi Wiśniowiecki, Prior Kordecki and Stefan Czarniecki, and, above all, Jan Sobieski—play an integral part in the story. No less vivid are the portraits of such enemies of the Republic as Bohdan Chmielnicki, the Cossack and rebel chieftain, and the traitor Janusz Radziwiłł. If Sienkiewicz over-idealizes the heroes whose names are household words to the Pole, it must be remembered that he is no psychological student of character. His object is to take the best qualities of such men as an illustration of patriotism at its noblest. His method with events is different. He depicts in unsparing language such stains on the national conscience as the treason that brought about the easy conquest of Poland by the Swedish armies: and the scene in Radziwiłł's banqueting hall when the prince rises, goblet in hand and proclaims his allegiance to the king of Sweden, is one of the most dramatic pieces of writing in the whole of the Trilogy.

Sienkiewicz is too human to restrict his plot to the grand lines of epic. In the midst of his colossal stage he always has a love story, of a pure and healthy if conventional nature. His men and women are not usually very profoundly drawn; the women especially are, as a rule, types rather than individuals, yet they live vividly before us, whether they take their share in the great events of history or in the little doings of daily life. With the exception of the love of the young pagan Vinicius in *Quo Vadis?*, which has a subtle spiritual development, the love story in Sienkiewicz's historical novels runs more or less on the same pattern: the knight's loss of his lady, who is swept from him by war or abduction, for whom he searches through fire and flood, and to whom of course he is finally united! for Sienkiewicz generally prefers a happy end to his romance. In one respect he was something of a pioneer in Polish fiction, for his pages are full of humor, which has never been the strong point of Polish literature. The immortal Zagłoba introduces an atmosphere of laughter wherever he goes: and even beyond his burly form amusement may be constantly met with in other figures of the book. The little knight with his flirtations and his mastery of fencing, the gigantic Lithuanian Podbipienta who has vowed not to marry until he has cut off three heads of the enemy at one blow, Skrzetuski's servant, devoted but always on the make, Kowalski, the stupid dupe of Zagłoba, who in a headlong race across the Polish plains nearly captures the king of Sweden —these are some of the characters who give the reader ample entertainment.

After the immense success of the Trilogy, by which Sien-kiewicz became one of the greatest figures in the Poland of his day and one of the leading novelists of the world, he proved his versatility by bringing out a modern study of character. Although

Sienkiewicz's novels of contemporary life are not so attractive as his historical romances, nor on so high a literary level, *Without Dogma* is nevertheless one of the best psychological studies in Polish fiction. The title of the book Sienkiewicz wrote to counteract a tendency he perceived in the Polish youth of the day explains itself. The man who analyzes his character in a diary, who is brilliant, wealthy, with all the gifts of the world at his feet, is like a ship without a rudder because he lacks the controlling power of principle. He therefore comes to shipwreck after a contest with a woman immeasurably his mental inferior, whose happiness together with his own he destroys, but whom he cannot conquer, because she has principle or dogma to strengthen her resistance, and he has none. Sienkiewicz's second novel of contemporary life, *The Polaniecki Family*, lacks the distinction of *Without Dogma* and was the first of his novels to receive unfavorable criticism. Although it upholds such moral and social principles as the sanctity of marriage and the dignity of work, and although the back-to-the-soil movement is placed in counterpoise to the exaggerated disposition of the hour that was apt to find salvation exclusively in trade and business, a want of cohesion and consistency in the story prevents its being a masterpiece. But that Sienkiewicz's powers had not waned was proved when he returned to the medium in which he was most at home, and the following year produced *Quo Vadis?*

Quo Vadis? was the first Polish novel that traveled all over the world. It became a cosmopolitan property. In this romance, a brilliant picture of the reign of Nero, which was read in all European and in several Oriental languages, Sienkiewicz's thoughts were still with his country. The heroine of the book, who is the center of one of Sienkiewicz's finest psychological situations, comes from Sarmatia, otherwise Poland. Her servant Ursus is called a Sarmatian, the adventurer Chilon a Greek; but the former shows all the characteristics of a Polish peasant, and Chilon those of the Polish Jew. Half a century earlier Krasiński, in his drama *Iridion*, had allegorized the figures of Hellas and Rome, and it was the intention of Sienkiewicz to give courage to his compatriots by the recollection that a handful of Christians had sown the seed which was to bring a mightier power than Russia to the dust. This drama of imperial Rome at the height of her glory and vice, with its antithesis of Christ's first followers worshiping in the catacombs, captivated Sienkiewicz's imagination; and he poured into *Quo Vadis?* all the riot of color and splendid writing of which he had already proved himself a master. In such descriptions as that of the fire of Rome, where without descending to melodrama he presents an unsurpassable picture of horror and cataclysm, Sienkiewicz is at his greatest. If he fails in penetrating the spirit of the early Christian martyrs, and is eminently unsuccessful in his delineation of the two apostles, yet the principle of *Quo Vadis?* remains the same as the words which close Krasiński's drama of a perishing civilization: *Galilaee, Vicisti!*

Sienkiewicz's last great historical novel, *The Knights of the Cross*, is of a different type from the Trilogy. It deals less directly with historical events, although it introduces two of the national memories most treasured by the Pole, the figure of Queen Jadwiga and the victory of Grunwald which forms the epilogue. The story is not conceived on so great a scale as the two first parts of the Trilogy, nor does it possess the peculiar fascination of the eastern borderlands or the romance of the warfare between Cross and Crescent that the Trilogy gives us. The characters are less vivid and well contrasted than those of the Trilogy or *Quo Vadis?* and they fail to win the reader's personal affection as do those in the earlier novels. Nor is there anything to equal Zagłoba's humors. But the lives of the actors in the story are projected against the sinister background of the Teutonic Order, the immemorial and deadliest enemy of Poland. Therefore the book appeals peculiarly to the psychology of the Pole as representing the agelong struggle of Poland against Prussian aggression. Many of its scenes rank with the finest in Sienkiewicz's writings, and one at least, the duel of Zbyszko and the Knight of the Cross, with the cry: "Remember Danusia!" has been cited as a watchword to Polish patriotism. The noble ending, when a Polish army rides into Malborg, the stronghold of the Teutonic Order, by one gate, as the vanquished Grand Master with tears in his eyes rides out of the other, speaks straight to every Polish instinct.

Sienkiewicz's further attempt at the first part of another Trilogy, *On the Field of Glory*, and his subsequent social novel,

Whirlpools, in which he showed himself out of touch with the young generation, did not add to his renown. But even as old age crept upon him his powers revived in another direction, and he wrote one of the best books for children in Polish literature, based on his personal knowledge of Africa: *Through Forest and Jungle.* This book coincided with the rise of the Boy Scout organization in Poland, and contributed to its development.

That the last efforts of Sienkiewicz's pen were devoted to the theme of the Polish Napoleonic legions was characteristic of his Polish blood. Like many another Pole he had been brought up on the traditions of Napoleonism, and his grandfather was an old legionary. But he had only written a few chapters of this book, *The Legions,* when the Great War broke out. One more task remained for him to do. It was a labor of love that set the seal on his long service for his country, and one that he himself said he rated higher and prized more than all the writings his pen had given to his nation. While the soil of Poland was being ravaged by three armies and her children were starving by thousands, Sienkiewicz, with all the influence of his world-wide fame, dedicated all his remaining energies to the collection of funds for these Polish derelicts. The death that overtook him in the midst of this labor was in the nature of a national calamity. When in 1926 his remains were transferred from their temporary grave in Vevey to the cathedral in Warsaw, they were accompanied by an outburst of unanimous homage that proved what Sienkiewicz had stood for to the Polish nation.

He still retains that place. With the passage of the years, and changed conditions, his works were bound to lose something of their popularity even during his life. His peasant stories have been surpassed by others, his social novels at least equaled. As a master of historical romance he still stands unrivaled in the literature of Poland, and in the forefront of that of the world. The moral position he occupied among the leaders of his nation in her captivity remains unassailable by time. His country was always his first object. He was, in his own words, the "ambassador of Poland"; that is, of a nation whose very name had been blotted out, who had none (besides Paderewski) to represent her or defend her, who was ignored by the world as though she had ceased to be. It was Sienkiewicz who pleaded before the bar of Europe for this forgotten country. More than once he addressed open letters to the governments and prominent men of Europe protesting against the acts of injustice of which his nation was the victim: notably in 1901, when he exposed in burning words of indignation the persecution of Polish school children at the hands of the Prussian government, and in 1907 when he drew public attention to the iniquitous Prussian Law of Expropriation. All the magnificent gifts of his genius were dedicated throughout his life to the task of saving his compatriots. He protected them against apathy and despair. He prepared them to be citizens of a reborn country to which he pointed the way, but which he did not live to see.

JÓZEF CHEŁMOŃSKI

(From a pastel sketch by Leon Wyczółkowski, in the National Museum in Kraków)

XXIV

JÓZEF CHEŁMOŃSKI
"An Epic Painter of the Polish Countryside"

1850-1914

by
TADEUSZ SEWERYN

THE role played by Józef Chełmoński in Polish art is best represented in his picture "Racławice," a splendid composition of marvelously subtle import. In a moment the battle is to begin. In a moment, the history of the Polish struggle for freedom will begin to be written in blood. Through the soft mists of that April morning there looms in the distance the silhouette of the commander, Tadeusz Kościuszko, on horseback. Behind him is his staff in their colorful uhlan uniforms; before him are the armed and picturesque peasant folk. At the call of the commander the mountaineers, arrayed in garments white as snow, have come down from the Tatra hills, armed with their hatchets; peasants from the region of Kraków have appeared, with the points of their scythes fastened firmly to long poles. In a moment they are to set forth, to oppose Russian cannon.

Yet it is not history that is the substance of this picture. In the breeze quiver banners brought from the churches, with the picture of Our Lady, Mother of God. The spring morning mist is pervaded with the quiet whisper of prayer. A religious fervor is depicted in the faces of all. Some gaze into the heavens, others in ardent love kiss the earth, as the Polish peasant is wont to do during the adoration of the Sacrament. They vow to give their blood for that beloved earth!

And that is the real substance of this picture, as it is the chief characteristic of the soul of Chełmoński, and the most peculiar feature of his talent. Love of his native soil, of nature, and of the country folk.

On his huge canvases Matejko immortalized the days of the glory of Polish chivalry, the purple and majesty of kings. Chełmoński is the mouthpiece of that great value in art which is created by feelings coming from the heart; he is the Walt Whitman and the Rousseau of Polish painting. Matejko was a historical interpreter of the past, a Shakespeare of great individualities. Chełmoński was fascinated by nature and in her discovered worlds unknown but close at hand, revealing to everybody that beauty which till then was known to poets only.

His colleague, the great Polish critic and painter, Stanisław Witkiewicz, said of him that "nature spoke to the sensitive mind of Chełmoński with the whole diversity of its phenomena; it was not only form, color and light that concerned and interested him. He wished to express the music of the approaching night, the whisper of the wings of the bat, the silent flight of birds, the croaking of frogs and the piping of the lover. He first, perhaps he alone, painted clouds of gnats droning in the air, and the buzz of the beetle speeding in its heavy flight. He wanted to make the wind in the picture rustle in the dry stalks of sunflowers, beat with the rain on the panes, and knock with the pail on its pole at the well. He made pictures through whose dense fogs the sound of the postillion's bell seemed faintly to echo and moan across the steppes slumbering in their grey haze, awakening the drowsy, wet bustards. He wished his painted fair to sound and jingle with all the clutter and bustle of real life. Girls dreaming longingly in the evening twilight, and buxom strong sensuous wenches laughing in the sun, little children, old men and shepherd boys—all types of people crowding the roads and by-ways of life."

Such was Chełmoński, thanks to the fact that his first teacher was not the printed word, but nature. He was born in the year 1850 in Boczki, a little village not far from Warsaw in the pretty Łowicz country, the land of Reymont's *Peasants*. He spent the years of his youth on his father's farm, and passed the most joyful moments of life in happy freedom. He watched the life of birds in the swamps, the shape of the crooked willows and the colors of "wide fields painted in diverse grain, gilded with wheat, with rye silvered again"—as the poet Mickiewicz wrote. He liked to wander through the woods and from childhood observed the fine horses of landowners and of peasants. He was never tired looking at the beautiful peasant dress, gleaming in the sun with its many colored stripes, which even today makes such an exotic impression on a foreign visitor.

And when he attempted to note down his observations on paper, his first lessons in drawing were given him by his father, who also instructed his son in music. Chełmoński's love for drawing did not wane when he attended school in Łowicz, and consequently the father soon sent his thirteen-year-old son to the School of Art in Warsaw, and later to the private studio of W. Gerson.

The choice of the teacher was happy. Gerson, whose Bible of art was the writings of Leonardo da Vinci, worshiped nature with a special devotion and constantly pointed out to his pupils the profound depth of the words of the great artist: "The art of painting is the daughter of nature and kin to God." He gave the young painters advice in the words of Leonardo: "And thou, O artist, who dost desire to attain the highest level of practical skill, shouldst understand that if thou basest it not on a true acquaintance with nature, thou shalt create works which will bring thee little honor and less profit; but if thou acquirest knowledge thy works shall be many and good and shall bring thee honor and profit."

In the studio of the master reigned an atmosphere of intense work. As a result all the pupils of Gerson, amongst whom many were to occupy important positions in Polish art, were splendidly prepared, when they had finished their academic routine, to grasp and re-create the forms and fleeting phenomena met with in nature, while their acute observation and visual memory were astounding. Chełmoński towered above them all in talent.

When his happier colleagues, upon finishing their studies with the master, left for Paris or Munich, he had to remain at home, as if to exphasize the principle that need and true talent go together. Then Chełmoński, full of inexpressible grief and resentment toward the world, painted a stirring picture: above the native meadows, above the furrows veiled in the haze of an autumn morning, flies a flock of cranes, westward, into the rosy beams of the sun, to another life, and only one of the flock remains behind. Standing on one foot amidst the faded weeds, hiding his broken wing, he sends a longing glance in the direction of his brothers who are fast disappearing. . . .

But he also was destined to good fortune. Thanks to the help of a friend, the painter Brandt, he went to Munich, where his first drawing executed in the Academy won him a medal and fame. He brought with him from Poland so much artistic skill that his talent was developing independently, far from the rigors of the Academy, far from those "crutches for cripples," as the French philosopher of art, Taine, expressed it. In Munich Chełmoński painted his wildly speeding horses, drawing the sleigh with the huntsman across the broad expanse of snow in the depths of the Polish country. He painted Polish peasant folk coming with their complaint to the bailiff, and other subjects he had stored away in his remarkable visual memory.

But his Munich surroundings did not give him satisfaction. He complained to Gerson in a letter: "Dear Teacher of mine, longing for our skies and fields tortures me now in all its intensity . . . and this place of my dreams has become the place of my suffering." He disliked the municipal gardens with their carefully weeded greens, trimmed trees, and flowers well drilled by the gardener, and with a joy reminding him of the years spent with unrestrained nature he preferred to observe the profuse nettles growing at liberty beyond the fence of the garden. "The partridges with their call at eventide," he wrote longingly, "once when I was in the country awakened in me a multitude of desires; when will it be possible to return home? for there everything is so different, so different."

The fever of longing for his country began to consume him more and more persistently until he decided to return. He left his unfinished canvases and returned home, like the mythical Antaeus, to find new creative strength in contact with his native soil. He worked in Warsaw, but often went to the Ukraine, that Texas and Arizona of former Poland, and there imbued his imagination with pictures of life, full of poetry and the primitive power of nature. The soul of the artist in these times is well reflected in a beautiful picture, steeped in poetry, which is entitled "The Night Watchman." It depicts a moonlit night, the sky resplendent with stars, and in the distance beyond the hedges cottages sleep in the silence of the summer night. The watchdogs have left their places and are playing gaily on the wide village green beyond, while the night watchman, leaning on his cane, gazes at the stars, muses and dreams. . . .

In another mood the laughing shepherd girl dreams, when, musing on love, she throws her fine healthy body on the grass, and picks at the silver threads of gossamer floating above her. In these pictures, as in his others, Chełmoński, lover of the simplicity and beauty of life, of physical health and the poetry of the human heart, reflects beauty in moods which no other artist has treated before him. Thus his works, glorifying the romantic charm of the Polish countryside and nature, occupy a peculiar position in the history of art in general.

As a genre painter he was never satisfied with the outward recreation of reality in a picture. Let us but look at his splendid picture "The Farmstead." Stacks of corn, a multitude of people working, a farm hand leading some trotting horses away, and in the foreground the unusual scene of a mute conversation between a man and an animal. In the wide courtyard of a farmstead an old Polish nobleman is reviewing his horses. A large black well-shaped horse stands before him; he has stretched out his neck to his master, pulled back his ears, thrust forward his wide open nostrils, fixed his bloodshot eyes on him, and planted his hind legs stubbornly on the ground. This is a conversation which in the speech of human beings would mean reproach, menace and malediction.

Abroad, Chełmoński was known chiefly as a splendid painter of horses. Paris admired the Polish artist's three- and four-in-hands harnessed to peasant sleighs and carts; everybody was delighted with his hunting scenes, his horses wildly galloping past gay vagrants, or reined in by the driver as the hunter fetches his kill, with muzzles bridled in and noble heads flung high, his kennels, the dread attacks of wolves, the furious gallop of his hunters across the wide stretches of snow-covered country.

Polish love of horses and the tradition of famous Polish horse-manship live in the pictures of Chełmoński. In these subjects also live the memories of the childhood years of the artist and the charm of the Polish borderland, to whose romanticism various Polish poets and painters have succumbed. The strength and temperament evident in all his canvases, triumph in the gigantic picture entitled "The Four-in-Hand." It astonished the Parisians, as today this four-in-hand, leaping from the frame of the picture and galloping with unheard-of fury straight at the onlooker, still astonishes every visitor to the National Museum in Kraków. The enormous bodies of these horses, represented in violent foreshort-ening, the powerful silhouettes outlined against the background of a drizzly sky, mud flung out from under their hoofs, the cart hurled onward with elemental force by the racing horses—this always makes an unforgettable impression. This is no dramatic episode, but the ordinary manner of driving in the Polish border-lands, in the Texas of Poland. For while the driver with difficulty retains in his hands the reins of the speeding four, the old gentle-man sitting in the cart bends to one side and calmly lights his pipe. It is just the Polish style of driving.

In Paris, where Chełmoński lived for nearly ten years, oc-curred simultaneously a great revolution of aesthetic conceptions and the development of new ideals of beauty. Artists turned away from the historical costume which had been a requisite of art for so long, turned from all kinds of academic conventions imitating the pose of classical sculpture to current life, as a subject for art. This movement, called impressionism, was also termed the cult of sun and light, for its characteristic was the noting of visual light impressions gathered from the outer world. The aim of the painter became not the re-creation of a thought fancied or studied from books, but the observation and reflection of the constantly changing values of light in nature. Artists turned in great numbers to the study of landscape in the open air and of light-vibration, to the artistic analysis of the phenomena of light; thus breaking away from the old painting which made use of conventional colors and studio lighting, together with the former type of landscape with its artificial mood and story.

This movement made a great impression on Chełmoński. At

"PRAYER BEFORE THE BATTLE"

Józef Chełmoński portrays here Polish peasants armed with scythes in prayer before the Battle of
Racławice—led by Kościuszko (first on horseback)

the time when the works of the French impressionists called forth
at the exhibitions storms of protests from the public, and artists
boldly experimenting proved that no color in nature is autonomous, but is dependent upon the reflexes and colors of its nearest
surroundings, that shadow is neither gray nor black, nor is it the
result of the lack of light, but may be blue, violet, greenish, that
the chief value of the picture is not the drawing but the color—
then Chełmoński, recognizing himself as an impressionist, decided
to be himself, to borrow from nobody, to paint as his own sensitive eyes and his own feeling dictated. He realized that for several
years he had been creating paintings in Paris out of reminiscences
of impressions carried away from his country, his native soil and
the Ukraine, land of the steppes, of the sun and of the most
melodious song on earth. In Paris, the capital of art, where for a
new talent and a foreigner especially, it is so easy to be drowned
in the sea of neglect and hateful competition, Chełmoński had won
recognition, honor and a good income. His works, purchased for
American collections, increased in price, as the temperament and
force of the Polish artist won for him more and more adherents
among the Anglo-Saxon patrons of art. In spite of this he decided
to break away from the painting of memories, to which he had
been devoted until then. Here no observations could enrich his
ingenious visual memory, which was superior to that of even the
great masters of the brush. He watched the elegant carriages driving up before the buildings of the *Opéra*, the elegant riders in the
Bois de Boulogne, the smooth sidewalks of the boulevards, and in
his fine studio full of precious antiques he painted peasant sleighs
drawn by fiery horses, tearing over swampy roads, and similar
subjects which were sought after eagerly by art dealers with the
famous Goupil at their head.

From this type of painting he decided to break away; from
now on he would return no more to his spirited steeds, to the
silhouettes of human figures against the background of the landscape, nor to the crowds of perfectly arranged figures. And once
again, after a longer stay abroad, he returned to Poland to delight
in his native country and to absorb its innumerable colors. The
homesickness of the artist finds expression in a picture full of the
feeling of joy: amidst the gay poppies and starry sunflowers of a

country garden close to a thatched cottage stands a shapely Łowicz girl in her beautiful native dress, gazing at the flowers and into the sunlit world; she has shaded her eyes with her hand and watches in rapture.

And again, as in his youth, the artist paints a flock of flying storks, but he no longer confides to them his resentment towards the world. In his picture a peasant is seated on the autumn grass; during his noonday meal he has seen storks flying above. He and the boy who has brought him his dinner in an earthen pot, open their lips in mute curiosity. The old man gazes into the sky with care and sorrow for times past, and the boy with joy, as a child who looks at the first snowflakes or a butterfly above him. There is a great sincerity in it and great simplicity in the means with which the artist expresses himself; and every picture, pervaded with personal experience, becomes an episode in his autobiography. For he also returned, like those wandering storks and cranes. Having exhausted the store of impressions he had carried away from Poland, he now returned there for new pictures.

Taking up his abode in a small country house in Kukłówka near Warsaw, in unbroken contact with nature and the country folk, he experienced an increasing joy in life, in the flowers, the animals, and the people. And again, as in his youth, with a broad straw hat on his head, in a red waistcoat, high boots and a dark jacket, he wanders through woods, meadows and swamps, listening to the call of shepherds and of quail, and to the murmur of the streams. He paints not the sentimental theatrical peasant for the amusement of the noble, but a peasant who lives with primitive nature, with the storms, the winds, and the blizzards. In one picture he has presented a Mazovian peasant, walking in his long white smock-frock behind the plow drawn by two oxen, with crows flying before him, awaiting the worms turned up by the blade. It is an epic of work. In another picture he has interpreted the feelings of shepherd lads overtaken by a storm in the fields. From the red-brown clouds the first drops of rain are falling, forecasting a deluge. The dry grass whirls in the wind. The cattle, stretching out their tails behind them, speed blindly ahead. Then lightning pierces the heavens. One small shepherd scurries off, the second covers his head with his apron, to protect himself from the storm, and the third has stopped, has taken off his hat, and crosses himself devoutly, as is the custom of the people when lightning shows in the sky. Again blue smoke, rising from a fire lighted by the shepherds on a low stretch of pasture, also catches his interest; or peasants gathering sticks in the woods sprinkled with snow. Or he shows us a girl weaving a wreath of cornflowers to be placed on a shrine by the wayside, and a small shepherd boy, lyric in his charm, in a ragged brown cloak, standing amidst the stubble and playing on the fiddle. White lambs feed quietly in the distance, half hidden by the autumn mist. A white shepherd dog has seated himself close by and listens.

In these pictures there is nothing of fantastic invention, nothing of dissonance either in drawing or in color; the story is told simply but with a noble gesture and with strength of feeling, on a broad scale. The untiring sensibility of his industrious mind and sharp observation create for him a treasury of constantly new pictures. No longer does nature herself attract him, but only that which he finds of himself in her. So he characterizes the rhythm of the life of Polish nature, her moods, her charm and her soul. He paints the melancholy of the lowlands, the forests and the marshes, the charm of quiet moonlit nights, pale rose dawns, lily-covered ponds, flooded spring meadows dotted with buttercups, sylvan lakes with their whispering rushes, flocks of heron on marshland half-veiled in the morning mist, storks and cranes holding parliaments, the ecstatic love-call of the blackcock, the ribbons of silver rivers, cottages by quiet waters, orchards of blossoming apple trees, sands and woods covered with snow, and frost sparkling in the sun. The pictures of Chełmoński are "the song of our soil," an expression of devoted love for the Polish countryside, a love lost in the listening contemplation of its beauty. They are an expression of the Polish impressionism born of temperament and the realization that only in this way may one paint. French art refined his manner of observation, but Chełmoński had been an "open-air painter" from the time when, as a pupil of Gerson, in accordance with the instructions of Leonardo da Vinci, he studied the secrets of form and color in nature. As the artist's talent develops, a constantly growing simplicity dominates his pictures, and the force of expression increases. We have again a very characteristic picture depicting the moment before sunrise when nature has not yet awakened from her sleep. In the sky is a deepening rosy light, the stars have already paled, but the morning star still shines. A wood becomes visible in the morning twilight and on the limitless stretch of meadows the dew sleeps. The landscape, uninteresting from the point of view of drawing, has so much atmosphere in its coloring and so much sincerity of feeling that this picture should be numbered among masterpieces. In another picture, "The Frog Concert," night is lurking in the dark outlines of rushes. Widely spread pools burn with the reds of sunset and on the bright surface of the water, like spilled music notes, the black heads of frogs appear, while here and there about them small wave circles spread. Here even the colors have acquired musical values.

Chełmoński has taught us that the most ordinary subjects taken from nature have in them poetry and inspiration for painting. His picture of a stream in spring will always be the expression of this truth. It shows monotonous lowland and a brook, and it would seem there could scarcely be a subject less paintable. However, the artist has so masterfully reflected the mood of early spring that we almost feel how the snow melts in the earth and hear how the damp earth breathes, while the cold water breaking into spheres of waves, splashes against the bushes at its edge. In another picture, widely flooding masses of water threateningly sway and rise in sharp wave crests, while above this spring deluge herons hover.

The landscapes of Chełmoński are near to us also because they bring back to us our own memories, or awaken feelings which come at the sight of interesting phenomena of life in nature. They are works not only of the eyes and hands, but of the heart. Whose heart is not moved with the fate of his painted quail in the snow? The poor birds crowded closely together, trembling from the cold, hop with little red feet over the frozen snow, the cold wind stirs their feathers and they go meekly on, in quiet resignation, through the icy blizzard. So simple in coloring, in composition, and so human in feeling. These values in the art of Chełmoński won him the great esteem of the world. For his works he received in the Paris Salon in 1889 *"mention honorable"*; at a general exhibition in Paris he received the *Grand Prix;* in Berlin in 1891 he won the highest award in the form of a diploma of honor, and a year later he received a gold medal in Munich; in San Francisco in 1894 he also received the gold medal; at the General Exhibition in Lwów he won the highest distinction, and in Kraków the award of the Polish Academy of Sciences was given him.

Chełmoński turned the eyes of the world upon the beauty of Poland; he was an epic painter of Polish life, and he set a new direction in Polish painting. He never lost his peculiar force of expressing himself, even when the long beard falling upon his breast became tinged with gray. He was indefatigable in work and always youthful, like that nature he so dearly loved. When he died in the year 1914, his loss was deeply felt in all Poland, for not only a great artist but an educator of his nation lay buried in the quiet country cemetery in Ojrzanów near Warsaw, amidst Mazovian fields, peasant huts, and lofty poplars. Through his achievement Chełmoński contributed to the consciousness of the Polish nation in the realization of the beauty of its country.

Translated from the Polish by Mrs. Clifford Corbridge (née Patkaniowska), London, England.

XXV

JOSEPH CONRAD

(*Józef Teodor Konrad Korzeniowski*)

1857-1924

"The Marvel of a Polish Country Gentleman . . .
Becoming a Great English Writer"

by

ROMAN DYBOSKI

I. THE MAN

THE conditions in which Poland was placed during the century and more of her division and her domination by foreign powers were such as to bring into full play a certain spirit of restlessness and a romantic love of adventure, which centuries of constant warfare against Turkish and Tartar invaders had produced in a race of idyllic tillers of the soil. It was naturally among the country gentry of Poland's southeastern borderlands, which had for ages been the scene of those frontier wars, that the adventurous and romantic streak in the Polish temperament became most marked. And from that border gentry—passionate of mood and wide of outlook, as indeed most border populations in the world are bound to be—Joseph Conrad was descended.

But it is a far cry from the knight-errantry of Polish exiles fighting for the liberty of other nations in all the world's revolutions during a hundred years, to the strange phenomenon of avocation for a seafaring life asserting itself with elemental force from adolescence in the son of an inland race which had never produced great sailors. And even more amazing than the seafaring career

JOSEPH CONRAD

(From an autographed photograph, signed twice—revealing the original
Polish spelling and the simplified version or pseudonym by which he
became famous)

of a Polish country gentleman in the British merchant service is the subsequent fact that this Pole, who until the age of twenty-one did not know a word of English, should, after enforced premature retirement from the life of a sea-captain, use the accumulated experience of that life to make of it the texture of twenty-eight volumes of great literature in the English language. However much—or little—incidental circumstances may contribute to elucidate this marvel of a Polish country gentleman who became a British sailor and then a great English writer, it is, in the last resort, the ever-inscrutable secret of the workings of inborn creative genius which must account for the unique personality and career of Joseph Conrad.

Józef Teodor Konrad Korzeniowski, born on December 3, 1857, in a country manor of the Ukrainian border province of the old Poland (then under Russian rule), was the son of a father who combined literary culture and ability with a fiery and adventurous disposition. Apollo Nałęcz Korzeniowski was a gifted writer of Polish prose and verse, and a prolific translator of Shakespeare, Victor Hugo, Alfred de Vigny, and other foreign masters. He showed neither capacity nor inclination for those agricultural occupations which constituted the life of his class, and abandoned the country, first for a provincial town, and then for Warsaw, to make a living by his pen, as a journalist and a man of letters. His wife came from the Bobrowski family, who differed from the Korzeniowskis by greater steadiness and resolution in their pursuits, though somewhat lacking in imagination and enterprise; her brother Thaddeus was to become Conrad's paternal protector, adviser, and benefactor throughout the stormy years of youth and early manhood. In Conrad's own temperament the romantic eccentricity of his father seems to have been blended with something of the determination and self-command of the Bobrowski stock, which helped him to work his way through all obstacles toward the seemingly fantastic aims, first of a sea-captaincy, and then of literary success.

Apollo Korzeniowski's activities in the Warsaw of the early sixties were political as well as literary. Hopes for the emancipation of Russian Poland from Tsarist rule were running high under the new reign of Alexander II, and public opinion was seething with the excitement of controversies as to ways and means of achieving that end. Conrad's father naturally found himself on the side of the "Reds," who were conspiring for an armed rising against Russia. A few months before the ill-fated insurrection of 1863 broke out as a result of these activities, Apollo Korzeniowski was arrested and was soon sentenced to exile. From the dreary distance of far-off provincial Russian towns the exile anxiously followed the disastrous course of the national struggle. Two of his brothers were killed in the insurrectionary war, and a third was sent to Siberia. His own wife, who had nobly and dutifully followed him into exile, died by his side in the bloom of her youth, a victim of hardships and privations.

The broken man, left alone with the little boy, was at last allowed to leave Russia, and settled in Austrian Poland, where he soon died in Poland's ancient capital Kraków. "It was in that old royal and academical city"—so Conrad himself tells us in *Poland Revisited*—"that I ceased to be a child, became a boy, had known the friendships, the admirations, the thoughts and the indignations of that age." And it was probably from the manifold and indiscriminate reading in which he indulged by the bedside of his dying father, particularly of stories of travels (to be remembered in Conrad's essay *Geography and Some Explorers*), that the passionate desire for a seafaring life arose in the boy's mind. When the wish was revealed to the family, soon after the father's death, it appeared to them as little short of willful treason to the national and class tradition of life on the forefathers' soil.

But the boy's persistence, and his uncle's wisdom and kindness, at last led to an arrangement under which Conrad, in 1874, at the age of seventeen, was sent to France—the country of Poland's traditional sympathies—to begin a sailor's life on French ships. Some of the most romantic adventures of his youth have the old harbor city of Marseille for their scene. There he found the "guide, philosopher, and friend" of his seagoing novitiate in the person of the Corsican sea-wolf Dominic Cervoni, who is vividly portrayed again and again in Conrad's works, from *The Mirror of the Sea* and *The Rescue* to *The Rover* and *Suspense*. At Marseille Conrad lived through the great early passion so vividly depicted in *The Arrow of Gold;* and there, in connection with that love affair, he engaged in gun-running for the Carlists on the Spanish coast, saw the beloved ship *Tremolino* perish, and received a bullet wound in a duel. That crisis in Conrad's French experiences drove him away from France and into the British merchant service, which he entered at the age of twenty-one as an ordinary sailor, facing all the hardships of service before the mast.

Within the next eight years (1878-86), while sailing all the seas of the globe under the British trading flag, he passed successfully the three service examinations and reached the rank of master mariner. In the course of those years he became particularly familiar, through numerous voyages, with the Malay Archipelago, which became the favorite scene of his literary masterpieces both early and late, from *Almayer's Folly*, *An Outcast of the Islands*, and *Lord Jim*, to *Victory* and *The Rescue*. Weary at last of this region, he tired even more of it through the distressful experiences of that first command of his (commemorated in *The Shadow Line*), which made him "feel old" at thirty-one (1888)—that voyage on which Conrad, with a sick crew and many other adversities to overcome, with one mate constantly sick and the other a fool, with only the ship's cook for a real stand-by at his worst moments, fought one of the most bitter struggles in his whole career against elemental forces without and the demon of despondency within his own breast. At Mauritius, shortly afterward, he experienced the pathetic love adventure recorded with melancholy in *A Smile of Fortune*, and resigning his command after it, turned his back on the East forever.

Having reached the top of his profession, with his master's certificate in his pocket, Conrad had to spend wearisome periods of waiting for employment. Partly as an escape from the perplexities of such anxious uncertainty, and partly following his innate bent for ever-new adventures he, who had at one time thought of whaling in the Arctic, and at another had been tempted by a business position in Canada, undertook in 1889 a mission in the service of a Belgian company in the Congo, and went in a wretched little steamer up the mighty river into that very "Heart of Darkness" which he describes with fascinating power in one of his greatest shorter works. The severe attacks of gout, to which he was henceforward a lifelong victim, began soon after the long illness which was the consequence of the Congo expedition. But perhaps the same unfortunate Congo journey definitely gave a great writer to the world. In the long hours of contemplation to which the illness doomed him, for which he had never before had much leisure, his first novel, *Almayer's Folly*, begun years earlier, and carried as an unfinished manuscript into the heart of Africa (where he nearly lost it), reached maturity and completion. And since the half-hearted attempts of a permanently enfeebled man to go to sea again were only intermittently successful, Conrad not only followed the call of inspiration, but submitted to the dictates of necessity, in ultimately exchanging his seafaring career in 1894 for that of a man of letters, at the age of thirty-seven. His way into the new profession was opened up for him by Mr. Edward Garnett, who, as reader to the firm of Fisher Unwin, recommended Conrad's first novel for publication. Soon after the issue of his second book, Conrad married Miss Jessie George (1896) and made a home for himself in the southern English countryside.

The remaining twenty-eight years of his life (1896-1924) are an unbroken record of struggles not less heroic than those against the hostile element of the sea in his earlier days. There were continuous struggles, now against serious financial difficulties at first, against afflictions in the shape of frequent illnesses in the family constantly, but above all, against his own constant and painful ill health, coupled with the equally painful strain of literary composition. Conrad never wrote with ease, and at the very summit of his career, in 1922, after writing the prefaces to a collected edition of his works, had a period of blankness and anxiety when, like the old sea-captain going blind in his own story, he seemed to himself to be at "the end of the tether." The crown of complete literary success came late—in fact only after *Chance* in 1912, with the dark days of the War to follow soon. But the garland of friendships with some of the best men of his time—writers and others, in England and elsewhere—never ceased to adorn Conrad's toilsome literary life with its refreshing verdure. Content with such personal relations, conducting a large correspondence, and intensely absorbed in his creative work, Conrad never stepped into the limelight of London, except perhaps on the occasion of several unsuccessful attempts to produce dramatic versions of some of his narratives. Politics he only touched at rare intervals, when he foretold the crash of the corrupt Russian system after the Russo-Japanese war,[1] or when he made himself the advocate of the cause of his native Poland in several articles of wartime.[2] These utterances on behalf of Poland—the only ones in Conrad's work, apart from a short story on a Polish theme [3] had been preceded by a visit to Kraków and to the Tatra mountains in 1914, on the very eve of the War. The wistful record of this visit [4] is not the only piece of evidence among his later works for what his friend John Galsworthy so tellingly described as "the cradle calling to the grave" toward the end of Conrad's life. Thus several masterpieces of his last years—*The Arrow of Gold, The Rover, Suspense*—are either based entirely on his strange youthful experiences at Marseille, or are set on the shores of what he calls [5] "the sunlit sea of my boyhood dreams"—the Mediterranean, "that old sea of magicians, slave-dealers, exiles and warriors, the sea of legends and terrors, where the mariners of remote antiquity used to hear the restless shade of an old wanderer weep aloud in the dark." And we have Mrs. Conrad's authentic testimony that Conrad, who liked until the end to shift his dwelling-place time and again, in the fashion of an old sailor, thought and spoke of returning to Poland to live there in the evening of his days; that, in fact, "for a long time before his death he felt the call of his native land—though he was as good an Englishman as any born and bred, as loyal to her interests and as devoted to the English people." [6] England early in his life had become his chosen "home" in that particular sense in which he speaks of it in a letter from Singapore to a Polish friend in England,[7] as of a country that offered quiet and friendly shelter to one for whom personal happiness was impossible in his own land "in the presence of national misfortune." And his patriotic attachment to the "free and hospitable land"

[1] *Autocracy and War*, 1905.
[2] A note on the Polish Problem, 1916; The Crime of Partition, 1919.
[3] *Prince Roman*, 1911.
[4] *Poland Revisited*, 1915.
[5] In *The Mirror of the Sea*.
[6] *Joseph Conrad as I Knew Him*, by his wife, Jessie Conrad, Heinemann, 1926.
[7] *Life and Letters of Joseph Conrad*, ed., by G. Jean-Aubry, 2 vols., Heinemann, 1927.

which had made "relative peace and a certain amount of happiness" possible to him, became vocal in wartime, when the privilege of visiting some of the vessels of the British Navy on patrol duty in the North Sea was proudly recorded in his articles *Well Done* (1918), *Tradition* (1918), and *Confidence* (1919).

II. THE WORK

When Conrad died suddenly on August 3, 1924, while at work on his unfinished great novel *Suspense*, the array of his works amounted to twenty-eight volumes. Novels and volumes of stories had followed each other in almost uninterrupted sequence since 1895. The material for all of them, however modified in the telling, was supplied by Conrad's memories of the men and women he had met, the tales he had listened to, and the events he had acted in or witnessed during the nearly twenty years of his early seafaring life. Some of his very greatest work in the form of fiction is almost undisguised autobiography (*Youth, Heart of Darkness, The Shadow Line, The Arrow of Gold*), and some contain autobiographical records of his inmost self under a symbolic veil (*Lord Jim, Nostromo*). If, in accordance with the facts of his own life, the sea is the scene or the background of most of his great stories, Conrad is not on that account to be disposed of merely as a writer, however distinguished, of novels about the sea and the life of sailors. When asked, in my presence, toward the end of his life, whether he ever wished to go to sea again, he replied, with a gesture of revulsion: "No, I have had enough of the sea!" His attitude is more fully revealed in a key passage of *The Mirror of the Sea*, of which these are characteristic fragments: ". . . The sea has never been friendly to man. . . . Its fickleness is to be held true to men's purposes only by an undaunted resolution and by a sleepless, armed, jealous vigilance, in which, perhaps, there has always been more hate than love. *Odi et amo* may well be the confession of those who, consciously or blindly, have surrendered their existence to the fascination of the sea. . . . The love of the sea, to which some men and nations confess so readily, is a complex sentiment wherein pride enters for much, necessity for not a little, and the *love of ships*—the untiring servants of our hopes and our self-esteem—for the best and most genuine part."

If, however, Conrad the sailor loved not so much the sea as ships, and if he loved them with a tender affection which often makes him speak of them as of living beings, it is essentially not the ships, but the "men in 'em" [8]—men, in fact, whether on sea or land (and women too)—that stand in the center of Conrad's creative interests. An approach toward a comprehensive view of that pervading human interest in Conrad's work is sought by those who emphasize the fact that, being himself a son of the Russian-Polish border, he liked to place his stories in the borderlands between different national civilizations, remote from each other by race and tradition. Such is his preferred scene of action, the Malay Archipelago, that "corner of the world, where the clash of two races and many religions, the passions, follies, principles and failures of men wove those intricate plots, of which he was to become the astonishing dramatist." [9] Such, again, is the South America of *Nostromo*, in which the clearheaded and generous Englishman's enterprise is engulfed in the irrational passions of that semi-Latin, semi-Indian Southern world. Such, finally, in *The Secret Agent* and *Under Western Eyes*, are the vast and mazy territories of Russian mentality, in which European and Asiatic standards of thought and conduct meet in perplexing association.

However, not even in surveying Conrad's work from this angle do we get nearer to its core than in classifying him as a great writer of sea stories. His deep and sympathetic insight into the ways of thinking, the traditions of belief, the codes of behavior, of widely different races all over the face of the earth does, indeed, make him a great cosmopolite in the world of letters, far superior in his wisdom to the comparative narrowness and partiality of the panoramic view of "East and West" in their everlasting contrast, and to the complacent dogma of the "White Man's Burden." But even these are all things of the surface. What matters most to Conrad is not humanity in crowds or tribes, but man in his sublime solitude, such solitude as he himself deeply experienced three times in his life: first as a foreign youth plunged into a strange

[8] *The Mirror of the Sea.*
[9] G. Jean-Aubry, *Joseph Conrad: Life and Letters*, I, 98.

Western world, then as a sailor facing the lonely immensities of the sea, and lastly as a newcomer from the world of action in the world of letters. That solitude—the common destiny of man at the decisive moments of his life—is to Conrad invariably a solitude of heroic struggle, and man's heroism in it, though outwardly ending in inevitable tragedy, is his supreme achievement on earth. "Man versus the element" is perhaps the fittest formula—if there is any—for summing up the spiritual essence of Conrad's manifold tales. That element surrounding solitary man and heroically combated by him, is often the sea—that "heartless and impenetrable" sea which he knew so well in its worst moods; sometimes it is a foreign community, which increases the pathos of solitude by its baffling strangeness and its desolating indifference; and sometimes —in particularly poignant stories, such as *The Shadow Line*—the stern enmity of the element around man seems allied to a chaos of dark and unruly forces in the abyss of his own subconscious mind, which he must face and fight and keep under.

As if to emphasize his conception of the struggle against elemental circumstance as the substance of man's tragic destinies, Conrad, with a persistent preference, chooses for his hero a type of man who has "lost caste" either through his own fault or through adverse chances, and who finds himself thrown out of his natural orbit and cast away amidst an alien world. On this uniform foundation Conrad builds up a variety of presentations of the mystery of human failure and defeat—the subject of his unending curiosity and unfailing compassion. Thus, in *Almayer's Folly*, we behold in masterly and painful detail the picture of the degradation of a white man through marriage with a woman of another race—the nemesis of the action finding cruel expression in the runaway match of Almayer's cherished daughter, whom he wished to bring up for European society, with a noble and chivalrous Malay. In *An Outcast of the Islands*, the moral degradation of a white adventurer in colored surroundings is even deeper, because it proceeds from ingrained baseness of character, and the task of retribution is carried out by the blind and cruel force of tropical nature. In *The Nigger of the Narcissus*, on the contrary, the recurrent figure of the solitary assumes heroic stature: here, it is the lonely Negro, dying a lingering death among the white crew, who by sheer power of soul inspires a fellow-feeling of revolt in them all. In *Heart of Darkness*, shrouded in mystery as its central figure is, we seem to find once more, as in the *Outcast*, moral guilt conspiring with the dark power of the tropics to break a man with the capacity for greatness in him. In *Lord Jim*, the outcast is one who has sentenced himself to a lifetime of heroic exile for his own tragic fault of deserting a sinking ship—an unmistakable allegory of Conrad's own lifelong uneasiness over his secession from the ranks of the defenders of his ancestral soil. Echoes of the drama of Conrad's abrupt severance of his early Polish connections, with mellowed memories of a schoolboy love for a well-born, patriotic Polish maiden, play beneath the South American surface of *Nostromo*, that grandiose epic of the multifarious feverish passions of greed for power and wealth in a setting of exotic and mixed civilization. In *The Secret Agent*, and again in the later novel, *Under Western Eyes*, the solitary is a Russian abroad, and "the element" the omnipresent dark force of autocracy. Tragedy here is rooted both in the unreality of revolutionary extremism and the futility of the intelligentsia in action, and it finds ultimate expression in service to an authority which under the mask of law and order conceals chaos and corruption.

In the midday of Conrad's creative career, a certain change came over his permanent conception of man's solitary struggles against elemental force; on the one hand, the dark forces now often become dramatically personsified in the demoniac figure of a villain; on the other hand, the hero's moral triumph, even in the midst of apparent defeat, is more positively asserted. In *Chance* the intriguer is De Barral, who seems animated by a desire of revenge on all humanity for the imprisonment to which his financial speculations led him; but his victims—his daughter and his son-in-law—emerge triumphant in actual fact, while he perishes; we even get what must pass for a "happy ending," unique among Conrad's otherwise invariably tragic denouements. In *Victory*, the noble lovers indeed meet their death through pursuit by a particularly villainous enemy; but the moral triumph indicated by the title is more definitely assured than ever. An even higher note of moral exultation is reached in the grand finale of *The Shadow Line*, where the young captain, having acquired the bitter wisdom of age through the trials of his first command, is confirmed in the sense of its lasting value by these words of an old seaman: "A man should stand up to his bad luck, to his mistakes, to his conscience, and all that sort of thing. Why—what else would you have to fight against?" And there is all the sadness of Conrad's own life of unceasing strain and effort in the old man's later words: "Precious little rest in life for anybody. Better not think of it."

Returning to the scenes of his youth in his later novels, from *The Arrow of Gold* onward, Conrad also returned both to his original antithesis of solitary man versus the circumambient element, and to his earlier, uncompromisingly tragic view of it. Thus, in *The Rescue*, begun long ago on Conrad's honeymoon trip, resumed repeatedly in his later life, and finished only a few years before his death, we once more meet a hero very like "Lord Jim," an exiled white in a position of authority among the Malays, whom the mirage of return into the world of European civilization only dazzles for a brief while before a final adieu. In *The Rover*, again, the sturdy figure of the marine mentor of Conrad's youth, Dominic Cervoni, re-emerges under the shape of the lonely old ex-pirate, who, at a moment of supreme crisis for the young people around him, heroically sacrifices his life to save them. Heroism and tragedy are inseparably associated once again.

Although the figures and events of Conrad's works are all derived directly from the real experience of his seafaring days, both figures and events are unusual in the extreme: all belong in the category of that truth which is proverbially "stranger than fiction." "The world of the living," so Conrad himself says in his preface to *The Shadow Line*, "contains enough marvels and mysteries as it is; marvels and mysteries acting upon our emotions and intelligence in ways so inexplicable that it would almost justify the conception of life as an enchanted state." There is always, in Conrad's novels, a prolonged central situation, almost weird in its tension, to which approaches from several points are laboriously worked up by a deliberately involved and complex method of narration. It is in accordance with this conception of the main theme—a conception rather ballad-like and dramatic than epic and novelistic in its character—that a realism of detail which is sometimes almost as ruthless as the glare of the sun in the tropics, is coupled with a technique of fantastic splashes of color in the description of scenery, of costume, and of the variegated human population of the tales.

This organic blend of romance and realism, inherent as it was in the exotic subject matter of Conrad's tales, was also rooted in his own personal nature and nurture. Trained in literary realism by his wide and judicious reading in the masterpieces of French and English fiction, he possessed at the same time a vein of romanticism in his temperament, which was a Polish inheritance [10] strengthened both by his adventurous life and by his permanent residence in England. For it is on a common plane of romantic idealism that the standards of character and conduct established for centuries among the chivalrous Polish gentry approximate closely to the English notion of a gentleman, as it grew up, ages ago, out of medieval tradition and Renaissance culture. The convergence of both national codes of honor on the idea of loyalty as its essence finds perfect expression when Conrad, in his "Familiar Preface" to *A Personal Record*, says: "Those who read me know my conviction that the world, the temporal world, rests on a few very simple ideas; so simple that they must be as old as the hills. It rests notably, among others, on the idea of Fidelity."

In the case of Poland in her century of captivity, that fidelity was exacted by a cause irrevocably doomed in the eyes of the world, by a country—as Conrad himself expresses it, with deep feeling, in *Prince Roman*—"which demands to be loved as no other country has ever been loved, with the mournful affection one bears to the unforgotten dead and with the unextinguishable fire of a hopeless passion which only a living, breathing, warm ideal can kindle in our breasts for our pride, for our weariness, for our exultation, for our undoing." It is not fanciful, accordingly, to assume that Conrad's gloomy upbringing in the shadow of national disaster largely accounts for that profoundly tragic view of life which his works consistently breathe from beginning to end. Pessimism was a settled feature of Conrad's disposition long before his writing days. His friend Galsworthy ascribed his habitual gloom to the lingering Congo fever in his blood. But four years

[10] See *The Polish Heritage of Joseph Conrad*, by Gustav Morf, S. Low Masten, London (1930), 248 pp.—*Ed.*

before the unlucky Congo expedition, Conrad, not yet thirty, in discussing the world's political and social outlook in a letter to a friend, could incidentally drop the statement: "I look with serenity of despair and the indifference of contempt upon the passing events." [11] And in a period of particular depression, due to ill-health and unemployment after the Congo experience, his uncle, who knew him better than any man on earth, remarked in a letter to him: ". . . this tendency to pessimism was in you as long ago as the days when you were at Marseille." [12] Conrad's biographer is right, therefore, when he states that the enforced leisure after Conrad's retirement from searfaring "drew up, little by little from the depths of his being, that inborn melancholy and energetic despair which underlie his work, and which twenty hard, adventurous years had kept beneath the surface." [13] And we are fully justified in believing that the tragic pessimism of one of the greatest of modern novelists—a pessimism surpassed, in grandeur of literary expression, only by Shakespeare's in English letters, and equaled in intensity only by Hardy's among writers of fiction—is the princely if melancholy gift which Poland, out of the bitter wealth of her misfortunes and sufferings, presented to the literature of England with the genius of Conrad. As in the strains of Chopin's compositions, which speak to all humanity in the ancient universal language of music, there rings, perennially inseparable from them, the note of Polish folk song and folk dance and of the folk soul, so in the immortal works of Conrad, speaking to all the nations of the globe in the modern world language of English, ages to come will hear the note of the chivalrous idealism and of the infinite woe of heroic and suffering nineteenth-century Poland.

[11] December 1885; *Life*, I, 84.
[12] *Life*, I, 148.
[13] *Life*, I, 147.

IGNACE JAN PADEREWSKI

(From a photograph taken in 1934)

XXVI

IGNACE JAN PADEREWSKI

1860-1941

The Artist, Composer and Man of Action

by

HENRYK OPIEŃSKI

Morges, Switzerland

IN JUNE of 1872 Stanisław Moniuszko died in Warsaw; in September of the same year twelve-year-old Ignace Jan Paderewski entered the Warsaw Conservatory as a student of the piano and the theory of music. These two dates indicate the continuity characterizing the development of Polish creative musical art in the nineteenth century. However, the maintenance of this continuity did not rest solely on the shoulders of Paderewski. In the intervening years between the death of Moniuszko and the appearance of Paderewski as a creative artist (his first composer's concert took place in Warsaw in 1885), names of outstanding composers had dawned upon the horizon of Polish musical life: Zygmunt Noskowski, Władysław Żeleński, Alexander Zarzycki. Fame at home and abroad came to the virtuoso of the violin and composer, Henryk Wieniawski. Juljusz Zarembski, Paderewski's senior by six years, who had studied abroad and who at an early age had begun his career as a professor in the Conservatory in Brussels, showed promise of developing into a first-rate composer, but died at the early age of thirty-one. The other highly talented contemporaries of Paderewski, the composers Antoni Rutkowski and Eugenjusz Pankiewicz, likewise died young. All these composers, indeed, the entire group of young musicians studying in Warsaw, were dominated by the traditional ideals of national music; folk songs as well as the works of Chopin and Moniuszko fired these young artists to creative enthusiasm. Pankiewicz left behind interesting and original adaptations of folk songs; Zarembski, with the bravura of virtuosity, composed works based predominantly on Polish themes; the mazurkas of Wieniawski found their way to the repertoires of all violinists, Polish and foreign alike.

Paderewski sensed the significance of these national currents with all his soul and enthusiastically carried on these traditions, which Chopin himself had received as a heritage from his predecessors of the last decades of the eighteenth century.

Paderewski was also destined to become in his time the most eminent interpreter of these ideals and to enrich musical literature by a series of compositions which are Polish in character but international in scope. In his very earliest works—the *Impromptu* (1879), the *Valse Melancolique*, Opus 2 and the *Elegy*, Opus 4— he sought no inspiration in national rhythms as did Chopin, nor did he, like Liszt, strive for virtuosity. Following these beginnings, devoid of a definite national character, Opus 5 brings up a group of several Polish dances (two *Krakowiaks* and a *Mazur*). Simultaneously, Opus 1 and Opus 2 reveal a budding interest in the old musical styles. Although all his early compositions bear the imprint of the old musical language and the old form, they always contain a Polish note elusive for precise description, but undeniable. This can be easily felt in the famous *Minuet*.

Paderewski's style, inherited from Chopin and his predecessors, may be termed peculiarly Polish, for it blooms on a substratum of Polish rhythm and melody. But also manifest in this style is a very personal expression of the artist's musical temperament. Whether in the *Chant du Voyageur*, the *Maytime Album*, the themes of the *Variations*, the *Polish Fantasy* or the *Concerto for Piano*, the lyrical quality of Polish song and Polish rhythm is constantly apparent in the harmonious and melodic patterns of which Paderewski alone was capable. Paderewski never composed unless he had something to say and never utilized original folk motifs to lend "color" to his style. His only musical composition directly based on folklore, but harmonized with great poetic imagination, is his *Tatra Album*, a collection of songs and dances of the Polish Tatra mountaineers. In the opera *Manru* he evoked the music of Polish Gypsies, but this music is spun out of the composer's own imagination with the help of the tones of the so-called "gypsy" scale (with one and a half notes interval). He also mingled with his astonishingly fertile poetical fantasy a fragment of the melody from Dąbrowski's *Mazurka*, "Poland is not yet Lost," which serves as one of the recurring motifs of the *B minor Symphony*. Thus, stylistically, Paderewski is a thoroughly original creator; his individual melodic and harmonic ideas may be recognized after listening to a few measures.

But the compositions of Paderewski have a still deeper meaning. If we probe their inner significance, they stand before us in the guise of a chronicle, mirroring the smiles, the moments of joyous exaltation and of tragic disappointments in the composer's life. This is truly art, art lived through. From the youthful, romantic lyricism of the *Traveler's Songs*, the *Maytime Album*, and the reflective-poetic mood of the *Piano Concerto*, Paderewski turns to the realization of the raptures of his national temperament in the *Krakowiaks* and the *Polish Fantasy*; then becomes serious and dramatically engrossed in *Songs to Poems by Mickiewicz*, bursts forth into lofty and somber longing in *Manru*, until in the *Sonata in E flat minor*, the *Songs to Poems by Catulle Mendès* and the *Variations in E flat minor*, he sheds "pure, copious tears" for his "manly age." And when the wind of the first Russian revolution blew into this "century of defeat," the vision of the frosty nights of national slavery evoked within him by the fortieth anniversary of the 1863 Insurrection was suddenly brightened by a cry heard deep within his soul: "Poland is not yet lost!" The active faculties of the artist-poet were convulsed with a volcanic surge of inspiration and the *B minor Symphony* came into being. Its last triumphal fanfares marked the end of Paderewski's musical creativeness; they became instead a call to action. Paderewski the composer ceased to live in a fantastic vision of the tonal world and began to create a Symphony of Life, the finale of which—not musically expressed but actually accomplished—was to be the rebirth of Poland.

The creative work of Paderewski, which came to a premature end, is bound up with the past and the future of Polish music: with the past, because it reflects the tradition of Chopin; with the future, because by its very modern character it revitalized the style of national art and became a golden bridge between the former romanticism and the new Polish creativeness.

One who desired to compile everything that has been written about Paderewski the virtuoso would undoubtedly create a many-volumed work filled with superlatives. Today we have only the memory of that inspired playing. For some time before his recent death the great virtuoso no longer played in public, preferring, despite his advanced age, to place all his strength at the service of the National Cause, as he did during the first World War.

Before Paderewski attained the pinnacle of success as a concert artist, he had to devote long hours of tedious, difficult work to the study of technique. Even when he reached his goal, he never neglected his hours of practice. This perseverance enabled him to achieve an unprecedented freedom in the expression of his conceptions and subjective feelings as he interpreted his own works or those of others. To Paderewski every concert was the giving of a portion of himself, a fusion of himself with art in the greatest concentration of spirit. That is why his concerts were an uplifting ceremony and a great festival. We understand why he wished to be left to himself immediately before each appearance, to be separated from the outer world for a brief period of intense concentration. His playing, of course, varied in quality from performance to performance, depending on his nervous tension; but his every concert was always a period of tremendous action.

It has aptly been said that Paderewski's playing cannot easily be described, that it must have been lived through! It is an entirely natural phenomenon that as an interpreter of Chopin Paderewski should have been unequaled. His sensitivity, his spiritual kinship with Chopin, his warm emotionality and thoroughly Polish temperament were factors making for a sympathetic rendition of Chopin's works in the spirit in which they had been conceived. Apart from the Polish creator of mazurkas and polonaises, Robert Schumann, that charming romantic, was a composer whose pieces Paderewski also played with the fondness of a kindred spirit. Bach and Beethoven were played by him with stylistic, lofty and noble simplicity. In the scintillating *Rhapsodies* of Liszt he revealed the charm of his technical brilliance. In Schubert's *Impromptu* or in Mendelssohn's *Songs without Words* he reconstructed the atmosphere of romantic poetry.

It is impossible to list all the older and newer composers whose works Paderewski rendered with incomparable craftsmanship; his performance was always characterized by an unrivaled innate genius, and his playing was always a revelation of beauty.

Saint-Saëns once said of Paderewski: "He is a genius who happens to play the piano." This is one of the happiest characterizations that could have been made. But we must stress the fact that Paderewski was also a man of action. He was endowed with a dynamic inner initiative, and with the necessary will power, endurance and unswerving tenacity to attain his goal. Everything he tackled he carried through, whether it concerned matters of art, political activity, the acquisition of knowledge, or even relaxation and recreation. Despite the poetry and tenderness of his nature and the enthusiasm of a passionate temperament, Paderewski knew how to be governed by cold reflection, since his was an extremely realistic mind which embraced with unusual thoroughness all the aspects of a given task. The influence he exerted directly upon his environment as well as the charm of his personality, were an expression of that spiritual force which is to be found only in genius.

In Paderewski greatness and goodness were combined in towering proportions. He would not have presented a rounded picture of a great man if his talents and qualities of mind had not been supplemented by attributes of soul and of heart—all of which made him in public as well as in private life a figure of noble, magnanimous gestures and inexhaustible goodness. His philanthropic sense of duty struggled within him for victory over a heartfelt compassion for poverty and misery. If one were to write down all his benefactions intended to allay human poverty, if one were to sum up all his scientific and artistic assistance, his foundations, stipends, gifts, the figures would run into a sizable fortune. His was a wealth earned by personal work and given away in accordance with the dictates of his heart, in the ideal spirit of Christian love for one's fellow men. For Paderewski considered his possession of material goods merely as a means of accomplishing beautiful, useful, good and great deeds. His goodness was occasionally abused, but this apostle of goodness and beauty preferred to err on the side of excessive trust and continued his good work.

Of a sunny and radiant disposition, full of simplicity in everyday intercourse, Paderewski drew people to him; his servants remained at his side for many years, and he was their protector and friend. He could play with children without tiring, falling into a frolicsome and gay mood; this doubtless accounted in part for his spiritual youth, and for the fact that despite the severe inner experiences to which his sensitive soul must often have been subjected, Paderewski always remained a cheerful and happy man.

Translated from the Polish by Halina Chybowska.

IGNACE JAN PADEREWSKI
In America

by

RICHARD ALDRICH
New York

WHATEVER the course of the world's history may have demanded of Paderewski as a statesman, and however patriotically and brilliantly he may have responded to those demands, he will remain, for the vast majority of his American admirers, the great musician. His place in their admiration and affection is, first, that of the master pianist, the conjurer with the magic of tones; and then that of the composer of strong individuality, tinged deeply with the color of his Polish nationality. The history of his conquest of America has hardly been paralleled in the history of music. There came other artists before him, but Paderewski's achievements were of a different and a higher sort, more deeply grounded in the nobility, the poetry, the pure artistic quality of his musicianship. He touched the deepest and tenderest feelings and tugged irresistibly at the heartstrings of a whole people.

He came to America in the autumn of 1891 and gave his first concert in New York's Carnegie Hall, with an orchestra, on November 17. The impression he made on the American public was deep and poignant from the very first; there was no mistaking the quality of the man and his art. It was a unique impression, of a sort, it might safely be said, such as no other solo artist ever quite achieved. He seemed to speak a new language in music; he raised its poetry, its magic, its mystery, its romantic eloquence, to a higher power than his listeners knew. To every one of them it seemed as if he spoke directly in an individual appeal, touching the heart as never before. There was a beauty of line as well as of color and atmosphere, a poignance of phrase, a quality of tone, a lyrical accent such—so it seemed—as to make of his playing something never till then quite divined.

Public interest grew so greatly that it was soon necessary for Paderewski to return to Carnegie Hall for his solo recitals—a new thing, then, to present a single performer in a vast audience-room with no associate to bring relief or contrast. His tour of the country, his return season after season, gave rise to an increasing series of popular demonstrations in New York and other cities, such as had never been witnessed here before. For over forty years this went on, interrupted only by the turbulent years of the war. And in those years Paderewski took a part unique in the history of art: his appearance here, and elsewhere, first as an eloquent pleader for the rights of his native land in a speech of impeccable and burningly eloquent English; and then, after a few moments' breathing spell, his reappearance on the platform in an equally impeccable and burningly eloquent interpretation at the pianoforte of some of the greatest works of his fellow countryman, Chopin.

Paderewski garnered the laurels not only of a great interpreter but also the more lasting, if less dazzling fame of a composer. At his first American concerts he played his own concerto and his *Polish Fantasia*, works which became lasting items in his repertory. Many of his lesser pianoforte solos, rooted in the soil of Poland, fragrant with the blossoms of Polish national art, were amongst his best beloved offerings. Many will remember the superabundant popularity of his melodious *Minuet*, the exotic charm of his *Chant du Voyageur* and of his *Nocturne*. His *Sonata for Pianoforte and Violin* had made its way to America before he did. Later in his career he brought hither his Polish opera *Manru*, produced in his own presence at the Metropolitan Opera House. Still later he gave to the Boston Symphony Orchestra his symphony, for its first performance. It was work of a somber spirit, of grandiose and moving power, denoting a new direction and a new development of his creative activity, and was followed by a profoundly felt, if gloomy, pianoforte sonata and a set of variations for pianoforte solo.

Many are the virtuosos who have come to America to exploit a European reputation, not infrequently animated by pecuniary considerations. It was impossible to conceive of such a spirit in Paderewski, or of his viewing his American triumphs with any such purpose. He reaped great fortunes repeatedly in America; but he felt himself so much a part of America as to wish to leave here a permanent impress of his personality. He gave lavishly with both hands, for charity; many were the benefit performances which he proffered in the interest of worthy causes; many are the artists he has helped and encouraged. He founded as a perpetual reminder of his interest in American art and in its progress, the Paderewski Prize for compositions of outstanding merit in various forms by American composers.

For two generations Paderewski's profoundly poetic and heartfelt art was a benison to America, a country too often swept by the unthinking worship of the virtuoso. It is good to think that the American public's reaction toward one who always put his technical powers so completely at the service of the highest ideals in music, remained so immediate, so direct and so lasting; and that the influence Paderewski exerted gained him lasting affection in the minds and hearts of the American people.

IGNACE JAN PADEREWSKI [1]
As Statesman and Patriot

by

FRANK NOWAK

PERSONALITY, genius, character, call it what you will, enabled Ignace Jan Paderewski to hold the attention of the world for half a century. Beloved as a great personality, admired as a consummate pianist and composer, and deeply respected as statesman and patriot, he gained an ever-widening circle of friends who today speak of him with veneration. Perhaps it was the unassuming simplicity of genius and the deep sincerity of a man of profound convictions which made this universal appeal and gave him the power to stir the highest emotions and aspirations of mankind. In a sense Paderewski belonged to no one country, but to all the world. A modern Erasmus, he embodied the highest culture of Western civilization and was a true citizen of the world.

The World War which shook Western civilization to its foundations and brought tragedy to millions of homes affected Paderewski deeply. He could not go on with his music while all the world was in arms, and humanity lay prostrate before the Moloch of war. A great decision had to be made. Heartrending as it was, he resolved to sacrifice his music and to use it in the service of humanity. He toured North and South America again and again as a distinguished international beggar, using the concert stage to attract audiences who contributed dollars for the relief of the starving and the dying. In this work he spared neither

[1] The reader will find fuller information (carried to 1933) about this "modern immortal" in the only full-size biography that has so far appeared in the English language, a work by the late Professor Charles Phillips: *Paderewski— The Story of a Modern Immortal* (The Macmillan Company, New York, 563 pp.). The Kosciuszko Foundation de luxe limited edition (now long exhausted), with the Introduction by President Henry Noble MacCracken, appeared in 1933. The trade edition, of which there are several reprints, with the Introduction by the late Colonel Edward M. House, first came out in 1934.

Paderewski's own *Memoirs*, written jointly with Mary Lawton and brought out by Charles Scribner's Sons in 1938 (397 pp.), are carried to the outbreak of the first World War.—*Ed.*

himself nor his own private fortune, but labored incessantly at the noble task of alleviating the suffering of his fellow men.

What tortures of the spirit Paderewski endured from 1914 to 1917 can be understood only by those whose sensitive natures can respond to the kind of patriotism that moved this man, who during the period of American neutrality was condemned to silence upon the cause nearest his heart, the Polish question. When the United States entered the war in April 1917, Paderewski at once assumed a new role, as spokesman for the Polish people, devastating critic of the Central Powers and ardent crusader in the cause of Poland. No nation could ask for a more intelligent or a more skillful advocate. His patriotism proved contagious, while his popularity and prestige in America made him *persona gratissima*, and enabled him to represent and serve his people very much as Benjamin Franklin served the American Colonies at the French court during the American Revolution.

Most surprising to many an American audience was the masterly manner in which this musician marshaled facts of history to prove his contentions, yet neglected none of the artifice of the orator in playing upon emotions to make conviction doubly sure. His manner was simplicity itself, a disarming simplicity, the simplicity of all great art. A master of understatement, he never labored a point already made but drove it home with a humor that was sometimes grim and at other times of so delicate and whimsical a nature that his hearers were at once disarmed and charmed, as in the instance of his opening words in a speech delivered at San Francisco. "I come to speak to you of a nation which is not yours, in a language which is not mine." It was soon apparent to every audience that it was listening to "a genius who happened to be a musician." Music was not the only means of expression that Paderewski knew how to use for the purpose of expressing his highest thoughts and aspirations with masterly precision and calculated effect. He was a great orator, or as Colonel House would have it, "the greatest orator of our time." Henceforth, to millions of Americans, the cause of Poland was so closely associated with his name that the words Paderewski and Poland were uttered in the same breath as inseparable synonyms.

But the transition from musician to orator, diplomat and

statesman, was not nearly as sudden as the American press would have us believe. No Pole of intelligence could live under the yoke of foreign domination without indulging in dreams of political freedom, least of all Ignace Jan Paderewski, whose grandparents were Siberian exiles, whose mother was born in Siberia far away from her native land, whose father suffered imprisonment for complicity in the insurrection of 1863. Indeed, one suspects that young Paderewski, who was born in Podolia in 1860 into this atmosphere of intense patriotic sentiment and family sacrifice for the cause of Poland, might have turned to music as the best medium for expressing his own personality and as a means of serving his country to the best of his ability. It had been done before, for many a Pole who was restricted in his political activities turned to the fine arts for expression of his longing for independence and to glorify the heritage of his race. Sienkiewicz fired the patriotism of his people by means of the historical novel; Matejko, the great painter, did the same with his expressive brush; and it remained for Paderewski to reveal the innermost soul and longing of the Polish nation by his own compositions and by inimitable exposi-tions and interpretations of the music of Chopin. The concert stage became a rostrum from which the great artist addressed the civilized world, won its sympathy, and gained countless friends for himself and his country.

Close personal friendship with many men in high places afforded Paderewski numerous opportunities for discussing in practical and realistic fashion the political outlook for Poland. He was no novice in politics and was regarded by statesmen, diplomats, and politicians as one of the best-informed political observers of his day. A brilliant and witty conversationalist, he knew how to charm his hearers as well as to command their respect.

Long before the outbreak of the World War Paderewski had prepared himself as a public speaker and on a number of occasions addressed his countrymen on political issues. The keynote of his speeches seemed always to be the theme, "in union there is strength"; harmony and co-operation and a strong moral determi-nation would lead to self-preservation and ultimate independence. His first important political address was delivered in Warsaw in

1898, while his most dramatic appearance as orator and statesman was in 1910 in the ancient capital of Poland, Kraków, at the dedication of a monument which he presented to the Polish nation. Thousands of Poles from the German, Russian, and Austrian Partitions and from beyond the seas had gathered on Wawel Hill, the Westminster Abbey of Poland, to do homage before the tombs of their great kings and to celebrate the five hundredth anniversary of the great victory of King Władysław Jagiełło over the Teutonic Knights at Grunwald in 1410. Paderewski, who had commissioned the sculptor Antoni Wiwulski to fashion a magnificent monument to commemorate this moment of solemn consecration, was scheduled to deliver an address presenting the work of art to the city of Kraków. From the point of view of Russia, Germany, and Austria it was a tense and provocative political situation, a possible prelude to another insurrection long overdue since the uprisings of 1831 and 1863. Amid subdued cheers, Paderewski arose to speak. "This work of art which you gaze upon did not arise from hate," he began. "It was born of a deep love of the fatherland, not only in its past greatness, its present powerlessness, but its certain powerful future." Love and gratitude rather than hate was the theme of his discourse. Confident of the ultimate triumph of justice and right, he counseled no insurrection, but the cultivation of the virtues that give moral strength, such brotherly love as brought union and co-operation between Poland and Lithuania and gave them the power to resist invaders. It was a vigorous presentation of the Polish question and a dramatic appeal for justice to the civilized world.

Three months later, on October 23, 1910, Paderewski addressed his countrymen at the Chopin Centenary Festival in Lwów. Again it was a speech more akin to poetry than prose, full of poetic imagery, a beautiful tribute to Chopin, and yet it contained political implications of a far-reaching nature and a keen analysis of Polish character. Referring to the moody character of his fellow countrymen, he declared:

"Here may be found, perhaps, the secret of a certain enveloping charm that is ours; here, too, may be our greatest demerit. Change follows change in us almost without transition; we pass from blissful rapture to sobbing woe; a single step divides our

sublimest ecstasies from the darkest depths of spiritual despondency. We see proof of this in every domain of our national life;
we see it in our political experiences, in our internal developments,
in our creative work, in our daily troubles, in our social intercourse, in all our personal affairs. It is palpable everywhere. Maybe
this is only an inherent characteristic; yet when we come to
compare ourselves with other happier and more satisfied races,
it strikes us rather as being a pathological condition; if this be so,
it is one we might specify, perhaps, as inborn national *arhythmia*.
This lack of rhythm would serve to explain the instability, the lack
of perseverance with which we are generally accredited; we might
therefore find the source of our, alas, undeniable incapacity for
disciplined collective action; therein, doubtless, lies some of the
tragedy of our ill-fated annals."

Here was the clarion call of the leader who commanded his
people to put their own house in order in preparation for the new
day that was dawning.

When the war began in Europe in 1914, Paderewski was at
his home in neutral Switzerland, whither numerous Polish leaders
fled as exiles from Germany, Austria, and Russia that they might
more readily watch the international political situation and make
plans in behalf of their own country. In the home of Paderewski
at Morges, at Vevey in the home of Sienkiewicz, and in Lausanne,
patriots gathered to debate the course of action the Polish nation
ought to follow. Naturally counsels were divided in so complicated
a political situation and various groups were organized, each with
its own platform and plan of action. All were agreed, however,
regarding the most immediate necessity for aiding the victims of the
war in Poland and co-operated in setting up under the leadership of
Paderewski and Sienkiewicz a "General Committee of Assistance
for the Victims of the War in Poland." Later Paderewski established branches in Paris and London and sailed for America, where
he could be of most service in collecting funds, informing the
American public on the Polish question, and furnishing leadership
for the four million Polish-Americans who desired to aid Poland
but were divided in counsel as to the best method to pursue.
We have already noted the phenomenal success attained by the
virtuoso-diplomat in all these things. He won the sympathy and

support of the American public, united under his leadership the activities of most of the Polish-American committees, and made possible the formation of an expeditionary army that was an important nucleus around which developed the Polish army of General Haller in France.

A distinctly personal achievement was the success of Paderewski in making contacts with men in high places; contacts which soon developed into loyal friendship based on mutual admiration and respect and which served him in good stead in many an hour of need. Early in 1916 he sought and obtained an interview with Colonel Edward House, the close personal adviser of President Wilson. Although very different in temperament the two men became close friends. "It has been the dream of my life," wrote Paderewski to House, "to find a providential man for my country. I am sure that I have not been dreaming vain dreams." That providential man was indeed the hardheaded and taciturn colonel who frequently dropped in for tea at the Polish pianist's New York apartment. There they discussed the Polish question for hours. In the words of Colonel House, "we pored over maps—his maps and mine—of Central and Eastern Europe, and together we traced what we thought should be a homogeneous Poland. . . . The Poland we outlined during these fervid periods proved to be practically the Poland created by the Versailles Conference."

In the summer of 1916 Paderewski attended a dinner at the White House. After dinner, as the guests gathered in the drawing room, someone opened the piano, and the great pianist consented to play, upon the request of the President. It was an all-Chopin program, through which he spoke to the assembled guests of the sufferings and hopes of his people. Everyone, including the President, was visibly moved. For the rest of the evening Poland was the chief topic of conversation.

On November 6, 1916, President Wilson received Paderewski in his New Jersey residence, where he was awaiting election returns, thanked the Polish leader for his support, and asked his opinion about the German declaration of November 5 regarding the independence of Poland. Paderewski replied that in his opinion it was an insincere offer made for the purpose of securing recruits for the German army. Wilson agreed with this interpretation absolutely, and the two men held a conversation that lasted nearly an hour. Again Paderewski emphasized the importance of the Polish question since the Partitions of the eighteenth century, while Wilson the historian listened with keen interest. When they arose, Wilson has been reported to have said: "My dear Paderewski, I can tell you that Poland will be resurrected and will exist again. For Poland the miracle of independence will come from the West, as my own victory will come today through a miracle from the West."

Two months passed. On January 8, 1917, Colonel House called upon Paderewski and asked him to prepare a memorandum on Poland for the President. Since House was leaving for Washington in a few days, the Polish leader shut himself in his room and wrote continuously for thirty-six hours. It was this memorandum that the Colonel "read and re-read four or five times" on his way to Washington and the arguments of which he repeated to the President, who seemed to be in complete agreement.

On January 22, 1917, President Wilson appeared before the Senate of the United States and declared that it was the duty of the United States to take part in restoring international harmony on the basis of certain principles. He advocated "peace without victory," declared that "statesmen everywhere are agreed that there should be a united, independent and autonomous Poland," and insisted upon the right of nationalities to liberty and self-government. One year later this pronouncement took on more definite form in the famous speech of January 8, 1918, advocating a settlement of the war on the basis of fourteen points enumerated by the President. The thirteenth point concerned Poland and provided that "an independent Polish State should be created which should include the territories inhabited by indisputably Polish populations, which should be assured a free and secure access to the sea, and whose political and economic independence and territorial integrity should be guaranteed by international covenant."

After this extraordinary success as a statesman and diplomat in America Paderewski sailed for Paris in December 1918 to report to the Polish National Committee which he had represented in America since 1917. This Committee, headed by the brilliant

National Democrat, Roman Dmowski, represented the conservative and pro-Ally sentiment of a large part of the Polish population residing principally in western Poland, and was regarded by the Allies as the *de facto* government of Poland. After the Armistice it sought *de jure* recognition as the government of Poland. France was ready to accord recognition but delayed action for lack of British approval. The British government rightly pointed out that there was already a government in existence in Poland, headed by Józef Piłsudski, and although the Allies mistrusted and suspected the policies of this "Socialist" government, it could not be ignored.

The Polish National Committee now sent Paderewski to London, where he was most cordially received by his close friend, Arthur Balfour, Foreign Secretary of Great Britain. In the course of their interview Paderewski asked Balfour whether he still stood by his promises of 1915 regarding Poland, and the foreign secretary replied, "Of course I stand by them. We all want an independent Poland. In my personal opinion Poland is at present in both a very lucky and unlucky position. Although in England Poland's independence is most sincerely desired, I don't see how she can be represented at the Peace Conference in which her fate will be decided. You know that his Majesty's Government have not recognized the *Comité National* as the responsible Polish Government. But neither have we recognized the present Polish Government in Warsaw, and the latest news from Poland is anything but reassuring. Yet Poland must be properly represented at the Peace Conference. It is your task, Paderewski. I want you to go to Poland to unite the Polish hearts."

For a man like Paderewski, whose love of country had become a ruling passion, acceptance of this new mission was nothing less than a sacred duty as well as a great opportunity, and he proposed to make the most of it. He insisted upon being taken to Poland on a British warship in order that he might carry with him some of the enormous prestige of the victorious Allies to hearten his own people, and he proposed to reach Warsaw by way of the old Polish province of Poznań, which was still in the hands of the German army.

On Christmas Day 1918 the British cruiser *Concord* landed her distinguished passenger at the port of Danzig and the triumphal progress of Ignace Paderewski through his native country began. At Poznań the enthusiasm of the people was unbounded. The mere presence of their beloved leader provoked an uprising which resulted in the dispersal of the German army of occupation.

At Warsaw on January 3 he was accorded a reception equaled only by that given to Józef Piłsudski several weeks earlier upon the latter's release from a German prison. The next day, however, brought disillusion, for the interview with Piłsudski proved futile, and Paderewski moved on to Kraków. Meanwhile an unsuccessful *coup d'état* against the Piłsudski government on the night of the fourth and the morning of the fifth of January paved the way for the recall of Paderewski to Warsaw and the formation of a new government. Piłsudski remained Chief of State while Paderewski accepted the post of Premier and Secretary of Foreign Affairs. Thanks to the good political sense of both Polish leaders, civil war was avoided, the country was united and ready to take its place at the Peace Conference scheduled to meet five days later, January 19, 1919. The Polish delegates to the Conference were to be Ignace Paderewski and Roman Dmowski, former head of the Polish National Committee in Paris.

The ability of Paderewski as a statesman and negotiator appeared to best advantage at the Peace Conference, from which few men emerged with greater reputation and prestige than he. Summoned to Paris at a most critical moment in the settlement of Poland's frontiers, he seemed to succeed where others had failed. Roman Dmowski with characteristic brilliance had already presented the claims of Poland to the Big Four. Even Clemenceau had commended him upon the clarity of his exposition and the inescapable logic of his argument, yet something seemed to have gone wrong. Dmowski knew how to convince his hearers with sound argument, but he failed to win them over to active support of his contentions. Apparently his personality was too uninspiring, his manner too sophisticated, to arouse sympathy. Besides, he had incurred the enmity of Lloyd George, who listened to rumors to the effect that Dmowski had accused him of being pro-Jewish. Finally Lloyd George, who was astonishingly ignorant of the geography of eastern Europe, for reasons of his own decided to appease Germany at the expense of Poland, whose claims were mainly sponsored by France. The decisions of the Big Four now proved unfavorable to Poland and Dmowski began to feel that the situation was hopeless. It was at this juncture that Paderewski arrived in Paris in April 1919, and despite the pessimism of his colleague proceeded at once to make plans for reopening the questions already supposedly settled.

Paderewski brought to the Polish delegation his great personal influence together with a human sympathy and an understanding of human nature which Dmowski lacked, despite his impeccable logic. He was exactly the right man in the right place at the right time, notwithstanding the sarcastic jibe of Lloyd George, who remarked, "What can you expect of a country that sends as her representative a musician?" At a formal dinner given in honor of Paderewski by the French Foreign Secretary, M. Pichon, the Polish orator and statesman delivered an address that proved to be one of the high lights of the Conference. His breadth of vision, which transcended the narrow national bounds of the mere politician, and his emphasis upon idealism and harmony in the interest of the future of civilization itself, swept even the most cynical and prosaic of men off his feet. A new atmosphere of hope and idealism pervaded the great hall, and a surprise at the masterful exposition of the diplomat-musician gave way to sincere admiration. There was no longer any doubt in the minds of the Polish delegates that decisions of the Big Four regarding Poland would be reconsidered. Indeed, the representatives of the major powers never replied to Paderewski's views with an unqualified "no."

Moreover, the personal friendship of Paderewski with such men as Wilson, Clemenceau, Balfour, House, Foch, and even, eventually, Lloyd George, was hardly less important than his public appearances. They felt his personal presence, responded to his human appeal, and admired him for his profound sincerity as well as for his wide information.

In a letter signed by Wilson, Clemenceau, Lloyd George, and Orlando, the Big Four stated: "No country could wish for a better advocate than he." The reference was to Paderewski's activities at the Conference. Even more illuminating was the experience of Robert Lansing, Secretary of State of the United States, who distrusted the Polish statesman. Writing some years later, Lansing stated: "My original impression was not one of a complimentary nature. . . . When the famous musician came to see me at my office at the Department of State, I could not avoid the thought that his emotions were leading him into a path which he was wholly unsuited to follow. In truth, I thought he was making a mistake. . . . My second impression—and it is the impression that I still hold—was that I.P. was a greater statesman than he was a musician. . . . He was wonderfully resourceful and apparently had an instinctive sense of the possible. . . . He held his imagination in leash as he did his emotions. . . . His views were essentially sane and logical. What M. Paderewski has done for Poland will cause eternal gratitude. . . . His career is one which deserves to be remembered not only by his countrymen . . . but by every man to whom love of country and loyalty to a great cause stand forth as the noblest attributes of human character. . . . In history as in memory there will live two Paderewskis—Paderewski, the master of music, and Paderewski, the statesman of Poland."

"The vision of a strong independent Poland has always been the lodestar of my existence. Its realization is still the great aim of my life," declared Paderewski some years before the outbreak of the World War. He lived to see that vision realized, partly as a result of his own strenuous activity. It remained for him to return to Poland after the Peace Conference as Prime Minister to engage in the co-operative effort with Piłsudski, the newly created Polish Diet, and the Polish people, to unite the three fragments of Poland into a united country. It was a tremendous task that demanded every moment of his time and every ounce of his energy. He labored incessantly, but failed to win the continued confidence and support of the political factions in the Diet and officially resigned on December 5, 1919. His countrymen, inexperienced in parliamentary government, divided in counsel, and narrow in political outlook after nearly a century and a half of foreign domination, perhaps had not yet grown sufficiently in understanding to grasp the motives and the ideals of a statesman who could influence and convince the most experienced leaders of the West. Too far ahead of his times to be understood by his people, he could not descend to the level of a mere politician, and therefore withdrew from active political life.

Life is full of paradoxes. Even those who opposed Paderewski could not but admire his lifelong sacrifices for his country and today he lives in the hearts of his countrymen, admired and loved by all.

Having done so much to win the independence of Poland and to establish the state a quarter of a century ago, this great Pole was not spared in his old age the tragedy of witnessing the destruction of his country. In November 1939 he was called to the position of President of the National Council, a legislative body of the Free Polish Government temporarily located in France, which moved later to England. Despite his frail health he answered the call, went to Paris, and inaugurated with a stirring message the first session of the Council. This patriarch of statesmen, exemplary citizen, and peerless master of tones and of words, spoke again to his compatriots and the conscience of the world. A year later, in November 1940, this great citizen of the civilized world revisited America to gain a much-needed respite in the New World from the turmoil of the Old and to join with the moral forces working here for the liberation of all oppressed nations. His voice was heard again in the stirring call for Polish independence.

His feeble health strained by a public appearance in behalf of a Polish cause, he contracted pneumonia and after a brief illness died on June 29, 1941, in the country that gave him asylum, which he loved next best to his native land. In this grand finale of his life and work his parting words were: *"Polska Powstanie"*—"Poland will live again." His mortal remains rest temporarily in the Arlington cemetery, pending their removal to his native land when Poland is free again.

MARIA SKŁODOWSKA CURIE

An autographed photograph dedicated to the students of Vassar College.

XXVII

MARIE SKŁODOWSKA CURIE

"Self-effacing and devoted scientist, teacher and author . . .
inspired and inspiring idealist, practical dreamer."

1867-1934

by

MARY LANDON SAGUE

MARIE SKŁODOWSKA, youngest of the five children of Władysław and Bronisława (née Boguska) Skłodowski, was born in
Warsaw on November 7, 1867, and died at Sancellemoz, France,
on July 4, 1934. The families of her father and mother, who were
Roman Catholics of purely Polish stock, were among the small
landed proprietors, a class notable for its intellectual interests.
True to this tradition, Mme. Curie's paternal grandfather directed
the management of his own lands and at the same time was
president of the *gimnazjum* of Lublin. Both her father and her
mother were distinguished educators in Warsaw. In 1895 she
married Pierre Curie, Professor of Physics in the School of Physics
and Chemistry of the City of Paris. They had two children, Irene,
born in 1897, and Eve Denise, born in 1904.

Mme. Curie received her early education in the schools of
Warsaw, which were subject to the oppression and restrictions
imposed by Russian domination. She graduated at the age of
fifteen at the head of her class. While doing private teaching she
continued her preparation for university work by self-instruction.
Of the opportunity to use a laboratory which came to her during
this period, she wrote: "On the whole, though I was taught that
the way of progress is neither swift nor easy, this first trial confirmed in me the taste for experimental research in the fields of

333

physics and chemistry." In 1891 she was finally able to undertake the study at the *Sorbonne* of which she had dreamed. For four years she lived in a garret room, practicing the utmost economy but happy in her independence and "entirely absorbed in the joy of learning and understanding." In 1893 she graduated with first rank as *"licenciée ès sciences physiques"* and in 1894 with second rank as *"licenciée ès sciences mathématiques."*

After her marriage, while working in the laboratory with her husband, she continued to prepare for the examination for the certificate to teach in schools for young girls; in 1896 she obtained first place in this examination. In 1897 she completed and published a piece of research on the magnetic properties of steel. Professor and Mme. Curie announced the existence of polonium in July 1898 and in the following December that of radium. Mme. Curie, the first woman to hold a full professorship in France, was made professor at the *École Normale Supérieure des Jeunes Filles* at Sèvres in 1900. In 1903 she completed her thesis, *Recherches sur les Substances Radioactives*, and was granted the doctorate. She was made *chef de travaux* in the laboratory planned for M. Curie when he was named to the new chair of physics at the Sorbonne in 1904. After his tragic death in 1906 she was asked to succeed him in this professorship, the first time such an honor had been accorded to a woman. While fulfilling the obligations of this position she continued her research in collaboration with others, and in 1910, with André Debierne, succeeded in isolating metallic radium. In 1911, appointed by a commission of scientists representing different countries, she prepared the international standard of radium chloride, which is preserved in the International Bureau of Weights and Measures at Sèvres. In 1912 she aided in establishing a radium laboratory in Warsaw and saw arrangements completed for and work begun on the Institute of Radium in Paris. During the war, in addition to much of her regular teaching, she made an invaluable contribution in the organization and maintenance of a radiological service which, after the armistice, developed into a national service of radiumtherapy. The building up of an Institute of Radium to the memory of Pierre Curie and carrying further her investigations in the study of radioactive substances occupied the last years of her life.

In 1903 the Nobel Prize in Physics was awarded to M. and Mme. Curie and to M. Becquerel for the discovery of radioactivity and of the new radioactive elements; in 1911 Mme. Curie was awarded the Nobel Prize in Chemistry. Other honors and recognitions came to her from all parts of the world, honorary degrees from colleges and universities, honorary membership in academies of science, medals of great distinction from learned societies, and the homage and admiration of the whole scientific world.

Twenty years before the discovery of radium by Mme. Curie, Sir William Crookes had studied the cathode rays produced in an evacuated tube by the passage through it of a high voltage current. In 1895 Roentgen, carrying further the work in high vacuum tubes, discovered the now familiar X-rays of great penetrating power. The association of the X-rays with fluorescence of the glass walls of the vacuum tube led to the investigation of phosphorescent and fluorescent materials to determine whether or not they produced any rays similar to X-rays. Becquerel discovered in 1896 that a compound of uranium affected a photographic plate in the same manner when it had been kept in the dark as it did after it had been exposed to the sunlight. He further showed that this substance was capable of discharging an electroscope. Radioactivity had been discovered, though it was not so named until later. In 1897 Mme. Curie determined to make a study of the phenomenon of radioactivity the subject of her thesis. It was not long before Professor Curie abandoned his work on crystals to join his wife in her quest and together they devoted their energies to the problem whose triumphant solution was to bring them world-wide and lasting fame.

The fact that the rays given off by uranium caused the discharge of an electroscope indicated that the air had been made a conductor, that it had been ionized. This process of ionization, which had been studied to a considerable extent in connection with X-rays, furnished the best medium for Mme. Curie's measurements in the study of radioactivity. To obtain sufficiently precise quantitative results it was necessary to have an instrument of sufficient delicacy to measure the very feeble currents carried by air ionized by uranium. Such an instrument was at Mme. Curie's command, the result of earlier work of her husband and his brother, namely a Curie electrometer and a piezoelectric quartz. With the addition of an ionization chamber Mme. Curie was enabled to balance on the electrometer the current carried by ionized air against that furnished by a piezoelectric quartz. She soon demonstrated that with this new device it was possible to measure the radiations with great precision. Using a variety of compounds of uranium she found that they all produced the same rays and that the intensity of the radiations depended only on the quantity of uranium in the compound, while neither the nature of the compound nor the temperature and light conditions of the experiment had any effect. From these observations she reasoned that the radioactivity shown by uranium compounds was a fundamental property of the uranium atom. Of this finding Soddy says: "On the theoretical side, the conclusion that had most to do with the rapid progress made was the recognition that radio-activity is a fundamental and unalterable property of the atom. . . . This brilliant generalization, at once clarifying and simplifying the whole subject, was made quite early, in the face of much apparent evidence to the contrary. . . . In spite of the discovery of many new phenomena, at first sight quite out of keeping with it, it has survived and remains as the central pivot on which the whole science turns."

To determine whether or not atoms of other elements have this same property Mme. Curie began a systematic examination of all other known elements, either free or in compound, to find that only one other, thorium, gave off rays similar to those from uranium. Another and more important observation made by Mme. Curie was that the ores of uranium and thorium which she had examined had shown greater radioactivity than was consistent with their content of these elements. To explain this unexpected behavior she suggested that the ores contained, in addition to the uranium and thorium, small quantities of an unknown element, more radioactive than either of the known elements possessing this property. At this point Professor Curie joined in the work in order, as Mme. Curie thought, that the search for the predicted element might be quickly completed. As she said later: "Neither of us could foresee that, in beginning this work, we were to enter the path of a new science which we should follow for all our future."

For their investigation they chose an ore of uranium known as pitchblende, the material being generously presented to them by the Austrian Government. The recently made discovery of radioactivity furnished the tool for a new method of chemical research, without which the new radioactive element, present to less than one-millionth of a per cent, would not have been found. The separation by the usual methods of chemical analysis was first employed and then all the fractions were tested for their radioactivity. As purification proceeded and the element became more concentrated the radioactivity increased and, at the same time, the chemical identity became apparent. In July 1898 they announced the existence of polonium, named for Mme. Curie's native Poland. Chemically much like bismuth, it was concentrated in the bismuth fractions from the ore. As the barium fraction also showed great radioactivity, search for a second new element was carried forward and in December 1898 the existence of radium was announced. Evidence for the two new elements seemed conclusive, but it still remained to separate them from their companions, bismuth and barium, and to obtain them in the free form.

To accomplish the separation of the traces of polonium and radium present in pitchblende was a task requiring a tremendous amount of raw material and labor, for both of which money was needed. Although they were later assisted by various grants, the purchase of the material was at first financed by the Curies themselves from their slender resources, and the work was done with very little aid. They were fortunate in being able to buy advantageously from the uranium plant at the St. Joachimsthal mines in Austria a supply of the residues, previously treated as waste, which they were convinced, by their experiments with pitchblende, would contain radium. As adequate quarters were lacking, this great undertaking was begun in an old shed, across the court from the room containing the electrometric apparatus. This shed had a leaky roof and the most primitive equipment; because it offered no ventilation facilities to remove fumes from the chemical reactions the work was done in the adjacent court whenever the weather permitted. However, in spite of its disadvantages and the grueling toil of the work done there, Mme. Curie wrote of this room: "Yet it was in this miserable old shed that we passed the best and happiest years of our life, devoting our entire days to our work. . . . I shall never be able to express the joy of the untroubled quietness of this atmosphere of research and the excitement of actual progress with the confident hope of still better results. The feeling of discouragement that sometimes came after some unsuccessful toil did not last long and gave way to renewed activity. We had happy moments devoted to a quiet discussion of our work, walking around our shed. One of our joys was to go into our workroom at night; we then perceived on all sides the feebly luminous silhouettes of the bottles or capsules containing our products. It was really a lovely sight and one always new to us. The glowing tubes looked like faint, fairy lights."

While Mme. Curie, the chemist, wrestled with the problem of separating an unbelievably small portion of the precious product from great masses of raw material, M. Curie, the physicist, devoted himself to the study of the physical properties of the rays. Fortunately, industrial facilities were before long made available for carrying out the earlier steps in the separation of the radioactive materials, thus relieving Mme. Curie of the heaviest of the toil. By 1902 she had prepared one-tenth of a gram of pure radium chloride and the properties and atomic weight of radium had been determined. In other words, indisputable proof of the existence of the element had been presented. The thesis which Mme. Curie submitted for the doctorate in 1903 was based upon this work, in recognition of which the Royal Society of London awarded the Davy Medal to M. and Mme. Curie. Later in the same year the Nobel Prize was awarded to them and to M. Becquerel for the discovery of radioactivity and of the new radioactive elements. The existence of radium was undeniably proven but the work, instead of being completed, was only well launched.

From the beginning M. and Mme. Curie, at congresses of science, in private conferences and in their publications, had freely given information concerning all their processes and results, without any attempt to acquire for themselves patents or copyrights.

Greatly aided by such complete information put at their disposal, workers in other countries as well as in France, singly and in groups, carried on investigations suggested by the work of M. and Mme. Curie. Their generous and high-minded attitude becomes particularly significant when one realizes that it meant almost certainly relinquishing a large income, the possession of which would have left them free to devote their whole time to research. Though one must wish that they might have been spared financial burden and that they had not been called upon to do work beyond their strength, one cannot but be glad that teaching claimed part of the attention of both these gifted scientists and that many came under their influence and guidance. Until his death M. Curie, with his co-workers, continued his study of the properties of radium and of its emanation, a gaseous substance produced from radium itself, and also conducted investigations of the heat given off by radium. Although assuming the exacting duties of her husband's professorship after his death Mme. Curie continued her research and, by 1907, had again carried out the time-consuming preparation of very pure radium chloride which was used in making a new determination of the atomic weight of radium. In 1910 she and Debierne made one gram of the element in metallic form, which she now saw for the first time and which, in accordance with the wishes of her husband, she gave to the laboratory. It was Mme. Curie who was chosen by a commission of scientists in 1911 to do the precise work of making the international standard of radium, so essential for physical, chemical and medical research. The award of the Nobel Prize in Chemistry in 1911, this time to her alone, brought to Mme. Curie the unique honor of having received this prize twice.

The knowledge that rays were produced by radioactive substances early suggested the question of the source of the energy involved in their production. The later observation that radium constantly gives off heat, though it undergoes no apparent change itself, was further evidence for energy change involved in radioactivity. As early as 1900 Mme. Curie had suggested that, if the energy evidenced by the radiations did not come from an external source, it must result from the breakdown of the atom, since radioactivity is an atomic property. Such an explanation involved discarding Dalton's theory of the existence of atoms as the ultimate indivisible units of matter, a theory which had been accepted for nearly a century. In 1903 Rutherford and Soddy enunciated their theory of atomic disintegration to account for radioactivity and thus gave complete corroboration to the suggestion advanced by Mme. Curie. By this process of atomic disintegration atoms of the radioactive elements lose either α or β particles, producing residues different from the original atoms. The final product of the change is lead, which is not radioactive. The half-decay period of the radioactive elements, the time required for one half of a sample of an element to undergo its characteristic change, varies greatly, from millions of years to fractions of a second. The phenomenon, which is a spontaneous and uncontrollable process, is one of transmutation of elements. Such a concept of the nature of the radioactive process brought with it the necessity of revising that of the atom and there followed the vast researches leading to new theories of the structure and nature of the atom. To go into these and the related problems is impossible here, but suffice it to say that our ideas have been revolutionized. It has recently been shown that artificial transmutation of elements is within the reach of man's most powerful experimental tools, thus opening up valuable possibilities of research into the secrets of nature. As Mme. Curie's discovery of radium and its products furnished an invaluable source of great intensity of α, β and γ rays, so her later work in developing methods for obtaining powerful sources of polonium in thin films furnished a tool so successfully used by Mme. Irene Curie Joliot and her husband in their recent investigations in the field of artificial radioactivity. Mme. Curie's own researches on the physical and chemical properties of radioactive substances were carried on to the end of her life. To have realized, as she had the opportunity to do, how ably the work would be continued by M. and Mme. Joliot must have meant much to one who had labored so long and so valiantly.

That Mme. Curie's interest was not primarily in practical use of radium was shown when she said in her speech at Vassar College at the time of her first visit to the United States: "But we must not forget that when radium was discovered no one knew that it would prove useful in hospitals. The work was one of pure science. And this is a proof that scientific work must not be considered from the point of view of the direct usefulness of it. It must be done for itself, for the beauty of science, and then there is always the chance that a scientific discovery may become like the radium a benefit for humanity." However, in 1914, after having personally taken her laboratory supply of radium to Bordeaux for safekeeping, Mme. Curie gave up her research and undertook her splendid work for the army, in all of which she had as her companion and able assistant her daughter Irene. As facilities for X-ray examination and trained operators were both very scarce the establishment of the radiological service which she proposed had to be begun from the foundation. By means of private donations and of army support radiological cars as well as installations in hospitals were financed, making possible X-ray examinations both at ambulance stations and hospitals. Not only did Mme. Curie organize the work and train operators but she also visited widely separated army zones and made many radiological examinations herself. In 1915, when it was thought safe to bring the radium back to Paris, she added the service of radiumtherapy, using not the radium itself but the emanation, the tubes of which were prepared in her laboratory, at first by Mme. Curie and later by workers she had trained. The value of both services was so great that the Radiographic Nurses' School, established by Mme. Curie in an effort to obtain trained operators, was continued after the war and a national service of radiumtherapy developed.

Although she lived the greater part of her life in France, Mme. Curie never lost her love for the land of her birth. Brought up under the bitter burden of Russian oppression, she had as a child dreamed of the re-establishment of the Polish nation. As a young girl, employed as governess in a family in the country, she had shown her interest in the betterment of others and her fearless and independent spirit by organizing classes for the village children who were denied the privilege of education under the Russian government. After her return to Warsaw she became a member of a secret organization of Polish young people "who believed that the hope of their country lay in a great effort to develop the intellectual and moral strength of the nation, and that such an effort would lead to a better national situation. The nearest pur-

pose was to work at one's own instruction and to provide means
of instruction for workmen and peasants. In accordance with this
program we agreed among ourselves to give evening courses, each
one teaching what he knew best. . . . You cannot hope to build
a better world without improving the individuals." To this end
they worked with great diligence.

Although she never lived in Poland after 1891 her interest in it
never flagged and she rejoiced that she had lived to see her dream of
a united Poland come true. Her loyalty to her native land and affection for it were deep and abiding. Her learning and ability were
always at its service. In 1912, although unable to leave France, she
gave great assistance to the Scientific Society of Warsaw in the
establishment of a radium laboratory and of the courses in it. She
used the fund given her for her private use by the women of the
United States, when they presented her with a gram of radium
in 1921, toward the rental of another gram of radium for the
laboratory in Warsaw. When she visited the United States
again in 1929 to dedicate the Hepburn Hall of Chemistry at St.
Lawrence University, at the door of which is a beautiful bas-relief
of Mme. Curie, American friends presented her with money to
purchase the gram of radium for Warsaw, thus freeing the original
fund for her use. In 1932 she paid her last visit to her beloved
Poland to attend the dedication of the Radium Institute of
Warsaw, the cornerstone of which she had assisted in laying in
1925. On each occasion she was received with great acclaim and
rejoicing. It seems eminently appropriate that she was elected a
foreign member of the Academy of Science of Poland and was
appointed honorary professor in the University of Warsaw.

A little child with a scholarly heritage and an eager mind,
a young girl working alone to prepare herself for advanced study
and later living a most Spartan existence in order to enjoy that
study, and finally the accomplished, brilliant research worker, so
we may picture the discoverer of radium. But to think of her in
this way alone would be to have merely a partial picture. Her
own exhaustive investigations, bringing to the service of science
new tools for research into hitherto unexplored regions and for
the relief of human suffering, were supplemented by the great
contribution she made in the field of teaching and in the vigorous

school of research of which she was director at the Radium Institute, as well as by her co-operation in congresses and conferences and her activities as a member of the Committee of Intellectual Co-operation of the League of Nations. That she was able, while engaged in such exacting work, to give her most thoughtful and constructive attention to the education and health of her children, was due not only to her unusual abilities but also to the capacity which she shared with her husband of not spending herself in the less important concerns of life. One of the greatest scientists of all time, the first woman of France to enter an Academy, she was also a woman whose joy in the simple, lovely things of life and whose serene fortitude in sorrow and perplexity, as well as her great contributions to science, call forth our admiration. In his citation when St. Lawrence University conferred the honorary degree of Doctor of Science on her, President Sykes spoke of Mme. Curie thus: "Self-effacing and devoted scientist, teacher and author, exemplar of the art of living while directing to beneficent ends powerful forces of nature, single and persistent in purpose, triumphant in research, hastening the march of civilization by the discovery of radium, inspired and inspiring idealist, practical dreamer."

XXVIII

JÓZEF PIŁSUDSKI

Soldier, Statesman, Patriot—"Liberator of Poland."

1867-1935

by

Stephen P. Mizwa

Had it not been for the present war, which brought about a temporary occupation of Poland by her enemies, and the need for living generations of Poles to acquire their freedom anew, the subtitle of this story would have been "The George Washington of Poland." For Józef Piłsudski did more than any other single Pole, working primarily with Poles and on Polish soil, to achieve the independence of Poland after the first World War and to set up the national housekeeping.

The Piłsudski era in Polish history, the era of struggle and achievement and of disappointments—because the thing hoped for was not as perfect in reality as some had imagined it would be—closed in the early hours of September 1, 1939. The curtain is drawn and when it rises, there will be a new scene and new heroes; yet through the smoke of the present conflagration and the confusion of judgments, the Poles still see the towering figure of Piłsudski. Judged by any standard, he will remain one of the great men of Poland and of world history.

Józef Piłsudski, the fourth of twelve children of Józef and Maria (née Billewicz) Piłsudski, was born on December 5, 1867, at Zulów in the neighborhood of Wilno, in the old Grand Duchy of Lithuania that for over 400 years (from 1386 till the third partition in 1795) was united with Poland. He was descended from noble Polish-Lithuanian stock—"with a strain of Scottish

344

JÓZEF PIŁSUDSKI

blood from an ancestor who had belonged to the ancient house of Butler and had come out to Poland as a fugitive after the Jacobite rebellion of 1745." [1] He belonged to the class of people, as he later expressed it himself, that were "*bene nati et possessionati*" (well born and well-to-do). Like other families in similar circumstances, his people passionately loved the native soil and shared the common Polish-Lithuanian tradition of past greatness, present sadness and hope for a brighter future.

In 1874 the manor house at Zulów, together with its outbuildings, burned down, and the family, greatly impoverished, moved to Wilno. It was in that outpost of Western civilization and concentrated Russian persecution of every Polish manifestation, that Piłsudski attended the secondary school (*gimnazjum*) which was housed in the now closed Polish University of Wilno. Here, too, the Polish patriotism his mother taught him crystallized under the derision of his Russian schoolmasters into a program of rebellion. Later he described these *gimnazjum* days as follows:

"The atmosphere of the *gimnazjum* crushed me; the injustice and the politics of the schoolmasters enraged me and the way of teaching harassed and bored me. . . . How deep the impression of this school system was on my mind, may be judged by this one fact: although I have since passed through gaols and Siberia, and have had to do with a variety of Russian officials, it is still one of my Wilno schoolmasters who plays some part in every bad dream. In these circumstances my hatred for the Tsarist administration and the Muscovite oppression grew with every year. Helpless fury and shame that I could do nothing to hinder my enemies often stifled me; my cheeks burned that I must suffer in silence while my pride was trampled upon, listening to lies and scornful words about Poland, Poles and their history. I was constantly dreaming of an insurrection."

And so, secretly, he studied the French Revolution, pondered upon its success and tried to learn lessons therefrom that might be applicable to some future Polish uprising against Russia. He became a revolutionary and made up his mind to retaliate with force.

---

[1] Alexandra Piłsudska, *Piłsudski—A Biography by His Wife.* (Dodd, Mead and Co., New York, 1941), p. 152.

His mother, a fountain of spiritual strength and wise counsel, died in 1884 and he was left to his own devices. His father, formerly an experimenter in "scientific farming," did not prosper in the city and the family finances were strained. The idyllic country life was over, as were the school days of suppressed individual freedom and rebellious planning; strenuous years of action, of persecution—and of final triumph—lay ahead.

Upon graduation from the Wilno *gimnazjum* in 1885, Józef Piłsudski went to the Univeristy of Kharkov (Ukraine) to study medicine. Here he remained for only a year. Having become acquainted with some Russian revolutionaries, he came under suspicion for political activities and was expelled. He returned to Wilno with the intention of continuing his studies abroad later on. He was arrested in 1887 for alleged participation in an attempt to assassinate the Russian Czar, Alexander III. Though absolutely innocent, he was sentenced to five years in Siberia, and after serving the full term he returned to Wilno in 1892.

His Siberian experience, though accompanied by the usual difficulties with Russian officials, was not devoid of certain definite advantages. First, it gave him leisure to reflect upon the past and plan for the future—avoiding the mistakes of the past. The last insurrection of 1863 had failed, he thought, because of inadequate military preparation and because of the failure of the whole nation to rise. This must be remedied in the future. The proper approach must be through the masses. But how to reach them, educate them, arm them and drill them? He found the solution in socialism: not as a military instrument in itself, because its class program for economic betterment precluded sacrifice for national ideals, but as a springboard from which to reach wider masses to whom his own "romantic" program of armed struggle for national independence would appeal. Socialism then, to Piłsudski, was not even a means to an end, but a means to a better means. Secondly, his Siberian experience as an exile proved a desirable apprenticeship, a valuable passport in his later career as an agitator and a revolutionary. Now he could approach the masses with a badge of authority, as a victim of the Czarist regime.

Therefore, upon his return to Wilno in 1892, he joined the newly formed P.P.S. (*Polska Partia Socjalistyczna*—Polish Socialist

Party) as a full-fledged Socialist under the assumed name of Comrade Victor, and launched upon his task of agitation. For years he traveled through the three parts of partitioned Poland, learned much about the underground work and mastered the technique of secret organizations. In 1894 the party relegated to him the difficult task of running its official organ *Robotnik* (*The Worker*) of which he was the editor-in-chief, chief printer, business manager and the most active distributor, assisted by Stanisław Wojciechowski, later president of liberated Poland.

In six years he brought out thirty-five numbers by dint of superhuman efforts. "It was a hand-to-mouth existence. . . . He was constantly in flight from the Russian authorities; he could rarely remain in the same place longer than a few days. When he was in Wilno, he slept out in the forest night after night because none of his acquaintances dared to take him into their houses for fear of a search by the secret police. He used to spend such leisure as he had, sitting in some church; he could not walk in the streets without running the risk of being recognized and arrested." [2]

He started this paper in a small town near Wilno, then transferred it to Wilno and finally (in 1896) to Łódź, "The Manchester of Poland." The *Robotnik* was read by thousands of rebellious spirits. The Russian authorities began to feel its pronounced influence and searched for the source of this public disturbance. They discovered the printing press in Piłsudski's house in the year 1900, arrested him and threw him into the dreaded Tenth Pavilion of the Citadel of Warsaw, from which there was reputedly no way of escape. Piłsudski simulated insanity, was transferred to an insane asylum in St. Petersburg for observation, and escaped with the aid of a Polish staff doctor who had purposely worked himself into the hospital staff. Incidentally, twenty years later, that doctor, Władysław Mazurkiewicz, became professor of mental diseases at the University of Warsaw when his "patient" was Chief of State.

Five years of Siberia to his credit, a sojourn in the Tenth Pavilion (a place of confinement for the most dangerous political prisoners), and finally an escape from a heavily guarded insane asylum in St. Petersburg—these episodes made Piłsudski a half-legendary figure in his party. After a brief business trip to London

[2] Piłsudska, *op. cit.*, p. 165.

in the winter of 1901-2 Piłsudski settled in Kraków, the ancient capital of Poland, which was under Austria and enjoyed comparative freedom. His influence among the masses grew rapidly and he was soon recognized as the acknowledged head of the whole Polish revolutionary or insurrectionist movement.

Now, as from the beginning of his revolutionary career, he was confronted by and had to contend with a strong current of Polish thought that militated against his conception of direct solution of the Polish question. Recalling the tragedy of the last insurrection against Russia in 1863 and the folly of making war barehanded against a well-armed Great Power, many of his influential compatriots counseled moderation and advised intellectual and economic improvement of the people as the best national policy for the time being. But Piłsudski was impatient. Force, he believed, was the only means by which wrongs brought about by force could be righted. His first chance came, he thought, when Japan declared war on Russia in 1904. He went to Tokyo and asked assistance of the Japanese Government for an insurrection in Poland with a view of attacking the Russian rear in Europe. Having no army at his disposal, his arguments could not have been convincing. Besides, he was blocked by a representative of the Polish realists—those who counseled moderation—in the person of Roman Dmowski. Dmowski, the leader of the National Democrats, argued that Piłsudski's plan was not only utopian but would be detrimental to the Polish cause in the long run.

This was the first open conflict between Polish patriots, leading representatives of the two divergent schools of political thought, both of whom loved Poland but could not agree on practical means for her liberation. Piłsudski was an insurrectionist and a revolutionary, and represented the Polish romantic tradition that viewed direct action through force as the best means of liberation. Dmowski was a realist who believed in gradual gaining of advantages through appeasement and by such means as occasions might present, without running the risk of needlessly spilling Polish blood.

Piłsudski came back to Kraków defeated and disappointed, but not cured of his conviction that the independence of Poland could be secured only by fighting for it and that the Poles themselves must do the fighting. Nobody else would do it for them and for their interests exclusively. Taking advantage of the Russian Revolution of 1905, he organized his first fighting corps, a militant organization of the Polish Socialist Party, known as the *Organizacja Bojowa* or *Bojówka*. For three years this *Bojówka*—composed of artisans and nobles, university professors and students, doctors, engineers and wealthy landowners—waged incessant guerrilla warfare against the Czarist government. They carried on by attacking detachments of Cossacks here, raiding police and military posts there, releasing Polish prisoners by bribery or force, eliminating Russian spies and *agents provocateurs* and, above all, by making the enemy pay for this work in occasionally relieving the Russian government of various sums of roubles. For such "unethical" acts Piłsudski was later criticized by the uninitiated abroad and the realists at home, and was called all kinds of names. Suffice it to say here that he did not take a penny of the proceeds for himself, that he regarded Poland as at war with Russia and, finally, that the money thus procured was used for a good purpose: to purchase arms and ammunition and to finance a new military organization that was being secretly founded at Lwów in Austrian-Poland.

By a split in the Polish Socialist Party, the *Bojówka*, haphazardly put together for guerrilla warfare, ceased to exist in 1908 and Piłsudski, with the aid of Kazimierz Sosnkowski, organized in its place the Union for Active Struggle (*Związek Walki Czynnej*). Under Piłsudski's leadership, the purpose of the Union was to train soldiers and officers, especially officers, but in accordance with military discipline, so as to create a skeleton organization for a Polish army capable of a successful national insurrection. Students and peasants, farm laborers and bank clerks, pooled their resources to buy a few old revolvers, obsolete rifles, and books on military tactics. Piłsudski lectured to them and drilled them. He taught them all he knew, and what he knew of military science he had learned from books. They gathered secretly and drilled in backyards and orchards, in meadows and vacant lots. The townspeople of Lwów—whose patriotism shown ten years later was surpassed only by that of Warsaw in 1939—and the wits, when they got wind of the secret army, laughed at the military antics of young people who might spend their time more profitably; and their "commander in chief" got his share of ridicule. But the "army" grew from a few to a few hundred; and in two years, to a few thousand. From a handful of boys that played at soldiers, there developed well-drilled companies that went through regulation military exercises and invoked both admiration and uneasiness; admiration from those who were formerly amused and uneasiness on the part of the Austrian police authorities. The upshot was that Piłsudski was given the choice of disbanding or reorganizing the Union. In 1910 The Union for Active Struggle was reorganized into The Union of Riflemen's Clubs (*Związek Strzelecki*), which became an open organization, legally constituted, and to which the Austrian authorities gave their approval.

Now Piłsudski could train his riflemen more easily. He expanded his work until he had established in Kraków what amounted to a staff college in miniature. He even obtained the right to one old Austrian rifle for every twenty of his riflemen. His success inspired the more conservative elements of Austrian Poles to organize their own Riflemen's Companies (*Drużyny Strzeleckie*). Under the impact of events in 1914 these two rival riflemen's organizations composed their political differences and merged into the Polish Legions under Piłsudski's command.

When the war broke out in 1914 the Poles found themselves in a tragic situation. Friends and enemies were in juxtaposition. Austria was reasonable; discussion with her on problems of interest to the Poles was possible, and at the same time she was at war against Russia—but Austria was a junior partner of imperial Germany, which had plans of its own. Russia, on the other hand, in Piłsudski's opinion the biggest enemy of Poland, was an ally of France and England—traditional or potential friends of the Poles. Furthermore, hundreds of thousands of Poles were drafted into the armies of Austria, Germany and Russia and were arrayed against their own brothers, all of whom were fighting for the respective interests of their enemies. Foreign powers, whether traditional or potential friends, were interested in their own problems and not in the independence of Poland—a measure of which could be secured only at the expense not of their victorious allies, but of their defeated enemies, if, when and as their enemies were defeated. Every nation was fighting for its own interests;

the Poles were forced to fight for the interests of their enemies; nobody seemed ready or prepared to fight directly for the interests of the Poles—except Piłsudski and his handful of enthusiasts.

Piłsudski's political ideology and his "military" policy—in this instance as in many others—were misunderstood and misinterpreted by his critics in other countries, and by his own compatriots at home, His critics might have been justified at the time, but later events proved that he was right. While others followed complicated and indirect methods to secure compromised advantages, he wanted unconditional restoration of Poland's independence within her historical boundaries. And to gain that, he wanted the Poles themselves to fight for Poland and on Polish soil. "When swords were being thrown into the scales of destiny, I would not allow the Polish sword to be among the missing," said he. But how could integral Polish independence be secured when one of Poland's enemies, either Russia or Germany, was bound to be victorious? In February 1914, Piłsudski delivered a lecture in the hall of the Geographic Society at Paris, in which he made this prophetic statement: "The problem of the independence of Poland will be definitely solved only when Russia shall be beaten by Germany—and later Germany beaten by France. It is our duty to lend our help to that aim; otherwise we shall have to pursue a very long and almost desperate struggle."

That miracle did happen and Piłsudski's subsequent actions must be viewed only in the light of his prophecy, in which very few believed.

At dawn on August 6, 1914, before Austria declared war on Russia, Piłsudski's first detachment marched out of Kraków to fight against Russia. He had several thousand well-drilled riflemen ready to fight under his command, but he had no equipment for them and the Austrian government would furnish none. He started with three skeleton companies numbering exactly 172 men, equipped for the most part with discarded rifles that had been used for training purposes. The "army" included eight cavalry men, five of whom carried their saddles with the hope of finding horses on enemy territory. The sublime and the ridiculous perhaps seldom found a more perfect union. One hundred and seventy-two boys, carrying ammunition in their pockets but with a sparkle in their eyes and an abiding faith in their hearts, were going "to do a job" on the Russian Empire! A few carried extra guns for other Poles they might find on the way after they had crossed the Russian frontier. They got as far as Kielce, some seventy-five miles northeast of Kraków, well into Russian-held territory. Here, having arrived before the Austrians and the Germans, Piłsudski unfurled his Polish banner and used the town as a base for his "military operations." Later on several thousand more legionnaires joined him in Kielce. In contact with detachments of the Russian Army, Piłsudski's Legions met with occasional successes. But this handful of men had much greater psychological importance than its real or even its nuisance value in a war where millions were pitted against each other: it was a symbol of the Polish army, the first armed force since the insurrection of 1863, composed of Poles, fighting for Poland on Polish soil. Based on a Polish romantic tradition, it was a demonstrable expression of the belief of a group of Poles that the mighty Russian army was not invincible.

Almost simultaneously political movements began to work at cross purposes. In Austria a Polish Supreme National Committee (*Naczelny Komitet Narodowy*) was formed on August 16, advocating Polish Legions under the Austrian Supreme Command, with a view of uniting Austrian and Russian Poles against Russia. In Warsaw, on November 25, a similar Committee (*Komitet Narodowy Polski*—Polish National Committee) was created with the purpose of organizing all the Poles under Russia against Germany, according to Dmowski, the biggest enemy of Poland. Polish Legions were also to be raised. As a basis for the Russian Poles' initiative was the manifesto issued by the Russian Commander in Chief, promising the Poles a united and autonomous Poland under the Russian scepter. Later on, when the Germans entered Warsaw, they, too, issued manifestoes, asked for Legions and promised freedom under German hegemony, at the expense of Russia. Piłsudski was caught in the vortex of gratuitous promises of all three partitioning powers, each anxious to get Poles to fight for their respective interests. Piłsudski himself was a problem to all three, especially to the Austrians, since his own Legions were small and his demands high. He wanted all Polish Legions merged into one independent Polish Army, exclusively under Polish command; and his goal was a united and independent Poland. He wanted definite guarantees and not promises. He was neither pro-Austria nor pro-Germany; he was definitely anti-Russia and pro-Poland. Finally, when misunderstandings with the Central Powers increased and reached a point when compromise with his purely Polish objectives was inevitable, he presented his resignation to the Austrian High Command in September, 1916.

Meanwhile, as difficulties with the Central Powers were developing, friends and subordinates of Piłsudski had begun to build for him a secret organization in Russian-Poland that was to be independent of external influences. It was known by its initials as P.O.W. (*Polska Organizacja Wojskowa*—Polish Military Organization). Thus, while his legal Legions in Austrian-Poland were on the verge of dissolution, illegal military cadres in Russian-Poland were in the process of formation, led by other enthusiasts and even officers, whom Piłsudski had previously trained in his Riflemen's Clubs and in the Legions. But within several months two great events took place: the Russian Revolution brought the recognition of Polish independence by the temporary liberal government, and the United States of America entered the war with a definite commitment with respect to the independence of Poland. Now Russia was down and out—out of Poland—but in her place came the German and Austrian armies of occupation. The only enemies that remained to be defeated now were Austria and Germany, especially Germany. Austria had been willing to solve the Polish problem to the satisfaction of the majority of Austrian-Poles, but her dual partner, Hungary, strenuously objected. A triple arrangement with Poland as the third partner would have weakened the position of Hungary and have given undesirable ideas to other minority nationalities under Austria-Hungary.

Events moved swiftly to a climax. The remaining legionnaires, who still wore uniforms, were required to take a new oath of loyalty to the Austrian and German thrones. Piłsudski advised them to refuse the oath, and 5,200 out of 6,000 that had come from the former Russian Poland followed his advice. They were interned. As to Piłsudski, the Central Powers did not know whether he was their ally or their foe. They soon made up their minds when they heard that he was planning to lead new Polish military formations—this time against them—grouped around the secretly organized P.O.W. The Germans arrested him at Warsaw on July 22, 1917, and kept him in the fortress of Magdeburg for the duration of the war. Many patriotic Poles tasted prison life in Czarist Russia, and Siberia was often called their second home, but it was given to few of them to enjoy such "hospitality" both in Russia and Germany. Those who had formerly believed Piłsudski to be an Austrophile or Germanophile were no longer sure of their conviction.

This incarceration in the fortress of Magdeburg proved a blessing in disguise for Piłsudski and perhaps for the country. Legends began to grow around his person, around his exploits and those of his Legions. They multiplied in number and grew in importance. In short, he grew into a national hero, into a leader of all the people and not of the handful of revolutionaries alone.

When the revolution broke out in Germany, Piłsudski was released and, escorted by German dignitaries, arrived at Warsaw by train on November 10, 1918, on the eve of the memorable Armistice Day. He was immediately acclaimed as the hero and leader of independent Poland.

Now the story of Józef Piłsudski becomes a part of the history, trials and tribulations of the Republic of Poland from 1918 till his death in 1935—in fact, the story continues to 1939. It is a tale replete with momentous events. The woes and hopes of generations of Poles had converged into this brief span of time allowed for building a State. The Polish Rip Van Winkle had been put to sleep in the days of kings and emperors and autocratic systems; he suddenly awoke, dazed, in the bright sunlight of freedom when the old order collapsed and a new democratic system came into being. There were other actors on the stage, collaborating or conflicting with the role of Piłsudski: some were towering personalities that made Polish history, some played more or less conspicuous roles and vanished from public view, still others said their lines, retired and were later catapulted by events into leading roles. But it can be safely said that the history of the New Poland revolved around the person, the deeds, the tradition and legends of Józef Piłsudski.

When he arrived at Warsaw on November 10, 1918, he

found a temporary government in the form of a Council of Regency which had been set up by the powers of occupation in the fall of 1917. Some 100,000 German troops were still in occupation of Polish soil. Radical and conservative elements were vying for power. In Lublin a separate government, headed by Ignacy Daszyński, had been set up by the Socialists, challenging the authority of Warsaw and pretending to speak for the whole country. There was literally no one strong enough to unite the whole nation, save Piłsudski, who alone possessed the moral authority and the national prestige. The Council of Regency immediately turned over its power to him, nominated him Chief of State and General in Command of the Polish forces, which consisted of the remnants of his Legions and the P.O.W.

His first tasks were to disarm and drive out the German forces from Polish soil—which he succeeded in doing so far as central Poland was concerned—and to win the confidence of the Western Powers, a much harder undertaking. The Allies knew very little of him and what they knew was not very favorable. They knew of him in a general sort of way as ex-Socialist agitator, ex-political prisoner, ex-anti-Russian when Russia was their ally, and ex-Austrophile and ex-Germanophile when Germany was their deadly enemy. Paderewski came to Poland, with the blessing of the Allies, to form and head the new Polish Government. The invincible met the irresistible. Piłsudski represented tears, sweat, and blood; his patriotic passport bore in indelible ink the earmarks of Siberia, of the Tenth Pavilion and Magdeburg; Paderewski, on the other hand, confident of his position, brought the message of the Allies: Wilson's "Thirteenth Point," the backing of France and England, the hurdle of the Peace Conference which the New Poland still had to clear, possibilities of food from America for the hungry, economic and financial aid to rebuild the devastated country. There is no use trying to evaluate the respective contributions of Piłsudski and Paderewski, to compare the two contrasting characters or to enumerate their differences. Each had millions of friends, and as many opponents. But they were both patriots; they differed on practical forms of free government, just as Poles had differed on practical means of attaining freedom, but they both loved Poland and soon composed their differences.

Paderewski became Prime Minister and Minister of Foreign Affairs, and later, with Dmowski, represented Poland at the Peace Conference. Piłsudski remained Chief of State and Minister of War until the constitution was adopted. It was most fortunate for Poland that both could serve her in this formative, critical period.

In the years that remained for Piłsudski to live in the free Poland he had helped to create, he was for some time Chief of State, twice Prime Minister, Minister of War, Inspector General and Commander in Chief of the Polish Army, and First Marshal of Poland, but he declined the highest office, that of President, which was twice offered him.

Was Piłsudski a dictator? It is one of the anomalies and paradoxes of history that actual dictatorship was unanimously conferred upon him, whereupon he voluntarily divested himself of power by setting up the most democratic system of government; and when that system failed, he fought to regain power, ending his regime as a moral dictator.

When Piłsudski arrived at Warsaw from the fortress of Magdeburg, the temporary Regency Council transferred its full powers to him until the formation of the new government, and this act met with popular approval. Piłsudski, as Chief of State, became a full-fledged dictator. The Regency Council ceased to exist. His edicts became the law of the land, since there was no other source of authority. He had supreme power, to hold and to use—to abuse even, had he so willed. Without the use of force, without firing a shot, without even as much as asking for it, he became a dictator. Piłsudski the revolutionary created a Polish army before there was a Polish State, and then Piłsudski the dictator started to create a democratic government.

We are too near these historic events and lack perspective for their proper evaluation; certain forces set in motion have not yet run their course; or to use a more homely figure of speech, we cannot see the forest because of the trees. Disregarding, for our purpose, the one thousand and one problems that faced Piłsudski as state-builder—organizing and equipping the army, setting up the administration, rebuilding the country, opening schools, starting the railroads running, making one state out of the former three

partitions, rectifying frontiers which the big Powers had left un-
rectified, gaining the confidence of minorities within and making
treaties with Powers without and neighbors close by, etc., etc.—
let us choose for a brief outline two basic problems which interested him very deeply and served as leitmotivs of his creative
statesmanship: internal political organization devoid of ancient
weaknesses, and foreign policy based on the old Jagiellonian idea
of federalism.

Whatever else history will say of Piłsudski as a leader of
Poles, it will say this: that he knew his Poland, past and present;
that he knew his own compatriots, their weaknesses and, perhaps
to a lesser extent, their potential strength, as very few other Poles
did. The keystone of the structure he undertook to erect, both in
its internal and external aspects, was his clear perception of Poland's geographic position, her past experience and unavoidable
dangers in the future. And he knew how to draw consequences
from this situation. Time and again he stated his conviction with
the relentless logic of a mathematical formula. It may be para-
phrased as follows: When the hand of destiny distributed lands
and continents, the Poles happened to receive as their share a relatively poor portion of flatlands—north of the Carpathian Mountains, west of the Russians and east of the Germans. Both of these
strong neighbors were at the same time endowed with the desire
to expand toward the west and east respectively, at the expense
of the Poles, while the latter were not provided with natural
frontiers and a keen sense of cohesion for self-defense. Thus the
chief problem of Poland has always been a struggle for national
existence. So it has been from the very dawn of Poland's recorded
history down through the centuries, so it is today and so it will
always be. Whenever the Poles were morally united, physically
strong, had an adequate army and a central government with
authority, they fared well; otherwise, they fared badly.

And so, having all the powers of a dictator, Piłsudski wanted
to organize the Polish State in such a way that it would possess all
the necessary elements of strength for self-preservation, combined
with the requisites of modern democracy but minus those vices
of the Poles which, under the guise of extreme individualism,
had weakened the Polish State in the past. He was a liberal and a

democrat, and wanted Poland to have a democratic form of government, because he firmly believed that this form was best suited to the Polish temperament. He apparently thought that the miracle of freedom would produce a very high patriotic temperature and in this miraculous retort of freedom, all the ancient faults would disappear and the best traits would be distilled into a solid amalgam of civic virtues. Poland was to be a democracy, with the regulation Parliament of Lower and Upper House controlling the general policies of the Executive; but the latter, represented by one bearing the accepted title of President would have sufficient power to make quick decisions in emergencies that might often arise because of the precarious position of Poland.

With all this in view, one of Piłsudski's first steps was to order a general election for the first democratic Parliament that would serve as the source of legal power in Poland, that would adopt the Constitution and provide for a legally constituted successor to the dictatorial Chief of State. The general election was set for January 26, and the first or Constituent Parliament (*Sejm*) met on February 10, 1919. The franchise was the most democratic imaginable; equal and direct, including both sexes regardless of race and secret, based on proportional representation; the voting age began at twenty-one. The direct representatives of the people met. On February 20 the *Sejm* unanimously (305 votes) confirmed Piłsudski's position as Chief of State but reserved to itself the sovereign power of the State, so that the Chief could do only what the *Sejm* told him to do. Paderewski, who had in the meantime agreed to serve as Prime Minister and Minister of Foreign Affairs, and had formed a Cabinet, was also given a vote of confidence by the *Sejm*. The first Constitution (not counting a series of laws passed *ad hoc* that served as the "Little Constitution") was adopted in March, 1921. According to this Constitution, the President was to be chosen by the National Assembly composed of both Houses of Parliament for a period of seven years. Piłsudski declined to be a candidate for the Presidency, but accepted appointment as Chief of the General Staff of the Polish Army.

Piłsudski's hopes for "moral regeneration" in politics were doomed to failure. The legislative body became supreme and the powers of the executive branch were trimmed into insignificance.

The President was to serve as a symbolic representative of the nation, but had no power to make important decisions even in a crisis. Political parties multiplied, political differences grew even more acute and the result, as Piłsudski put it, was not a democracy but a "Sejmocracy." The Poles were not different from any other people who try to govern themselves, and extraordinary civic virtues could not be evoked either by wishful thinking or by legislation. They simply acted like human beings, while Piłsudski wanted them to act like heroes in everyday life, simply because that life called for continued heroic deeds.

Besides, they were at a tremendous disadvantage. For nearly 150 years they had been subjects of three hostile powers and had become accustomed to suspect every governmental act; to oppose the government was regarded as every Pole's patriotic duty. It was only natural that as free citizens, now that they had a government of their own, they should try to adjust their relationships to that government from the point of view of their own rights and privileges rather than of their duties and responsibilities.

Piłsudski continued to serve as the head of the Army, but political trends in the country overtaxed his patience and he retired in the summer of 1923. Rightly or wrongly, he believed that the ancient Polish weaknesses, plus a few modern ones—common to other democracies—were gaining the upper hand and that he, no longer having influence over the course of events, could not share the responsibility for failures. He retired to his modest country cottage near Warsaw (Sulejówek) and devoted his time to writing, occasional lectures, and not infrequent teachings and preachings on historic topics and current problems. He kept in constant touch with his friends, especially former comrades-in-arms, and watched political developments very closely. In May, 1926, he decided to reach for power again—this time by force of arms, as in his opinion there was no other way. The *coup d'état* took place on May 12. Analysis of motives for this radical step would lead us far astray into controversial paths. The immediate motive for the overthrow by force of arms of the legally constituted government, which was indirectly of Piłsudski's own creation (the President, Stanisław Wojciechowski, was his former collaborator and co-editor of the underground paper *Robotnik*), was a report that all of Piłsudski's former legionnaires, now officers in the Polish Army, were to be summarily discharged. He could not stand the thought of politics in the Army, his beloved child.

In less than two days the issue was decided, unfortunately not without bloodshed. Although Piłsudski could have become actual dictator, such as he was in 1918, he reserved to himself only the Ministry of War and launched on the task of reorganizing the democratic machinery of government. He was anxious to give Polish democracy another chance. In two weeks after his forceful intervention the National Assembly met to elect a new President, in place of Wojciechowski, who had resigned. The National Assembly, composed of the two Houses of Parliament, elected Piłsudski President of the Republic by 292 to 193 votes. Piłsudski declined. Ignacy Mościcki, a prominent scientist, was chosen on the second ballot. By tendering the Presidency to Piłsudski, the people's representatives legalized his *coup d'état;* and by not doing it unanimously, gave proof that democracy and not dictatorship was in the saddle. The political atmosphere became clearer. The Cabinet was composed for the most part of experts. Ministerial changes became less frequent; certain policies, especially Foreign Affairs, assumed aspects of continuity; the number of political parties began to decrease and the heat of controversy subsided. Piłsudski continued as the moral power behind the throne: training men for key positions, advising them when important decisions were under consideration, teaching his nation their new duties as citizens, but he himself declined the highest office in the State. In the sense that no important move was made by high government officials without consulting him, he was a moral dictator. More than that, his chief rôle was that of a teacher of his nation. He brutally castigated all symptoms of vice in public office and advocated moral renaissance, respect for law and social justice regardless of race or creed.

Did Piłsudski want to be a dictator? The answer is, No!

A few days after the *coup d'état* he made this illuminating observation:

"When I consider the history of my country, I cannot really believe that Poland can be governed by the stick. I don't like the stick. Our generation is not perfect, but it has a right to some respect; that which will follow will be better. No, I am not in favor of a dictatorship in Poland. But, we live in a legislative chaos. Our State inherited the laws and prescriptions of three States, and they have been added to. The authority of the President must be increased in order to simplify things. I do not say that we should imitate exactly the United States where the great force of the central power is counterbalanced by the large autonomy of the different States. But something in that order of ideas should be sought for that can be applied to Poland."

The fact is that the Polish Constitution of 1921 was even more democratic than that of the United States in that the President had less power, the Legislature was supreme, and there was no Supreme Court to serve as the balance wheel between the two. From 1926 until his death in 1935, Piłsudski used all his moral influence to have the Constitution changed in order to strengthen the Executive. The new Polish Constitution with all the essential changes he advocated was finally adopted nineteen days before his death.

In his foreign policy (also based, as indicated above, on his perception of Poland's geographic position) Piłsudski reverted to the old Jagiellonian idea of federalism. If and when the Poles are morally prepared, they should play the leading rôle in the proposed federation; but he viewed the safety of Poland assured by federal union with Lithuania, White Russia and Ukraine. For that reason he wanted those countries also to be free. When in the early days of Poland's independence Piłsudski succeeded with the aid of the Ukrainian General Petlura in clearing its southeastern provinces of Bolshevik troops, he pushed as far East as Kiev. Piłsudski's idea was to help set up an independent Ukrainian Government there, to start the nucleus of his federation, and then to proceed to do the same thing for the White Russians with Minsk as their capital. Lithuania, strong in its resurgent nationalism and desirous not to compromise its complete sovereignty by any union or federation, was a hard nut to crack; that problem was to be tackled later.

It was a great idea, this East Central European Federation, and statesmen now are seriously thinking of such a federation as the only bulwark against Russian and German expansion and the only salvation for each of the countries involved. But the whole scheme toppled in 1918-20 like a house of cards. The Poles were sick and tired of war and did not see why they should fight for Ukrainian independence. The Ukrainians themselves, though having no objection to being independent, suspected Piłsudski's motives. The White Russians had no pronounced national consciousness and, frankly, were not ready for complete independence. The Allies, England and France, accused Piłsudski of imperialism at the expense of Russia and did their best to make things difficult for him. Their conservative statesmen regarded Bolshevik Russia as a temporary arrangement, which would soon be replaced by the return of a conservative Russian Government toward which they had moral obligations. Hence they felt they should protect future Russia's interests against Piłsudski's "imperialism." The Czarist Russian *émigrés* also carried on propaganda in western European capitals on this line of reasoning. The British Laborites and French Syndicalists, who sympathized with the Russian proletarian revolution and its war against Polish "bourgeois landowning capitalists," exerted pressure on their respective Governments.

Taking advantage of all these factors in their favor, the Bolsheviks struck back before Piłsudski had a chance to establish an independent Ukrainian Government in Kiev and, in the flush of victories, threatened Poland with destruction and Europe with Communism. In August 1920, their armies appeared at the very gates of Warsaw. The "Miracle of the Vistula" saved Poland and, perhaps, the rest of Europe. It was a decisive victory—"The Eighteenth Decisive Battle of the World," Lord D'Abernon calls it. Lord D'Abernon, who was a member of the Allied Advisory Mission to Poland together with General Weygand, says in his diary that "the boldest measures included in the scheme were due to the personal initiative of Piłsudski." General Weygand later said: "The military operations were executed by Polish Generals in accordance with a Polish plan."

There was enough glory to cover many a hero, and many other Polish military leaders made important contributions to this Polish victory. General Józef Haller, who commanded the Second Brigade of the Polish Legions in Austrian Poland and later on became Commander in Chief of the Polish Army in France, in the Polish-Bolshevik war was appointed to the Chief Command of the Northern Armies. General Władysław Sikorski, now (1941) Premier of the Polish Government in Exile and Commander in Chief of the Polish Army, was in command of the Fifth Polish Army around Modlin. His victory of August 16, on the River Wkra, routed the Bolsheviks so completely that they retreated in disorder. This victory relieved the pressure on the Warsaw bridgehead and served as an important psychological factor, proving that the Bolshevik armies were not invincible.

The Bolsheviks were badly defeated, yet Piłsudski's idea of a federation failed. His guiding principles in foreign policy now were: not to desire other people's territory and not give up one's own; to keep Russia and Germany from uniting, as their understanding would mean the end of Poland's independence; to insure Poland against possible attack from East and West by alliances with friendly nations (with France for defense from Germany; with Rumania, from Russia); to maintain as strong a defensive army as economic conditions would permit; to follow an independent policy and to refrain from aligning Poland with one strong neighbor against another, so as not to become a victim of the victor; and, if possible, to enter into nonaggression pacts with both neighbors.

That was perhaps the best policy under the circumstances and Piłsudski lived long enough to see it work. After his death his policy was carried on, but in 1939 the whole structure fell to pieces. Russia and Germany did reach a temporary understanding. France was too weak to defend even herself and Rumania did not come to Poland's aid. However, two things remained as monuments to his life's labors and the twenty years of Poland's independence: later events showed that the Polish Army, though inadequately equipped for modern warfare, gave a good account of itself; and in the hour of trial, the nation was morally united as perhaps never before in the history of Poland.

Józef Piłsudski died on May 12, 1935, and was laid to rest in the ancient Wawel Castle in Kraków, among many of the Polish kings and national heroes. On behalf of the nation President Mościcki said: "Though his head bears no crown and his hand carries no scepter, he was king of our hearts and master of our desires."

Colossal as Piłsudski's contributions were to the New Poland of 1918-39, they were not devoid of shortcomings and weaknesses. He was neither the sole liberator of Poland, as his most zealous followers would have one believe, nor was his statesmanship crowned with unvarying success in every respect.

When he could not persuade some of his opponents, he tried to quiet them with arbitrary imprisonment and jail sentences of questionable legal validity. Although no opponent of his was ever "liquidated" through this means and numerous protests on general principles against such arrests brought no reprisals (which is a favorable testimony against the charge of dictatorship), faith in the independence of the courts of justice was unavoidably weakened.

Personally Piłsudski tolerated no nepotism, corruption or personal gain in public office, but his former officers in the Legions received preference in the Army and in government service, not infrequently out of proportion to their ability. In time there grew around him an entourage in the government that did him no credit and was of no particular benefit to the country. "The Government of Colonels" was one name for it. After his death this entourage continued in power. When the guiding and restraining moral influence of Piłsudski was gone, his epigones used their power in a way that tended to compromise the tradition of their great master.

The press was theoretically censored, but both he and his government were freely criticised there and elsewhere. He had a sense of humor and he did not kill that sense in the nation. Cartoons, jokes and racy stories at his expense were constantly circulated and he enjoyed them no less than his fellow countrymen. Millions of Poles called him "*dziadek*," which means "grand-dad."

On ideological grounds and because of the way in which their personal affairs were affected, he had only rabid admirers and bitter enemies, none indifferent, but he moved freely throughout the country and abroad with no more protection than any important government official would have.

He was a conspirator, a revolutionary and a soldier all his life, and could not free himself of the habit of secrecy and the method of direct action even when applied to constructive legal problems. He was impatient with legislative bickerings and slow legal procedures moving from precedent to precedent. Life, he insisted, has its own laws and he always tried to take short cuts —to the consternation of legalistic minds.

He was a revolutionary (and a Socialist at one time) because he saw the way to Poland's independence through revolution, but in spirit and substance he always remained a conservative Polish nobleman, a country squire. He did not seem to grasp the economic implications of the relationship of industrial to rural economy. Poland made tremendous economic progress in her twenty years of independence, but her economic position was not commensurate with her size, moral standing and historic importance.

The government under Piłsudski's authoritarian democracy was considered by protagonists of pure democracy as too authoritarian to allow its citizens complete freedom of action in every respect, so that they could learn by trial and error, and it did not go far enough to harness the maximum productive energies of the nation by edicts of authority. It was strong enough to meddle in the people's business but too timid or not willing to assume complete control.

In national defense, which most of the time absorbed his undivided attention, he emphasized the moral qualities of the Army. The Army he created was a school for the training of citizens. He grasped the importance of the war of movement, did not neglect the cavalry, but he thought in terms of the past and underestimated the danger of a modern mechanized war. Even if he did not underestimate this danger, the actual mechanical equipment of the Army was under par. Yet he was not isolated in this respect. Besides, even under ideal economic conditions Poland could not match in equipment the armies of her enemy-neighbors.

Whereas contemporary dictators attracted to their programs the youth of their respective countries, Piłsudski failed to capture the youth of Poland. Once independence was won and the Polish romantic tradition was played out, there was nothing he could offer except the prosaic task of rebuilding the country. He asked for toil and honest sweat, but promised no empires to be conquered and no prizes to be won.

Piłsudski was a liberal with respect to Polish minorities, and the Jews sincerely mourned his passing, but somehow neither he nor his collaborators were able to solve the biggest of the minority problems: the Ukrainian question. And although he was of Lithuanian extraction, he was never able to establish the good neighbor policy with Lithuania, because of the irreconcilable attitude of that country's statesmen.

With all his real or alleged faults and shortcomings, the nation still recognized in Józef Piłsudski one of the greatest and most effective leaders of the one thousand years of Poland's recorded history.

WŁADYSŁAW REYMONT

(From a charcoal drawing by Antoni Kamieński in 1896)

XXIX

WŁADYSŁAW REYMONT
"The Vagabond Actor Who Became Nobel Laureate in Literature"

1868-1925

by

Julian Krzyżanowski

"Had Reymont belonged to the Anglo-Saxon race, had he been an American writer, then only those marks of his character which made him an ideal of independence and self-help, would have raised him to the summit of renown, and his life-history would have been taught at schools for the encouragement of younger generations."

In these concise and significant words, Zdzisław Dębicki, Reymont's close literary friend, underlined the fundamental traits of his character, at a moment when the Nobel Prize brought the author of *The Peasants*, little known outside Poland before 1925, to international fame. In fact, these words accurately illustrate the so-far unwritten romance of the life of Reymont, a novel which would have been no less interesting than the best of his works, the novel which he lived. It is indeed a matter of regret that Reymont, although he recounted his own life-story to his small circle of friends more than once, describing his adventures as well as the silhouettes of people with whom he had come into contact, and the many-colored situations he had found himself in, did not put them down on paper. Such a biographical account would, no doubt, have been an excellent supplement to his works.

It is hardly necessary to reproduce the biography of Reymont, built up on the fragmentary remarks of the author himself

367

and the casual evidence of others. These remarks, though not systematic and not too picturesque, contain facts which speak for themselves. I am, however, citing here a considerable section of this outline, changing only some minor details:

I was born on the Seventh of May, 1868, in the village of Kobiele Wielkie, in the environs of Piotrków, where at that time my family rented a small farm, called "ecclesiastical," being situated on church lands. But a year after my birth, my parents migrated to a settlement called Tuszyn, seven miles from Łódź. My parents were entirely indigent, though finally they succeeded in possessing a property of thirty acres. My childhood was rather sad. We were nine children, and seven were girls. My oldest brother was sent to the *gimnazjum*, which was before the awakening of my consciousness. So I was brought up among girls, far from people, and I was not allowed to know or mix with the children of the nearest town-dwellers. At home, following the old tradition, there reigned a profound and sincere religiousness, and severe discipline. Father ruled us all with an iron hand. He was inexorable to our childhood's offenses, so that my early years were full of fear, terror, and inward torment, coupled with a sense of revolt.

An escape from that was into the enchanted land of books, of which I found a sufficient number. We had inherited a small library from my mother's uncle, a priest named Kupczyński, and I let myself be completely drowned in it. I could, however, read those books only by stealth, as father had put a strict ban on them. But I remember what an unforgettable impression the first books made on me. I read Skarga's *Lives of the Saints*, which I knew almost by heart. In the seventh year of my life, I got a copy of *Robinson Crusoe* and some works of Scott, and I went mad over them. When I was eight, I was sent to school. I wanted that myself, just to be able to break away from home, and go to that 'world,' shut out from me by all kinds of paternal restrictions, to that wide world.

The following year I had to appear at an examination to be admitted into the lowest class of a high school at Łódź, but failed. It was a sad and shameful tragedy. . . . And then? Then came years of vagabondage and of being chased about from school to school, as I could not abide in one place for long. I was given over to handicraft, but did not stay, then to trade, and I bolted, then to school again, but I did not stay there either. Thus about six years passed. It all ended in my being thrown out of Warsaw by the police, and I was compelled to stay with my parents for a year. I was eighteen then. . . . My family looked upon me as its open wound, and I was lamented as lost and wasted. In fact, I did not know what to do with myself.

I wrote verses from time to time, but I did not send them anywhere, as I felt shy and feared lest they should be sent back as fit only for the wastepaper basket. My compulsory confinement in the country, under the cruel, severe and vigilant control of my father, was slowly killing me. I fled from home to Warsaw, but was arrested and sent back. Then I wanted to go to a college for priests, but my father was against that.

What was I to do? I had a school friend at a provincial theater. I fled from home penniless, and went to him, traveling a distance of more than thirty-five miles. I was taken into the company. Neither my companions nor the play itself dazzled me particularly, but I could have a free life at any rate. I changed my name, and tramped about with my theatrical company, all over the country, from small provincial towns to the remotest parts. My poverty was gnawing, but I began to like that freedom and that life full of unexpected wonders, movement and fantasies. I did not possess any histrionic talents, but played all kinds of parts. My vagabondage with that theatrical troop lasted for more than a year. In the end it bored me, and I returned home. No one paid any more attention to me, as all hopes of my ever being a respectable man had been given up. My father helped me only this much, that he found me a post in the Warsaw-Vienna railway. I stayed there for more than a year, then it began to pall: that sheep's life, the surroundings, my colleagues and all that mechanical existence.

I made the acquaintance of a certain Pushow, an ardent spiritualist, and went away to Germany in order to devote myself entirely to spiritualism. I went to Breslau, where the spiritualists had their principal church. However, I did not stick to it for long, as very soon I saw through the naïveté of this pseudoscience and its votaries. Pushow wanted to keep me by force, and chased after me to bring me back to his fold. Then we came to an understanding that I should go to America, and there I should propagate that doctrine among the Poles.

Again I had to run away against the wind. At Częstochowa I came across another theatrical company and joined it. I changed my name again and tramped about the world. And then once more I threw up everything for a time, and returned to the railway.

I changed to many other jobs and professions, till at last I returned to my railway employment for the third and the last time. As I had often left my job, they employed me as a railway apprentice, with the lowest grade of pay, and posted me near Skierniewice. There I stayed for more than two years. I shall not describe what I lived through, as I am only sketching the bare contours. It may suffice to say that in spite of all struggles and endeavors, I still found myself at the very bottom of life.

I ceased writing poetry and started on prose, the results of which

are embodied in my book, *Meeting,* written in the country, where
I lived with peasants in the same small house for such a long time.
I was to marry the daughter of my landlord, and remain there permanently. I had no friends nor any well-wishers. I was not a good
employee, and my literary efforts were laughed at. My employers
advised me to find a more suitable job. Then, in utter despair that I
should have to start vagabondage again, I collected all my writings
and sent them for an opinion. I waited for the answer about six months
and then came a favorable reply. Now I felt my strength and saw my
goal. *Głos* (*The Voice*) a weekly paper published my *Death* in 1893.
I began to write correspondences from the country for that paper,
which made my position in the railway still worse. I was urged to
leave my job. I had had enough of it myself, of that service, that
misery and those awful people.

I shall not confess how much I suffered. In the autumn of the
year 1893, I thanked the authorities for my job, and with a new
capital of three roubles and fifty kopeks (about $1.75), I went to
Warsaw to conquer the world. In the opinion of my family I was a
completely lost man. I shall not describe the first years of my literary
career. They were unhappy because of my misery, the worst form of
misery, which I had to suffer on the city pavements. But somehow
or other, I lived through that suffering.

Those times, however, did not last too long, for from the
year 1895 Reymont had already made his position so secure that
his writings were accepted by the best paying papers. Thanks to
this he could work very intensively, and could allow himself such
luxuries for a young littérateur as travel abroad, to France, where,
without interrupting his work, he led the life of a typical Bohemian. An unexpected accident put Reymont on his feet, when
he had already five novels and one volume of short stories to his
credit. The compensation for a nervous shock suffered in a railway accident furnished him with some funds, while his keen
practical sense enabled him to realize fair sums of money as royal-
ties. His frequent travels to Italy and France did not exert any
arresting influence on the intensivity of his literary productions,
but enriched it with new ideas, increasing the inner maturity of
the author. They created in him a happy counterbalance to the
unrest and disorder so characteristic of the early twentieth-century
Polish life, shaken by the Russian revolution of 1905, the revolution in which Poland, as belonging to Russia, took part. In fact,

just in that period Reymont rose to the zenith of his career and wrote the best works of his life.

The author of the huge novel in three volumes, dealing with the life of a wandering theatrical and a rural intelligentsia (*The Comedian* and *The Fermentations*), as well as two volumes of short stories on the industrial life of Łódź (*The Promised Land*), all written in the first five years of his astonishing career, devoted the next ten years of his work to his enormous and panoramic novel *The Peasants* (1901-09). This novel consolidated his position in Polish literature as well as in the literature of the world. *The Peasants*, however, did not entirely exhaust his creative vein, for between the appearance of its volumes, he published collections of short stories dealing with the current problems of contemporary life, with the portent of revolution, among others. Directly after finishing *The Peasants*, Reymont successfully tried his hand as a journalist. He visited the so-called "Chełm Territory" (the country around Chełm), which the Russian government sought to annex to the empire, to complete its long process of political and religious Russianizing. The author's impressions of that visit shocked his readers, and exposed him to an unpleasant political trial which, however, ended in his exoneration. Reymont then started his next, rather ambitious work, *The Year 1794*, an enormous historical novel in three bulky volumes, dealing with the insurrection of Kościuszko and the years preceding it. Together with it, he published further collections of short stories, which showed that in spite of his ill health, the author worked intensively till death literally snatched away his pen from his fingers, for his manuscripts contained the unfinished sketch of the religious legend of *The Goose-Girl*.

These works, though they seemed to occupy the whole of Reymont's time, did not take him away from other engagements which life demanded of the famous and popular writer, which his sense of duty did not allow him to shirk. When the newly formed Polish State turned to writers, asking them for special services, a voyage to the United States fell to Reymont's share. He was acquainted with that country through a flying visit in 1919. He then crossed the Atlantic again, as a member of a commission having for its object the raising of a loan in America. In the company of

Francis Stefczyk, the famous organizer of village co-operative banks, and of the editor Zdzisław Dębicki, he took an active part for four months in meetings held in New York, Washington, Philadelphia, Baltimore and Chicago, and visited a number of the larger Polish colonies in America. He studied the life of emigrants, and kept in touch with American society also, through publishers such as Mr. Putnam, writers, such as Mr. Rupert Hughes, and with emigrant painters, such as Władysław Benda. His work did not prevent him from gathering materials which interested him as a writer, and out of which he meant to write a great novel on the life of Polish emigrants in America, on his return to Poland. These materials, however, he utilized only in a few sketches or short stories.

Reymont's popularity reached its height by the end of the year 1924, when he was awarded the Nobel Prize. He followed Sienkiewicz in the history of Polish literature, as the second recipient of the distinction. That international recognition, putting Reymont in the forefront of outstanding Polish writers, awakened in him the ambition of playing some political role in the new Republic of Poland. A few months before his death, for instance, Reymont, in spite of his heart disease, accepted an invitation to take part in the peasant harvest festival, a political manifestation organized by the contemporary leader of the Peasants' party, the then Premier, Witos, in his own village, Wierzchosławice. As a writer rather than a politician, the author of The Peasants attached a considerable importance to the festival, for he saw in it the realization of those ideals he served in his own creations. In a letter to his friend Dębicki he wrote about that manifestation:

> Did you hear what the "Piast-ites" are organizing on the fifteenth of August? As I learned yesterday, 30,000 people from all parts of Poland wanted to take part in it. . . . Should it not assume a wider significance? Should we not make this gathering into a pro-Polish and All-Poland conference? Think of it!
>
> I myself think that it might be the only way of reconciling all the classes of Poland, and of forming some sort of a holy confederation of permanence and defense. . . .

That letter, so strongly accentuating the unification of the entire nation, has the significance of being the political testament of Reymont, and shows him as a man deeply concerned about the future. It is indeed a testament, for on December 5, 1925, the author's heart ceased beating forever.

The works of Reymont, as opposed to those of his contemporaries, with the single exception of Żeromski, encompass an extraordinarily wide field of thought, reaching the farthest corners of Polish life, within the country and beyond its boundaries. In his novels and short stories, side by side with pictures of life in Poland, we come across problems connected with the emigrants, such as for instance in the novel *The Vampire*, which deals with the turns of fortune of an Anglicized Polish writer in London; and in the novel *The Dreamer*, which describes poor emigrants in Paris, as well as in his last short stories dealing with the life of American Poles.

Reymont's imagination, however, was caught more by the problems of his own country than by anything else, problems which the author knew well from the observation of long years, from his youthful recollections, from stories told by others, and through reading. He was interested in the social and economic processes current in the Poland of his time, which gave him the outward form of his work and built up the psychology of his characters. He was interested in the formation of new classes and groups in the Polish society, in the disappearance of some and the rise of others. In other words, Reymont was more of a novelist-sociologist than a psychologist. And thanks to his interest in these matters, his novels and short stories can be regarded as a sort of document recording the slow changes in the social structure of the Poland of the end of the nineteenth century, changes more easily seized by the author's imagination than by the mind of a learned historian.

For instance, in Reymont's first two novels (*The Comedian* and *The Fermentations*) we see a very explicit description of the process of infusion into the old nobility of the new peasant element. The heroine of the novel, after passing through a number of difficulties arising from her artistic temperament, marries an educated and energetic man of considerable means, whose father, once an innkeeper and wood-merchant, made a fortune and gave his son an aristocrat's palace in which he himself was unable to live. What for the most progressive writers of the preceding generation, for Sienkiewicz or Bolesław Prus, would have been a subject of satire, is for Reymont just an ordinary statement. Instead of satirizing the upstart, Reymont gives a warmly sympathetic but not too idealistic picture of the process of change in Polish social life, a process which he considers not only normal but also extremely profitable for society. Reymont's point of view is almost an apologia for the philosophy of material well-being such as is seen in Sienkiewicz's *The Polaniecki Family*. Sienkiewicz unconsciously apotheosizes the energy of a member of the nobility who makes his fortune through trade and industry, while Reymont exalts the energy of a peasant who becomes rich through agriculture, which a nobleman had to abandon. Both Sienkiewicz and Reymont, although they belonged to different classes of society and to different generations, were very near to each other in the nature of their talents, and agree astonishingly in their cult of an American attitude to life. That cult was one of work as the source of individual and social prosperity, and an aversion to indolence, which in those times adorned itself with the plumes of an artistic calling.

Sienkiewicz, however, idealized industry as a workshop for labor, looking at it only from the point of view of the owner; while Reymont took a strongly hostile attitude to the industrialization of the country, an attitude even more extreme than that of English writers, such as Ruskin or Morris, to whom he bore a striking resemblance in his ideas. His *Promised Land* is a powerful condemnation of an industrial town, the abode of Satan, who lies in wait to deprave human souls by streams of gold, gained by an inhuman exploitation of the worker. One characteristic of Reymont's point of view, however, is that he does not look upon that town from the angle of vision of socialistic doctrines, which then were gaining ground speedily, but from that of Christianity. His later short stories, written after the revolution of 1905, when socialistic and communistic conceptions were already in evidence in society, bear testimony to the fact that Reymont opposed such theories with all his might. According to Reymont, industry is the perdition of man, whether it remains in the hands of the capitalist or is transferred to those of a communistic government. Thus the picture of life seen in his *Promised Land* is not painted from the point of view of the exploited worker, but from that of an observer believing in the humanitarian principles of Christian ethics; principles that are violated, at every step, by the worshiper of the golden calf. The lives of the textile manufacturers of Łódź, who have no ties with the land on which their factories stand, where they are but foreign elements, are a damnation in themselves; for these people recognize but one god—money, and one right—that of the strongest, the right of might. The industrial town grows into the proportions of some apocalyptic polyp, sucking the lives of those who are drawn by the mirage of the promised land into its pales. The town is a dark spot on the earth from which it grew. It is not a blessing of God, but an impending curse on all that come into contact with it. Thus Reymont's attitude to industry is not that of a biblical prophet threatening evil, but of a cold and quiet observer-sociologist who thinks that the development of industry is a transitory phase of social existence and of humanity, a phase which will appear to future generations as a thing of incredible barbarism, of the slavery of man captured by the demon of capitalism. This standpoint is not that of a fanatical preacher, nor of a violent speaker at a workers' meeting, but one that shows the objective picture of modern great industries in a terrifying light. It corroborates the view that *The Promised Land* is not a party manifesto clothed in the form of a novel, but the artistic vision of a historical reality.

Reymont's next novel, *The Peasants*, carries his attitude much farther. This novel is an epic vision of the problem of work in its age-old forms, as the permanent and unchangeable foundation of all societies. On this Mother Earth, "the holy earth" which is the universal and natural workshop, agricultural labor is a particular way of linking man with eternity. The peasant, as a particle of nature, depending on and fulfilling its laws, becomes *ipso facto* a symbol of all workers. His whole life is strictly governed by nature's laws, from the moment of his birth to the hour of his death, when what once sprang from the earth returns to it as its natural component. One of the most impressive pictures in that striking novel is the death-scene of the old farmer Boryna. Rising from his bed, he goes to the fields and, collecting some earth in his shirt-tail, scatters it about, just as he had sown seeds all his life, as had his ancestors through centuries. Mother Earth accepts this symbolical seed-sowing, and calls him, old and weary, back to her. This picture of peasant life as painted by Reymont fills four volumes, divided according to the seasons, so that it is something like the *Erga kai hemerai* of Hesiod, a kind of calendar-novel dealing with man's yearly life with nature, his constant relation with and continual dependence on her. The expression of that relation is work done by the hands of man, and to a smaller degree, by his intelligence; his discovering nature's demands and trying to create within their frame the best conditions for his existence. On that work is based Reymont's theory of right, the right of hands on the earth, determining its ownership by the ability to cultivate it.

These conceptions present themselves as an invisible range of forces, as it were, forces which find their expression in the wonderfully executed scenes of country life, valuable historically as well as artistically. The French translator of *The Peasants*, Franck L. Schoell, said that the novel was a document of peasant life to which the great war put an end, by changing and mechanizing the methods of agricultural labor. This statement needs some modification, for the war did not alter the forms of country life so radically as was expected at its termination, although even in the most conservative societies the life of the peasant underwent considerable changes. The documentary value of *The Peasants* consists in its reviewing in epic dignity the ancient structures of society, which have already disappeared or are in the process of disappearing. These archaic structures assume a perfectly artistic form through the pen of the novelist. It is a form full of plastic pictures, profoundly dramatic conflicts, eternal and permanent, such as love and duty, the passions of individuals and the collective will, shown in extraordinarily colorful and exceedingly absorbing action. The pictures appear on a canvas of country nature studied in its minutest details, and described in such a manner that the author's pen seems to vie with the painter's brush. This explains why this novel of Reymont entered into the gallery of world's literature, as undoubtedly the greatest and the best picture of peasant life.

It is not insignificant, however, that *The Peasants* is the work of a writer who was of half peasant origin, and that in this work he erected a monument to that class of society with which he was linked by his origin and by the reminiscences of his youth, the class in which he saw the assurance of his nation's rebirth. In brief, Reymont's works are a realization of that program of the great author's political testament, known to us already, and an expression of his conviction that literature is that branch of art in which desires and endeavors are formulated which life fulfills as the years roll by.

XXX

STANISŁAW WYSPIAŃSKI
Poet, Painter, Dramatist

1869-1907

by

Tadeusz Mitana

Stanisław Wyspiański, Poland's greatest dramatic poet, is also the most extraordinary personality in the history of Polish art. His sixteen plays, extremely popular when first written, are still frequently acted in all Polish theaters. Of all of them the poetic drama, *The Wedding*, is considered by his countrymen the supreme achievement in the field of Polish dramatic writing. Acted for the first time in 1901 at the Kraków Theater, it electrified Poland by its exquisite and revealing study of national character and by its tremendous emotional intensity. It took the nation by storm, arousing an enthusiasm which was the more significant because the play contained a bitter and severe arraignment of contemporary Polish life.

Many of Wyspiański's readers, however, are unaware of the fact that he was also an excellent and very original painter. His pictorial works total more than five hundred pictures and drawings. Representative selections from these have recently been made available in a magnificent folio volume of some two hundred reproductions. Reviewing this publication for *The Studio*, an English magazine of fine and applied art, a British critic ventured to say: "Wyspiański is certainly the most original and universal artistic genius since Leonardo da Vinci."

As a Pole, I might be expected to endorse most heartily a judgment so ardently expressed. But, to be on perfectly safe

STANISŁAW WYSPIAŃSKI

A pastel autoportrait. In the National Museum in Kraków.

ground, this Englishman's statement may well be taken with a saving pinch of salt. And after all, in the kingdom of art, as in the Kingdom of Heaven, there are many mansions.

Wyspiański, however, did possess an artistic range which recalls that of Leonardo da Vinci. In the city of Kraków alone the variety of his genius is evident in churches, in the National Gallery, and in the Kraków Theater. In two Gothic churches, for example, one can find his superb mural decorations and admirable stained-glass windows. In a somewhat related field, the cartoons which he drew and elaborated for the reconstruction of the ancient royal castle of Wawel, reveal an extensive technical familiarity with architecture. Again, associated by ties of lifelong intimacy with the Kraków stage, he discovered new emotional values in scenery and costumes which he himself designed. If we add that he inaugurated a new movement in decorative, applied, and typographical arts, and that he gave detailed suggestions for the musical instrumentation of the lyric parts of some of his dramas, we may gain a fairly adequate conception of his astonishingly many-sided interests. An eminent Jugoslavian poet and critic, Dr. Zdenka Markovic, in her penetrating book on the dramas of Wyspiański, places him side by side with Wagner, Ibsen and Maeterlinck, and discovers him to be a precursor of the drama of the future.

Within the limits of this paper I can only sketch briefly the chief influences in the development of Wyspiański's creative powers, particularly his dramatic gifts. But something must be said of this phase before his work as a dramatist can be understood.

Stanisław Wyspiański, the son of a noted sculptor, spent most of his life in Kraków, the ancient capital of Poland; it was here, "in the city of living stones," that he received his first and most enduring impressions. From earliest childhood the sensitive boy was stirred and haunted by the many old churches and historical monuments. However, it was the Royal Castle of Wawel, with its gorgeous Renaissance cathedral, that inspired him most of all.

After completing the usual training in the *gimnazjum*, he spent a summer as an artist-pilgrim, sketching picturesque old village churches in various parts of Poland. Shortly thereafter he entered the Kraków Academy of Fine Arts, then under the guidance of Poland's great painter of historical subjects, Jan Matejko. Soon this master painter discovered the marked talent of his youthful pupil, and gave him the responsible task of assisting in the decoration of Kraków's finest church, St. Mary's. A year later he won a scholarship from the Academy, enabling him to continue his studies in Paris and in Italy. Then opened before the young painter the impressive vista of western European art. Under the stimulus of the new surroundings he studied, almost feverishly, painting, sculpture, and architecture, as well as literature and the art of the theater. The Louvre and the French Cathedrals at Rheims, Chartres, Rouen, and Amiens, and a little later, the Italian cathedrals, had an intoxicating effect upon him. It is significant of his outreaching artistic nature that he found the paintings of Puvis de Chavannes as absorbingly interesting as the great tragedies of Corneille, Racine and Shakespeare. He also threw himself into the study of Greek art and civilization, of Gothic architecture, of the Shakespearean and French theaters, and of contemporary painting and sculpture. It was out of this enlarging experience that he came gradually to his most congenial means of expression—the theater.

Upon his return to Kraków, Wyspiański's passion for creative work ran far beyond his slender physical strength. No man of his frail constitution could for long give himself without stint to the writing of plays at the rate of more than one a year, and to painting, sculpture, stagecraft, and applied arts. His intense overactivity was undoubtedly responsible for his premature death at the age of thirty-eight.

This paper's chief concern is with Wyspiański's dramas and with his conception of tragedy. The whole of his literary achievement is bound up with his overwhelming vision of the theater. With Goethe, he believed that dramatic poetry is man's greatest accomplishment on earth, and with the early Bernard Shaw he looked at the theater as fundamentally a cathedral of the spirit, the chief function of which is to create for men a sublime vision of life. Possessed as he was of the genuinely critical mind, a mind deepened by long experience and by profound knowledge of history of the drama, Wyspiański found the stage his most natural and psychologically indispensable means of self-expression. As a synthesis of various arts the theater provided a perfect vehicle for a man who, by accident of genius, was in one person poet, painter, architect, sculptor and musician. This was all the more true, since besides being a born artist, he was also gifted with fine intellectual audacity, distinct originality in his philosophic outlook on life, and with that rare historical sense which made it imperative that he should become a prophet and an interpreter of the national dreams.

The dramas of Wyspiański may conveniently be divided into two groups: those definitely Polish in subject, in characters, and in setting, and those based on subjects drawn from the literature of ancient Greece. The majority belong to the former group. Three of these—*The Curse* (1899), *The Wedding* (1901), and *The Judges* (1907)—would probably be of greatest interest to foreign students of Wyspiański's plays. The Greek dramas, four in number, are *Meleager* (1894), *Protesilas and Laodamia* (1898), *Achilles* (1903), and *The Return of Ulysses* (1906).

In any analysis of the Polish dramas, it must be remembered that they all sprang from two sources—the heroic past of Polish history, and the painful consciousness, ever present with Wyspiański, of Poland's subjection after the Partitions. It may perhaps be useful to keep in mind the fact that the problem of freedom, political as well as moral, never ceased to be an issue of paramount moment to any creative individuality in Poland throughout the nineteenth century. It was the burning bush out of which rose Poland's most sublime and fiery inspirations. No wonder then that in the case of Wyspiański, Poland's most dynamic and powerful artist, the issue had cut itself deeply into the very roots of his mind and of his heart. His peculiar social environment and national characteristics could not but profoundly influence his product. On the one side were the historic traditions, picturesque and glorious; and on the other, the national degradation at the hands of foreign conquerors, a subjection desperately and unrelentlessly resisted. It is only natural that the problem of Poland's political destiny should have become his one overwhelming theme.

Wyspiański, ever seeking heroic values in life, was first drawn to the eternal source of such values—to legends and myths, particularly to the immortal Greek legends. Their primitive simplicity and power led him naturally to utilize the mythology and heroic early history of Poland. Three plays, *The Legend, Boleslas the Bold,* and *The Church on the Rock,* express this absorbing interest. As a result of his preoccupation with these remote times, Greece and Poland became blended in one splendid vision, the Greek Acropolis symbolizing the Royal Castle of Wawel, and the Greece of Achilles symbolizing Poland in the time of Boleslas the Bold.

Yet his sure sense of truth made him realize that in contemporary Polish life at least one element possessed a similar primitive heroism and beauty—the Polish peasant. Artistically, one of the results of this blending is a startling vividness and simplicity in his contemporary Polish plays, *The Curse* and *The Judges.* Both have peasant life as their subjects, but both possess an intensive tragic concentration essentially Greek.

The master idea back of most of Wyspiański's dramas was the presentment of various aspects of modern Polish life, particularly those weaknesses that delayed the hour of political deliverance. This idea is intimately linked with the poet's attitude toward Romanticism. Few Poles seemed capable of freeing themselves from its occasionally morbid charm. Wyspiański himself was drawn to Poland's great romantic poets, especially Mickiewicz and Słowacki. But his critical mind soon protested violently against this poetry which, in his estimation, induced the Poles to acquiesce in the pathos and beauty of political martyrdom. For example, the hero of his profound imaginative play, *The Deliverance,* speaks vehemently against Romanticism and urges his countrymen toward the goal of an actual Polish state. His rebellious shout, "Away, Poetry, thou art a tyrant!" is a protest against the Messianic dreams of romantic writers.

Having thus passed judgment on the morbid habit of indulging in dreamy contemplation of the past, Wyspiański turned to the interpretation of the realities of everyday life. In doing so he wrote *The Wedding,* a deeply moving allegorical drama, of which a distinguished critic says: "No literary work, in fact no appeal in any form in modern Poland, and no event in national life since the insurrection of 1863, has shaken the consciousness of the nation so strongly as did Wyspiański's *Wedding.*" To give any comprehensive account of its plot or contents would be fruitless, for there is scarcely any plot in it, and scarcely any discernible connections between the incidents. A poet of repute in Kraków artistic circles, the dramatist's personal friend, has stirred the Polish elite by his marriage to a simple peasant girl. To the wedding ceremony, gay and colorful, a great variety of guests, representing different social classes, are invited. The poor peasant cottage in which the ceremony takes place thus becomes a meeting-ground for poets, journalists, artists, town ladies and peasant men and women. There is delightful, lively folk music, to the tunes of which the guests dance, there is a spontaneous outburst of free and animated talk, a genuine riot of bright peasant costumes, the pervading melancholy of winter scenery, and above all an ever-increasing tendency on the part of the guests to unbosom their innermost feelings and moods, their dreams and fears, their likes and dislikes, thoughts and aspirations, griefs and joys. The imagination and the emotions rise high, and an all-pervading feeling of some mysterious spiritual unity seems to have come upon the group. Accidental differences of social rank and education appear to have vanished, and an undefinable feeling of some metaphysical and racial identity seems to bind them all into one spiritual entity. The rare intensity and beauty of this peculiar psychological situation gives Wyspiański a marvelous opportunity for a searching and merciless analysis of Polish national character. With exquisite humor and irony, biting sarcasm and delicate melancholy, and occasional flashes of love and tenderness, the dramatist reviews through the medium of dialogues and gestures, emotional symbolism and half-fantastic devices, all the deficiencies and peculiarities of Polish temperament. Through his uncanny power over words, the superb beauty of his language, and the hidden music of his verse, his vision creates a perfectly harmonious and admirable work of art. The drama vibrates with life and passion, with tremendous intensity of human emotions, and is shot through with lyricism and loveliness of description. Personages reveal themselves through a natural display of their traits, giving the drama an unmistakable Polish flavor and a distinctive national note.

All of Wyspiański's Polish plays tend to create life over again.

They are all vigorous protests against the weaknesses of Polish character, the incapacity for united action, the substitution of misty moods for clear and fearless thinking, and passive resignation as to the future of Poland. Absorbed though he often was in the great traditions of bygone days, he centered his creative efforts on problems of the living present.

I have so far said little of Wyspiański's conception of the tragic. This aspect of his dramas can best be understood, I think, by a reading of his four Greek tragedies. Here, more than in his strictly Polish plays, the hero is sharply set apart, his inner struggle completely revealed. The plots are classically simple, and the peculiar treatment given them by the Polish writer can be better appreciated because of our familiarity with Greek literature.

From his Greek plays it can be seen that intensity of external action is not dominant in the life of Wyspiański's heroes. Their spiritual energy wastes itself in inner struggle. They live in their own worlds, within the confining circle of their introspective thinking. They are consequently destined for conflict and ultimate catastrophe. But punishment never comes from without; it springs from the very nature of the heroes' thoughts and acts. The effects of evil actions turn upon the souls which conceived them. And a life made intolerable by unappeasable remorse, a life broken by the ruin of man's moral self—that is the profoundest form of human tragedy.

The idea that life under certain circumstances may be more abhorrent than physical death is frequently stressed in Wyspiański's dramas. He regarded death as an avenue of escape to a higher form of existence. We may see this even in his stained-glass windows, which are almost a hymn of adoration to Death. Though he was a painter deeply sensitive to the beauty of form and an admirer of the splendor of Greek civilization and the Renaissance, in his attitude toward death he is a follower of St. Francis of Assisi.

To summarize this cursory study of Wyspiański as a dramatist, I quote a characteristic remark of his, explaining how he began the writing of a new play: "In order to begin writing, I must first determine two things: *the line* and *the tone*. As soon as I grasp these, the rest is but a question of execution. The line usually appears in my mind as a vault in which I can see in advance the dimensions, the shape, and the exact position of each stone. And when I know this, it is wholly indifferent to me in what order I am to carve the stones."

Wyspiański's genius has left a specific imprint on the consciousness of contemporary Poland. His influence upon the national mind has been extraordinarily profound and lasting. This should not be surprising to students of his work. For, apart from being a great and original artist, one of the Lord's Anointed, he possessed a keen and penetrating intellect and was also gifted with the peculiar superabundance of heat and patriotic ardor that springs only from a heart brimming with social sympathies and divine compassion. He was born with the soul of an apostle. In him, Poland's racial dream, her glory and her tragedy, her greatness and her weaknesses, found their most brilliant interpreter. His dramas are all full of the nation's blood and tears. He alone, with the possible exception of his distinguished contemporary fellow writer, Stefan Żeromski, was tacitly granted the supreme privilege of probing the national wounds. However, Wyspiański's mind was far too profound and constructive to stop at the crossroads of mere pessimism. He had a definite message to his countrymen, a message that never failed to arouse their immediate emotional responses. If his dramas stirred and electrified the public mind and held it spellbound, it was chiefly due, apart from the sheer beauty of their form and contents, to the fact that Wyspiański never wished to offer direct observations on the country's political, social or economic life. Instead, his heart and soul were focused on something incomparably more important—on strengthening and clarifying the nation's sense of values, on stimulating its instinct for the valid, the permanent and the central. Deep under the crust of everyday Polish life his searching eyes saw in the darkest recesses of the national mind, problems wellnigh metaphysical and religious in magnitude. Radical and almost revolutionary as he was in his political and social outlook, an apostle of his country's complete independence, an enthusiastic supporter of Piłsudski's audacious military dreams, Wyspiański nevertheless stressed one supreme, all-embracing idea, that of an intense, heroic and creative individual life. For him, the paramount problem of Poland's political freedom was inextricably bound with ethical and religious virtues of which the crowning flower was man's personal heroism. To the Polish people, oppressed and bleeding, he unburdened his heart and, keenly concerned in their problems and conflicts, in their longings, triumphs, and despairs, he offered them, in a series of magnificent works, a message that was to stir up their sense of human greatness. He did so, and with splendid success, through his unparalleled power over words, through the beauty of his language, the splendor of his imagination, and his extraordinarily extensive knowledge of the national psychology. Even his slashing criticism of the weaknesses of the contemporary generation sprang from the fullness of his heart. No wonder then, that he took captive the Polish reading public and that to the youth of the country his name became a synonym of prophet and saint of the new Poland.

"Apollo, the King that Smiteth Afar"

(Adapted from Wyspiański's charcoal sketch of Apollo, one of the illustrations for Homer's *Iliad* in Polish translation—Book I, verses 45-53.)

INDEX

Adalbert St., missionary to Prussia, 3

Adams, Maude, actress, 253

Agriculture, encouraged by Zamoyski, 96; at beginning of Machine Age, 163f; co-operative farming, 167

Alexander of Russia, sought Kościuszko's support, 142; friendship with Czartoryski, 171f

"Almagest," by Ptolemy, 46

America, Polish colony, 250f; immigration of Modjeska, 257f; visited by Sienkiewicz, 278; by Paderewski, 319, 325ff; by Marie Curie, 340f; by Reymont, 371f; appreciated Chełmoński, 295; attitude toward Polish independence, 353

American Revolution, service of Kościuszko, 130ff; of Pułaski, 150ff

American stage, golden age, 253

"Ancestors," by Mickiewicz, 193

Andrews, physicist, 264

Angevins, Hungarian rulers, 15

Anne, Princess, wife of Batory, 92

Antitrinitarians, in Poland, 63

Aristarchos of Samos, astronomer, 49

Army, German troops for, 6; led by Jadwiga, 32; fortress commanded by Copernicus, 41; ideas of Modrzewski, 61f; commanded by Zamoyski, 89; mutiny in time of Wiśniowiecki, 108; size in "last crusade of Christendom," 109ff; expanded in 1789, 135; service of Pułaski, 146f; under Congress Kingdom, 176; formation helped by Paderewski, 325f; work of Marie Curie, 341; corps organized by Piłsudski, 349

Art, Matejko's philosophy, 241; Matejko's paintings, 248; Chełmoński's paintings, 289ff; National Museum in Kraków, 294; impressionism, 294f; Paris Salon, 298; "Grand Prix," 299; contribution of Wyspiański, 378f

Astronomy, Copernican theory, 42f; Pythagorean theory, 42f; Ptolemaic theory, 46f

Austria, intrigues with Sigismund III,

94; alliance with Poland, 105; enemy of Turks, 105f; partner of Germany, 350; relation to Poland at beginning of World War, 350; war with Russia in 1914, 351

Avignon, site of Papal Court, 21

Bach, interpreted by Paderewski, 316

Balfour, Arthur, friend of Paderewski, 328

Bancroft, George, comments on Kościuszko, 132

Basil II, contact with Bolesław, 8f

Batory, Stefan, admired Kochanowski, 73; influence on Skarga, 82

Bautzen, Treaty of, 7

Bavaria, trouble with Germany, 5

Bècu, Dr. August, step-father of Słowacki, 209f

Beethoven, interpreted by Paderewski, 316

Bellaigue, Camille, comments on Chopin, 229

Bemis Heights, selected by Kościuszko, 130

Benedictines, brought from Prague, 35

Berlioz, friendship with Chopin, 230

Bernhardt, Sarah, actress, 253

Bishop of Merseburg, chronicle about Bolesław Chrobry, 10f

Bobrowski, Thaddeus, benefactor of Conrad, 301

Bodin, Jean, comments on Modrzewski, 55

Bohemia, patron saint of, 3; attempted conquest of, 5; reconquered by Henry II, 6; under Charles IV, 14f

Bolesław the Brave, see Bolesław Chrobry

Bolesław Chrobry, King of Poland, story of, 1-13; birth, 1; promoted Catholicism, 2ff; conference with Otto III, 3f; undertook missionary work, 5; wars with Germany, 5ff; added Lusatia to realm, 7; domestic policy, 8f; policy toward Russia, 8ff; ideas for Eastern Central European

387